The Economy of Paraguay

CAPITAL CITIES OF PARAGUAY

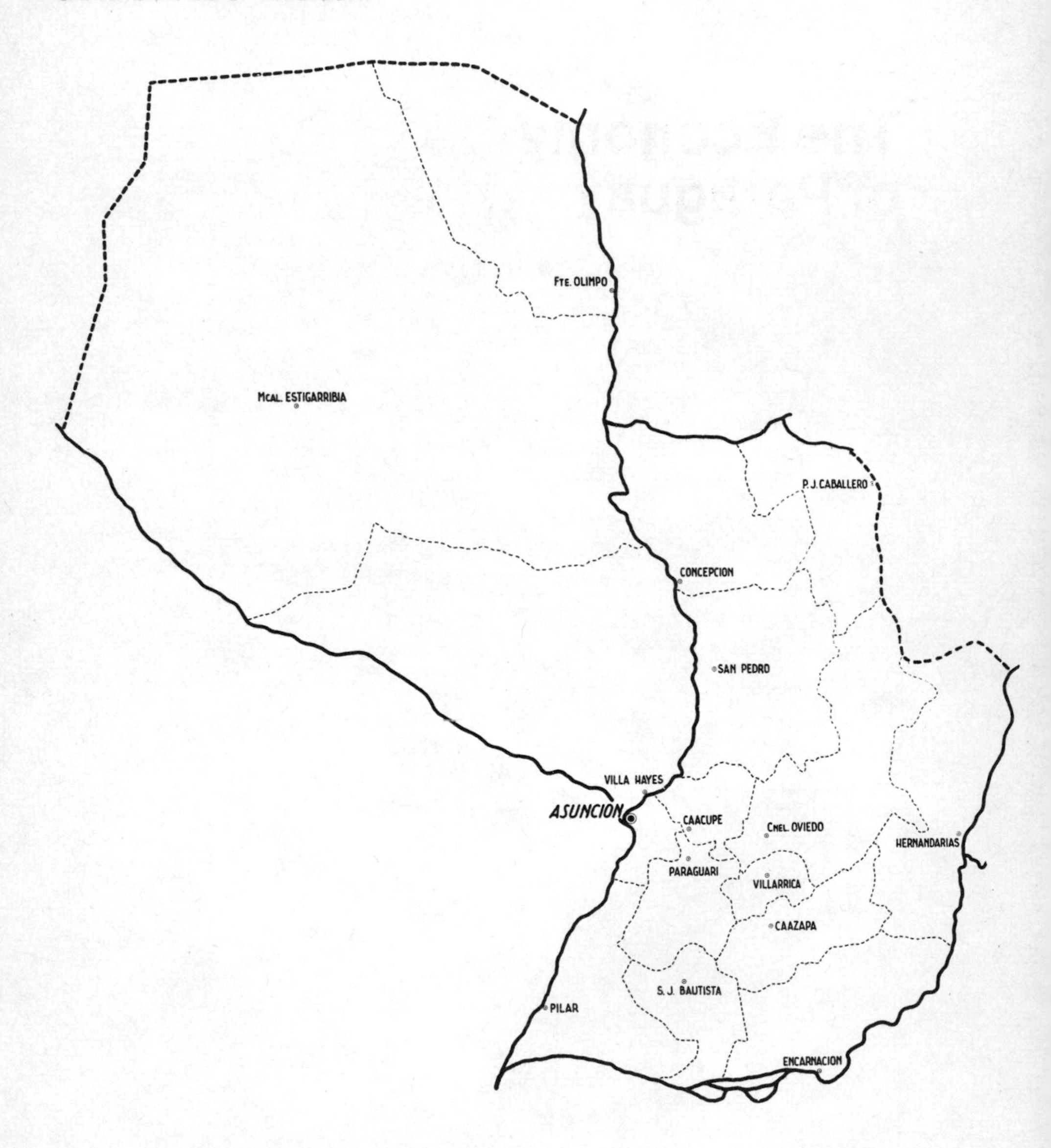

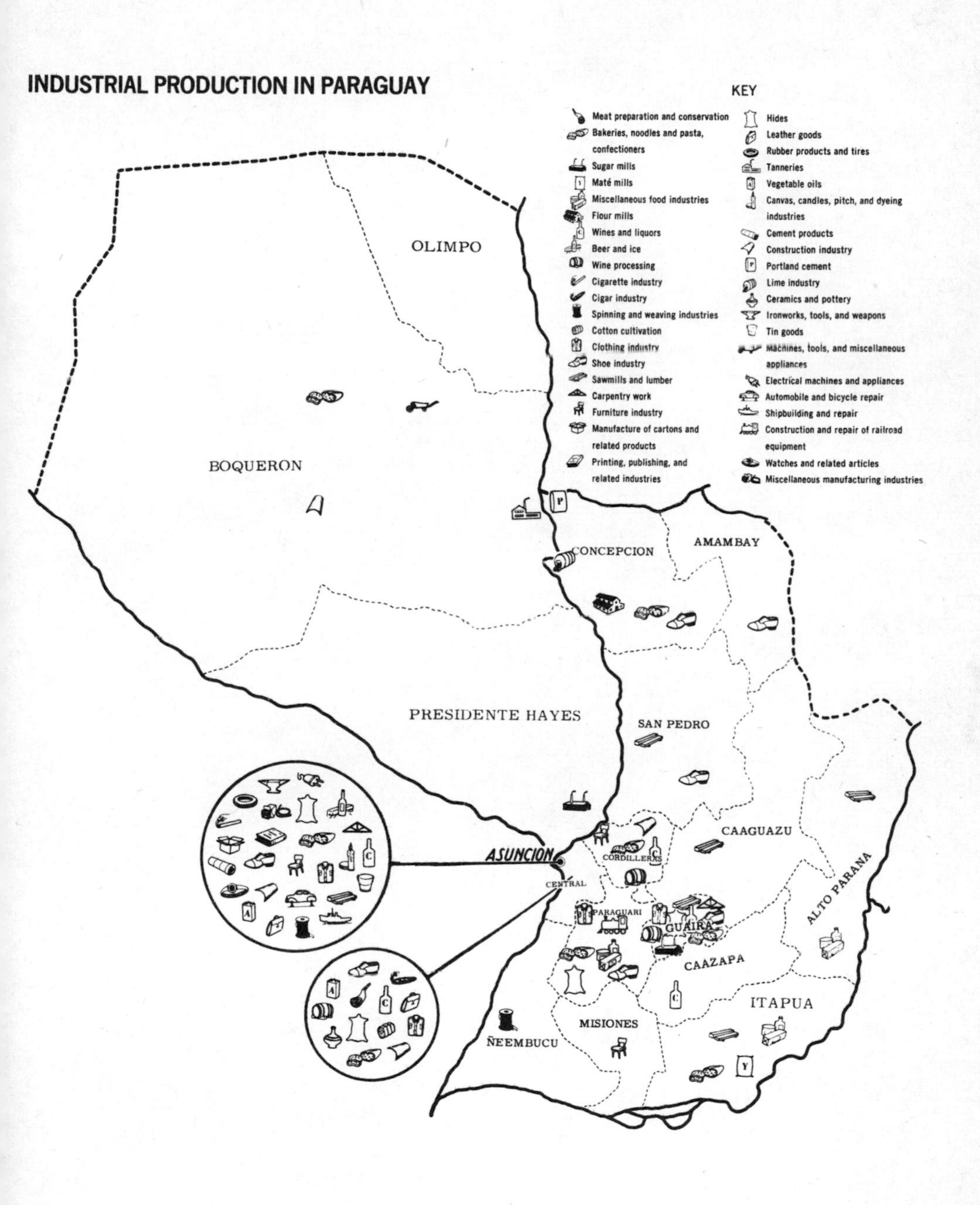
INDUSTRIAL PRODUCTION IN PARAGUAY
KEY
Meat preparation and conservation
Bakeries, noodles and pasta, confectioners
Sugar mills
Maté mills
Miscellaneous food industries
Flour mills
Wines and liquors
Beer and ice
Wine processing
Cigarette industry
Cigar industry
Spinning and weaving industries
Cotton cultivation
Clothing industry
Shoe industry
Sawmills and lumber
Carpentry work
Furniture industry
Manufacture of cartons and related products
Printing, publishing, and related industries
Hides
Leather goods
Rubber products and tires
Tanneries
Vegetable oils
Canvas, candles, pitch, and dyeing industries
Cement products
Construction industry
Portland cement
Lime industry
Ceramics and pottery
Ironworks, tools, and weapons
Tin goods
Machines, tools, and miscellaneous appliances
Electrical machines and appliances
Automobile and bicycle repair
Shipbuilding and repair
Construction and repair of railroad equipment
Watches and related articles
Miscellaneous manufacturing industries
OLIMPO
BOQUERON
CONCEPCION
AMAMBAY
PRESIDENTE HAYES
SAN PEDRO
CAAGUAZU
ASUNCION
CORDILLERAS
CENTRAL
PARAGUARI
GUAIRA
CAAZAPA
ALTO PARANA
ITAPUA
MISIONES
ÑEEMBUCU

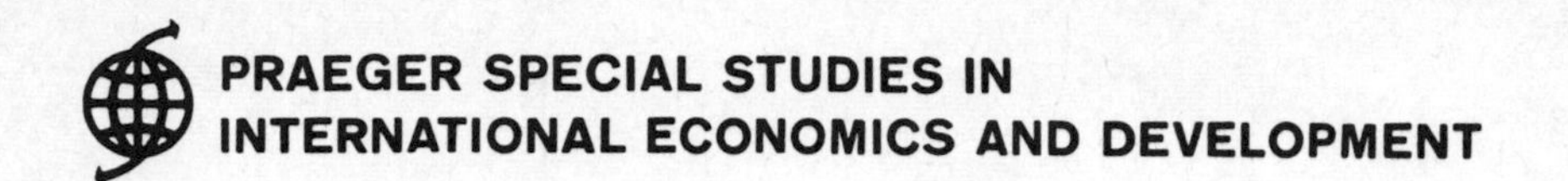

PRAEGER SPECIAL STUDIES IN INTERNATIONAL ECONOMICS AND DEVELOPMENT

The Economy of Paraguay

Joseph Pincus

FREDERICK A. PRAEGER, Publishers
New York · Washington · London

The purpose of the Praeger Special Studies is to make specialized research monographs in U.S. and international economics and politics available to the academic, business, and government communities. For further information, write to the Special Projects Division, Frederick A. Praeger, Publishers, 111 Fourth Avenue, New York, N.Y. 10003.

FREDERICK A. PRAEGER, PUBLISHERS
111 Fourth Avenue, New York, N.Y. 10003, U.S.A.
77-79 Charlotte Street, London W.1, England

Published in the United States of America in 1968
by Frederick A. Praeger, Inc., Publishers

Library of Congress Catalog Card Number: 68-14163

Printed in the United States of America

TO MY WIFE

CONTENTS

Chapter Page

LIST OF TABLES

Table Page

TABLES IN APPENDIXES

LIST OF MAPS AND CHART

INTRODUCTION

Paraguay is advancing--politically, socially, and economically--but few outsiders, even those in high places, appear capable or willing to discard the romanticized notions of Paraguay during the reign of El Supremo[1] or the notorious "Woman on Horseback," Madame Eliza Lynch.[2] War, revolution, ignorance, poverty, and disease have been Paraguay's heritage from its Spanish conquerors. Its right to exist has been challenged repeatedly by its larger and more powerful neighbors. Even contemporary observers--ignorant of Paraguay's role as a jumping-off place for the founding of Buenos Aires and other cities in Argentina, Brazil, Bolivia, and Uruguay--have claimed that there appears to be little justification for the country's independent existence other than historical accident, and that its territory should have been part of the adjoining countries which border on the Atlantic Ocean.[3] Nevertheless, a new Paraguay is emerging, with a growing middle class, a dynamic private sector, a stable government, a stable currency, and a genuine will to progress. Paraguay is a staunch supporter of the Alliance for Progress and appears to take its obligations under the Charter of Punta del Este seriously, even if implementation of required reforms is slower than many observers consider desirable.

Unless the threat of a Communist takeover of the country should develop, Paraguay will remain one of the least strategic countries in the world, with a geography and resource base of only marginal interest to the free world's leading nations. There is little doubt that this inland country ranks near the bottom of the geopolitical scale in world affairs. Nevertheless, Paraguay is a member of the United Nations complex, including the Organization of American States. In this role the vote of Paraguay is as important as that of any other nation, and Paraguay's attitude toward achieving a peaceful and prosperous world society within the framework of political democracy is important to the United States.

It thus is very important for Americans to recognize that Paraguay is changing and is taking limited measures to enter the twentieth century way of life. The degree of change that has occurred since the mid-1950's, together with a description and evaluation of current economic developments and policies and of the country's economic growth potential, are discussed in this study. Because so little information on the economy of present-day Paraguay is available, at least in English, we hope that the present effort will make a contribution to the knowledge of the American public. For in our view, as well as in that of Paraguay's leading commercial bank,

> Few Latin American nations have worked harder than Paraguay to brighten their prospects for achieving significant long-term economic growth. Emerging from a protracted period of political stability and economic stagnation, Paraguay during the last decade has been engaged in establishing the foundations upon which an industrial economy can be built. Under the government of President Stroessner, a sorely needed program of monetary reform has been instituted and relative monetary stability has been achieved. Attracted by Paraguay's potential, foreign governments and private investors are channeling substantial amounts of capital resources into both the public and private sectors of the economy.

> Some results of Paraguay's concentrated development efforts are already in evidence. The economy is being transformed by highway and road construction, the expansion of air services, the creation of a domestic river fleet, the development of land resources, and the enlargement of health and educational services. In the opinion of many observers, more has been accomplished in less than a decade than had been achieved in the previous half century.[4]

The past decade--especially since the signing of the Charter of Punta del Este on August 17, 1961--has witnessed a remarkable change in the attitude of the Paraguayan business community. Young new leaders have emerged to assume leadership roles in the major enterprises and economic associations in the country and to spark its growth. These leaders, many of whom have been trained abroad, are dedicated to private sector development through its own initiative, with or without governmental assistance. Since 1961, the private sector has found its voice, and the present administration is permitting it to have its say.

The private sector, no longer willing to sit back and oppose those governmental actions which allegedly threaten its welfare, is now requesting and receiving official permission to cooperate with the government in formulating policy and framing legislation. The results of this recent and remarkable development in Paraguay's political economy are evidenced in the recent expansion of infrastructure facilities; new private investments in the country; a surge in tourism; improved displays in store windows; increasing Paraguayan participation in international expositions and the sponsorship of such expositions in Paraguay; some expansion in the heretofore miniscule budgets of certain government development agencies (such as the Technical Planning Secretariat, the Ministry of Agriculture and Livestock, and the Ministry of Industry and Commerce); and the incursion of foreign businessmen, news reporters, and economic missions.

In facing the future, Paraguay's basic development problem will be to convert its geographic location and climate--heretofore serious obstacles to development--into positive growth factors. This will require that the country: (a) develop unique products that will have wide acceptance in world markets; (b) process its raw materials into higher unit value products suitable for transportation by air; (c) encourage the establishment of specialized services capable of being sold to other countries in South America (e.g., computing center; research center in special fields); and (d) develop a highly trained labor force and managerial sector to carry out these essential programs.

Notes to Introduction

1. José Gaspar Rodríguez de Francia, dictator of Paraguay during 1814-40.

2. Irish mistress of Francisco Solano López who lived in Paraguay during 1855-70.

3. R. H. Whitbeck and Frank E. Williams, Economic Geography of South America (New York: McGraw-Hill Book Company, Inc., 1940; Third Edition), p. 312.

4. The First National City Bank of New York, Foreign Information Service, "Paraguay: Building Foundations for Growth," (December, 1964), p. 1.

The Economy of Paraguay

CHAPTER 1 PERSPECTIVE ON PARAGUAY

GEOGRAPHIC FACTORS

Paraguay, one of the two landlocked countries in South America (Bolivia is the other), is located at the heart of the continent between the latitudes 19°18' and 27°30' South and longitudes 54°19' and 62°38' West of Greenwich meridian. Its area of 157,047 square miles is slightly smaller than that of California and supports a population slightly over 2 million (1966). The density of population is less than 13 per square mile. According to the 1962 census, 35.6 per cent of the population live in urban areas and 64.4 per cent in rural. Roughly 4 per cent of the land area is in farms, 40 per cent in grazing land and ranches, 54 per cent in forests, and 2 per cent in cities and wastelands. Less than 1 per cent of the total land area is in cultivation (including fruit crops) and more than two thirds of the timber lands are virgin forests.

The country has access to the sea by river, road, and rail. Its two river systems--the Paraguay and the Paraná--rise in neighboring Brazil and join the Río de la Plata at the southwestern tip of Paraguay, whence they flow to the Atlantic Ocean. The Paraguay River is 1,580 miles long, of which 1,426 miles are navigable; the Paraná River is 2,914 miles long but has a navigable distance of only 1,276 miles. A road from Asunción reaches to Puerto Presidente Stroessner and continues across the new international bridge into Brazil and eastward to the Atlantic port of Paranaguá where Paraguay has free port privileges. The total length of the road is about 700 miles, of which 203 miles lie in Paraguay and 497 miles lie in Brazil. The Presidente Carlos Antonio López Railway, owned by the Paraguayan Government, links Asunción with Encarnación, some 230 miles distant, and continues by way of a railway ferry across the Paraná River to the Argentine city of Posadas and from there to Buenos Aires.

Over most of its territory, Paraguay has a continental subtropical climate similar to that of southern Florida, ranging from 63° to 80° and with an average temperature of 74.5° Fahrenheit. However, variations are found between zones. Average rainfall, which increases from west to east, ranges from 20 to 68 inches a year.

The Paraguay River, running from north to south, separates the country into two distinct zones. The Chaco, with 95,000 square miles, is the larger of the two zones; it forms a part of the Gran Chaco which lies in Argentina, Paraguay, and Bolivia. It is an area of undulating plains with a maximum recorded elevation of 754 feet above sea level, and it is covered with marshes, lagoons, and dense tropical forests. The soil and physical characteristics are suited chiefly to hunting and livestock raising.

Eastern Paraguay, between the Paraguay and the Alto Paraná rivers, is a region of rolling plains with swamps in its low-lying river areas and fertile plains with maximum altitudes of 2,000 feet in the northeast and east central regions. Heavily wooded sections cover less than half the area. East of the Paraguay River lies the more developed area of the country and the majority of its population. It includes most of the cultivated lands.

POLITICAL FACTORS

Paraguay was discovered about 1524 by a Portuguese, Alejo García, a survivor of the Juan de Solís expedition dispatched by King Ferdinand of Spain to find a passage between the Atlantic and Pacific oceans. However, Asunción was not founded until thirteen years later, in 1537, by the Spanish explorer Juan de Salazar. Paraguay gained its independence from Spain in 1811, the first Latin American province to do so.

The Spanish settlement of Paraguay differed in several characteristics from that in other countries of Latin America. As Paraguay had little movable wealth (gold, silver, spices, etc.), it was used as a way station by the Spanish conquerors in enlarging and consolidating their colonial empire in the New World. Those Spaniards who remained in isolated Paraguay not only married local Indian women, but assimilated the Guaraní customs and language as well. To this day most Paraguayans are bilingual, speaking Spanish and Guaraní. The latter tongue is spoken almost exclusively in the countryside, although Spanish is taught in the schools.

The Spanish took over the agricultural economy of the Paraguayan Indian and gradually improved production methods and introduced new crops. The intermingling with the Indian stock, combined with the concentrated settlement in the Central Zone in order to obtain a labor supply, served to restrict the formation of a Spanish landholding aristocracy such as occurred in other countries of the Western Hemisphere. The small holdings, or <u>minifundia</u>, became the established pattern of land tenancy in Paraguay. To the native cotton, tobacco, <u>mandioca</u>, corn, peanuts, potatoes, beans, and squashes, the Spaniards added wheat, rice, and other cereals, as well as oranges, sugar cane, grapes, and temperate zone fruits. Their major contribution to the Paraguayan economy was the introduction of livestock--cattle, horses, pigs, sheep, goats, poultry, etc.

During the first century of the colonial period, Paraguay's commerce--internal as well as foreign--consisted almost entirely of agricultural and forest products. Unlike the other Spanish colonies in America, whose commerce was controlled by the mother country, the foreign trade of Paraguay was regulated and monopolized by Buenos Aires. This factor tended to keep Paraguay from European markets and influence and established the economic, political, and cultural isolation of the country which the dictator Francia was to confirm by his policies.

It has been said that Paraguay liberated itself from the Province of Buenos Aires rather than from Spain, and that the persistent efforts of Francia, Carlos Antonio López, and Francisco Solano López to consolidate its independence were against the pretensions of Argentina.

This enforced isolation, broken only intermittently during its history, has created a special Paraguayan mentality different from that in other Latin American countries. This mentality is characterized by an inordinate nationalism and the cultivation of the aboriginal language and culture as a defense mechanism against the encroachments of its neighbors. The absence of important inflows of immigrants until recent years has tended to preserve this pristine nationalism--based on cultural differences--and partly accounts for the small population of Paraguay compared with the demographic explosions taking place in Argentina and Brazil. Paraguay's increasing struggle to consolidate its independence, defend its frontiers, and integrate the national territory into a defensible political unit has created and perpetuated the tradition of strong personal, authoritarian rule and a highly centralized paternalistic administration of the country.

The slow--and at times--negative growth rate of the Paraguayan economy since its independence has been largely the result of its turbulent history: It has had to recommence its development effort four times, and each time the effort was interrupted by war or internal strife that put any previous progress to nought. Under Dr. Francia (1814-40) the national frontiers were closed, the national economy was almost entirely agricultural, and output was sufficient only for the needs of the producers. This pattern of producing at a low level and only for one's own (or family) needs prevails to this day in a large segment of Paraguayan agriculture.

Attempts by Carlos Antonio López to open up the country and to broaden its social, cultural, and economic perspectives were halted by the Triple Alliance War (1865-70) during the regime of Francisco Solano López. At the end of this war, "Paraguay lay all but lifeless."[1] Its population had declined from about 1 million in 1863 to about 221,000 in 1870; of these, 5 per cent were men and the rest women and children. Substantial territorial losses were suffered. At the time of its independence in 1811, Paraguay had an area of 237,173 square miles. During the Triple Alliance War, it lost 60,392 square miles (36,328 to Argentina and 24,064 to Brazil). As a result of the Chaco War with Bolivia (1932-35), the present area of 157,047 square miles was established; 61,719 square miles (39.3 per cent) lie east of the Paraguay River and 95,328 square miles (60.7 per cent) lie west of the river.[2]

After the Triple Alliance War, the country was occupied by Brazil and Argentina. Paraguay had to begin again to build the country. During the occupation period, the national monetary system was replaced by that of the conquerors, whose money circulated freely until a national monetary system was restored in 1944. The small labor force, consisting almost entirely of women, returned to its basic self-sustaining agricultural production. The ancient Guaraní system of mutual aid (minga) in agricultural activities, including home construction, was particularly important in this rebuilding effort in view of the labor shortage.

During the war and occupation periods,[3] the records of land titles were burned or lost, so there is still considerable confusion about ownership. The dire need to re-establish a national treasury resulted in the auctioning and sale of vast tracts of government lands in the Chaco and Alto Paraná, the areas of present-day large landholdings (chiefly ranches). The best and most suitably located lands were acquired by foreigners, particularly Argentines and Englishmen. In addition, the government floated two loans in London, in 1871 and 1872, which totaled

Ⱡ3 million. However, after prediscounts, commissions, and reparation claims of the Allies were deducted, the government netted only Ⱡ527,000 from these loans.[4] The country at the same time was opened to foreign investments, and an externally oriented commercial class was created in Paraguay. Also during this period, political instability became the rule.

During its interwar period from 1870 to 1932, Paraguay's economy recovered slowly. Its orientation remained inward, to supply local requirements. Foreign trade continued to be unimportant, amounting in 1934 to only slightly more than U.S. $4 million (equivalent), with exports slightly exceeding imports. Consequently, unlike the other Latin American countries, Paraguay's isolated economy was virtually unaffected by the Great Depression of the 1930's.

The Chaco War (1932-35) brought economic activity in Paraguay once again to a halt. Some 30,000 persons were lost in the war (including 20,000 youths) out of a population estimated at 1.5 million. Also, as previously mentioned, nearly 20,000 square miles of territory were lost. Livestock declined from a reported 3.984 million in 1932 to 3.052 million in 1935.

During the Chaco War, many conscripts from rural areas had been trained in the cities. As a result, an urbanization trend was begun after the war. While this brought more people into the market economy, at the same time it probably aggravated the parcelization of lands into small tracts in the Central Zone, because few job opportunities were available in the capital city.

The Constitution of 1940 provides for separate executive, legislative, and judicial branches. It also enables the President to govern under a "state of siege" under certain conditions. This power was generally exercised until 1963, when the state of siege was lifted in ten of the sixteen departments, or the bulk of the national territory outside Asunción. It was lifted for one day in the remaining areas to permit the municipal elections held on October 24, 1965, in all parts of the country.

The Government of Paraguay is republican in form. The Executive Branch consists of the President, a cabinet of ten appointed ministers, a Council of State, a National Economic Coordination Council, a less formal Economic Group (Equipo Económico), and a Technical Planning Secretariat for Economic and Social Development. Under the Constitution, the President is to be elected by direct vote for a term of five years and may be re-elected for a second term.

A unicameral congress of sixty members and twenty alternates exercises the legislative functions. Judicial power is vested in a Supreme Court of Justice of three members appointed for five-year terms, in a Tribunal of Accounts, and in lower courts.

The country is divided into sixteen departments and the capital city of Asunción. Of the sixteen departments, three are west of the Paraguay River: Presidente Hayes, Boquerón, and Olimpo. Thirteen departments lie east of the river: Concepción, San Pedro, La Cordillera, Guairá, Caaguazú, Caazapá, Itapúa, Misiones, Paraguarí, Alto Paraná, Central, Ñeembucú, and Amambay.

The Government of Paraguay under the Alfredo Stroessner Administration operates as a more or less benevolent autocracy through a republican form. The elite group is the military, which assures stability of the regime. There is little doubt, however, that the regime has the support of the majority of the people. A substantial degree of individual freedom is permitted and, by February, 1967, all major political parties in Paraguay had been recognized by the government.[5] Thus all important groups were able to participate in the process of revising the 1940 Constitution, which began in 1966. The major purpose of the constitutional revision presumably was to permit President Stroessner to run again for that office in the 1968 elections.

Opposition newspapers are vociferous in their criticism of the Administration and are quick to point out instances of corruption and inefficiency in the public sector. Nevertheless, there is an unwritten but well-understood proscription against direct criticism of the President, his family, and his friends. Political satire and caricatures are absent in Paraguay. A state of siege continues in certain parts of the country, and a number of political prisoners reportedly are held in jail.

The Asociación Nacional Republicana or Colorado Party exercises political control. Basically, it is in the hands of a rural class of popular origin. While no landed aristocracy is found in the country, a rural economic bourgeoisie may be said to be constituted by the large ranchers and lumbermen, many of whom are foreigners. There also is a growing merchant and industrial middle class. Although these businessmen have considerable economic power, until the decade of the 1960's they had little influence in national politics.

The businessmen and ranchers in general have supported the opposition parties (Liberal and Febrerista). This cleavage between the capitalist groups and the Administration until recently constituted a major impediment to Paraguay's economic development. Only within the past six years, coincident with the signing of the Charter of Punta del Este, has a real beginning been made to bring the public and private sectors into an effective working relationship. The business community has come more and more to adopt an apolitical attitude in its dealings with the Stroessner Administration. Political and monetary stability have been found profitable. By 1966, various major business organizations (e.g., Federation of Production, Industry, and Commerce [FEPRINCO]; Unión Industrial Paraguaya) were working with government officials in the preparation of draft legislation on new income tax and industrial incentive laws.

The lack of a traditional aristocracy has made for a rather open society in Paraguay. The isolation policy instituted by Dr. Francia offered little opportunity or incentive for the accumulation of wealth, and such wealth as had existed was soon reduced by forced austerity or confiscation. Until rather recently in Paraguayan history, the chaotic condition of the country made the accumulation of wealth precarious. As late as 1952, savings deposits in the banking system amounted to less than 25 million guaranies (about $500,000 at the then free market rate of 49 guaranies to the dollar).

The public sector is by far the largest and most important source of employment in Paraguay. Organization on the Central Governmental level comprises more than 29,000 public employees, not including the military. Employment by the Ministry of Education and Worship alone accounts for over 14,000, including over 13,000 school teachers. The next largest ministry, the Ministry of Interior, accounts for about 8,600 employees, including the police forces which total over 8,000. In addition to the Central Governmental organization, local governments throughout the 152 municipalities employ an estimated 1,650 persons, and the 21 autonomous agencies (including public services) have an additional 7,400 employees. The total governmental and semigovernmental work force, excluding the military, exceeds 38,000 persons. However, continuity of employment from one regime to another is not assured because there is no civil service system in effect and no formal merit system. In some of the autonomous agencies, however, there are elements of modern personnel administration in effect. The Central Government itself has no central personnel agency (other than, perhaps, Colorado Party headquarters) and no standard policies or practices for training of employees and for regulating employment, promotions, benefits, vacations, and evaluation of capabilities. Several past attempts to formulate civil service laws have bogged down, either before they were introduced into the legislature or during the legislative process.

The prime criterion for employment in government positions is political affiliation, past and present; members of opposition parties or their friends and relatives have little chance of being employed in the governmental organization, particularly in supervisory or professional posts. The almost universal method followed for securing government jobs (i.e., for appointment to the positions specified in the government budget) is through family members or friends already in influential government positions. The steady employment (while the regime is in power), short hours (most government offices work only in the mornings from 7 to 12), and opportunities to make lucrative contacts--rather than the salary level--are the main attractions. The government employees' afternoons and evenings are available for other employment, study, or leisure. Only in a relatively few offices and in policy positions is afternoon work necessary, usually for two or three hours.

Apart from the foregoing factors, the principal handicaps in the evolution of effective administration are: (a) the ingrained habits of having authority overcentralized in a few key and command positions; (b) the lack of delegation to lower echelons (due to fear of competition, of proliferation of authority, and of opening the door to excessive corrupt practices); (c) the general shortage of qualified middle-management personnel; and (d) the scarcity of qualified supporting staff. This overcentralized pattern of management tends to delay decision-making and to produce highly subjective executive decisions, rather than logically evolved policies, plans, and procedures. Staff preparation is lacking or inadequate. Although these problems prevail in other Latin American countries, the scarcity of trained and reliable administrative talent is particularly pronounced in Paraguay.

The conditions characterized above and the absence of modern methods and routinized administrative practices are particularly serious in their effects upon fiscal administration, particularly in the management and enforcement of revenue collections, budgeting, and controlling expenditures and floating debt.

A few examples will illustrate these conditions. The program budget system's elaborate classification does not correspond to the fiscal accounting breakdown and numbering system; the latter was not revised when the program budget was adopted. Therefore, the budgeted figures cannot be reconciled with summaries of the expenditures for a given period. The budget provisions are not "executed" by a systematic accounting for the amounts expended against the budget figures. Disbursements of certain categories hinge upon individual pressures, weighing of current contingencies, and executive authorizations. Budgeted expense items, without the needed pressure or support behind them, remain unexpended.

In the area of tax collections, the declared incomes subject to income tax are actually audited only in a small percentage of cases. The clerical processes called "office audits" consist mainly of routine checking and arithmetical verification of the figures filed, rather than scrutinies of the methods of accounting used or of the adequacy or totality of the declarations. Property tax bills are not mailed to all taxpayers. Taxes are collected on only about 45 per cent of the properties located in the capital and on about 25 per cent of those outside the capital. Follow-up on delinquent property tax payments is fragmentary and unsystematic, if done at all. Customs duties and charges, the major source of revenue, are substantially reduced by the traffic in smuggled goods. These are sold openly on the streets and in hundreds of business establishments without tax stamps and with virtually no fear of penalties. Tax enforcement in general tends to be selective, depending upon the status and influence of the taxpayer.

The development plans prepared by the Technical Planning Secretariat are not coordinated with the budget process. The annual budget preparation is largely a revision of the previous year's budget, taking into account current pressures and the degree of unsatisfied past needs. Because of the absence of a systematic budget execution process and of a detailed accounting reconciliation of actual outlays with the budgeted figures, the new annual budgets cannot be reconciled in accurate detail either with the requirements of the development plans or with the various past years' actual expenditures.

In summary, it can be said that there are major problem areas in every field of Paraguay's public administration. Lack of administrative capability is the primary problem in almost every field of governmental activity, and the prospects of wholesale administrative reforms are dim. Cultural barriers, tradition, and political considerations are major inhibiting factors to be overcome in virtually every area. In the past, overambitious attempts from external aid sources to achieve quick results either have failed completely or have left behind a backlog of unfinished business and a number of written reports whose recommendations are "on file." The most successful projects, resulting in the development of new institutions, had their groundwork well laid; these institutions are continuing to function well. Recently, local self-help efforts have begun to have an impact on improved administrative effectiveness in the interior of the country.

The economic philosophy of the Stroessner Administration, as expressed in various editorials in the Colorado Party's organ, _Pátria_, purports to be that of economic liberty (_libertad económica_) rather than--or as opposed to--orthodox economic liberalism (_liberalismo económico orthodóxo_). The characteristic of economic liberty, in _Pátria's_ use of this term, is that economic and financial policies and actions derive from and are directed toward the needs of the country, and transcend the selfish needs of private interests, individuals, or sectors.[6] The private sector is encouraged to organize into business associations and to cooperate with the State in establishing unselfish policies of national benefit. Implicit in this philosophy is the idea that State intervention in the private sector is justified when the private sector becomes self-seeking, greedy, exploitative, etc., or when it fails to do what the government deems necessary to develop the nation. Conversely, "orthodox economic liberalism," in _Pátria's_ conception of the term, means selfish exploitation of the nation's resources and people, disregard for national and social objectives, and conservative rugged individualism (_egoísmo_).

The policy of permissive freedom of private enterprise is reflected also in the Constitution of 1940. Article 13 provides that in no case shall private interests have primacy over the general interest of the Paraguayan nation. The most sweeping provision, however, is Article 15, which states that "the State shall regulate the economic life of the nation." Combinations tending to monopolize (corner) the market for consumer goods, artificially raise or lower prices, or obstruct free competition are prohibited. The State may nationalize the public services, with payment of indemnity, and establish monopolies for the production, distribution, and sale of articles of prime necessity. A monopoly may be established only by special law.

While Article 21 guarantees private property, it nevertheless authorizes the State to specify the maximum content and limit of holding in accordance with their social functions, and to expropriate or require a public sale of lands in excess of this limit. The right of eminent domain is also established, with the form of compensation to be fixed by law. Foreigners enjoy the same civil rights as Paraguayans (Article 36) and may engage in all legitimate business and own property without the obligation of acquiring citizenship.

The President of the Republic, in whom the Executive Power resides, in addition to his functions similar to those of the President of the United States, may also declare a total or partial state of siege. During the state of siege, he may order the arrest of any persons, move them to various parts of the national territory, or eject them from the country. He may also dissolve the House of Representatives[7] and remove the Councilors of State.

Any bills sent by the Executive Departments to the Congress must be dealt with within the same year; if not, they automatically become laws. During the recess of Congress, the President--with the approval of the Council of State--may issue decrees with the force of law. These decrees must be submitted to the next session of the Congress. The Executive Power is authorized (Article 56) to adopt plans for the redistribution of the population for economic, social, public health, or national defense reasons. Moreover, it not only may participate in preparing the laws, but it also is empowered to sanction and publish them (Article 51,3), as well as to issue the instructions and regulations required to execute the laws (Article 51,2). Any law passed by the Congress must receive the President's approval to become law (Article 78). If the proposed law is disapproved in its entirety by the President, it may not be reconsidered by the Congress in the same legislative year (Article 79). Proposals disapproved only in part may be reconsidered by the Congress and, if approved by a two-thirds vote, in two successive readings three days apart, become law. There is no known instance in which the Congress has used this authority. In short, the authority of the President of Paraguay is almost absolute. While theoretically he might not always get the legislation he wants, it is certain that legislation he does not want will not be enacted into law.

The 1940 Constitution provides for a Council of State (Article 62), to be composed of the ministers of the various departments of the government, the rector of the national university, the Archbishop of Paraguay, a representative of commerce, two representatives of the agricultural and livestock industries, a representative of processing industries, the President of the Bank of the Republic (now the Central Bank), and two retired members of the armed forces (one from the Army and one from the Navy, at least of the rank of colonel). The Council of State is authorized (Article 63) to (a) rule on proposed decrees with the force of law that the Executive Power may enact during the adjournment of the House of Representatives; (b) rule on matters of international policy submitted for its consideration by the Executive Power; (c) give consent to the appointment of members of the Supreme Court, diplomatic representatives abroad, and military promotions for the rank of colonel or above; (d) rule on financial or economic matters, for which purpose it may be advised by technical committees; and (e) act as a court for trying impeached members of the Supreme Court.[8] Thus, in certain respects, the Council of State exercises functions similar to those of the United States Senate, but without the attributes of being popularly elected and representative of particular areas of the country.

Juan Natalicio González, a noted Paraguayan writer and former President of the Republic, has termed the Council of State "an organism typically oligarchic and plutocratic."[9] He has charged that the representatives of the private sector are selected by the small oligarchic associations in the capital and thus the small farmers (_campesinos_) in the interior have no idea of who is representing them--representation in their name but generally not in their interests.[10] He termed the Council of State "a type of Senate established at the margin of the popular will," having as its tacit purpose the elimination of political parties from public life, as this elimination is the basis of its life and its success.[11] González believed that the private sector representatives in the Council of State represent political pressure groups that are trying to take the power of decision away from the government, and he has characterized the so-called private sector as a self-centered, myopic oligarchy of the capital, incapable of considering a problem in national or global terms. He claimed that the true "private sector" is composed of the farmers, who represent 75 per cent of the population, and includes also the small industrialists and merchants of the interior, who are the sole sources of credit for the _campesino_. However, this group is not represented in the Council of State but is controlled by the iniquitous pressure groups, and these irresponsible groups threaten democratic party government in Paraguay.[12]

The foregoing extremist attitude toward the private sector in the past was held widely in government circles. It is small wonder that the First Congress of Economic Entities of Paraguay, sponsored by FEPRINCO and held in April, 1951, was not repeated until August, 1964.

A National Economic Coordination Council was created by Law No. 47 of November 25, 1948. It is headed by the President of the Republic and comprises all the Ministers of State and the presidents of the two government banks, the Central Bank and the National Development Bank (formerly the Bank of Paraguay).[13] The Council has very broad powers and its decisions in the economic field are final. It has the following functions:

- Review of proposed legislation relating to taxation, the budget, and the public debt;

- Coordination of financial policy with the economic development of the country;

- Direction of the national economic policy and its planning;

- Settlement of banking, credit, and monetary questions in keeping with the laws regulating these matters;

- With the recommendation of the Department of Labor in the Ministry of Justice and Labor, establishment of minimum wages and authorizing wage increases, and in general regulating industrial and labor legislation;

- Issuance of directives regulating the distribution of articles of prime necessity and their maximum prices, if necessary;[14]

- Review of the texts of proposed commercial treaties or other international agreements relating directly or indirectly to the national economy or finances;

- Establishment of the minimum prices paid to farmers for agricultural products;
- Proposals of solutions to administrative problems, including recommendations for the reorganization of government departments;
- Supervision of the administration of the autonomous agencies;
- Study of the financing of the economic plans of the Central Government and the autonomous agencies;
- Supervision of the operations of the public services; and
- Proposals of the concession terms to be accorded industrial enterprises or public services.

Ceiling prices have been established for such articles of prime necessity as bread, biscuits, meat, sugar, and fuel. Minimum prices have been established for surplus agricultural commodities.

Within the National Economic Coordination Council is an Economic Group (Equipo Económico), headed by the Minister of Finance, and comprised also of the Ministers of Agriculture and Livestock and Industry and Commerce, and the presidents of the Central Bank and National Development Bank. The Economic Group deals with economic matters that can be handled at the ministerial level and also formulates recommendations on matters that require the action of the National Economic Coordination Council.

A recent addition to the government structure is the Technical Planning Secretariat for Economic and Social Development, created by Decree-Law No. 312 of March 6, 1962, and confirmed by Law No. 841 of September 14 of that year. Its head is an Executive Secretary (currently Dr. Federico Mandelburger) appointed by the President. The

Secretariat is a dependency of the Office of the President and provides advisory services to the President and the National Economic Coordination Council, as well as performing its planning activities of a global, sectoral, and regional nature. Since its inception, the Secretariat has received technical assistance from a Tripartite Advisory Group comprised of designees of the Organization of American States, the United Nations' Economic Commission for Latin America, and the Inter-American Development Bank.[15] Financial assistance, in the form of Public Law 480, Title I loans, has been made available annually to the Secretariat by the U.S. Agency for International Development (USAID) Mission for the purposes of expanding the staff and material of the Secretariat. This assistance was scheduled to terminate after 1968. The operations and performance of the Secretariat and its technical advisors are discussed in Chapter 16.

Outside the Central Government there are a number of autonomous agencies performing public services, social services, and economic development functions. The most important public service institutions are the National Electricity Administration (ANDE), the State Merchant Marine (FLOMERE), the Sanitary Works Corporation (CORPOSANA), and the National Telecommunications Administration (ANTELCO). In addition, there is a publicly owned railroad (Ferrocarril "Presidente Carlos Antonio López"), two airlines (Lineas Aéreas de Transporte Nacional, and Lineas Aéreas Paraguayas), and a recently organized port administration.

In the economic field are the Central Bank and the National Development Bank. The administration of the agrarian reform program and colonization projects of the government is in the hands of a Rural Welfare Institute (IBR), while low-cost housing and urbanization projects are the responsibility of the Paraguayan Housing and Urbanization Institute (IPVU). There is a government-supported National University of Asunción, a National Institute of Technology and Standards, and a National Atomic Energy Commission. A Social Insurance Institute provides social services to a growing number of Paraguayans. The foregoing agencies are discussed in the chapters dealing with their respective fields of activity.

SOCIAL FACTORS

Paraguay's population in mid-1966 was estimated at 2,094,100, with a growth rate of 3.1 per cent a year, compounded. During the intercensal period from 1950 to 1960, the population rose from 1,343,100 to 1,751,200.[16] Some 60 per cent of the population is rural. Virtually half of the people are located in the capital city of Asunción and in the Central Zone of eastern Paraguay. Asunción and surrounding areas account for 47 per cent of the urban population; the remainder of the urban dwellers are found in small cities, usually of less than 20,000 inhabitants.

The economically active population amounted to 615,630 persons in 1962, or 33.9 per cent of the total. A total of 70 per cent of the employed population was engaged in agricultural pursuits, largely within a radius of 60 miles of Asunción. Some 50 per cent of the employed population was self-employed. The more recent foreign elements in general are the most dynamic elements in the country, being the prime movers in its agricultural, commercial, and industrial growth. The relatively large number of such persons in the country augurs well for Paraguay's future. The initiative and know-how of these elements are gradually overriding the static qualities of the _mestizos_.*

Contrary to what is usually said of the population of Paraguay, it is not entirely homogeneous. Although the majority of the people are _mestizos_,

---

*The mixture of Spanish and Indian blood.

being admixtures of the Spanish and Indian (Guaraní) races, since the 1850's there have been additions of German, Italian, French, Swiss, Canadian, Polish, Russian, and more recently, Japanese and Korean stock.[17] It is estimated that only 3 per cent of the population is pure Indian. Nevertheless, Guaraní is an established language along with Spanish; both exist in spoken and written form. The lower classes, especially in the interior, may speak and understand Guaraní rather than Spanish. The state religion is Apostolic Roman Catholic. However, the Paraguayan Constitution guarantees liberty of worship to all faiths.

In response to growing labor demands for improved working conditions, the Liberal Administration of Dr. Félix Paiva instituted the eight-hour day and forty-eight-hour week on January 6, 1938; the law applied to all workers except farm labor, domestic servants, and higher company officials.[18] Legislation granting maternity benefits and assistance to working mothers in lower wage brackets was put into effect; the Department of Labor was organized as a permanent part of the Ministry of Justice and Labor, and strikes and lockouts were forbidden unless all attempts to settle labor disputes by conciliation and arbitration had failed.

Labor unions have had considerable difficulty in becoming established in Paraguay: Decree No. 39436 of 1931 dissolved workers' associations on the grounds that their aims had been perverted; in 1939, authorization was granted to the then National Labor Department to suspend the registration of employers' or workers' associations; and Decree No. 1217 of 1943 resumed regulation of the right of association. Freedom to organize trade unions was restored by Decree-Law No. 15,465 of 1947, and a Labor Code was enacted in 1961.[19] This Code for the first time provided regulations concerning the manner of organizing unions, both of employers and workers.

Current labor and social legislation are contained in the 1940 Constitution, the Labor Code, a

Code of Labor Procedure, and various social security laws. Article 14 of the Constitution proscribes the exploitation of one man by another and requires State inspection and supervision of all labor and social security contracts, as well as of health and safety conditions in places of employment. All inhabitants of the country are obligated to earn their livelihood through lawful work (Article 22).

The Labor Code (Law No. 729) was enacted together with the Code of Labor Procedure (Law No. 742) on August 31, 1961, and became effective April 1, 1962. The Labor Code provides for an eight-hour day and forty-eight-hour week,* a weekly rest day and holidays, and a system of paid vacations based on length of service.

Articles 250-61 of the Labor Code deal with the establishment of minimum wages. Such wages must be reviewed at least every two years, in the light of studies prepared by the Central Bank on trends in the cost of living since the previous minimum wages were established. The Department of Labor formulates its recommendations on the basis of these studies and forwards them to the National Economic Coordination Council for approval. If approved, the Department, through the Ministry of Justice and Labor, then issues a Resolution with the force of law. The change in the cost of living in any two-year period must exceed 10 per cent if the minimum wages are to be raised. Increases were effected on April 1, 1962 (15 per cent), and on April 1, 1964 (5 per cent in Asunción; 10 per cent in the interior). Supplemental payments and profit sharing by workers may be provided in labor contracts. The Labor Code also establishes and regulates health and safety standards and special working conditions for women and minors.

---

*In the case of night work the hours are reduced to seven per day and forty-two per week. Agricultural laborers may work twelve hours per day.

For the most part, labor activities in Paraguay are closely controlled by the government. The Paraguayan Labor Confederation (Confederación Paraguaya de Trabajadores, or CPT), with which most of the unions in the country are affiliated, is governed by a General Assembly whose head (Raimundo Pizurno) has been a Colorado Party Congressman. The two divisions into which the CPT is divided--Shore Unions (Sindicatos Terrestres) and Maritime Unions (Sindicatos Marítimos)--likewise have been "advised" by top government officials. Volta Gaona, Paraguay's Postmaster General, has been the adviser to the Shore Unions, and Dr. Nelson Villate, Subsecretary of Interior, has been the adviser to the Maritime Unions.

Recently, a church-supported Young Christian Workers' Union (Confederación Cristiana de Trabajadores--CCT) has appeared, working mainly in rural areas. It has been highly critical of the CPT as a State-dominated confederation whose member organizations have little freedom. The Catholic weekly Communidad publicizes the activities of the CCT and also criticizes the CPT.

Under the Labor Code the appropriate authorities may regulate individual and collective labor contracts, recognize labor unions and employer organizations and govern their formation, and stipulate the conditions under which strikes and lockouts are lawful. These functions are exercised by the Department of Labor of the Ministry of Justice and Labor. This Ministry has primary responsibility for implementing Article 32 of the Constitution, which confers on the State the power to supervise and regulate the organization, functioning, and activities of groups or entities of a public character. Outside the capital, the enforcement of the labor laws rests with the government delegates or delegations and political authorities appointed by the Minister of the Interior (Decree No. 9,442 of 1945 and Article 354 of the Labor Code). Thus, a written petition must be filed with the local political authorities who, in turn, must notify the proper labor authorities in the capital before any redress of grievances may be sought by the individual workers or the unions outside the capital. Indications are that enforcement of the Labor Code is not strict, especially in the rural areas.

In Paraguay, employers as well as workers are free to form unions, and they are entitled to protection against interference from each other. Employer unions are based on the branch of industry in which they are engaged. Unions of workers may be formed on the basis of their craft (occupation, trade, or specialty) or by enterprise (including all occupations). Such unions are formed for the purpose of the study, protection, development, and defense of professional interests, as well as for the social, economic, cultural, and moral benefit of the members.[20] The unions negotiate collective labor contracts and attempt to enforce them. While the Labor Code recognizes the right to strike and to a lockout, the conditions under which these may take place are limited specifically by the laws and by the Constitutional provision that in no case shall private interests prevail over the national interest.

The Code of Labor Procedure establishes procedures for the settlement of labor disputes by a permanent Board of Conciliation and Arbitration. Disputes must first be submitted to conciliation; failing this, arbitration is compulsory. If the parties cannot agree on how to implement the arbitration award, an enforcement procedure is established by the Board. Review of the Board's decisions may be had from a Labor Appeals Tribunal, whose decision is final.

The foregoing State controls over labor activities, combined with the predominance of company unions and the small number of industrial enterprises in Paraguay, have prevented the labor movement from attaining significance in this country. Labor disputes almost invariably have involved the intervention of the government. The official policy has been to prevent strikes or other labor disturbances whenever possible, especially when there were indications of serious complications. Nevertheless, there have been a few strikes in recent years, involving such issues as payment of overdue wages, wage increases, layoffs, or the transfer of workers from one type of work to another.

The government from time to time has organized seminars, both in Asunción and in the interior of the country, to train labor leaders. Some thirty such leaders attended a three-week course sponsored jointly by the Paraguayan Confederation of Workers (CPT) and the government, held at Encarnación in February, 1966.

The establishment of a social security system in Paraguay dates from 1943 (Decree-Law No. 17,071 of February 18), when a Social Welfare Institute was established as the central agency for social security in the country. This Decree-Law was amended by Decree-Law No. 1,860 of December 1, 1951, which is the organic law on social security. It provides benefits for nonoccupational illness or accidents, maternity, work-connected accidents or illnesses, death, and old age. Workers, wage earners, and employees engaged in private enterprise are covered by this Decree-Law, which was finally approved by the House of Representatives as Law No. 375 on August 26, 1957. By Law No. 1,085 of September 8, 1965, social security coverage was extended to teachers in private schools (effective March 2, 1966) and to domestic servants (effective January 2, 1967).

Railway employees are covered by a Retirement and Pension Fund established by Decree-Law No. 1,550 of May 29, 1940. Bank employees are covered by a similar fund established by Law No. 105 of August 27, 1951. Government employees and officials are covered by various special retirement and pension laws (e.g., for teachers, judicial officials, war veterans, and members of the armed forces and police).

The State, employers, and insured wage earners and workers contribute to the social security fund.

The monthly amounts of contribution stipulated in the most recent revision of the law (No. 1,085 of 1965) are as follows:

Salaried workers	6	per cent of salary.
Employers	13	per cent of workers' salaries.
State	1½	per cent of the wages for which employers are liable.
Teachers	5½	per cent of earnings.
Domestic servants	₲	150
Private schools employing teachers subject to social security	2½	per cent of payroll subject to local security contribution.
Employers of domestic servants	₲	75
Independent workers	8	per cent on minimum salary for 25 days.

A worker who reaches age 60 and has paid at least 780 weekly installments to the social security fund is entitled to an annual life pension.

Notes to Chapter 1

1. Philip Raine, Paraguay (New Brunswick, N.J.: Scarecrow Press, 1956), p. 185.

2. Juan Natalicio González, Geografía del Paraguay (Mexico City: Editorial Guarania, 1964), p. 615; and Ministerio de Agricultura y Ganadería, STICA, Manual Estadístico del Paraguay, 1941/1961, Publication No. 254, Asunción, September, 1963, p. 3.

3. Occupying troops were finally withdrawn on June 22, 1876.

4. Raine, op. cit., p. 209.

5. The "Radical Liberal" Party, the largest opposition group, was recognized on February 27, 1967.

6. ". . . . las actividades económico - financieras hacia las conveniencias del país, que están por encima de los egoísmos de los intereses privados, individuales o sectoriales." Pátria, Asunción, September 16, 1965, p. 1 (editorial entitled "Importantes Medidas").

7. However, he is obliged to call new elections within two months of this action.

8. Raúl Sapena Pastor and Raúl Sapena Brugada, A Statement of the Laws of Paraguay in Matters Affecting Business (Washington, D.C.: Pan American Union, 1962), p. 11.

9. Juan Natalicio González (President from August 15, 1948, to January 30, 1949), op. cit., pp. 637-38. He died in December, 1966.

10. Ibid.

11. Ibid., p. 638.

12. Ibid., pp. 641-42.

13. Members of the Finance and Budget Committee and of the Industry and Commerce Committee of the Congress may be invited to attend meetings dealing with the particular fields of interest. However, they have no vote in the Council.

14. The supervision of such activities has been delegated to the Ministry of Industry and Commerce.

15. By an agreement with the Government of Paraguay signed November 20, 1962.

16. Projections of the population through 1970 are as follows:

1967 2,161,200
1968 2,230,500
1969 2,303,500
1970 . . . . . 2,379,000.

17. The first foreign colony established in Paraguay was settled by French immigrants in May, 1855. (Raine, _op. cit._, p. 297.)

18. _Ibid._, p. 251.

19. Pastor and Brugada, _op. cit._, p. 131.

20. Articles 281 and 286 of the Labor Code.

PART I

AGRICULTURE

CHAPTER 2 FARMING

Agricultural experts agree that Paraguay has substantial amounts of excellent soil and forest resources of certain hardwoods, and they believe that the potential is great for crop, orchard, and pasture development and livestock improvement.[1] Although agriculture is performed in the main under pioneering conditions, fields and herds reportedly are fairly well cared for. Some 60 per cent of the farms in Paraguay utilize animals as their source of power, and 36 per cent still rely entirely upon human energy for their operation. Only 1 per cent derive their power entirely from mechanical means, and 3 per cent from a combination of animal and mechanical sources. Fertilizer is employed on less than 15 per cent of the farm properties, almost entirely in the form of manure.

The great mass of farmers are self-sufficient, clean, fairly well housed (compared with other Latin American countries), and reasonably well fed except for some deficiency in minerals (chiefly iodine) and vitamins. The staple foods of the country are meat and _mandioca_ (also known variously as manioc, cassava, and yuca). The dietary need is to increase the intake of dairy products, eggs, fruits, and vegetables. Most farmers in Paraguay regard themselves as being in the money economy.[2]

IMPORTANCE TO THE ECONOMY

Paraguay's agricultural sector, which includes the production of field crops and forest products, livestock, game, and fish, accounted for at least

36 per cent of its Gross National Product in 1965 and (in 1962) employed about 53 per cent of the economically active population. The economically active population totaled 599,000, of which 258,000 (43 per cent) were in agriculture, 27,000 (5 per cent) in ranching, and 28,000 (5 per cent) in forestry operations. Productivity per person employed in the agricultural sector (in 1962), as estimated by the Technical Planning Secretariat, varied considerably, averaging $271 in farming, $417 in forestry, and $1,211 in ranching. As Paraguay's exports consist almost entirely of agricultural sector products and of commodities derived from them (e.g., meat products; vegetable and essential oils; quebracho extract), these productivity relationships directly reflect the importance of the respective components in the country's export trade.

Paraguay's manufacturing industries, with a few exceptions, are based upon the processing of agricultural products. Thus, the national economy is almost entirely dependent upon agriculture and, according to agricultural experts, Paraguay is a classic case of low-level equilibrium based on subsistence agriculture. It must rely on the importation of essential capital goods to change its present system of production. The subsistence level of agriculture is demonstrated further by the fact that, according to a 1961 sample census, nearly 70 per cent of the farms in Paraguay were less than 10 hectares (25 acres) in size, but some 91 per cent of the farms, regardless of their size, had less than 10 hectares in cultivation (see Tables 1 and 2). Moreover, 45 per cent of the properties enumerated were held by squatters, who accounted for 8 per cent of the total farm area (see Table 3). The bulk of the subsistence farmers is found in the Central Zone near Asunción.

TABLE 1

Distribution of Enumerated Farms, by Size, Crop Year 1960/61

Size of Farm, in Hectares	Number of Farms	Per Cent	Cumulative Number of Farms	Cumulative Per Cent
0.1 - 9.9	112,294	69.9	112,294	69.9
10 - 19.9	26,451	16.4	138,745	86.3
20 - 49.9	13,700	8.5	152,445	94.8
50 - 99.9	3,053	1.9	155,498	96.7
100 - 499.9	3,009	1.9	158,507	98.6
500 - 999.9	641	0.4	159,148	99.0
1,000 - 4,999.9	1,081	0.6	160,229	99.6
5,000 - 9,999.9	270	0.2	160,499	99.8
10,000 -19,999.9	132	0.1	160,631	99.9
20,000 and over	146	0.1	160,777	100.0
TOTAL	160,777	100.0		

Source: Ministry of Agriculture and Livestock, Agricultural Census of 1961.

TABLE 2

Size of Tracts Under Cultivation, Crop Year 1960/61

Area Under Cultivation, in Hectares	Number of Farms	Per Cent of Total	Cumulative Per Cent
Without arable land	2,807	1.7	1.7
0.1 - 0.4	4,480	2.8	4.5
0.5 - 0.9	8,887	5.5	10.0
1 - 1.9	24,364	15.2	25.2
2 - 2.9	24,694	15.4	40.6
3 - 3.9	21,974	13.7	54.3
4 - 4.9	17,996	11.2	65.5
5 - 5.9	40,843	25.3	90.8
10 - 19.9	11,766	7.3	98.1
20 - 49.9	2,489	1.5	99.6
50 - 99.9	328	0.3	99.9
100 or more	147	0.1	100.0
TOTAL	160,777	100.0	

Source: Ministry of Agriculture and Livestock, Agricultural Census of 1961.

TABLE 3

Number and Area of Enumerated Farms, by Type of Occupancy, Agricultural Year 1960/61

Type of Occupancy	Number of Farms	Per Cent	Area in Hectares	Per Cent
Owner-occupied:	59,994	37.3	14,200,935	81.3
With definite title	48,688	30.3	13,839,055	79.2
With provisional title	11,306	7.0	361,880	2.1
Rented:	12,000	7.5	726,798	4.1
For cash payment	9,700	6.0	713,671	4.1
Share-cropped	2,300	1.5	13,128	. .
Squatter	66,643	41.5	1,235,656	7.1
Multitype occupancy:[a]	22,130	13.7	1,310,084	7.5
Owner-occupied	8,391	5.2	1,059,285	6.1
Rented	5,124	3.2	95,615	0.5
Share-cropped	2,617	1.6	19,914	0.1
Squatter	5,998	3.7	135,270	0.8
TOTAL	160,777	100.0	17,473,474	100.0

[a]Distribution based on type of occupation of principal area.

Source: Ministerio de Agricultura y Ganadería, Censo Agropecuario por Muestreo, 1961 (Asunción, 1964), pp. 10-11.

TABLE 4

Distribution of Farms by Type and Size, 1960/61

Type and Size of Farm	Number of Farms	Per Cent
Crop farms	158,391	98.5
Very small	18,026	11.2
Small	37,548	23.4
Medium	94,925	59.0
Large	7,892	4.9
Livestock ranches	981	0.6
Medium	429	0.3
Large	552	0.3
Mixed farms[a]	1,405	0.9
Medium	1,177	0.7
Large	228	0.2
TOTAL	160,777	100.0

[a]Livestock and crops combined.

TABLE 5

Number and Size Classification of Farms by Department, 1960/61

Department	Very Small	Small	Medium	Large
Capital	610	316	116	3
Concepción	433	1,317	5,094	156
San Pedro	617	2,505	6,112	230
La Cordillera	2,450	6,288	13,939	1,360
Guairá	3,030	3,152	7,278	442
Caaguazú	1,404	2,007	7,890	361
Caazapá	1,150	2,783	7,410	301
Itapúa	1,727	2,386	10,912	1,653
Misiones	156	1,442	3,671	422
Paraguarí	2,025	6,290	16,542	782
Alto Paraná	97	504	744	27
Central	2,332	6,252	8,728	675
Ñeembucú	1,269	1,479	3,920	308
Amambay	32	74	1,527	444
Presidente Hayes	308	583	501	---
Boquerón	317	95	485	728
Olimpo	69	75	56	---
TOTAL	18,026	27,548	94,925	7,892

LANDHOLDING

Because of the predominance of small holdings, Paraguay's agricultural land is mainly (87 per cent) owner-occupied, as shown in Table 3. Less than 5 per cent is rented, and there is virtually no share cropping. Squatters occupy about 8 per cent of the farmland area. According to the sample census of 1961, 98.5 per cent of the properties were devoted to field crops, 0.6 per cent to ranching, and 0.9 per cent to both field crops and ranching, as shown in Table 4.

Crop farms have been classified according to size, as follows:

Class	Size
Very small	Less than 0.5 hectare
Small	0.5 to 3 hectares
Medium	3 to 10 hectares
Large	10 or more hectares

It is clear from the foregoing data in Table 5 that, not only are nearly 94 per cent of the crop farms in Paraguay of uneconomic size (under 10 hectares), but the majority of these *minifundia* or small holdings are located within an area whose radius extends about 90 miles eastward from Asunción, on the uplands above the flood plain. Some 40 per cent of the rural population is concentrated in a pie-shaped wedge extending from Asunción northeastward to San Estanislao, thence southward through Villarrica, southwest to San Juan Bautista, and thence northwest to Asunción. The diversified output of these farms consists primarily of items for auto-consumption (*mandioca*, corn, beans, sugar cane, vegetables, fruits) and perhaps some small surpluses for nearby urban markets. Even on these holdings, room for additional production exists as not all the land is under cultivation. The pressure of people on the land that characterizes this Central Zone does not exist elsewhere in Paraguay. The *minifundia* problem is the principal reason why only some 60 per cent of the farm labor force is gainfully employed; the remainder of the farm labor force is either underemployed or unemployed. This surplus labor supply serves to perpetuate the low level of farm wages and to limit the size of the national market.

Most of the large farms are located south of the highway running from Asunción almost due east to Puerto Presidente Stroessner on the Paraná River. The other important area for large farms is the Department of La Cordillera lying across this highway, just a few miles from the capital city. Its capital is Caacupe where the country's major agricultural experiment station is located.

Ranches were divided into only two size classifications in the 1961 sample census of agriculture: medium and large. These classifications were based upon land area and the number of cattle grazed, as shown in Table 6.

Most ranches lie along the Paraná and Paraguay rivers; the largest-sized ranches are in the Chaco. The reasons for this are discussed in Chapter 3.

While the 1961 census reported nearly 95 per cent of the properties to be owned by Paraguayans, it did not relate this figure to the area of farmland they control. It is reasonably certain that the 5 per cent of farm properties owned by foreigners, including the major meatpacking establishments in the country, account for a very substantial proportion of the land devoted to field crops and especially to livestock raising.[3] The allocation of farms by nationality of ownership was reported to have been as shown at the top of page 44.

TABLE 6

Number and Size of Ranches, 1960/61

Zone A[a]	Medium	Large	Total
Concepción	13	41	54
San Pedro	21	30	51
La Cordillera	8	8	16
Guairá	25	8	33
Caaguazú	11	16	27
Caazapá	2	19	21
Paraguarí	47	39	86
Central	2	6	8
Subtotal	129	167	296
Zone B[b]			
Itapúa	38	16	54
Misiones	44	78	122
Alto Paraná	--	--	---
Ñeembucú	159	66	225
Amambay	2	6	8
Subtotal	243	166	409

Zone C[c]			
Presidente Hayes	9	209	218
Boquerón	24	10	34
Olimpo	24	--	24
Subtotal	57	219	276
TOTAL	429	552	981

[a]In Zone A, large ranches must be of 50 or more hectares each and pasture 250 or more head of cattle; medium ranches must have 3 to 50 hectares and more than 250 head of cattle.

[b]In Zone B, large ranches consist of 100 or more hectares each with 500 or more head; medium ranches range from 3 to 100 hectares and carry over 500 head each.

[c]In Zone C, representing the vast Chaco region, large ranches are those having 5,000 or more hectares and pasturing at least 1,000 head each. Medium-sized ranches are those below 5,000 hectares but having more than 1,000 head each.

Nationality	Number of Farms Operated	Per Cent of Total
Paraguayan	152,600	94.9
European	2,872	1.8
Argentine	1,759	1.1
Asiatic	1,351	0.8
Mennonite (various)	1,346	0.8
Brazilian	760	0.5
Other Americans	89	0.1
TOTAL	160,777	100.0

LAND USE

Paraguay's area of 157,047 square miles is equivalent to 40,675,200 hectares (101,688,000 acres).* Only 2 per cent of this area is devoted to farming. About 60 per cent of the land area is in forests, 34 per cent in livestock, and the remainder in various kinds of wasteland (see Table 7). The total acreage devoted to farming and livestock raising amounted to 17,473,474 hectares in 1961. However, the opening of new agricultural areas in recent years with the aid of a partially United States Government-financed feeder road program, combined with colonization efforts by the Government of Paraguay, undoubtedly have increased this figure.

Because of their major importance to Paraguay's economy, ranching and forestry activities are treated in separate chapters. The remainder of this chapter discusses field crops.

COMPOSITION OF FARM OUTPUT

Paraguay produces both field crops and tree crops. Its principal field crops include corn,

*One hectare equals approximately 2.5 acres.

TABLE 7

Land Use in 1962
(In Thousands of Hectares)

	Eastern Region	Western Region	Total	Per Cent
Farming	838.0	25.0	863.0	2.1
Cultivated	672.0	21.0	693.0	
Fallow	166.0	4.0	170.0	
In Livestock	5,770.0	8,652.0	14,332.0	34.2
Permanent pasture	2,814.0	2,337.0	5,151.0	
Seasonal pasture	2,020.0	2,569.0	4,589.0	
Artificial pasture	14.0	2.0	16.0	
Swamps, mountains, brush, etc.	922.0	3,654.0	4,576.0	
Forested	8,757.0	15,466.0	24,223.0	59.6
Other Uses	618.0	639.0	1,257.0	3.1
TOTAL	15,983.0	24,692.0	40,675.0	100.0

Source: Technical Planning Secretariat, *Plan Nacional de Desarrollo Económico y Social para el Bienio 1965-66* (Asunción, 1965), Vol. II, p. 14.

mandioca, sugar cane, beans, peas, rice, sweet potatoes, onions, potatoes, peanuts, wheat, various kinds of melons, and alfalfa, which are produced for internal consumption. Cotton and tobacco are important field crops which also enter the export trade. The major tree crops are citrus fruits (grapefruits, oranges, tangerines, lemons), *yerba maté* (Paraguayan tea), oilseeds (coconut, tung), bananas, and coffee. All of these also are exported, the *yerba maté* and *petitgrain* oil being the most important of the tree crops sent abroad.

The country is virtually self-sufficient in food production, in spite of the fact that yields per hectare appear to have varied relatively little during the past twenty-five years (see Table 8).* Imports consist almost entirely of wheat and wheat derivatives; salt; dried, powdered, and condensed milk; temperate zone fruits; and spices, as shown in Table 9.

The maintenance of virtual self-sufficiency in spite of a population growing at the rate of 3.1 per cent a year has been due almost entirely to the expansion of the cultivated area. Substantial capacity exists for further increases in farm output through a choice or combination of methods: (a) further increases in the area under cultivation; (b) the application of better production techniques (more animal and mechanical power; utilization of fertilizer on a wider scale; more extensive crop rotation); and (c) improvement in the economic position of agriculture by means of price incentives and better marketing facilities.

---

*As in the case of the national income statistics, those for agricultural production also are highly unreliable. There is no crop reporting system in Paraguay, and the production figures are "made up" in the Ministry of Agriculture and Livestock. Moreover, the figures published in various sources vary as much as 100 per cent. Consequently, we have reported those data which are the product of agricultural censuses as being the best available.

The following discussion of individual crops is based mainly on two U.S. Government-sponsored reports, Agriculture In Paraguay[4] and Encuesta de Salud, Nutrición y Alimentación, Republica del Paraguay, Mayo-Agosto, 1965.[5]

1) Mandioca -- The major cultivated crop produced in Paraguay is mandioca. The areas of highest production are the Departments of Paraguarí, Itapúa, Central, La Cordillera, and Caazapá. It is the universal crop of the subsistence farmer and, together with meat, forms the basic diet of the population. In spite of this, the majority of the output (including the roots) is used to feed cattle, oxen, and pigs. Mandioca is a cheap source of carbohydrates of high caloric yield per acre. Relatively small quantities are industrialized into flour, starch, and tapioca. Further industrialization of this product would permit a substantial increase in its output. Mixed with other locally produced by-products, mandioca could make an excellent improved animal feed.

A basic problem is to expand the cultivation of those low-fiber content varieties of mandioca having the greatest industrial potention (e.g., pomberí, yerutī, caballero-ī, concepción, and cano). In many areas, inferior varieties are being grown[6] because they are easier to cultivate.

2) Corn -- Corn ranks as the second most important cultivated crop. Along with mandioca and sugar cane, it is a major source of carbohydrates. The Departments of Paraguarí and Itapúa are the leading producing areas, although corn is grown in every part of the country. A yellow variety (venezolano) and two white varieties (pepi and blanco) are grown in Paraguay. Corn is raised as a cash crop, as well as for subsistence, and is consumed by both humans and animals. Its use in poultry feed has been increasing in recent years, and with a rationalization of poultry production the demand for corn for this purpose could become quite important.

TABLE 8

Yield of Principal Crops, In Census Years 1942/43, 1956, and 1960/61

(In Kilograms per Hectare)

Crops	Agricultural Census of 1942/43	Agricultural and Livestock Census 1956	Sample Agricultural and Livestock Census of 1960/61[a]
Cotton	774	604	800
Rice	1,603	1,963	2,100
Green peas	622	448	600
Sweet potatoes	9,700	9,800[b]	8,800
Calabashes	1,400	1,530	1,878
Sugar cane	21,600	29,700	30,000
Onions	2,079	2,150	3,100
Lima beans	842	595	830
Corn	1,068	1,172	1,200
Peanuts	914	823	1,000
Mandioca	14,500	15,450[b]	16,000
Potatoes	2,980	3,514	3,600

Beans	790	659	800
Soybeans	734	589	1,100
Tobacco	1,208	1,243	1,300
Castor beans	1,011	1,103	1,100
Wheat	821	776	800
Tung	1,800	2,000	5,600[c]
Coffee	500	600	800[c]

[a]Yields are from farms specializing in the respective crops. On farms where these crops were grown in combination, yields were uniformly lower.

[b]Datum from the Ministry of Agriculture and Livestock.

[c]Yield per plant.

TABLE 9

Principal Imports of Foodstuffs, 1962-66
(In Metric Tons)

	1962	1963	1964	1965	1966
Wheat and derivatives	88,897	79,174	68,716	71,793	71,864
Onions	2,287	397	2,152	---	74
Salt	16,401	17,446	15,777	21,616	20,495
Spices and conserves	519	429	229	121	272
Fruits	804	976	857	803	913
Dairy products	1,656	3,152	671	769	644
Sweets	78	66	41	42	42
Coffee	10	15	7	4	--
Others	5,111	5,715	5,041	3,592	4,039
TOTAL	115,763	107,372	93,491	98,840	98,343

Source: Central Bank of Paraguay.

Corn, when planted on newly cleared lands, gives high initial yields. However, because little fertilizer is used and crop rotation is not practiced widely, the yields decline with time. The Ministry of Agriculture and Livestock and the Inter-American Technical Service for Agricultural Cooperation, known as STICA, have been very successful in their efforts to increase yields. However, better cultural practices, especially in the use of fertilizers, could increase production materially. As most farmers have no storage facilities, they lose a sizable share of their output to insects and rodents. According to the 1961 sample census of agriculture, some 229,000 metric tons of corn were produced but only 50 per cent was sold. Even so, small amounts of corn are exported annually.

3) Sugar cane -- Sugar cane is an important source of cash income for numerous small growers whose plantings may range from 5 to 10 hectares. However, the larger sugar mills produce substantial amounts (perhaps one third of their requirements) for their own use as a means of stabilizing their operations. These large sugar growers raise varieties best suited to their soils and are among the largest users of fertilizers in the country. If adequate markets were available, Paraguay could raise sugar cane production materially by the appropriate use of credit, fertilizer, and improved varieties. Unfortunately world sugar prices have fallen in recent years, Paraguay is a marginal exporter to the world market, it has failed to obtain a quota in the United States, and internal demand for the product has been limited by its small population and purchasing power. Unless additional internal uses for sugar are developed--which would appear likely with increasing industrialization--it would seem to be advisable to shift the small producers into more economic cash crops rather than continue to subsidize them through the national budget.

Guairá is the center of sugar cane production, with the highest yield per hectare (about 40 metric tons) in the country. Paraguarí and Central are other important cane producing departments.

4) Wheat -- Paraguay's consumption of wheat in 1966 was estimated at about 100,000 metric tons. Production has ranged between 5,000 tons in 1957 and 14,000 tons in 1959. Thus far, wheat has been grown on small farms, thereby making it difficult to mechanize production and increase its scale. Yields are low, running about 800 kilos per hectare. This is considerably below that of Argentina and only about half that of the United States. Consequently, costs of local wheat are high even when compared with imports. The Departments of Itapúa and Misiones produce over 80 per cent of the wheat crop.

To supplement its wheat requirements, Paraguay has been purchasing between 65,000 and 75,000 tons of wheat annually from Argentina, and has obtained virtually all of the remainder from the United States Government by means of Surplus Agricultural Commodity Sales Agreements under Public Law 480. The local currency proceeds of these sales agreements have been of major importance in the non-inflationary financing of capital projects of the Government of Paraguay, as well as in providing local currency for official U.S. Government uses in the country.

In 1965, the Paraguayan Government took the initial steps to expand domestic wheat production, with a view to attaining eventual self-sufficiency in this basic commodity. However, the government appeared to be emphasizing small-farm cultivation rather than extensive growing on large farms and ranches. This policy would perpetuate high-cost output in the country and would not raise production substantially.

STICA experts have recommended that the National Wheat Program be undertaken on ranches, utilizing the program at the same time to develop improved pastures. Thus, if the grazing area were divided into five parts, each year one part could be planted in wheat, on a scale large enough to permit mechanization, and at the end of five years, improved pasture would be attained over the total area through the rotation system. This cycle could then be continued. The quality of the wheat raised in

Paraguay is satisfactory for producing a good baking flour. It is a semihard variety having a high gluten content (about 48 per cent). Imports consist of hard winter wheat.

5) Cotton -- The output of cotton is vital to the economy of Paraguay. The fiber is used not only to supply the relatively efficient domestic textile industry, but also for export to West Germany, France, the United Kingdom, Spain, and Japan. The staple length of Paraguayan cotton fiber ranges from 15/16 of an inch to 1 1/6 inches, averaging 1 1/32 inches. It is comparable to the U.S. "middling" classification. The quality reportedly has great acceptance in the aforementioned markets.

Most of the cotton is produced by small farmers on tracts averaging between 1 hectare and 1½ hectares. There are few large cotton growers, and most of these are located in the Mennonite colonies in the Chaco. As most farmers do not have the money to finance the growing of cotton, its exporters in large part provide the seed and some cash for harvesting costs. Because the use of insecticides and fertilizers are most important in cotton production, the undercapitalization of this activity is a major drawback to increasing production. The average small grower obtains a yield ranging only between 350 and 700 kilograms per hectare. The cotton is packed by hand and is stored in his house until sold.

Except in the case of a few large growers, who sell directly to exporters or ginners, the cotton is purchased at the farm by agents (acopiadores) of exporters or ginners. Inasmuch as cotton is often his only cash crop, the farmer is under considerable pressure to sell at the agent's price to pay his accumulated debts. All of the cotton sold, except that marketed by the Mennonite colonies in the Chaco, is sold as seed cotton. Cottonseed oil is an important industrial product of Paraguay and is discussed in Chapter 6.

The Department of Paraguarí accounts for about one fourth of the national output of cotton; lesser amounts are produced in Itapúa and La Cordillera. Cotton production, exportation, and consumption in Paraguay over the past twelve years has been as shown in Table 10. About 32 per cent of the cotton goes for fiber, 60 per cent for seed, and 8 per cent for wastes. Between 12 per cent and 18 per cent of the fiber produced is consumed in the country; the remainder is exported very largely to Uruguay and to Europe, or is held as stocks.

6) Tobacco -- A relatively large number of small farmers rely on tobacco as an important source of cash income. However, the planted area varies from year to year in accordance with price expectations. Over a period of years, however, average production has not changed very much. The crop is sold in a manner similar to cotton, through intermediaries to exporters or manufacturers. The center of production is the Department of Caaguazú, followed by the Departments of La Cordillera and Paraguarí.

Two major types of tobacco are produced: One type, called *flojo*, is rather mild and is exported primarily to European markets for use in the manufacture of cigars and for blending with other tobaccos for making cigarettes. A darker, stronger tobacco, *criollo*, also is produced. It is used largely within Paraguay for the cigar and cigarette industries, but some also is exported to Argentina. The quality of Paraguayan tobacco is very uneven because of the primitive curing methods employed. Most growers hang the leaves in the open for drying, so that unseasonable rains or high humidity conditions cause substantial losses from mold or other infestations. The tobacco is graded only when it reaches the exporters, and there is no uniform grading system.

An article in the newspaper *La Tribuna* of January 4, 1966, reported on the recommendations of a commission to formulate a tobacco development plan. The commission had been created under the sponsorship of the Technical Planning Secretariat

TABLE 10

Production, Exports, and Apparent Consumption of Cotton Fiber, 1954-66
(In Thousands of Metric Tons)

Year	Production	Exports	Apparent Consumption[a]
1954	12.9	11.6	1.3
1955	13.2	9.5	3.7
1956	11.9	10.3	1.6
1957	11.0	8.9	2.1
1958	11.2	8.2	3.0
1959	8.8	6.4	2.4
1960	4.3	1.2	3.1
1961	8.5	5.0	3.5
1962	10.7	7.0	3.7
1963	12.9	8.9	4.0
1964	11.5	9.7	1.8
1965	14.3	10.8[b]	3.5
1966	n.a.	5.7	n.a.

[a]Including stocks.

[b]Valued at $4,687,000.

and the Tripartite Advisory Group (OAS-IDB-ECLA). This commission concluded that the best type of tobacco to be grown in Paraguay is the black tobacco known as tipo criollo. Not only are growers familiar with this variety but it has a good potential market in France, Spain, and other European countries. However, curing has to be improved and better classification needs to be instituted. The zones of greatest productivity are in the northern departments of the country (Paraguarí, Guairá, Caaguazú, and San Pedro), and these are the areas where efforts should be made to increase output.

The commission recommended the establishment of an intensive educational program for the tobacco growers to improve materially their techniques of cultivating, curing, and classifying their product. It was felt that the establishment of a producers' cooperative might be the best means of channeling technical assistance to the tobacco farmers and providing them with credit for constructing proper curing facilities. They also recommended the establishment of offices abroad to promote the sale of Paraguayan products directly to users, thereby avoiding the costs of dealing through middlemen.

The newspaper article reported that the tobacco industry was operating at only 50 per cent of its installed capacity because of the small demand for locally produced cigarettes. Cigarettes, particularly from the United States, are the major item of contraband imports into Paraguay.

7) Oilseed crops -- Cottonseeds, peanuts, and castor beans are the major field crop oilseeds produced in Paraguay. Cotton and cottonseed production were discussed under item (5) above. Peanuts are grown on small farms, chiefly in the Departments of Paraguarí and La Cordillera. The Mennonite colonies in the Department of Boquerón, in the Chaco, also produce small amounts. Because of better production techniques and greater specialization, these colonies obtain yields substantially greater than elsewhere in the country. Soybeans, thus far a very minor crop in Paraguay, nevertheless give promise of

becoming much more important, both as an export crop and as a local industrial raw material. The Department of Itapúa is the principal production area; other growing areas are Caazapá, Amambay, Caaguazú, and Guairá, in eastern Paraguay.

The castor bean (tártago) contains about 50 per cent oil which has many important industrial uses.[7] While some 80 per cent of Paraguay's output of castor beans is obtained from low-yielding indigenous varieties,[8] efforts are being made to expand the production of imported varieties. Brazil, India, and Thailand are the principal world producers.

Paraguay's climate in all parts of the country, except the westernmost Chaco, is ideal for castor bean production. The bean is grown either as a perennial plant or as an annual crop. On a perennial basis, the plants attain two or three times their normal growth and produce from four and one half months after planting up to three years, yielding beans almost every month. With this method of cultivation, however, only some 5,000 plants per hectare may be planted.

Annual crops of castor beans generally are produced on lands of average fertility that also are suitable for cotton and corn cultivation. In Encarnación and Alto Paraná, profitable crops of castor beans are grown in this manner, with plantings ranging from 15,000 to 33,000 plants per hectare. Important yields are obtained prior to the frosts (e.g., 700 kilos per hectare). The frost limit for growing castor beans is 3½° C. below zero. Two crops a year are grown.

In 1961, the main producing areas were the Departments of Concepción, Boquerón, and La Cordillera. Only about 9,000 hectares of castor beans were cultivated in that year and the yield amounted to about 9,000 metric tons.

Commercial varieties of seed are imported from Brazil ("I-A-C-38" and "7 Canadas Rajadas") and the United States ("Lynn," "Hale," and "Dawn"). When the United States and Brazilian varieties are interspersed, yields may reach as much as 3,500 kilos per hectare, compared with about 2,500 kilos per hectare in Texas from the U.S. varieties. In Concepción, the largest commercial producing area of this crop in the country, the National Development Bank is encouraging the cultivation of castor beans by distributing imported seeds to farmers and granting credit to cultivators.

Costs of production on family plots are reported at 3.50 to 5 guaranies per kilo, with output ranging from 1,200 to 3,000 kilos per hectare.* For mechanized operations, production costs in Paraguay rise to between 5 and 7 guaranies per kilo, compared with 8.82 guaranies (equivalent) in India and 7.56 guaranies in the United States. The selling price for Paraguayan castor beans has been around 8 guaranies per kilo.[9]

PROBLEMS OF PARAGUAYAN AGRICULTURE

Special agricultural problems pertain to Paraguay's Central Zone, where not only have the soils been depleted by centuries of light temperature and rainfall but the land in this zone has been fragmented by a rapidly multiplying farm population. This has produced the pattern of subsistence agriculture mentioned above. On these subsistence farms, diversified production for auto-consumption is the rule, and yields per hectare for all crops produced are uniformly lower than on specialized farms. Comparative yields reported in the 1961 sample census of agriculture were as follows, in metric tons per hectare:

---

*There are 126 guaranies to the U.S. dollar, or one guaraní equals U.S. $0.0079.

	On Specialized Farms	On Diversified Farms
Mandioca	16.0	10.0
Sweet potatoes	8.8	5.7
Corn	1.2	1.0
Beans	0.8	0.6
Peanuts	1.0	0.7
Green peas	0.6	0.5
Lima beans	0.8	0.6

The relatively small differences in yields per unit harvested of certain crops between the specialized and the diversified farms reflect the low productivity that pervades farming in Paraguay and highlight the urgent need for major efforts to improve this basic sector of the national economy. In crop year 1960/61, 76 per cent of the harvested area in the foregoing crops pertained to specialized farms which yielded about 79 per cent of the tonnage produced in the country.

Paraguay is very fortunate in having enough suitable underdeveloped agricultural land to meet the needs of its people. It is now concentrating on moving farmers out of the Central Zone to these new lands. The best lands, well-watered and suitable for both crop and livestock production, lie east of the Paraguay River. This region also is heavily timbered, with level-to-undulating forests and grassland plains. The area west of the river, known as the Chaco, is very sparsely populated and consists mainly of flat alluvial plains. However, forested areas are found along river banks. The Chaco suffers floods in the wet winter season and drought and intense heat during the summer. Insects, reptiles, birds, and wild animals make this region intensely interesting to hunters and scientists, but most unattractive to settlers. Forage for cattle is sparse so that only large ranches and farms can support efficient operations. In many parts of the Chaco the underground water is too salty even for cattle, so that surface water must be collected in man-made ponds during the wet season. In addition, the heavy bush growth native to the area (similar to the mesquite in southwestern United States) requires a major control effort on the part of ranchers and farmers.

Another plague of Paraguayan agriculture is a leafcutting ant, known locally as Ysaú. According to Dr. George T. York, a U.S. Government entomologist who worked with the Paraguayan Government in developing a control program for this insect, the Ysaú ant is responsible for a 20 per cent to 30 per cent crop loss in the country. Because they live in deep underground mines and spread over wide areas, these ants have been very difficult to control. However, new and more effective insecticides (e.g., Mirex Bait) and techniques of application give promise of more efficient control of this leafcutting ant and eventually should return millions of dollars to Paraguayan farmers.[10]

In spite of the rudimentary state of its agriculture, Paraguay's basic agricultural problem is not that of production but of marketing. The inadequacy of essential services and facilities for handling, grading, storing, processing, transporting, and distributing existing output from its farms and ranches prevents the effective utilization of the country's productive resources.[11] The farmer, cut off from the main consuming centers and needing cash to purchase necessities and to pay his debts, sells his products with virtually no bargaining power to the middleman (<u>acopiador</u>). The middleman often advances credit to the farmer and sets the price at which he will purchase the next crop. As a result, the farmer generally gets little benefit from his production. Most of the gain goes to the intermediary who brings the products to market and resells them to the exporter or retail vendor. Therefore, while the producer has little incentive to increase his production, the market price to the consumer is raised. Thus, improvement of the marketing system is of the highest priority in raising agricultural income, production, and productivity.

All segments of Paraguayan agriculture are grossly undercapitalized. In spite of sizable external resources made available to the National Development Bank and the Rural Welfare Institute in the past few years, credit facilities continue to be inadequate for the majority of farmers, lumbermen, and ranchers who operate small- to medium-sized properties. There is no dependable cheap source of credit adapted to the needs and repayment abilities of these farmers. Technical assistance to accompany agricultural credit also is very inadequate.

If all the obstacles to agricultural production discussed in this chapter were overcome, there would still remain the problem of the small size of the national market. Of some 2 million population, only 36 per cent live in urban areas. Many of these have farms in the country and bring in much of the food they require. Thus the number of persons depending entirely on what is offered in the marketplace is quite small, and given the high costs of transportation and wastage en route, large increases in the output of staple foodstuffs would only drive prices down without a corresponding increase in sales.

Because of this situation, the Technical Planning Secretariat correctly has stressed the need for giving an export orientation to the national economy--"crecimiento hacia afuera." But this requires a change in government policies which currently place various controls and taxes on exports and imports. Such measures serve to increase costs and place Paraguayan products at a competitive disadvantage in foreign markets. These measures are discussed in greater detail in Chapters 12 and 15.

Notes to Chapter 2

1. Report of U.S. Department of Agriculture, Land Grant College, and Agency for International Development Survey Team, Agricultural Development in Paraguay, February 17, 1965, p. 4.

2. Ibid.

3. The author attempted to obtain this information from the Ministry of Agriculture and Livestock in May, 1966, but was informed that the tabulations (cards) had been thrown away.

4. Prepared by a survey team from the U.S. Department of Agriculture, Land Grant College, and Agency for International Development. The team members were E. N. Holmgreen, Team Leader (private consultant); Dr. Floyd Andre, Iowa State University; Nathan Koening and Dr. A. J. Nichols, U.S. Department of Agriculture; and J. B. Slack, Consultant.

5. Published by the U.S. Department of Health, Education, and Welfare, Public Health Service, December, 1965. (Preliminary Report.)

6. La Tribuna, June 17, 1966, p. 9.

7. Castor oil is a basic and essential ingredient in manufacturing certain types of paints and varnishes, greases, plastics, hydraulic fluids, printing inks, artificial leathers, urethane foams, pharmaceuticals, and many other compounds and products. (Raymond D. Brigham, "Castorbeans--An Industrial Crop with a Future," in Texas Agricultural Progress, Vol. 9, No. 2 (March-April, 1963), pp. 33-35.

8. Informativo Agrícola Ganedero, November, 1963, p. 3a.

9. El Agricultor, Asunción, August, 1964, p. 7.

10. George T. York, End of Tour Report to the U.S. Aid Mission to Paraguay. His two-year tour of duty ended April 17, 1965.

11. Agricultural Development in Paraguay, op. cit., p. 7.

CHAPTER 3 RANCHING, DAIRYING, AVICULTURE, LIVESTOCK, AND FISHERY RESOURCES

The livestock industry accounted for about 12 per cent of the gross domestic product and for about 36 per cent of the value of Paraguayan exports in 1965. Since 1958, livestock products, principally canned corned beef and beef extract, have been the country's leading exports, lumber having declined to second place. Of the three livestock enterprises--ranching, dairying, and poultry--only ranching is being done on any semblance of an organized basis, and even in this field there is substantial room for development. Experts agree that beef has the best market prospects among all of Paraguay's exports. Hog and sheep raising have been of minor importance but could be increased.

RANCHING

Cattle were introduced into Paraguay in 1556 by the Spaniards. The existence of large tracts of land suitable for grazing helped to establish the livestock industry in the country. However, the War of the Triple Alliance and the Chaco War reduced herds substantially. There also was a reduction reported to have taken place during World War II, when the slaughter rate was permitted to exceed the vegetative growth of the cattle population in order to provide meat to the armed forces of the Allies. There is no reliable information on the number of cattle in the country. Current estimates range between 6 million and 9 million head over an area of 14,332,000 hectares.

Cattle in Paraguay are produced almost entirely on range grasses and because of seasonal factors tend to gain weight slowly. Most of the cattle are mixed breeds, with the native Criollo strain predominating. However, experimentation with various imported breeds and cross-breeds has been going on for some years, encouraged by STICA and the Cattlemen's Association. The agricultural and livestock census of 1956 showed 94.4 per cent of the ranchers having herds of fifty head or less, whereas 5.6 per cent of the ranchers had herds larger than fifty head. While the census did not tabulate the number of head in each classification, it is understood that between one fourth and one third of the herds consisted of over 10,000 head, indicating the large size of certain ranching operations in the country. The 1961 sample census of agriculture enumerated 111,013 ranchers* with a total of 5,195,000 head of cattle, distributed as shown in Table 12. Some 3 per cent of these ranchers, located on large estates in the Chaco, ran approximately 40 per cent of the cattle, while 97 per cent of the cattle owners ran the remaining 60 per cent.

Since 1956, the cattle population has been increasing at an estimated rate of 3 per cent per year, and the annual production rate has been about 15.4 per cent.** This rate is very low when compared with 23 per cent in Argentina and 40 per cent in the United States. Following Dr. Kalnin's calculations, the trends in cattle population during the years 1956-65 have been as shown in Table 12. Because of flood damage to cattle in early 1966, the methodology cannot be used to project the cattle population and deaths in that year.

---

*Number reporting.

**The estimates are for the period 1956-63. Production equals slaughter plus the change in cattle population.

TABLE 11

Distribution of Ranchers and Cattle by Area, 1961

Eastern Paraguay	Number of Ranchers[a]	Thousands of Head of Cattle[b]
Capital	644	6
Concepción	4,764	391
San Pedro	6,412	266
Cordillera	15,069	291
Guairá	8,776	135
Caaguazú	7,843	156
Caazapá	7,665	241
Itapúa	11,653	251
Misiones	4,916	370
Paraguarí	18,043	380
Alto Paraná	748	10
Central	12,655	111
Ñeembucú	7,320	411
Amambay	1,218	51
Subtotal	107,726	3,071
Western Paraguay (Chaco)		
Presidente Hayes	1,385	1,743
Boquerón	1,677	312
Olimpo	225	69
Subtotal	3,287	2,124
TOTAL	111,013	5,195

[a]Excluding 166,420 oxen.

[b]Arvids Kalnins, Tentativa de Estimación de la Existencia de Ganado Vacuno del Paraguay, Años 1956-1964 (Asunción: Central Bank of Paraguay, September, 1964), p. 23, and Table No. 44.

TABLE 12

Estimated Increase in Cattle Population, 1956-65

Year	Number of Cattle on January 1	Annual Increase	Slaughter	Deaths[a]	Real Annual Increase
		(In Thousands of Head)			
1956	4,732	752	589	24	139
1957	4,871	774	587	24	162
1958	5,033	800	659	25	116
1959	5,149	818	678	26	114
1960	5,263	836	637	26	173
1961	5,436	864	712	27	125
1962	5,561	884	702	28	153
1963	5,714	908	666	29	214
1964	5,928	942	694	30	218
1965	6,146	977	724	31	222

[a]Estimated at 5 per 1,000 head.

Note: Totals may not add because of rounding.

Source: Arvids Kalnins, _Tentativa de Estimación de la Existencia de Ganado Vacuno del Paraguay, Años 1956-1964_ (Asunción: Central Bank of Paraguay, September, 1964), and Table No. 44, for years 1956-65. Slaughter statistics from the _Boletin Estadístico Mensual_ of the Central Bank of Paraguay.

The slaughtering rate during the period 1956-65 has ranged between 11.6 per cent and 13.2 per cent of the cattle population at the start of each year. The average beef cattle slaughtered in Asunción has weighed about 370 kilos (814 pounds) and has been about five years of age. The meat yield has approximated 48 per cent to 50 per cent of the carcass weight.

In October, 1964, the National Development Bank made an economic study of 656 ranches in Paraguay, relating size of herd to area pastured and to income and expenditure per head of cattle and per hectare of pasture land. The study showed that the intensiveness of stocking was inverse to the size of the herd, as shown in Table 13.

Thus, those few ranches having over 50,000 head each had a stocking rate of 4 hectares per head, whereas the numerous ranches with under 1,000 head each averaged only 1.5 hectares per head. The over-all density was about 3 hectares per head or only about one third of an animal per hectare.

The study also showed that gross income per head was greatest on the small ranches and tended to decline until herds above 10,000 head were reached. All ranches having about 10,000 head then had the same average gross income (₲ 725 per head). On the other hand, expenses per head were greater on the small ranches than on the larger ones. However, the range among incomes, expenditures, and profits was quite small.

Gross and net income per hectare were larger on the smaller ranches and the yield per hectare also was substantially higher on the more densely populated ranches. This would suggest that larger returns per hectare on the larger ranches could be obtained from increased stocking. Economies of scale apparently would serve to reduce costs per animal and per hectare and would maximize income on both counts. The relevant data of the National Development Bank's 1964 survey are given in Table 14.

TABLE 13

Survey of 656 Ranches, 1964

Number of Ranches	Size of Herd	Number of Head	Per Cent of Total	Pasture Land (Hectares)	Per Cent of Total	Hectares Per Head
263	500- 1,000	240,238	12	360,357	6	1.5
189	1,001- 2,000	291,801	14	583,602	10	2.0
112	2,001- 5,000	200,256	10	500,640	8	2.5
58	5,001-10,000	409,851	20	1,229,553	20	3.0
23	10,001-20,000	320,955	16	1,123,342	19	3.5
7	20,001-50,000	229,072	11	870,473	14	3.8
4	Over 50,000	345,123	17	1,380,492	23	4.0
656	TOTALS	2,037,296	100	6,048,459	100	3.0

TABLE 14

Operating Results on 656 Ranches, 1964

Size of Herd	Operating Results per Head[a]			Operating Results per Hectare[a]			Yield in Kilos per Hectare
	Income	Outlay	Profit	Income	Outlay	Profit	
500- 1,000	741	344	397	494	230	264	28
1,001- 2,000	720	291	429	353	141	212	20
2,001- 5,000	725	274	451	290	109	180	17
5,001-10,000	684	241	443	231	82	150	14
10,001-20,000	725	230	493	207	66	141	12
20,001-50,000	725	213	512	200	59	141	12
Over 50,000[b]	725	266	459	290	107	184	17

[a]In _guaranies_.

[b]Model ranch (possibly Barrerito Ranch).

While for the country as a whole, available pasture lands could support at least twice the presently estimated number of cattle, this increase would require better range management and control. Better and more widespread use of fencing, draining of swamplands, providing drinking water, and improving nutrition would be essential components of such an expansion program. Pasture improvements, particularly brush control and fencing, would be required to raise calving rates and reduce calf mortality.* Improved nutrition is believed to be the principal requirement for greater conception. These improvements can be expected to raise the livestock population measurably, so that the current slaughter rate of between 11 per cent and 12 per cent per year could be raised without prejudice to the supply of cattle.

The control of diseases and parasites is essential to prevent loss of animal weight and to preserve the hides for processing and export. The endemicity of hoof-and-mouth disease prevents the sale of Paraguayan beef, other than in processed form, to the United States. Cattle rustling is a major problem in certain areas of Paraguay, especially along its international frontiers.

Asunción is by far the largest meat consuming center in the country. The majority of cattle brought to the capital city, whether for local consumption or for export, come by boat from the upper reaches of the Paraguay River; others are brought in by truck, and a small percentage is trailed. All three means result in substantial carcass weight losses during transportation. It would be well to investigate the feasibility of locating slaughtering facilities in the Chaco in or near cattle producing areas and shipping the meat in refrigerated trucks to consuming centers. Simple slaughtering facilities already exist in eastern Paraguay wherever there are population centers.

---

*Currently reported at a 50 per cent calf crop (two calves every four years).

Because the supply of cattle is believed to be too small to assure that domestic requirements and unrestricted exports of meat products might be met, the National Economic Coordination Council, with the recommendation of the Corporación Paraguaya de Carnes (COPACAR), has set annual slaughter quotas for export. In most recent years these quotas have been established on a global basis and the meatpackers have competed for cattle to slaughter. For 1966, however, the government reverted to a system of individual quotas for each meatpacking plant (see Chapter 6). The result was a slow-down in buying by the export meatpackers accompanied by a decline in cattle prices. Inasmuch as meat exports provide a substantial portion of Paraguay's foreign exchange earnings, the Central Bank's foreign exchange reserves declined from U.S. $8.38 million at the end of 1965 to U.S. $7.64 million at the close of 1966.*

Until recently, special permits were required to move cattle from the Chaco across the Paraguay River into eastern Paraguay. This system gave the producer a choice of either selling his cattle to the meatpackers for export, or selling 60 per cent to COPACAR and the remainder to other buyers.** COPACAR, in addition to regulating the movement of cattle within the country, establishes minimum domestic prices on the basis of live weight; it also collects a fee (₲ 40 per head) on all cattle slaughtered for export and on the processed meat products derived therefrom.

COPACAR operates a former military slaughterhouse in Asunción and small slaughterhouses in other principal cities. Its principal slaughterhouse, in Barrio Tablada, Asunción, is very old, obsolete, and unsanitary. This organization in 1966 was preparing a loan project for the construction of a new facility in Asunción. It not only

---

*Excluding the IMF tranche (see Chapter 15).

**This control was removed by Decree No. 18,245 of May 6, 1966.

controls the prices paid to cattlemen and recommends the export quotas to be established, but also sells meat at retail in order to keep prices within the means of the domestic consumers.* The fixing of maximum prices (despite periodic upward adjustments) and export quotas has been a continuing source of dissatisfaction to the Cattlemen's Association (Asociación Rural del Paraguay).

COPACAR was established by Decree-Law No. 3810 of March 6, 1944. In order to receive a livestock loan from the International Development Association (IDA),[1] the Government of Paraguay re-organized COPACAR by Law No. 710 of July 25, 1961. It was made a commercial and industrial enterprise having both government and private capital participation, the latter coming from the cattle producers in the country, and its monopoly over cattle purchase and sale was abolished. Although the government's participation represents only 2 per cent of the capital and it nominally has only two representatives on the six-man governing board, the other four members also are selected by the Minister of Agriculture and Livestock from a list submitted by the directors of the Cattlemen's Association. The president of the board of COPACAR also is designated by the Minister from among the six board members. Thus, in spite of its minority stock participation, the government essentially controls COPACAR. Under Article 33 of Law No. 710, a plan for making COPACAR a completely private enterprise was to have been prepared within three years of the law's issuance. This was not done. In spite of the commitment to the World Bank (of which IDA is a subsidiary) to reform COPACAR, a Decree-Law No. 420 of March 29, 1966, repealed Article 33 of the 1961 law. This represented a victory for those elements within the government who are opposed to the private sector.

---

*COPACAR also supplies meat to Paraguay's armed forces. In fact, officers receive a part of their remuneration in the form of meat.

The Holmgreen Report of February, 1964, concluded that:

> When COPACAR was first established it probably was necessary to exercise certain controls in order to safeguard the public interest under conditions where cattle production remained relatively static or uncertain and meat supplies had to be assured for essential requirements. But with a changed situation in which positive efforts are directed at materially increasing cattle production and thus assure ample supplies, continued regulation by COPACAR and the burden that it puts on the livestock industry is open to serious question.[2]

The meatpackers were considering a proposal to the Government of Paraguay whereby they would guarantee domestic supplies of meat at reasonable prices provided the government eliminated the export slaughter quota system and permitted private enterprise to operate freely. This change might permit a year-round slaughtering operation for export instead of the existing five- or six-month slaughtering period, running from around March through August.

By an agreement between the Government of the United States and Paraguay, signed August 7, 1943, a demonstration ranch (Estancia Barrerito) was established some 90 miles from Asunción, near the Tebicuary River. This station has been operated by Paraguayans with the technical assistance of a livestock specialist attached to the U.S. AID Mission to Paraguay (USAID) or its predecessor agencies. Purebred cattle of various strains have been imported over the years for upbreeding local varieties, modern ranch management practices have been employed, and improvement in pasture has been undertaken. The results of these experiments have shown that, for the production of meat, the American Brahman variety of Zebu and the Santa Gertrudis are the most suitable to the Paraguayan environment. For "cutters and canners" meat, the Mellon variety of Zebu appears to give the best results. In 1953, STICA added an artificial insemination program and established a station for this purpose at San Lorenzo del Campo Grande, about eight miles from Asunción.

With the turnover of most STICA operations to the Ministry of Industry and Commerce in April, 1967,[3] the prospects for continuation of the Barrerito ranch were uncertain. A recently prepared fifteen-year breeding program for Estancia Barrerito, if implemented, would assure that more than two decades of investment would be permitted to provide conclusive results. This could be accomplished through a cooperative program between private ranchers and the Ministry of Agriculture and Livestock, or through a cattlemen's cooperative dedicated to the improvement of stock and range management. The work at Barrerito already has had noteworthy effects on the cattle industry, as evidenced in periodic cattle shows and sales in various parts of the country, with increasing rancher participation and rising prices paid for prize stock.

Development of other sources of meat--swine, sheep, poultry, and fish--and the inculcation of the habit of their consumption by the local population, also could serve to increase the availability of beef and beef extract for export. The production of these alternative sources of meat are as yet little developed in Paraguay.

DAIRYING

Paraguay has substantial possibilities for a dairy industry. Current output, however, is substantially below what the population should and can afford to consume. Consequently, relatively large imports of powdered milk, butter, and cheese, mainly from Argentina, are recorded. Additional amounts probably enter the country as contraband. The 1961 census reported the existence of 341,246 head of dairy cows. While these are distributed through most departments of the country, there is a heavy concentration around Asunción. Output is estimated at only 0.5 liter daily over an average lactation period of 300 days.

Locally produced milk is expensive and its quality is doubtful as there are no sanitary regulations governing the production and sale of milk products. The milk is marketed for the most part by direct sale from producer to consumer, although intermediaries are used to some extent in this industry, too. Large cans of milk are carried on muleback, by bus, or in trucks to the individual consumers and the milk is ladled out in the quantities desired. Very little milk is cooled prior to marketing. Consumers customarily boil the milk prior to its consumption, but this changes the character of its protein content. Manufacturers of ice cream in Asunción, who usually buy their milk directly from producers on the basis of butterfat content, also boil it prior to its utilization in the production of ice cream.

In 1944, STICA experimented with the production and distribution of pasteurized milk, producing between 800 and 900 liters daily. However, interest was insufficient for anyone to take over this project and the plant at San Lorenzo ceased to function. In recent years, several projects have been developed for producing pasteurized or sterilized milk in Paraguay. The first pasteurization plant in the Asunción area was inaugurated in June, 1966, with a rated capacity of 25,000 liters per day.[4] Its selling price was reported at ₲ 22 (U.S. $17) a liter. A similar cooperative had been formed in Encarnación to produce sterilized milk by an activization process.[5] Another milk treatment plant was being constructed in Asunción in 1966 to use the sterilization process. In the Chaco, one of the Mennonite colonies has been pasteurizing milk for some years and converting a substantial part into cheese for sale in Asunción.

It appears that the number of dairy animals and the volume of milk production have been increasing in recent years. The climatic conditions for expanding production and developing a reliable milk supply reportedly are quite good. Improved breeds and better management of dairy herds, including improved pasture, could result in a marked increase in the output of dairy products in Paraguay so that self-sufficiency might be attained in these items.

AVICULTURE

There is as yet little commercial production of poultry in Paraguay. Although chickens, ducks, geese, turkeys, and even guinea hens are found all over the country, only a few people raise fowl on a commercial scale. Production of types of fowl other than chickens is insignificant. Consequently, poultry is much higher priced than beef.* Nevertheless, Paraguay climatically is well suited to year-round poultry production on a large scale.

The internal market for broilers and eggs is not large but it is growing. This growth would be accelerated if a more modern poultry industry could be established and if distribution methods were improved, so that lower priced poultry could be offered to consumers. Under present methods of production it generally takes about fifteen weeks to get a broiler to weigh three pounds; this is nearly double the time required in the United States. A few producers using improved breeds and more advanced production techniques are achieving excellent results.

Feed for producing broilers can be made from locally produced by-products of the meatpacking and vegetable oil industries at reasonable cost, and this also is true of feed required for egg production. However, there has been a serious lack of know-how as well as of facilities for processing, freezing, and marketing, which has inhibited the development of commercial broiler and egg production.

---

*Dressed ("double-breasted") chickens sell for the equivalent of $.60 a pound, compared with $.40 a pound for tenderloin (<u>lomito</u>).

Interest in poultry raising has increased significantly in recent years. Several producers are establishing broiler breeder flocks, importing day-old chicks from the United States or nearby countries. The prevailing practice is for each poultry producer to produce his own flock replacements. Some also produce hatching eggs beyond their own requirements for sale to a few hatcheries that exist in the country. The usual ratio of roosters to hens is one to ten. There is little or no control over the quality of local hatchery chicks.

A poultry producers' cooperative (COVISA) was established in April, 1965, to serve Asunción and its environs, where the major part of poultry and egg production and consumption is concentrated. The cooperative was to supply its members with mixed feed, medicines, equipment, and other material, and to market eggs. Reportedly, the cooperative has not made much headway thus far. Its equipment for grinding and mixing feed is antiquated, so that costs probably are higher than they might be.

The Mennonite colonies in the Chaco have developed a substantial poultry industry, producing about 70,000 chicks per month. The Mennonite cooperatives also produce their own feed mixes, and their use of antibiotics in poultry raising is becoming more widespread. Leghorn male chicks are sorted out of egg-laying stock and are grown and marketed as broilers and fryers. They are packed in plastic bags and frozen in a chest freezer for shipment and sale in Asunción. While current production is far short of demand, material increases in chicken and egg output may be expected in these colonies. Construction of a killing and freezing plant was begun in 1966 so that poultry could be sent more economically to Asunción in the finished stage by refrigerated truck. In the past, whenever roads were closed because of rain, chickens died on the way, eggs spoiled, and considerable economic loss was incurred.

Paraguay's egg supply is very uncertain and marked price fluctuations occur between seasons, being some 50 per cent higher in the summer than in the winter.* Prices of eggs to consumers range between ₲ 60 and ₲ 150 a dozen in the capital city, for sizes equivalent to large and extra large U.S. grades. For mediums the price is between ₲ 10 and ₲ 20 lower per dozen. Internal quality of eggs from local producers is generally good, but little attention is paid to external quality factors. There is no packaging and promotion of eggs under a brand name. There is need to improve the strain of chickens for egg-laying purposes and to control temperatures to assure an even year-round production of eggs. This also will require the development of storage facilities in various parts of the country for the preservation of both poultry and eggs.

Problems confronting the poultry industry are the scarcity of prepared feeds and the lack of know-how in controlling poultry diseases (Pullorum and Newcastle disease). Because of the danger in purchasing chicks from local hatcheries, those who cannot afford to import them tend to produce their own flock replacements. Paraguay prohibits the use of live virus inoculations of poultry against Newcastle disease and at the same time prohibits the importation of chicks from areas where the disease is known to exist. Thus its sources of supply of baby chicks are limited and costs are high.

A project is being developed to establish a research center in poultry production at the Agricultural College. The U.S. AID Mission to Paraguay, through the fine work of its Marketing Specialist Robert P. Callaway, may provide assistance in incorporating facilities for poultry processing and egg grading into this project.[6]

Although Paraguay produces or is capable of producing most of the ingredients needed in a broiler or layer ration, most of the oilseed meals, bone meal, and dried meat scraps produced as

---

*As Paraguay is south of the equator, its seasons are the reverse of those in the United States.

by-products of local industries are exported. Corn and grain sorghum production could be expanded as needed, as well as soybeans for meal. Fish meal production also would be a possibility if the fishing industry were nationalized.

OTHER LIVESTOCK

Hogs, sheep, goats, horses, asses, mules, and oxen are found in Paraguay. The horses, asses, mules, and oxen are used as draft animals, and some 30,000 horses a year also are slaughtered and exported as frozen meat to Japan.

Pork consumption is very low and its price is higher than that of beef. There appears to be ample opportunity to expand hog production in Paraguay, utilizing low-cost feeds such as mandioca, supplemented with protein concentrates such as peanut cake, blood meal, palm kernel meal, and mineral mixture. All of these materials are produced in the country.

Hogs usually are slaughtered on the farm, either for family consumption or for immediate sale in nearby markets as fresh meat. Natural casing sausages are made both at home and in a few sausage plants. While there is no inspection of the meat at the time of slaughter, trichinosis reportedly is not found in Paraguay. Edible hog fats generally are used in the areas of slaughter, and quantities in excess of local needs are sent to the larger cities when possible.

FISHERY RESOURCES

In spite of some 238 species of fresh-water fish known to exist in its waters, Paraguay has virtually no organized fishing industry. Producers are generally small family enterprises employing rudimentary methods of fishing. The catch usually is sold fresh in the neighborhood where taken as there are few preservation facilities for transporting fish.

Names of Paraguayan fish differ among localities and, moreover, often exist in both Spanish and Guaraní. There are about fifty species generally used for food, of which the following are the most important: surubí, manguruyú, carimbatá, bagre, pacú, patí, dorado, armado, raya, and tararira.[7] Corbina should be added to this list. These edible varieties represent a good potential source of protein food for human consumption. Other varieties and fish waste could be used for the manufacture of fish meal.

At certain times of the year, the commercial fishermen must travel up to 250 miles north from Asunción for their catch. The surubí and manguruyú are the only fish that can withstand the trip back to the capital city. By rowboat, this trip takes from six to ten days each way, and about an equal time is spent in fishing. Only one catch per month is possible under such conditions. Of the total catch, approximately 30 per cent is not utilized. Moreover, the fish lose some 20 per cent of their weight in transit. The return to the fisherman is about 440 pounds of live fish from the month's work.[8] Obviously there is room for increased productivity in this field.

The new Compañía "Pesquera Pacú" S.R.L., in Asunción, is developing an integrated fishing operation, from refrigerated fishing boats to retail outlets. It advertises as the first modern fishing company in Paraguay, selling fresh, chilled, and frozen fish in Asunción and other parts of the country. A more widespread consumption of fish, as well as of poultry, pork, and veal, would serve not only to diversify the local diet, but would free more beef for export.

Notes to Chapter 3

1. Authorized in December, 1963.

2. Report of U.S. Department of Agriculture, Land Grant College, and Agency for International Development Survey Team, Agricultural Development in Paraguay, February 17, 1965, p. 36.

3. The agreement was signed on June 30, 1966.

4. La Tribuna, June 10, 1966, p. 9.

5. Ibid.

6. Mr. Callaway was on loan to the USAID from the U.S. Department of Agriculture. Much of the discussion on poultry and egg operations in Paraguay is based on his field notes.

7. C. J. D. Brown, Informe al Gobierno del Paraguay sobre los Recursos Pesqueros de Sus Aguas Continentales (Rome, 1959), (FAO/59/2/1336), p. 8.

8. Speech by Mr. Acisclo Miyares del Valle, Regional Fisheries Adviser of the Food and Agriculture Organization, on Radio Nacional del Paraguay, October 20, 1964.

CHAPTER 4 FOREST PRODUCTS AND TREE CROPS

Nearly 60 per cent of Paraguay's area is in forests. About three eighths of this forest area lies in the Chaco and five eighths lies east of the Paraguay River. The actual figures are 8.757 million hectares in eastern Paraguay and 15.466 million hectares in the west, for a total of 24.223 million hectares. From the viewpoint of forestry, as in other respects, eastern and western Paraguay constitute distinct economic areas. It is estimated that of the 24.223 million hectares of forest land, some 6 million hectares are commercially workable at this time.[1] Of this amount, 85 per cent is located in eastern Paraguay, especially in the Departments of Alto Paraná, Caaguazú, San Pedro, and Itapúa.

Although there are more than 500 identified species of trees in Paraguay, only seven figure importantly in the country's export trade, and only one--Spanish cedar--is well known in the United States.[2] Dr. Riveros counts only forty-five species as being commercially important at this time and estimates their aggregate supply at 900 million cubic meters; this figure he considers to represent the country's forest capital.[3] Thus, on the basis of an available 150 cubic meters per hectare and a thirty-year exploitation period, the annual yield should be 30 million cubic meters or a yield of 5 cubic meters per hectare. However, as 17 million cubic meters are in inaccessible areas and 8 million cubic meters are in areas of difficult accessibility, the feasible workable forest is reduced to 5 million cubic meters. All of them are hardwoods as Paraguay has no conifers in its natural forests. In 1963, lumber production was reported at only 680,000 cubic meters, of which 80 per cent consisted of Spanish cedar and lapacho.[4] This indicates clearly the underdeveloped state of Paraguay's forest industry, both in quantity of output and in species exploited.

Paraguayan forests, like most tropical forests in Latin America, are characterized by a profusion of species and a scattering of marketable trees. Although the preferred situation is one where a few desirable species grow in dense stands that are easily accessible, this situation may be realized only by reforestation and planting trees as a crop. Meanwhile, markets must be developed for the numerous species not yet exploited. This means that further investigation is needed to determine their properties and utilization possibilities, and a promotional program must be undertaken to familiarize U.S. and European markets with Paraguayan timber species.

Research has been started in five neighboring South American countries to identify and test timber species. This project will involve about U.S. $1 million of Public Law 480 funds and will be carried out in cooperation with the U.S. Forest Products Laboratory. Work already has been started in Peru. It is hoped that most of the species tested will be the principal species also found in Paraguay. The testing program was to take about five years. The Food and Agriculture Organization of the United Nations may undertake a similar investigation of Paraguayan timbers.[5]

The principal woods presently cut at sawmills and their major uses are as follows:[6]

Cedro: General use, sashes, doors, blinds, furniture, boxes, plywood.

Lapacho: Construction, railroad ties and sleepers, implements, cart and truck bodies, bridges, boats, woodworking.

Ivirapita: Interior construction, supports for tile roofs.

Curupay, iribaro, incienso: Same as lapacho.

Petereby: Furniture and plywood.

Lumbering is almost entirely an extractive industry in Paraguay. Little attention has been given to reforestation. A few tree "plantations" are being developed in eastern Paraguay by such firms as Azucarera Paraguaya (900 hectares), Manufactura de Pilar S. A. (200 hectares), and Fassardi Ltda. (136 hectares). These firms are cultivating chiefly eucalyptus and also some Spanish cedar. The STICA Experiment Station at Caacupe reportedly has an excellent plantation of Florida pine. The Presidente Stroessner Colony is cultivating Paraná pine for possible use in a paper industry. The firm of Fassardi Ltda. also is experimenting with the utilization of bamboo (tacuara) for making paper, but the results thus far have been unsatisfactory.[7]

Apart from lumber, Paraguay's forests yield many other economic products, most of which enter the export trade. These products include yerba maté (Paraguayan tea); coffee; petitgrain, palo santo, castor, tung, and coconut palm and kernel oils; caranday wax; tannin (quebracho extract); and heart of palm (palmito).

WESTERN PARAGUAY (CHACO)

Relatively little is known about the actual extent of forest in the Chaco. However, known principal species include quebracho, algarroba, coronillo, espinillo, samuhue, para todo, palo blanco, and palo santo, mixed with various palms of which the most important commercially is the caranday or palma negra. Apart from the palms, most of the species occurring in the Chaco produce very heavy hardwoods, usually dark in texture. Many of them contain tannin, but none in the proportion of the _quebracho colorado_, whose high tannin content (35 per cent) makes it the most valuable Paraguayan forest species.[8]

1) _Quebracho_ -- Although there are many tanniferous trees in the Paraguayan Chaco, the only one that has been exploited is the _quebracho colorado_ (_Schinopsis balansae_) from whose bark tannin extract is produced. This extract is used in the tanning of leather and gives it characteristics afforded by no other material.[9] The extreme hardness of the wood has caused it to be given the name _quebracho_ which means "axbreaker." Resistant to rot and insects, it is used for such purposes as railroad ties, mine supports, or other uses where hardwood is required. A cubic foot of _quebracho_ weighs 83 pounds. The tree may grow as high as 75 feet and generally grows on elevated ground.[10]

The _quebracho_ zone of western Paraguay extends from the Bolivian border on the north to some 210 miles southward, and inland about 120 miles westward from the Paraguay River. Its exploitation is centered in a region of over 4 million hectares west of the Paraguay River, opposite the mouth of the Apa River, between Puerto Pinasco and Puerto Guaraní, an area which also includes Puerto Casado.[11] Puerto Casado is owned by Carlos Casado, Ltda., an Argentine company. Puerto Pinasco was built by a U.S. firm, International Products Corporation, which is one of the major producers and exporters of canned corned beef in Paraguay and, until July, 1965, also operated a _quebracho_ extract plant at Puerto Pinasco. The plant was sold to Enrique Welbers, S.A.

Paraguay is the second largest producer of _quebracho_ extract (after Argentina), accounting for about one fifth of the world's supply. As this wood has been exploited for many years and takes about a century to reach maturity, the utilization rate has surpassed the growth rate, so that the cost of production is rising rapidly. It takes about 7.3 pounds of log to yield 2.2 pounds of _quebracho_.

2) Caranday -- Large stands of caranday palm (copernicia australis becc., also called palma negra) are located in the Chaco and in adjacent areas in northeastern Paraguay. The leaves of this tree yield an industrial wax similar to Brazil's carnauba wax, which is used extensively as an ingredient in the manufacture of polishes, coatings, laminates, inks, explosives, and other products. The wood is used for general construction and as a source of fiber and leaf straw for the manufacture of hats.

3) Palo santo -- Palo santo oil is produced by steam distillation, the input being the ground or shaved heartwood of the Bulnesia sarmentii or palo santo (holy wood) tree. This tree is one of the hardest woods indigenous to Paraguay and Argentina.[12] It grows wild in semi-arid sections of the Chaco. Production of the oil was begun in 1938, and since then two processing enterprises have been established by the Mennonite colonies in the Chaco, close to the source of raw material supply.

EASTERN PARAGUAY

Eastern Paraguay has an area of about 16 million hectares, of which nearly 9 million hectares (55 per cent) reportedly were in forests in 1962 (see Table 7), mostly with deciduous hardwoods. The main forest area extends southwestward from a point near Bella Vista on the northern frontier with Matto Grosso, Brazil, to within about 18 miles of the Paraguay River near San Pedro; from here it extends southeastward to Encarnación. This forest is predominantly a dense jungle, with entangled vines and underbrush, and occasional islands of open areas and low swampy grasslands that parallel the principal streams.[13] The major share of forests in this part of Paraguay is in private holdings. A very large percentage of these holdings is owned by foreigners, chiefly Argentines. Even those forestlands held by Paraguayans are exploited largely with Argentine capital. Consequently, the structure of the industry has remained basically extractive, logs being shipped down river to Buenos Aires for processing in Argentine sawmills.

In the major lumber zone, the Alto Paraná, twenty-nine loggers and sawmill owners have formed a cooperative to assist in improving their production and developing new markets. These members work 429,000 hectares of forest, of which not more than perhaps 20 per cent is actually owned by them. The remainder is rented, mainly from an Argentine proprietor and a small amount from the government (so-called fiscal lands).[14] The leases on the former lands are for a year, renewable at the discretion of the proprietor. The cooperative has built and maintains about 600 miles of logging roads from interior points to the Paraná River. Difficulties with Argentine buyers, who purchase only the varieties they want, when they want it, and at the price they care to pay, have encouraged the cooperative to seek other markets. In early 1966, this cooperative shipped a selection of logs to Belgium for trial, hoping to open a new, high-priced lumber market. The shipment included a number of relatively unknown species as well as those already established in Paraguay's export trade. If these new species are accepted, Paraguayan loggers will be able to harvest perhaps fifteen trees per hectare instead of the usual yield of only one per hectare.[15] Acceptance by European buyers could also open other markets to Paraguayan timbers without having to wait several years for the results of laboratory testing processes.

1) Yerba maté -- The yerba tree (Ilex paraguayensis St. Hilaire) also grows wild in Paraguay's forests. Its growing areas are widely scattered throughout the eastern part of the country. Most of the commercial production, however, comes from planted orchards. The leaves are picked, flame-blanched, dried, and finally ground and toasted to produce the maté or tea. The crop is harvested largely by hand and production costs are high. Paraguay is one of the principal producers of this product along with Argentina and Brazil. The maté is consumed chiefly in the River Plate area, but attempts are being made to develop markets in the United States and Europe through marketing the product in tea bags and paper cartons. The 1961 agricultural census reported 13.5 million yerba trees of bearing age, with an output of 41,387

metric tons. The largest producing zones were Itapúa, San Pedro, and Amambay, and the major producing firm is La Industrial Paraguay, S.A.

2) Coffee -- Coffee, a relatively new crop to Paraguay, is grown on a small scale in northeastern Paraguay, close to the Brazilian border. The varieties grown come from Brazil and are the genus Coffee L Rubiaceae. They are not as good as the excellent mocha variety from Ethiopia, which is well suited to the climate of Paraguay.[16] More than two thirds of the trees and of the output of coffee are attributed to the Department of Amambay. In 1961, there were over 4 million coffee trees of bearing age (out of 7.5 million trees), and production amounted to 3,521 metric tons. Paraguay's small exports to world markets are not now limited by international quota, although Paraguay hopes to join the International Coffee Organization.

The majority of the coffee is grown on a few large plantations which are owned by U.S. citizens and are highly developed. Occasional frost may cause some loss of production but does not constitute a serious problem. The International Coffee Agreement serves to provide an umbrella for Paraguayan production; without quota limitations on the surplus producing countries (such as neighboring Brazil), it is doubtful that Paraguay could compete in the world market.

3) Petitgrain -- Petitgrain oil, which is used as a base for perfume, scented soaps, and flavorings, is one of the more important export products of Paraguay. In fact, Paraguay is the major world producer and exporter of this product, accounting for about 80 per cent of total world output. At present, all of Paraguay's production is exported. The oil is produced from the leaves of the bitter orange (apepú) tree which grows wild in Paraguay but also is cultivated to some extent. The growing areas often coincide with those of the yerba tree. From the wild trees, between 550 and 990 pounds of leaves are required to produce 2 pounds of essential oil; from the cultivated trees only 396 to 660 pounds of leaves are needed to produce the same amount of

essence. In general, harvesting takes place throughout the year, although frosts may ruin the leaves at times. The major producing areas are Caraguaty, San José de los Arroyos, Coronel Oviedo, San Estanislao, and Villa del Rosario. In 1961, there were 52.4 million bitter orange trees enumerated, of which two thirds were of producing age. Output totaled 122,624 metric tons of leaves or about 8 pounds per producing tree.

The pioneer firms producing _petitgrain_ oil in Paraguay are Peña Hermanos, F. Krauch y Cia., and Burró Hermanos. The typical process of producing _petitgrain_ oil by these firms, as described by Jaime R. Peña of Peña Hermanos, is as follows:[17] In a cauldron holding between 200 and 600 liters, water is boiled, using firewood for fuel. The steam produced passes to a vat filled with bitter orange leaves and having a capacity of 300 to 600 kilos. The steam passes between the green leaves and cooks them, producing the essence mixed with steam that passes through a coil into another vat holding cold water. The mixture is then liquefied and the essence is separated from the syrup (_guarapo_) by specific gravity in a receptacle called an _esenciera_. The essence, being lighter in weight, remains in the receptacle and the liquor passes to the bottom of the vat and out through a pipe as waste matter. The consuming countries require the essence to contain at least 48 per cent of esters.

Other essential oils, such as _guayacán_, _cedron_, lemongrass, and peppermint, are produced and exported in small quantities.

The future of these extractive industries depends mainly upon the competition from synthetic products. Should the synthetics continue to replace the natural essences, Paraguay's exports of these products probably will disappear. However, should the local manufacture of perfumes and cosmetics develop, Paraguay's geographic position may give its essential oil producers a competitive advantage in the domestic market. The United States and Europe (France and West Germany) have been the principal markets for these essential oils. Southern France, Algeria, and Spain are producers of better quality _petitgrain_ oils that command higher prices because of their greater perfume value. Other important producers include India, Haiti, and Brazil.

4) _Tung nuts_ -- Tung nuts are produced in southeastern Paraguay, almost entirely in the Department of Itapúa. Some 28,000 metric tons were produced from slightly over 5 million trees in 1961, for an average of 123 pounds per tree. An experiment station in Encarnación (the capital of Itapúa) has been working with the tung nut tree and maintains extensive agents in the field to help in its production. The trees usually are planted in groves on cleared land. The Japanese and German colonies are the large producers. The German colonies operate a cooperative tung oil mill. However, the major portion of tung nuts produced in the country is sold by independent growers to several mills located in the Encarnación area. The millers purchase tung nuts either hulled or unhulled. Inasmuch as the hull accounts for approximately 40 per cent of the weight of the nut, some of the larger growers have installed hullers to reduce transportation costs in shipping the nuts.

Tung oil, produced from the nuts (16.5 per cent recovery rate), is used almost entirely as a dryer in the manufacture of paint. The Paraguayan product not only must compete with that of established tung producing countries (e.g., Communist China, Argentina), but is now faced with the competition of synthetic substitutes. The tung industry in Itapúa has been in a distressed state because of the decline in world tung oil prices and the resurgence of mainland China as a competitor in world markets; its sales reportedly are made through France. Tung oil cake is also exported. The United States is the largest importer of tung oil and from time to time establishes quotas for producing countries.

5) _Coconuts_ -- There were 23.8 million coconut palms (_cocoteros_) in Paraguay in 1961, mainly in the Departments of Central, La Cordillera, Paraguarí,

Concepción, Misiones, and San Pedro. The trees grow wild in forests or in open stands (palmares), but also are grown on cultivated land to provide forage for domestic animals. This palm yields a small fruit (coco) in large clusters. The fruit is about one inch in diameter. The small nuts are gathered after they fall from the trees and are accumulated until sold, usually to an intermediary who operates a truck and hauls his load for sale to the processing plant. Shelling and pressing plants convert the cocos into palm oil and palm kernel oil. These are the principal edible and industrial vegetable oils, respectively, in the country.

6) Heart of palm (palmito) -- The palmito (euterpe edulis) is a plant generally found in tropical countries. In Paraguay, the plant grows wild in the Alto Paraná forest, along the banks of the Paraná River, in a strip extending some 30 to 40 miles southward from the Carapá River to about Puerto Presidente Stroessner. The area of growth covers an estimated 100,000 hectares.[18]

The palmito grows in dense clusters similar to bamboo and in the same areas, where there are constant humidity, cool winds, and occasional frosts. The raw material (heart of palm or cogollo) must be processed within a week of cutting or it will decompose. Therefore, the industrialization of the product must be done in the growing area. Virtually the total output of palmito is exported.

The number of plants processing palmito has increased rapidly over the past five years. In 1962, there were only two factories with a combined annual capacity of 150 metric tons. By 1964, four factories were in production. The number rose to six in 1965. Production approximates exports, which in 1965 reached 2,499 metric tons valued at $1.225 million. The rated capacity of the six plants totals at least 7,000 metric tons a year, and the raw material is available to permit that level of production, provided markets can be developed.

Heart of palm is used mainly as a constituent of salads. Interest in this product developed about 1962 and has been increasing since that time. The major determinant of the rise in Paraguay's output of palmito has been the concessions obtained for this product in the Latin American Free Trade Association (LAFTA). Virtually all exports go to Argentina. However, trial shipments have been made recently to the United States and Europe.

The product is sold in cans of one kilogram (850 grams net). Its export price rose from U.S. $0.35 per can in 1963 to U.S. $0.42 in 1965. Each can contains two hearts of palm.

7) Grapefruit -- Paraguay has developed a market for the Marsh seedless variety of grapefruit in Great Britain, and production is increasing. Commercial production is largely on properties owned by the exporters themselves and by individuals who sell their fruit to the shippers. Maintenance of quality and improved handling and packing are basic to the expansion of this operation.

A wide variety of other fruits is grown in Paraguay: pineapples, bananas, oranges, tangerines, wine grapes, papayas, kumquats, avocados, mangoes, guavas, and strawberries. These either are consumed almost entirely within the country or go to waste because of the lack of transportation, storage, processing, and marketing facilities. Recently, the industrialization of some of these fruits has been undertaken (see Chapter 6), so that if quality and quantity can be assured, growing markets for these crops may be expected.

PROBLEMS OF THE PARAGUAYAN FOREST PRODUCTS INDUSTRY

The principal problems affecting Paraguay's forest products industry are (a) the absense of a general forestry law and forest service; (b) the absence of an inventory of the country's forest resources; (c) improper and uncontrolled exploitation of the forests, with the result that much valuable timber has been wasted and large areas have been depopulated of their timber resources; and (d) the country's lumber is exported primarily as logs, thereby losing substantial income that might be obtained from processing the lumber in Paraguay.

Uncontrolled cuttings over a long period have virtually denuded the Central Zone of its valuable timber.* Some of the finest woods are consumed as fuel wood, posts, and railroad ties, without thought to their value arising from the beauty of grain, variety of figure, or the intrinsically high quality of yield in burls or crotches.[19] Because of the incipient state of the lumber processing industry in the country, Paraguay receives in the main only the stumpage value of its lumber and such income as is paid for felling and skidding the logs to the river bank. Informed calculations indicate this value to be only about one half to one third of the value of sawn lumber. Thus one half to two thirds of the final value is earned by millers and manufacturers abroad.[20]

The dependence upon a single foreign market (Argentina) for the bulk of its lumber exports has worked to Paraguay's disadvantage, as noted above. The vagaries of Argentine policies and of the Argentine economy have immediate repercussions on Paraguay's lumber industry and, because of lumber's importance in the export trade, on the country's balance of payments. However, knowledge of foreign markets and foreign requirements has been largely lacking in Paraguay. Because Paraguay lacks a forest service to investigate problems of the industry, promote its development, and prevent wasteful exploitation of the nation's forest resources, the establishment of such a service ranks as the first priority in the forestry sector of Paraguayan agriculture.

---

*The Central Zone, comprising about 12,600 square kilometers, roughly includes the area extending 31 miles north and south of a radius drawn from Asunción to Villarrica.

Another problem has been the undercapitalization of the lumber industry. Lack of modern equipment, combined with increasing distances of hauling and shipping lumber to markets, has served to place this industry on a rising cost curve and to make increasingly difficult its ability to compete with other lumber producing areas, even in the nearby Argentine market. Consequently, there is a growing necessity to industrialize the lumber within Paraguay and to ship the higher-unit-value manufactured items abroad.

One of the difficulties in obtaining credit, however, is the landholding system in the forested areas. As previously noted, a very high percentage of the timber lands is foreign-owned, and Paraguayan renters--with only annual exploitation leases--are not good credit risks. To improve their creditworthiness the Paraguayans must obtain long-term leases (e.g., fifty years or more), go into partnership with the foreign owners, or be permitted to purchase a share of the foreign-held lands to use as security for loans.

Notes to Chapter 4

1. Nicolas T. Riveros, "Recursos Forestales del Paraguay," in Paraguay Industrial y Commercial, Vol. XXII, No. 258-259, (March-April, 1966), p. 30. (Publication of the Ministry of Industry and Commerce.)

2. Col. Arthur R. Spillers, "Forestry in Paraguay in 1966." Report given at USAID staff meeting on June 6, 1966.

3. Riveros, op. cit., p. 30.

4. Ibid., p. 31.

5. Spillers, op. cit.

6. The Institute of Inter-American Affairs, Food Supply Division, The Forest Resources of Paraguay (Washington, D.C.: December, 1946), p. 54.

7. *Ibid.*, p. 33.

8. *Ibid.*, p. 9.

9. Philip Raine, *Paraguay* (New Brunswick, N.J.: Scarecrow Press, 1956), p. 360.

10. *Ibid.*

11. U.S. Department of Commerce, *Investment in Paraguay: Conditions and Outlook for United States Investors* (Washington, D.C.: U.S. Government Printing Office, 1955), p. 38. *Quebracho* also is reported in eastern Paraguay, between the Jejuí and Apa rivers.

12. *Ibid.*, p. 46.

13. *The Forest Resources of Paraguay*, *op. cit.*, p. 10.

14. Cooperativa de Madereros del Paraná Ltda. Data as of March 23, 1965.

15. Spillers, *op. cit.*

16. Juan Natalicio González, *Geografía del Paraguay* (Mexico City: Editorial Guarania, 1964), p. 472, citing Dr. Moisés C. Bertoni, noted Paraguayan agronomist.

17. *La Tribuna*, March 30, 1965, p. 7.

18. Ladislao Bazán Ferreira, in *La Tribuna*, August 10, 1965, p. 10.

19. *The Forest Resources of Paraguay*, *op. cit.*, p. 76.

20. Eugene C. Reichard, *The Forest Resources of Paraguay and Their Possible Industrial Utilization* (Washington, D.C.: Inter-American Development Commission, July, 1946), p. 8.

CHAPTER 5 INSTITUTIONS, POLICIES, AND PROGRAMS

INSTITUTIONS

For a country as small as Paraguay there are too many institutions involved in agricultural development and agrarian reform. These include the National Economic Coordination Council, which is responsible for establishing and coordinating national policies in all sectors of the economy; the Technical Planning Secretariat, which analyzes the economic situation and prepares national plans for socioeconomic development; the Faculty of Agronomy and Veterinary Sciences of the National University of Asunción, which provides professional training to agronomists and veterinarians; the Rural Welfare Institute, the Puerto Presidente Stroessner Administration, and the Ministry of the Interior, concerned largely with colonization and land distribution; the Paraguayan Housing and Urbanization Institute, which is charged with constructing low-income housing units for urban and rural workers; the National Development Bank and the Agricultural Credit Bank, which deal with agricultural credit; and of course the Ministry of Agriculture and Livestock, which is charged with promoting agricultural production and the formation of cooperatives. While certain of these institutions are discussed below under the functional headings to which they pertain, the general functions of the Ministry of Agriculture and Livestock are discussed under this section.

The Ministry of Agriculture and Livestock, which formerly had been the Department of Agriculture and Livestock in the Ministry of Finance, was made a separate ministry by Decree No. 13,681 of August 4, 1950. Its organizational structure was established by Decree No. 1,000 of October 9, 1950. The major functions of this ministry are the protection and stimulation of agricultural, livestock, and forestry production; the regulation and economic coordination of such production; and the study of the country's natural resources, as well as their protection and control (except for subsoil resources, which pertain to the Ministry of Public Works and Communications). In addition, the Ministry is responsible for technical education and the diffusion of agricultural technology; certain agricultural credit activities and the development of cooperatives; the preparation of agricultural statistics; and matters pertaining to land distribution, colonization, internal migration, immigration, and repatriation.

The land distribution and colonization functions have been assigned to the Rural Welfare Institute, an autonomous appendage of the Ministry, and the agricultural credit function nominally has been assigned to the Agricultural Credit Bank, which is also dependent upon the Ministry. These dependencies are discussed more fully later in this chapter.

The Ministry itself is poorly administered, understaffed, and short of funds. Although Paraguay's economy is primarily agricultural, the Ministry receives less than 2 per cent of the Central Government's budget. Of this sum, some 90 per cent is consumed in paying salaries. However, by agreement with the U.S. AID Mission to Paraguay, the budget of the Ministry was to be increased over the next several years (beginning in 1967) to absorb STICA, most of whose functions passed to the Ministry in April, 1967. This transfer should improve the Ministry's operational capability.

In recent years, the Ministry of Agriculture and Livestock has carried out the agricultural census of 1956 and the sample census of agriculture and livestock of 1961. The results of both of these censuses appeared some five years after they were taken. Plans were being made in 1966 to undertake a badly needed livestock census in 1970. The Ministry's intercession in the Paraguayan Meat Corporation (COPACAR) was discussed in Chapter 3. The Ministry has a minuscule Cooperatives Department that attempts to promote the development of agricultural cooperatives.

Virtually all of the research and development work being carried on in Paraguay is performed by the Inter-American Technical Service for Agricultural Cooperation (Servicio Técnico Interamericano de Cooperación Agrícola - STICA), which was established in December, 1942, by agreement between the Government of Paraguay and the Institute of Inter-American Affairs, a former agency of the United States Government. Subsequent agreements concerning STICA were concluded in 1950 and 1960. The agreement for turning STICA over to the Ministry of Agriculture and Livestock was signed in June, 1966. This turnover terminated the last servicio in Latin America.*

The functions of STICA have been to improve agricultural production by imparting modern technology to farmers; training technicians to develop the nation's agriculture; collaborating with public and private entities for these purposes; and carrying out investigations of basic agricultural problems with a view to finding solutions to them. Research and experimentation, development of rural youth (4-C) clubs, economic studies, extension services,

---

*A "servicio" was a jointly funded organization sponsored by the United States and the government of the host country. Operated by technicians of the two countries, its objective was to inculcate modern technologies and train the nationals of the Latin American countries with a view to eventually passing the entire operation to the host government. Servicios had been operative in the fields of health, education, and agriculture since the early 1940's.

seed and plant distribution, brush control, control of the leaf-cutting Ysaũ ant, and tree farming, have been among the more important STICA activities in Paraguay. STICA established two Experiment Stations, the more important one being the National Agronomic Institute (Instituto Agronómico Nacional--IAN) at Caacupe, some 30 miles from Asunción. The other is the IAN Experiment Station at Capitán Miranda, near Encarnación.

As mentioned in Chapter 3, STICA has been operating a model ranch at Estancia Barrerito. This ranch covers 9,300 hectares and is divided into several pasture and breeding areas. It had about 5,600 head of cattle of various varieties, some 2,000 breeding animals, and 200 horses. Experiments have been conducted to determine those strains best suited for beef and for milk production in Paraguay. The work of Estancia Barrerito is supplemented by the Artificial Insemination Service operated by STICA at San Lorenzo del Campo Grande.

STICA also has operated an Agricultural Extension Center as an educational institution for improving agricultural and livestock production and for developing agrarian leaders, especially through the 4-C Clubs that it sponsors.* Eighteen Agricultural Extension Agencies were in operation in 1965. These were located at Concepción, Horqueta, San Pedro, Arroyos y Esteros, Pedro Juan Caballero, San Lorenzo, Caacupe, Coronel Oviedo, Caaguazú, Puerto Presidente Stroessner, Eusebio Ayala, Yaguarón, Carapeguá, Villarrica, Acahay, Caazapá, Estancia Barrerito, San Ignacio, Coronel Bogado,

---

*The 4-C Clubs in Paraguay are the counterpart of the 4-H Clubs in the United States. At the end of 1965, STICA reported the existence of 289 such clubs with an aggregate membership of 6,843 persons.

and Encarnación. Under the terms of both the Inter-American Development Bank (IDB) and the Agency for International Development agricultural loans to the National Development Bank (NDB), STICA also was to provide technical assistance to the sub-borrowers.

STICA had been experimenting with the planting of coniferous trees at its Caacupe Experiment Station. It reported considerable success with Florida pine (*Pinus elliottii*), Paraná pine (*Araucaria angustofilia*), and Arizona cyprus (*Cupressus arizónica*).[1] In early 1965, STICA assisted the Ministry of the Interior in establishing a Forest Demonstration Center in the zone of Alto Paraná. The primary purpose of this Center is to produce annually the quality of trees required to reforest Colony Stroessner (at Puerto Presidente Stroessner). The conifers planted in the zone may become the basis of a pulp and paper industry in the future.

AGRICULTURAL CREDIT

Paraguayan agriculture may be divided into three broad sectors: small-scale (largely *minifundia*) production for auto-consumption; medium-scale production for commercial sale; and large-scale (*latifundia*) production for export. The first has little credit available except from the agents who purchase the crops or the usurers. An Agricultural Credit Bank (Crédito Agrícola de Habilitación --CAH) was established in December, 1943, to serve farmers who could not qualify for loans from other banks. The CAH offered supervised credit, combining its loans with technical assistance in improving farming practices. It offered one-year crop loans; five-year loans for implements; loans for the purchase of breeding cattle; and loans for the purchase of land. The CAH also was authorized to promote the development of cooperatives and model colonies. However, it apparently was more concerned with social welfare than with sound credit practices, and by 1958 its capital had been dissipated completely; no new loans have been made since that year. The CAH failed to use its legal powers to enforce payment on its loans. Moreover, its interest rate of 10 per cent a year did not encourage prompt repayment; borrowers were able to relend the money at 5 per cent a month. However, the Ministry of Agriculture and Livestock lives in hope of finding new capital for this bank. The existence of two state banks in the agricultural credit field may be questioned seriously, especially in view of the difficulties each has had in the past. Perhaps a more flexible National Development Bank, operating through a system of Rural Credit Boards (such as in Costa Rica), might be a more effective way of solving the small-farmer credit problem.

In January, 1965, STICA initiated a Rotating Credit Program for members of its 4-C Clubs. By December 20, 1965, 151 loans had been made, totaling ₡ 1,493,335. The medium for extending these credits is the National Development Bank. Also, certain colonies have formed colony cooperatives or colony banks. The cooperatives in some Mennonite colonies, for example, operate as purchasing agencies through which most colonists do their buying, and also serve as the marketing agencies through which the members sell their produce.[2] These cooperatives have provided the colonists with better credit facilities, greater purchasing power, and more favorable marketing conditions than the farmers had enjoyed previously.[3] Where a cooperative exists, it also has much better chances of obtaining credit from banks than individual farmers.

One investigator has reported that, in the important agricultural zone of Itapúa, the major sources of credit to farmers are the small shopkeepers, who advance seeds, tools, food, clothing, and even spending money, in return for the pledge of the crop. Thus, the small farmers live on the margin of the monetary economy and are perpetually indebted to the shopkeepers. Moreover, as price information is lacking to these producers, the storekeepers often acquire the crops at the amount owed them by the farmers for accrued debts, rather than at the market price.[4] This system perpetuates subsistence agriculture, creates a feudal situation not in keeping with the independent Paraguayan character, and tends to generate social tensions. Therefore, other dependable means of financing need to be provided for the small farmer (campesino). While individual subsistence farmers do not generate cash savings with which to repay bank loans, the organization of such farmers into cooperatives tends to create improved production units and thereby enhances their ability to obtain credit and technical assistance.

The second group of agriculturists may be identified as the thousands of deserving farmers and ranchers who produce on a commercial scale and who qualify for bank loans.[5] With the provision of technical assistance in improving farming and ranching practices and facilities for storing and marketing their products, the accelerated development of this middle group as the backbone of a progressive private enterprise agriculture could be achieved. Recent external credits from the Agency for International Development, the Inter-American Development Bank, and the International Development Association (IDA) have been made to assist this group of farmers and ranchers.

For the third sector, the export agricultural sector, credit is available from the National Development Bank, the commercial banks, and customers abroad. The foreign buyers often will advance seasonal funds to producers of coffee, lumber, cotton, etc., for planting, harvesting, or marketing their crops. Of identified credits to the agricultural and livestock sectors, the National Development Bank (and its predecessor agency) has been the principal lender. The private commercial banks have made relatively few loans to agriculturists. They have been more inclined to lend to ranchers, who probably are better risks and are better known to these banks. Moreover, the private banks are not set up to administer this type of lending. The importance of the National Development Bank (NDB) in the agricultural credit field is shown in Table 15.

TABLE 15

Agricultural and Livestock Credit, 1953, 1959, 1965, and 1966[a]
(In Millions of *Guaranies*)

End of Year	Balances Outstanding, All Banks		
	Agricultural	Livestock	Total
1953	220.6	97.7	318.3
1959	602.8	271.8	874.6
1965	1,003.9	972.0	1,975.9
1966	1,134.0	1,327.1	2,461.1
	Balances Outstanding, National Development Bank[b]		
1953	181.6	70.0	251.6
1959	590.4	167.9	758.3
1965	985.1	626.6	1,611.7
1966	1,106.0	991.2	2,097.2
	Ratio of B/A, in Per Cent		
1953	82	72	79
1959	98	62	87
1965	98	75	85
1966	98	75	85

[a]Does not include short-term credits to these sectors classified as commercial loans.
[b]Prior to 1961, Bank of Paraguay.

Source: Central Bank of Paraguay.

Because of its predominant position in the agricultural credit picture, some discussion of the National Development Bank and its policies is in order. The NDB was created by Decree-Law No. 281 of March 14, 1961, to replace the Bank of Paraguay. The latter, through injudicious or politically motivated loans, had destroyed its cash position and become heavily indebted to the Central Bank.[6] The National Development Bank was established with an authorized capital of ₲ 1.5 billion, subject to revision at least every three years. The capital was divided among the Bank's operating departments as follows:

Department	Capital (₲ 1 Million)
Development	1,000
Commerce and Savings	200
Agriculture and Livestock	300
TOTAL	1,500

By April, 1966, the Commercial and Agricultural Departments had attained their authorized capital ceilings and authority was obtained to increase these ceilings to ₲ 400 million and ₲ 700 million, respectively. The Bank's total authorized capitalization thereupon was raised to ₲ 2.1 billion. In 1965, the NDB's deficit of ₲ 32.7 million was lower than in any previous year. By Ministry of Finance Decree No. 19,779 of July 8, 1966, the budget of the National Development Bank for calendar year 1966 was estimated at ₲ 1,954.6 million of obligations and ₲ 1,957.3 million, of receipts, providing an apparent surplus of ₲ 2.7 million, compared with deficits in prior years. Some 62 per cent of receipts were to come from domestic resources* and 38 per cent from the use of foreign credits. These

---

*Domestic resources include a percentage of exchange surcharges on imports, recoveries from the portfolio of the ex-Bank of Paraguay, increases in deposits, repayments of loans, and advances from the Central Bank.

foreign credits included an IDB loan for agricultural development; an IDB loan for industrial development; a Kreditanstalt für Wiederaufbau (KFW) loan for industrial development; an AID loan for agricultural credit; and an IDA loan for livestock development (made to the Central Bank but administered by the NDB).

The Bank's functions are comprehensive and would appear to provide the flexibility required for development lending. The Development Department is authorized to promote the organization of agricultural, livestock, forest, and industrial enterprises with a view to increasing national production. For this purpose, it makes short-, medium-, and some long-term loans to private persons and enterprises. With the consent of the Central Bank, the Development Department may obtain loans and issue development bonds and mortgage certificates (*cédulas hipotecarias*). It has not yet done so by the end of 1966. The Agriculture and Livestock Department makes production loans in limited amounts to small farmers and small industrialists, for short and medium terms.*

The Commerce and Savings Department conducts ordinary commercial bank functions. It receives sight, time, and savings deposits. This operation reportedly is the source of real profits to the Bank, as evidenced by the fact that the capital of this department is formed by its annual profits, and that its capital ceiling was reached within four and one half years of operations. On the other hand, the Agricultural and Development Departments have incurred continuous operating deficits. The deficits of the Agricultural Department, by law, must be made up by the Government of Paraguay. The Bank's balance sheet as of December 31, 1965, showed a cumulative loss of ₲ 120 million.

---

*By Law No. 1,117 of June 10, 1966, the authorized capital of the Bank was increased ₲ 600 million, of which the Agriculture and Livestock Department was to receive ₲ 400 million and the Commerce and Savings Department ₲ 200 million.

Because history seemed to be catching up with the National Development Bank by mid-1965--sizable bad debts were outstanding and the Bank's president was becoming increasingly subject to public criticism--a reorganization was effected in August, 1965. A new president was appointed and a new governing board was named shortly afterwards. Since that time, the NDB has taken steps to improve its administration in order to provide greater assistance to the private sector and to facilitate coordination with foreign lending agencies. Thus, the NDB established a new technical staff (gabinete técnico), responsible directly to the president of the Bank. This staff is to (a) assist private investors to prepare their loan projects in a suitable manner for Bank financing; (b) evaluate projects presented to the Bank for financing with external resources; and (c) identify and prepare new projects that are indicated by the priorities established in the national development plans.

The NDB also has established a "LAFTA Office" to provide information on opportunities offered to Paraguayan producers, exporters, and importers, in the LAFTA (Latin American Free Trade Association) market. This office also studies opportunities for establishing complementary and regional industries within the LAFTA framework. This move undoubtedly reflects the personal inclination and experience of Dr. Pedro Ramón Chamorro who, prior to becoming president of the NDB, served as Paraguay's Ambassador to the LAFTA in Uruguay.

In 1966, loans disbursed by the NDB approximated Ø 2.2 billion. Increases occurred in loans to the industry, commerce, and livestock sectors. On the other hand, substantial declines were shown in loans to the farming and forestry sectors, as shown in Table 16.

While the NDB's loans have increased very substantially in recent years its recuperations have lagged considerably behind. The gap between loan disbursements and recuperations on loans in 1965, for example, amounted to Ø 818 million. In

TABLE 16

National Development Bank Loan Disbursements, by Activity, 1962-66
(In Millions of _Guaranies_)

Activity	1962	1963	1964	1965	1966
Farming	139	166	235	486	379
Livestock	70	111	160	351	481
Industry	227	314	256	621	981
Forestry	184	73	136	122	- -
Commerce	76	247	398	277	349
Other	--	--	17	8	13
TOTAL	696	911	1,202	1,864	2,203
Annual Increase	- -	+31%	+32%	+55%	+18%
Number of Borrowers	1,369	2,045	8,957	9,397	n.a.
Annual Increase	- -	+49%	+338%	+5%	n.a.

Sources: Annual reports of the National Development Bank, 1962-65, and Central Bank of Paraguay, _Boletín Estadístico Mensual_, No. 103, December, 1966, p. 11.

addition, the NDB's accounts receivable in that year increased ₲ 923 million, a rise of nearly 76 per cent over 1964. In spite of this loss of liquidity, the NDB contemplated a loan program for 1966 amounting to ₲ 3.5 million, an increase of 85 per cent over 1965. To carry out this program, the National Development Bank attempted unsuccessfully to obtain substantial additional local currency resources for increasing its capital at a faster rate, especially the capitalization of its Agricultural Department. According to Dr. Chamorro's statement to La Tribuna,[7] the Bank's resources had been absorbed completely by its contractual commitments to international lending agencies. International loans made to the National Development Bank during the years 1961 through 1965 were as given in Table 17.

These loans required an NDB matching fund input of ₲ 665.6 million or 25.6 per cent. In June, 1966, the IDA extended a second loan in the amount of $7.5 million for livestock development. In addition to the foregoing long-term loans, the NDB had received three rotating lines of credit of six months each from foreign private banks (Chase Manhattan Bank; Deutsche Sudamericanische Bank; and Bankers Trust Company) to finance exports. The total of these credits was $2.5 million. The NDB has been negotiating with the IDB to augment its $2.9 million agricultural credit load by another $3 million loan. The KFW extended an additional loan of DM 12 million for industrial credit in January, 1967.

At the request of the National Development Bank, the National Economic Coordination Council, by resolution of January 26, 1966, effected the transfer of the current account, savings, and time deposits of certain autonomous entities of the government from the Central Bank to the National Development Bank. The autonomous agencies involved were the Social Security Institute (IPS), the National Electricity Administration (ANDE), the State Marchant Marine (FLOMERE), and the Asunción Sanitary Corporation (CORPOSANA). However, these new deposits, estimated at some ₲ 250 million, were

TABLE 17

International Loans to the National Development Bank, 1961-65

Lending Agency	Purpose of Loan	Amount in U.S. $1,000	Equivalent in ¢ 1,000
IDB	General operations	3,000	378,000
IDB	Loans to small farmers	2,900	365,400
IDB	Industrial development	4,000	504,000
AID	Agriculture credit	3,000	378,000
AID (P.L. 480)	Agriculture credit	980	123,480
KFW[a]	Industrial development	3,000	378,000
IDA[b]	Livestock development	3,600	453,600
	TOTAL	$20,480	¢ 2,580,480

[a]Kreditanstalt für Wiederaufbau, a German State Bank. The credit is for DM 12 million. A second credit in like amount was extended by the KFW in January, 1967.

[b]Loan made to the Central Bank but administered by the NDB.

to be employed through the NDB's Commercial Department for the typical short-term credit operations of financing imports. The emphasis was to be on financing imports for industrial needs. Thus the only effect on the Bank's local currency position for providing matching funds would be indirect--increased earnings from its commercial operations could augment its capital somewhat. Moreover, after various reserve provisions had been complied with, the NDB would have the use of only about half the funds (₲ 125 million), while having to pay interest of about 8 per cent a year on the whole ₲ 250 million. The Bank probably lends the ₲ 125 million at about 12 per cent interest. If these funds were to turn over four times a year, the NDB would earn a net return of only ₲ 40 million (pays ₲ 20 million in interest and receives ₲ 60 million in interest). The basic problem of the NDB, that of providing matching funds to present and future external loans, had not yet been solved by the end of 1966.

The NDB's loans outstanding at the end of 1965 amounted to ₲ 2,033 million and covered a clientele of 9,412 borrowers. The distribution of these loans by term and type of security was as shown in Table 18.

It appears from Table 18 that relatively little long-term credit has been available from the NDB. That which has been available rarely has exceeded ten years' duration and in almost all cases has been secured by prime mortgages. Of the total loan portfolio of the NDB on December 31, 1965, the Commerce and Savings Department accounted for 30 per cent, the Agriculture and Livestock Department for 21 per cent, and the Development Department for 49 per cent.

Loans backed by pledges (prendarias) may not exceed 50 per cent of the value of the security; those backed by mortgages may not exceed 60 per cent of the value of the property. Pledged items may consist of land, capital goods, animals, or crops. Title to these assets is reposed in the Bank when the loan is made.

TABLE 18

Distribution of National Development Bank Loans, by Term and by Type of Security, 1965
(In Millions of *Guaranies*)

Type of Security	No. of Borrowers	Short-Term (Up to 1 Year)	Medium-Term (1 to 5 Years)	Long-Term (Over 5 Years)
Personal	318	120	29	--
Fiduciary	--	--	--	--
Pledges	4,715	337	297	28
Mortgages	4,189	283	296	469
Other[a]	190	154	20	--
TOTALS	9,412	894	642	497
	(100%)	(44%)	(32%)	(24%)

[a]Irrevocable credits.

Source: National Development Bank of Paraguay

The National Development Bank has been a subject of considerable controversy. Its detractors have accused the NDB of making loans only to members of the dominant political party; of dilatory tactics in processing applications; of requiring excessive security for loans so that it was not really performing its development function; and of neglecting the interior of the country in making its loans. As a State institution, the NDB probably cannot withstand entirely external pressures concerning the use of its resources. Nevertheless, its lending activities definitely have encompassed borrowers of all political persuasions in Paraguay. Unfortunately, those persons or institutions who obtain NDB loans normally do not broadcast their satisfaction with the Bank, so only the unhappy voices are heard.

The NDB has been the recipient of substantial foreign technical assistance in connection with the loans made to it by international lending agencies. Many of the foreign technicians have reported that the Bank's personnel need considerable training in evaluating and processing loan projects, so that they may do a better job more expeditiously. On the other hand, these observers have noted the poor preparation of loan proposals by potential borrowers, requiring substantial negotiations between them and the NDB before the loans could be processed.

A tradition of central control that pervades all aspects of public administration in Paraguay affects also the operations of the National Development Bank. Although the Bank maintains seventeen branches and agencies throughout the country, these outposts deal largely in traditional commercial loans; development loans are still handled very largely by the central office.

Another point of contention has been the NDB's participation in commercial banking operations. The major portion of the Bank's bad debts have occurred in its Commerce and Savings Department, and this department definitely competes with the private commercial banks both for loan business and for deposits. On its part, the NDB considers its commercial operations a complementary function to its development lending, e.g., financing the exportation of products whose development it has financed. Nevertheless, the NDB has been more inclined to "roll over" its short-term credits than the private banks, so that many of its commercial loans have become medium-term credits.

Since its reorganization, the NDB has been trying to improve its operations and is having substantial success, as evidenced by its utilization of previous external loans and its contracting of new ones. Further reorganization of the Bank is required, particularly to provide a manager. At present, the president of the Bank also acts as an operating officer. Inasmuch as the NDB and the Central Bank are located in the same building, it should be possible to share the costs of maintenance rather than have each institution maintain supernumerary staff. In addition, the Bank could use additional trained technicians in its Development and Agricultural Departments to shorten the loan processing time and to provide greater assistance to its clients. In the future, as trained personnel are found, more autonomy might be given to branches in the interior to implement development lending.

COLONIZATION

In Paraguay, there is adequate public land available for settlement so that expropriation is only an infrequent occurrence. Much of the land to be used for redistribution and settlement is being made accessible by the extension of highways and feeder roads, mainly in eastern Paraguay. In order to move farmers off of subsistence farms in the Central Zone to more efficient production units in the newly available agricultural areas, to develop new socially and economically viable centers of production, and to take account of the semi-nomadic temperament and heritage of the Paraguayan campesino,[8] the colonization system has been utilized as the principal method of agrarian reform in Paraguay. Coronel Oviedo, for example, was founded by immigrants from other parts of Paraguay, and the people still travel back and forth to visit their old communities. Also, in various parts of the country (e.g., Pilar, Encarnación), the young people are leaving for lack of economic opportunities and are tending to move to Asunción or to Argentina, Brazil, or Uruguay. Thus the idea of establishing integrated colonies, economically and socially self-sustaining, makes considerable sense in the Paraguayan context. Also, the success of the Mennonite colonies might well have been an important consideration in choosing this means of agricultural development.

Private Colonies

Foreign colonization of Paraguay after its independence from Spain dates from the mid-nineteenth century. However, although efforts at colonization have been relatively numerous for this small isolated country, the net addition to its population has been quite small. Fretz has estimated the total number of immigrants for the past century at no more than 75,000.[9] The reasons for their coming were various: availability of agricultural land; almost complete religious, social, and political freedom offered to those agricultural immigrants who were willing to settle in remote regions of the country; exemption from military service; and the right to settle in closed communities.[10] According to Professor Fretz, Paraguay was unique in its openness to admitting idealistic groups for agricultural settlement in the second quarter of the twentieth century. Moreover, the immigrants have been accepted by the Paraguayan people and have been respected for their honesty, industriousness, and technical knowledge.

Those immigrants that have had the greatest impact on Paraguay came in groups, for the most part as ethnic bodies, e.g., the German and Dutch Mennonites and the Japanese. These settled in cohesive social groups and established their own societies to regulate their social, economic, and religious behavior. The Mennonites established their first colonies in 1927 in the heart of the Chaco; more recently, colonies also have been founded in eastern Paraguay. Recent data on the Mennonite colonies are given in Table 19.[11]

Each of these colonies operates an independent cooperative entity. Suffrage is limited to adult males who are property owners. Each village elects an administrator and a committee of four or five men who represent various facets of industry or agriculture. Tenure is for three years; re-election is quite common. The administrators are responsible for all phases of business, education, and medical activities of the colonies.

The Mennonite colonies are backstopped by the Mennonite Central Committee in the United States and Canada. Such backstopping includes purchases of materials on behalf of the colonies, sales of their products abroad, and negotiations of foreign loans for the colonies. The Committee has an office in Asunción.

The Japanese settlements in Paraguay began in 1936, at Colonia La Colmena in the Department of Paraguarí, and were formalized by an international agreement between the two countries in 1959.[12] This agreement provided for the immigration of 85,000 Japanese farmers over a thirty-year period. Japanese colonies thus far established (by the end of 1966) are given in Table 20.

The last three Japanese colonies in Table 20 are under the general supervision of a Japanese Immigration Corporation, formed in 1963 to implement the immigration agreement of 1959. Cooperatives

TABLE 19

Basic Data on the Mennonite Colonies in Paraguay

Name of Colony	Date Founded	Area in Hectares	Area in Cultivation (Hectares)	Number of Persons
In the Chaco				
Colonia Menno	1927	356,250	5,200	5,200
Colonia Fernheim	1930	262,500	4,100	2,624
Colonia Neuland	1947	206,250	3,000	1,596
In Eastern Paraguay				
Colonia Volendam	1947	32,000	n.a.	760
Colonia Friesland	1937	7,000	n.a.	993
Colonia Bergthal	1948	n.a.	n.a.	950
Colonia Sommerfield	1948	n.a.	n.a.	650

n.a. = not available

TABLE 20

Japanese Colonies in Paraguay

Name of Colony	Date Founded	Area in Hectares	Number of Families
Colonia La Colmena	1936	n.a.	...
Colonia Puerto Federico and Chavez	1954	n.a.	120
Colonia Fram[a]	1957	16,000	325
Colonia Alto Paraná (Pirapó)	1958	83,580	351
Colonia Yguazú	1960	87,762	35

n.a. = not available

[a]Apart from the Japanese families, the rest of the colony consists chiefly of White Russians and Ukrainians.

have been formed, a hotel (reception center) has been built in Encarnación, warehouses have been constructed, and a credit system for the colonies has been created, all of these financed by the Corporation.

The Mennonite, Japanese, German, and other major private colonies in Paraguay total eighty-five in number and include an area of 1.060 million hectares distributed over thirteen departments of the country. The area they occupy is approximately equal to that held by the officially established colonies.[13]

Other private colonies have developed as a result of (a) selling occupied lands to squatters and (b) selling off parts of larger tracts to private persons.[14] In the former case, owners often have found it cheaper to sell lands to the squatters than to pay them for improvements thereon in order to drive the people off. Moreover, owners have preferred to sell these lands than to have them expropriated by the government. The selling prices are regulated by the Rural Welfare Institute (IBR). Often, additional parcels have been sold at the same time to provide adequate-sized lots to the buyers.

In the case of certain large landowners, lands have been sold to settlers in order to obtain working capital, avoid expropriation, or encourage production of particular crops with reduced overhead. For example, a large landholder may subdivide a portion of his land and sell lots to small farmers who agree to produce a particular crop of interest to the subdivider. He may receive payment for his land either in cash or in kind, but in either case he is assured of the output which he will market.

Official Colonies

Apart from the private colonies that have developed in Paraguay, official policy has favored the movement of persons out of the Central Zone to the interior of the country. This policy is based on the political motive of "consolidating the national territory" and upon the economic motive of providing more viable family units of agricultural production and increasing the commercial output of farm crops. Implementation of this policy has been the responsibility of the Rural Welfare Institute (Instituto de Bienestar Rural - IBR) and predecessor agencies, the National Commission of Puerto Presidente Stroessner, and the Agricultural Credit Bank (CAH). These programs have resulted in a series of colonization movements (marchas) in various directions.

March to the East

A program designed to develop the rich agricultural area bordering the Brazil Road between Coronel Oviedo and Puerto Presidente Stroessner, in the Departments of Caaguazú and Alto Paraná, was begun in 1961. By the end of 1965, the area colonized covered some 300,000 hectares and contained about 30,000 farm families.[15] A plan issued by the Rural Welfare Institute in early 1966 called for the establishment of fourteen official colonies and two private colonies in this area, to cover 316,400 and 145,400 hectares, respectively.

March to the North

A second major colonization movement followed the opening of the road from Coronel Oviedo northward through Carayaó to San Estanislao and from there to the Jejuí River. Colonization by the end of 1965 had covered an area of 68,785 hectares and, by the end of 1966, was to reach a total of 118,400 hectares. This area was to include twelve official and two private colonies.

The three-year IBR program to colonize the north and east axes during 1966-68[16] was designed to establish fifty colonies incorporating 150,000 hectares of cultivated land, to create fifteen cooperatives, to increase crop and forestry production, and to raise the production of hogs and chickens for both home consumption and for sale in the marketplace. Credit was to be provided for the purchase of dairy cattle so that as many families as possible could have their own supply of milk. Some 40,000 farm families were expected to benefit from this program, and technical and credit assistance was to be provided by the IBR and the National Development Bank. The program is quite comprehensive in scope, having determined by soils and market analyses the kinds of crops to be grown in each colony. An analysis of the statistics, however, raises several important questions: Are the sizes of family farms adequate to create viable units (the range appears to be from 2 to 6 hectares per farm)? Also, only 8,000 of the 40,000 farms are scheduled to receive credit; what are the majority of farmers to do?

Estimates of costs for the first year of the plan (1966) involved an input of ₲ 22 million by the IBR and credit from the National Development Bank amounting to ₲ 170 million. Whether the IBR would be able to muster the necessary staff and finances to implement the plan remained to be seen. The plan bears further study with respect to size of family farms contemplated, the amount of credit required to meet the needs of the number of farmers envisioned in the program, and the wisdom of having each family provided with its own milk and poultry supply.

Colonization along Route V (East-West)

The road from Concepción eastward to Pedro Juan Caballero provides another opportunity for colonization. One of the colonies already established in this area (Colonia Cerro Memby) is formed completely by repatriates and veterans of the Chaco War.

March to the Chaco

The recently completed Transchaco Road, some 435 miles in length, will enable broad areas of territory in western Paraguay to be brought under settlement. The major potential for this region is cattle raising.[17] It is estimated that more than 3 million hectares are available for colonization, of which 400,000 hectares are to be settled in the first stage of the program. Beginnings already have been made in the area around Filadelfia, Department of Boquerón, adjacent to the Mennonite colonies.

March to the South

A program for colonizing southern Paraguay is in process of development. Its aim will be to provide land to landless farmers in the Departments of Itapúa, Misiones, and Ñeembucú. A census of landowners on lands in a fringe 18 miles wide along the coast of the Paraná River has been taken for the purpose of determining how such lands might be acquired legally for colonization purposes. A few colonies already have been established in the region.

In addition to the establishment of colonies, official policy, since 1962, has been to provide (through the IBR) small parcels of land and rudimentary agricultural implements to conscripts upon their completion of military or police service. The number of tracts granted during 1962-65 has been as follows: 1962, 1,072; 1963, 1,204; 1964, 2,610; and 1965, 4,913. While the policy seems like a good idea, reports are heard that the conscripts, once having been brought to large centers for training, find it difficult to return to the hinterland (campo), and many have abandoned the lands assigned to them. Also, lack of technical skill and of supervised credit have provided additional obstacles to their becoming successful farmers. The IBR also is responsible for resettling repatriates, migrants, and war veterans in various colonies around the country and for providing them with the social and economic necessities to start a new life.

There has been virtually no impartial evaluation of the IBR's efforts to date. However, Dr. Adlai Arnold, a colonization expert assigned to the U.S. Aid Mission to Paraguay, has stated:

> With about one-quarter million persons living in the colonies, the colonization program being administered by the Institute of Rural Welfare (Instituto de Bienestar Rural or IBR) is of considerable scope and significance. More than 200 colonies occupying one and one-half million hectares have been subdivided into more than 50,000 lots.[18]

The IBR, established by Law No. 852 of March 22, 1963, to replace the Agrarian Reform Institute, has thus far been concerned mainly with the distribution of land and the issuance of titles thereto. This agency and its predecessors, by the end of 1965, had distributed 56,018 titles to 1,612,940 hectares of land.[19] (From 1915 through 1954, only 11,705 titles and 269,226 hectares had been distributed.) The IBR also is responsible for the development and preservation of Paraguay's forest resources. In this respect the agency is in an anomalous position. On the one hand, it must clear lands for colonization purposes and, in the process, destroy certain forests. On the other hand, it is responsible for safeguarding and developing the national forests (Decree-Law No. 370 of 1964) and for collecting taxes on the commercial exploitation of privately owned natural forests (see Chapter 12). This conflict of interests within the IBR could be resolved through the creation of an independent Forest Service.

A government agency known as the Puerto Presidente Stroessner Administration was created in February, 1957, and was made an autonomous agency by Law No. 623 of August 22, 1960. Its functions are to plan, organize, and establish a city and colony at Puerto Presidente Stroessner, the eastern terminus of the road (Brazil Road) from Asunción to the Brazilian border. Part of the plan included the establishment of a colony on the outskirts of the city, between the Rivers Acaray, Monday, and Paraná, and a line running perpendicularly from the Brazil Road to Kilometer 294, cutting the Acaray and Monday rivers. The colony thus organized has an area of 30,000 hectares, of which 3,500 are in production. The land thus far distributed includes 800 lots averaging 20 hectares each. Land distribution in the Puerto Presidente Stroessner colony is linked with a program of technical and financial assistance and provision for the marketing of the colony's commercial production. Community facilities of an educational, recreational, and religious nature are provided. Six schools, four extension service offices, and a 10-hectare demonstration farm also have been established. The site of this colony, close to the Brazil Road and international bridge to Brazil, is also adjacent to the Acaray River where a new hydroelectric power station is being built.

The Inter-American Development Bank has loaned $910,000 to the Puerto Presidente Stroessner Administration ($250,000 in July, 1961, and $660,000 in July, 1965) for installing a sawmill, improving facilities for transporting logs from the forests to the sawmill, building access roads and a street system in the colony, constructing sewers and bridges, and establishing a tree nursery (including fruit trees). In addition, self-help construction of some 400 combination grain storehouses and dwellings was being undertaken. It was expected that 1,500 settlers and their families would be located in this colony, on economically feasible farm units, with better social conditions than in other rural areas.

It is curious, however, that this autonomous agency relates to the Executive Branch through the Ministry of the Interior rather than through the Ministry of Agriculture and Livestock or the Rural Welfare Institute. Along with the agricultural credit situation (discussed below), the arrangement reflects a general weakness pervading agricultural programs in Paraguay, namely, a lack of coordination within the government in the development of this sector which tends to hamper the efficiency of the projects undertaken. The limited manpower and financial resources are spread too thinly to do an effective job.

While the colonization is likely to be an effective means of increasing agricultural output, and in some cases agricultural productivity, this policy nevertheless creates problems in the lands left behind--the subsistence farms in the Central Zone. Unless legal provision is made for combining these tracts into economic units and providing the owners with adequate technical and capital assistance, farm production may actually decline for some years as the population leaves this key area. On the other hand, certain of these lands probably will be suitable for industrial development, perhaps as locations for industrial parks, and this possibility should be investigated by the business community and local officials in the affected areas.

AGRICULTURAL EDUCATION

With the exception of doctors and lawyers, Paraguay is short of technicians. More than that, persons who are able to combine theory and practice are very scarce in this country. Vocational agriculture is not taught in any of the public schools and only some basic training is given in a few private schools. At the university level, there were not more than seven individuals with the equivalent of a Master of Science degree in agriculture working in the Ministry of Agriculture, Faculty of Agronomy and Veterinary Sciences, and STICA combined, in 1966. Six technicians were studying in the United States and were to complete requirements for degrees by the end of 1968. By that time there would be less than fifteen individuals in the nation having the minimum technical training considered necessary to assume leadership roles in agricultural research and teaching. While the problem of training technicians is being addressed by the U.S. AID Mission to Paraguay and international organizations, and certain local institutions are able to contract foreign technicians for limited periods, the general shortage of trained teachers will require some time to be solved.

At the present time, government agricultural education and training efforts include five poorly administered agricultural schools (under the Ministry of Agriculture and Livestock), the vocational agricultural training to be included in four rural education centers (under the Ministry of Education and Culture), and the university level programs provided by the Faculty of Agronomy and Veterinary Sciences of the National University of Asunción. Also, informal agricultural training is provided by the Extension Service and the Rural Welfare Institute, and through cooperative and marketing programs. There also are two or three rudimentary private agricultural schools operated by the Silesian Fathers.

The most important source of trained agronomists and veterinarians is the Faculty of Agronomy and Veterinary Sciences of the National University of Asunción. This institution, established in 1956, is located near San Lorenzo del Campo Grande, across the road from the STICA Artificial Insemination Center. The Faculty graduated its first class in 1960. It has received technical assistance in administration, curriculum development, and training of professional staff from Montana State College (September 7, 1960 - June 30, 1963) and since then from New Mexico State University. Both institutions were contracted by the Agency for International Development. These contracts have assisted materially in establishing a program of higher agricultural education where none existed before.

The Faculty of Agronomy and Veterinary Sciences awarded only 172 degrees during 1960-65: eighty-eight in agronomy and eighty-four in veterinary science. Apart from the work being done at the Faculty, the Ministry of Agriculture and Livestock operates five so-called Regional Agricultural Schools located at Caazapá, Concepción, Guairá, Quiindy, and San Juan Bautista (Misiones). Their purpose is to provide two years of training to young agriculturists, combining theory and practice, and then to return these youths to their homes to practice agriculture more efficiently. Although the existing schools are in bad repair and poorly staffed, the Ministry was hoping to obtain external financial assistance to build fifteen or twenty additional ones.

The Ministry of Education and Culture, with the technical and financial assistance of the U.S. AID Mission, has constructed four Rural Education Centers (at Pilar, Encarnación, Villarrica, and Concepción) to provide secondary education to Paraguayan youths, including specialized training in agricultural activities. The advantages of this approach over the Regional Agricultural Schools operated by the Ministry of Agriculture and Livestock are (a) the training is provided by professional educators; (b) the students are better grounded (having completed elementary education) and thus are able to obtain a better over-all education to assist them in becoming good citizens as well as good farmers; and (c) the Ministry of Education receives more than eight times the budget of the Ministry of Agriculture, so that the former is financially (as well as technically) able to do a better job of education. The field of agricultural education is another example of duplicated government activity leading to inferior results and inefficient use of resources.

The Ministry of Defense operates several farms around the country at its various commands, and a seed and hatchery service at Asunción to supply its products to these farms. The commands in the interior produce food for the consumption of the troops and, in the process, training in agricultural activities is provided to the conscripts. The Ministry also operates a colony for Indians at Yvypyté, where a variety of crops is produced for commercial sale.

During the past twenty years a considerable amount of practical applied agricultural research has been done in Paraguay and is being put into practice on a limited scale. Nevertheless, the state of technical knowledge still is grossly inadequate for the host of existing farm, ranch, and forest problems confronting the country. For example, it has not been established if it is economically feasible to plant improved pastures; if it is profitable to clear thorny brush on the ranches and plant grass in its place; why cattle on some ranches fail to gain properly even though grass is abundant; what soils are deficient in mineral elements; and if it is profitable to plant and cultivate palmitos and coco palms for palm hearts and nut production, respectively. Research on the application of fertilizers to most Paraguayan crops and practical ways to increase their use is another field for development. However, even available information has reached relatively few Paraguayan farmers. Although the number of Extension Service centers has been increasing gradually, there were only twenty-two such offices for the entire country in July, 1966, and there was only one qualified Rural Extension Agent in each office.

Pests and diseases take a heavy toll of plants and animals. Nevertheless, there has been no opportunity for specialization in plant pest and disease control in the crops section of the Faculty of Agronomy and Veterinary Sciences. During 1963-65, an effective control was found for leaf-cutting ants, which in the past had destroyed as much as 30 per cent of the national production of some crops, but the method still remains to be exploited widely. Also, the Ministry of Agriculture and Livestock has neither the funds nor the staff for prompt effective action when outbreaks of infectious diseases (anthrax, foot-and-mouth, etc.) occur in the livestock herds.

Given the present primitive pattern of its agriculture and the importance of the agricultural sector in the national economy, there is an identified although unquantified need for more trained agricultural manpower, particularly below the university level. There is great need for a well-founded, integrated educational program wherein school-age children can obtain a sound primary education, proceed to secondary schools that incorporate specialized with general education, and then--if qualified--go on to a university for professional study in agricultural or veterinary sciences (including specialization in the various aspects of agriculture, livestock raising, and forestry). Such a program will require a delineation of functions between the Ministries of Agriculture and Education; the improvement of teaching staffs and curricula at all educational levels; assurance that such education will lead to higher incomes; and a coordination of primary, secondary, and university programs to assure continuity in subject matter and progressive acquisition of knowledge.

MARKETING

A U.S. Government-sponsored survey team[20] reported, in 1964, that "Paraguay has reached the stage of economic development where effective utilization of the country's productive resources is in large part dependent on material improvements in marketing."[21] The team recommended that a vastly increased amount of attention be given to the functioning of the marketing system and the availability of adequate essential services and facilities for handling, storing, processing, transporting, and distributing farm output so that the income needed as an incentive to increase production and purchasing power might be forthcoming.

At present, much of the output of farmers is lost or wasted because of inadequate marketing facilities. Access to both local and export markets is difficult because of the shortage of all-weather highways and feeder roads and seasonal drops in the level of the Paraguay River which involve transhipment of products and delays in transit. This situation increases costs and takes a toll from all concerned in the production and consumption of agricultural products. The loss and waste are reflected in widened margins of middlemen and other intermediaries in the distribution chain. This system reduces incentives to produce, deprives consumers of needed foods, and reduces available supplies for export.

No regular accurate source of agricultural market information is available to Paraguayan producers, processors, and exporters. There are no forecasts of market demand for various commodities, either for local sale or export, of planting intentions, acreage planted, crop yields, carryover stocks, or livestock numbers. Also, adequate and appropriate storage facilities are not available. This is particularly true for on-the-farm storage. Some farmers actually move out of their homes during harvest and use them to store crops until sold. Most of the corn and mandioca produced is left in the field until sold. Local wholesale and retail sales facilities, particularly for perishables (including milk), are highly inefficient and wasteful of commodities, time, and manpower.

The other side of the marketing coin is equally serious. Commodities that a farmer must buy in order to live and to produce a crop or a marketable animal are often expensive and difficult to find. For example, during 1966, ammonium sulfate fertilizer was not available in Asunción for several months. The costs of fertilizer and lime, when available, have been so high that, coupled with a scarcity of crop production financing, the widespread use of such items has been severely limited.

The National Development Bank inherited from the former Bank of Paraguay sixteen grain storage silos. Four of these are above ground, each with a capacity of 1,500 metric tons. However, only the one at Asunción is reported to be in usable operating condition. The remaining twelve silos consist of underground bins with capacities varying from 150 to 1,866 metric tons. The above-ground silos and some of the pit storage facilities have permanently installed grain drying facilities; the others utilize portable dryers when required. Most of the facilities have been idle for years. Shipments of P.L. 480 wheat, for example, must be stored in Argentina until required for local consumption, thereby adding to the already high cost of wheat imported from the United States. The Inter-American Development Bank is interested in making a loan to Paraguay for the development of silos and other crop storage facilities.

Paraguayan Government policy thus far has been directed towards developing main highways and feeder roads to open new agricultural areas and to connect existing productive areas with major markets. This road program has been in progress for a number of years, and although the system is still inadequate for the country's needs, results are evident in the increased truck and bus transport of produce to markets from as far north as Caraguaty. The road to Lima (Paraguay) has recently been opened to commercial traffic. The United States aid program has played a key role in the financing and construction of these vital roads. The program is discussed in more detail in Chapter 9.

Another major government policy has been to negotiate special concessions with other LAFTA members for certain exportable agricultural products. Also the Technical Planning Secretariat has undertaken a series of commodity studies designed to seek ways of stimulating production, alleviating marketing barriers for export, and/or substituting domestic production for imports on twelve items: wheat, cotton, tobacco, vegetable oils (peanut, soybean, and coconut), fruits (citrus and pineapple), kenaf fiber, vegetables, milk, poultry, hogs, and pine for pulpwood. None of these studies had been published as of July 31, 1966.

Paraguay taxes agricultural exports and levies heavy duties on most imports needed for crop and livestock production, as well as on supplies and equipment required for the establishment of essential handling, processing, and transportation facilities for farm, ranch, and forest products. These regressive taxes obviously are inconsistent with the government's professed policy of promoting economic development. In recent years there has been a growing, if grudging, awareness of this conflict in policies on the part of the Paraguayan Government. By Decree-Law No. 348 of March 25, 1963, imports of fertilizers, insecticides, and fungicides were liberated from import taxes. Previously, import duties on such products ranged between 40 per cent and 50 per cent ad valorem. Moreover, under the terms of various loan agreements signed with international lending agencies the Government of Paraguay has granted duty-free entry of many commodities required for agricultural, livestock, and industrial development if these were purchased with loan funds. The Minister of Finance, however, has not been reconciled to the short-term loss of revenue resulting from these exonerations and has not been disposed to revise the customs tariff to permit generalized free entry or nominal taxation of these development commodities.

For certain products--cotton, tobacco, fruit--national councils have been formed under the leadership of the Ministry of Agriculture and Livestock to consider matters relating to the planting, collecting, and marketing of these crops.[22] Such councils normally are comprised of representatives of the appropriate department in the Ministry of Agriculture and Livestock; the Central Bank and the National Development Bank; and the producers, agents, manufacturers, and exporters. Studies of the respective commodity problems by these councils are intended to lead to the adoption of official policies for improving their situation. Such councils may be created for other agricultural products whenever the need arises. Their recommendations are made to the Ministry of Agriculture and Livestock, which has responsibility for obtaining the desired government action.

Certain current developments undoubtedly will, in time, produce substantial increases in agricultural production and improvements in the marketing of farm products. The most significant of these developments are: (a) New roads are being opened up in most sections of the country and within a few years Paraguay will have access to the Atlantic Ocean port of Paranaguá via a hard-surfaced road through Brazil. (b) A major effort is being made to colonize new lands. The U.S. AID Mission to Paraguay has brought a colonization specialist to Paraguay to assist with colonization programs. (c) The Minister of Agriculture and Livestock had agreed in 1966 to a major reorganization of his Ministry and the Minister of Finance had verbally agreed to an increase in budget for that Ministry in 1967 in order to support the transferred servicio operations. If the integration of STICA activities were to be made without interruption, the Ministry of Agriculture would be strengthened greatly by the merging of functions. (d) Recent credits from AID, the Inter-American Development Bank, and the International Development Association have made substantial capital available through the National Development Bank for crop and livestock production and for production loans to medium-sized farmers. (e) Interest in cooperatives is high and the AID program, through a U.S. Department of Agriculture Cooperative Specialist, has been carrying forward an educational program designed to broaden the understanding of the administration of cooperatives throughout the nation. Interest in cooperatives is growing rapidly, and much understanding of the nature and functions of sound cooperatives is being developed. (f) The U.S. Aid Mission to Paraguay has brought a Marketing Specialist from the U.S. Department of Agriculture to this country to work on the marketing of a variety of products destined for internal consumption and for export, and to recommend improvements in growing, breeding, or processing methods. (g) Under Article 3 of Decree-Law No. 370, all forests, brands, and markings of forest products, as well as sawmills, are required to be registered with the Rural Welfare Institute. Also, all products removed from the forests must be marked with the brand of the producer. A special section to supervise these activities was established by IBR Resolution No. 391 of May 9, 1966.

In a move to spur colonization in the interior of the country, to stimulate reforestation, and to provide the raw material on which to base a paper industry, the Government of Paraguay decreed, October, 1965, that a demonstration plantation of pine be established at the Presidente Stroessner

Colony (Colonia Presidente Stroessner), with an area of 300 hectares. The species to be planted were Paraná pine and Florida pine because of their rapid growth characteristic (five to fifteen years).

Experiments with other types of trees, including eucalyptus, lapacho, tipa, chivato, and jacarandá, have been undertaken. Since 1961, a program of experiments with varieties imported from countries having climates similar to that of Paraguay has been in progress. Such experiments are being conducted at the National Agronomic Institute at Caacupe, the Agricultural Experiment Station at Capitán Miranda in Itapúa, and at Barrerito Ranch at Caapucú. Also, the Japanese Colony at Alto Paraná and the Mennonite Colonies in the Chaco are participating. Thus, the experiments cover the various ecological zones of the country and should provide much useful information for developing forestry as an agricultural occupation in Paraguay.[23]

Notes to Chapter 5

1. Ministerio de Agricultura y Ganadería, STICA--1965 (annual report), July, 1966, pp. 15-16.

2. Joseph Winfield Fretz, Immigrant Group Settlements in Paraguay (North Newton, Kansas: Bethel College, 1962), p. 163.

3. Ibid., pp. 164-65.

4. Tim G. Smith, Itapúa: Notes on the Economic Environment, October 17, 1965, pp. 12-13. Unpublished thesis submitted to the University of Oregon. (Mr. Smith was a Fulbright student who lived in Itapúa for six months to make his study.)

5. Frederick L. Kerr, "Report on Agricultural Credit in Paraguay," November, 1961, p. 4. Report submitted to the U.S. Operations Mission to Paraguay.

6. During the 1950's, the Bank of Paraguay had made many unsecured and uncollectable loans for consumption purposes to powerful political and military interests.

7. Published January 19, 1964, p. 10.

8. Fretz, op. cit., pp. 8-9.

9. Ibid., p. 187.

10. Ibid., pp. 187-88.

11. Ibid.; and Alberto Bravo G., et. al., Organización Administrativa y Contable del Instituto de Bienestar Rural (Asunción: Italconsult Argentina, May, 1965), p. 19.

12. Ratified on the part of Paraguay by Decree-Law No. 219 of October 19, 1959.

13. Bravo, op. cit., p. 22. The data do not include certain private subdivisions resulting from the parceling of portions of large properties.

14. Ibid., p. 17.

15. "Paraguay: Informe sobre La Evolución Económica y Social en El Quinquenio 1961-1965." Presented to the Fourth Session of the Inter-American Economic and Social Council (IA-ECOSOC) at Buenos Aires, March, 1966, p. 55.

16. Instituto de Bienestar Rural, "Program Regional de las Zonas de Colonización Trienio 1966-68," Asunción, 1966, p. 7.

17. However, Paraguay still hopes to discover commercial petroleum deposits in the Chaco.

18. Adlai Arnold, Paper on "Colonization and Agrarian Reform in Paraguay," 1966.

19. Statistics from the Rural Welfare Institute.

20. From the U.S. Department of Agriculture, Iowa State University, and the Agency for International Development.

21. Report of U.S. Department of Agriculture, Land Grant College, and Agency for International Development Survey Team, Agricultural Development in Paraguay, February 17, 1965, p. 33.

22. The Tobacco Council was created by Decree No. 9041 of January 19, 1952; the Cotton Council by Decree No. 31,231 of January 6, 1958; and the Fruit Council by Decree No. 4297 of April 30, 1957, and expanded by Decree No. 9676 of February 20, 1965.

23. La Tribuna, April 6, 1965, p. 5.

PART II

INDUSTRY

CHAPTER 6 THE INDUSTRIAL STRUCTURE

The Technical Planning Secretariat has described three systems of manufacturing in Paraguay: (a) rural artisans, producing chiefly at home between growing and harvesting seasons, to satisfy local needs for basic consumer goods; (b) urban artisan production of individual workers and small shops having less than four employees, producing hand-made or simply tooled end items of low quality for the lowest income bracket of consumers; and (c) factory-type production, producing items for the local market or for export. This third type of production is the most efficient.[1] However, there is little inter-industry relationship found in the country. Factory-type industrial production is discussed in greater detail below.

Paraguayan industry is still largely in the traditional Latin American pattern of small individual ownership, family employment, and low output. Of the 5,845 establishments recorded in the 1963 industrial census, 84.5 per cent (4,937) were individually owned; 63.0 per cent (3,681) had between two and four persons working, but 56.5 per cent (3,305) reported no salaried workers employed; and 68.7 per cent (4,013) of the establishments had no mechanical power. Also, 58.3 per cent (3,408) of the establishments had a value of output of less than ₲ 250,000 (U.S. $2,000) each per year. On the other hand, 174 establishments (3.0 per cent of the total) accounted for 74.9 per cent of the total value of industrial production, and for 70.5 per cent of the value added in manufacturing. For the country as a whole, the value of industrial production in 1963 was ₲ 15,461 million (U.S. $122.7 million), of which 63.2 per cent represented costs of inputs (excluding labor costs) and 36.8 per cent represented the gross value added in the production process.* The average value of production per establishment amounted to ₲ 2,645,231 (U.S. $20,994); and average value added per establishment came to ₲ 972,270 (U.S. $7,716). About 70 per cent of the value of materials consumed was of national origin and 30 per cent was imported.

Urban areas accounted for 57.4 per cent (3,355) of the establishments and rural areas for 42.6 per cent (2,490). However, Asunción alone accounted for 22.0 per cent (1,285) of the industrial enterprises, 36.5 per cent of the persons employed in them, 48.1 per cent of the value of industrial output, and 50.3 per cent of the value added in production. Also, nearly 38 per cent of the corporate enterprises were located in the capital city.

Five classes of industries accounted for 77 per cent of the total value of output in 1963. These are shown in order of their value of product in the 1963 census, in Table 21.

Within the major classes of industries shown in Table 21, a small number of subclasses stand out. In terms of value of product, the percentage contribution of these major subclasses to the total of their respective classes is given in Table 22.

The major industries of Paraguay tend to be highly concentrated in particular areas of the country. Table 23 shows the major locations of these principal industries in terms of percentage of value of production for each industrial class.

---

*If labor costs were included in the cost of production, the proportions would change to 75.7 per cent for inputs and 24.3 per cent for net value added. Raw materials represented 56.5 per cent of the value of product.

TABLE 21

Major Classes of Industry in Paraguay, 1963

Class of Industry	Value of Product (₲ Million)	Per Cent of Total
Food products	6,487	42.0
Chemicals	1,882	12.2
Textiles	1,779	11.5
Electricity, water, and steam	926	6.0
Beverages	831	5.3
Subtotal	11,905	77.0
All other	3,556	23.0
TOTAL	15,461	100.0

TABLE 22

Major Subclasses of Industry, 1963

Class	Major Subclasses
Food products	Meat processing (40.9 per cent); flour milling (23.0 per cent); baking (13.6 per cent); sugar milling (10.6 per cent).
Chemicals	Industrial oils and animal fats (nonedible) (62.3 per cent)
Textiles	Yarns, fabrics, and finished textile products (except knitted) (97.6 per cent)
Electricity, water, and steam	Electric power (70.8 per cent)
Beverages	Alcoholic beverages (56.3 per cent); beer (24.4 per cent)

TABLE 23

Geographic Distribution of Principal Industries, 1963

Class of Industry	Principal Departments
Food products	Asunción (50.9 per cent); Central (23.6 per cent).
Chemicals	Central (41.8 per cent); Asunción (22.2 per cent); Boquerón (18.8 per cent); Itapúa (11.5 per cent).
Textiles	Ñeembucú (37.9 per cent); Central (30.2 per cent); Asunción (23.2 per cent).
Electricity, water, and steam	Asunción (74.0 per cent).
Beverages	Asunción (73.2 per cent); Guairá (13.5 per cent)

TABLE 24

Geographic Distribution of Establishments and Persons Employed, 1963

Department	Number of Establishments	Per Cent of Total	Number of Persons Employed	Per Cent of Total
Asunción	1,285	22.0	13,024	36.5
Central	1,089	18.6	6,351	17.8
La Cordillera	992	17.0	3,750	10.5
Guairá	270	4.6	2,194	6.2
Itapúa	435	7.4	1,895	5.3
Paraguarí	372	6.4	1,409	4.0
Boquerón	166	2.8	1,306	3.7
Concepción	165	2.8	1,238	3.5
Ñeembucú	94	1.6	995	2.8
Caaguazú	249	4.3	633	2.3
Caazapá	161	2.7	736	2.1
San Pedro	226	3.9	599	1.7
Misiones	160	2.7	403	1.1
Pte. Hayes	50	0.9	366	1.0
Amambay	105	1.8	364	1.0
Alto Paraná	22	0.4	177	0.5
Olimpo	4	0.1	12	[a]
TOTAL	5,845	100.0	32,652	100.0

[a]Insignificant.

There is only one brewery in Paraguay, the Cervecería Paraguaya S.A., located in downtown Asunción. The major textile factory in the country, Manufactura de Pilar, S.A., is located in the city of Pilar, Department of Ñeembucú. Tobacco products manufacturing is found almost entirely in Asunción (52.3 per cent) and in the Central Department (47.2 per cent). Shoe and clothing manufacturing also are confined largely to Asunción (68.5 per cent of the value of output).

The most labor-intensive area of Paraguay is Asunción. Here is found 22 per cent of the country's industrial establishments containing 36.5 per cent of its industrial employment. Lesser labor-intensive zones are the Departments of Guairá, Ñeembucú, Boquerón, and Concepción. In all other departments of the country, the proportion of establishments to the national total exceeds the proportion of persons employed to the national total, as shown in Table 24.

Major U.S. investments in the country are represented by Esso's distribution of gasoline, gas, and petroleum products; a branch of The First National City Bank of New York; the International Products Corporation (meatpacking);[2] a new petroleum refinery; vegetable oil processing (Anderson, Clayton), and several coffee growing operations in northeastern Paraguay along the Brazilian border. Coca Cola began to be produced locally under license in 1965.

Other foreign investments are in commercial banking, insurance, import and export operations, shipping, ranching, lumbering, vegetable oil processing, extraction of _quebracho_, distribution of petroleum products (Shell), and wholesale and retail trade. Argentine capital is the major foreign investment component in Paraguay, and Argentina is the principal single market for Paraguay's exports. However, Brazilian, British, Spanish, German, and Dutch capital are also found here.

PROBLEMS AND PROSPECTS

There are numerous obstacles to industrial development in Paraguay, most of which are typical of underdeveloped countries. Such obstacles include (a) a shortage of trained businessmen, managers, foremen, and skilled workmen; (b) a small local market with relatively low purchasing power; (c) a shortage of credit for medium- and long-term lending; (d) limited mineral resources for industrialization; (e) inadequate transportation facilities and marketing systems; and (f) a general lack of know-how.

In addition, there are obstacles peculiar to Paraguay: geographical remoteness from world markets; high transportation costs for items of low unit value; restriction of credit to the private sector in order to control inflationary effects generated by chronic government budget deficits; and uncertain or unwise government policies (such as quotas on cattle slaughtered for export; taxes on exports and imports; and required prior import deposits of 100 per cent) that increase production costs and make Paraguayan products less competitive in foreign markets, given a fixed exchange rate.

The development of a broader internal market in Paraguay is dependent upon increasing the purchasing power of the population. As 65 per cent of the population is rural, obviously the greatest need is to raise the real income of farm families and to monetize that income at an increasing rate. This means establishing more viable family farms; improving varieties of crops; expanding transportation networks; providing storage, distribution, and marketing facilities; and making available sufficient credit for all of the foregoing activities. Concurrently, steps must be taken to provide markets for the agricultural output by increasing exports and installing new industrial capacity to process the raw materials and by-products thereof. The development of cheap hydroelectric power should permit greater diversification and dispersion of industry in the country.

In considering the establishment of factories to process agricultural products, the potential investor should consider the desirability of growing at least one fourth to one half of his raw material requirement in order to assure a stable operation. With part of his raw material supply assured, the investor will be better able to negotiate more favorable prices for his remaining needs, gauge his inventory size, and produce on a scheduled basis. There have been numerous instances of investments going awry because materials were unobtainable in adequate quantities or at previously estimated prices after the plants were built; the owners had not made prior contracts for these supplies.

The U.S. Investment Guaranty Program has been little used in Paraguay. Only three investment guarantees had been granted by the end of 1966, and the projects have had small success. While nine other applications reportedly were "in process" in AID/Washington, only two of the applicants had actually invested in Paraguay: one had constructed a petroleum refinery at Villa Elisa, and the Placid Oil Company had obtained concessions for petroleum exploration in the Chaco. Although now is the time to enter Paraguay "on the ground floor," no really desirable projects for U.S. capital investment have been developed thus far in spite of Paraguayan Government desires for such investment.

Major opportunities for investment appear to be in the cattle and lumber industries; fertilizers and insecticides; fruit and vegetable processing; vegetable oils; animal feeds; plywood and veneer; containers of all kinds; and possibly pulp and paper. Cereals, beverages, leather products, bakery products, dairy products (including ice cream), forged metal products, plastic products, and naval stores might be other possibilities. For all of these (as well as other) opportunities, adequate management and materials must be assured if the investments are to be profitable. Labor is available relatively cheaply and can be trained as required. There is room for import substitution as well as for exportable production. The new

Development and Productivity Center, inaugurated on October 6, 1966, and assisted technically and financially by the U.S. AID Mission to Paraguay, should assist materially in making investment opportunities known and in training management. A recent IDB loan of $700,000 to the Government of Paraguay to finance feasibility studies should help in the selection of sound projects; and the proposed establishment of a private development financing corporation hopefully will play a key role in their financing, along with the National Development Bank.

MEAT PROCESSING

Meat processing is Paraguay's major export industry. Most of the meat moving abroad is in the form of canned corned beef. However, frozen beef, beef extract, canned tongue, and other meat byproducts also are important exports. In 1965, exports of meat were valued at $18.7 million, exports of cattle hide at $1.4 million, and shipments of other meat products at $0.3 million. The total, $20.4 million, represented about 36 per cent of the customs value of exports.

Although Paraguay produces a high quality of canned corned beef and tongue, competition in world markets from other supplying sources is keen. The large meatpackers in the country have been making determined efforts to reduce production and distribution costs. However, their efforts have been limited by official policies that limit the slaughter season and impose various taxes on the animals slaughtered and meat exported. Meatpacking still remains an inefficient operation compared with similar activities in neighboring countries and in the United States.

The 1963 industrial census reported the existence of sixty-four abattoirs with a value of product of ₲ 2,656 million (U.S. $21 million). However, the Central Bank has revised these value data, charging that the census "included only industrial slaughter and a few municipal abattoirs in the interior of the country."[3] The Central Bank reported a gross value of meat production of ₲ 4,894 million (U.S. $38.8 million), and a value added of ₲ 1,829 million (U.S. $14.6 million) for 1963. These data include beef, beef products, and pork. The difference between the two sets of figures probably represents mainly estimated, unregistered slaughter in the interior of the country (i.e., untaxed slaughter).

Apart from the COPACAR abattoir, which supplies the armed forces and the civilian population of Asunción and its environs, other important slaughterhouses producing for domestic consumption are Segundo Antonioli S.A. (in Concepción); Bosafras S.A.; Copecuaria Nordeste Limitada (in Villarrica); and Industrializadora de Carnes S.A. Three major slaughterhouses produce meat and meat products for export. These are Liebig's Extract of Meat Co., Ltd. (British-owned); the Meat Products Division of International Products Corporation (American-owned); and the Industria Paraguaya de Carnes, S.A. (owned by private Paraguayan interests). These plants operate six or seven months a year, generally from about March through August, when the roads generally are open and the cattle can be brought to market. The export slaughter quota for the year 1966 was established as shown in Table 25.

Law No. 1114 of June 2, 1966, established the following tax system for meatpacking and/or meat exporting establishments for the 1966 slaughter season: (a) ₲ 750 per head slaughtered for export, whether from packer's own ranch or bought from third parties; plus (b) ₲ 250 transfer tax per head on cattle purchased from third parties for industrialization, this tax to be paid by the seller of the cattle; plus (c) ₲ 5 for each cowhide, salted or dried; plus (d) 2½ per cent on the value of exports of cattle hides; plus (e) real property taxes and road taxes; plus (f) stamp taxes; plus (g) any other tax not exonerated under this law.

Meatpackers or meat exporters were exempted from payment of customs duties and additional charges, and the sales tax created under Decree-Law

TABLE 25

Export Slaughter Quota, 1966
(Number of Head)

Company	Ordinary[a]	Extraordinary[b]	Total
International Products Corp.	80,000	12,500	92,500
Liebig's Extract of Meat Co.	80,000	12,500	92,500
Industria Paraguaya de Carnes	40,000	10,000	50,000
Others	15,000	---	15,000
TOTAL	215,000	35,000	250,000

[a]Resolution No. 2 of the National Economic Coordination Council (NECC), dated January 19, 1966. The quota was to be comprised 70 per cent of bulls and 30 per cent of cows over eight years of age (except pregnant cows of any age). The tax levied was to be ₲ 250 per head killed.

[b]Resolution No. 3 of the NECC, dated January 24, 1966. The tax levied was to be ₲ 750 per head killed.

No. 130 of 1957 for the importation of equipment, machinery, and parts for the installation or functioning of the slaughterhouses and of the refrigerated trucks for transporting the meat; income tax (Decree-Law No. 9240 of 1949); and whatever other customs duties and charges and exchange surcharges were levied on the importation of cattle destined for industrialization. Each enterprise had to apply for these benefits and obtain a special decree from the Executive Power.

By the end of July, 1966, only some 50 per cent of the export quota had been reached. This lag was attributable to a late start in the slaughter season and to restricted buying by the meatpackers who were unwilling to pay the prices asked by the cattlemen. Rain and floods in southern Paraguay early in the year also reduced the available supply somewhat. Because of these unusual circumstances, the slaughtering period was extended through October, 1966, but the quota was not met.

It is generally recognized that the official establishment of specific quotas for each abattoir reduces the competition to purchase available cattle. Under a global quota system, applied in prior years, the meatpackers competed for this supply, as they could slaughter at will until the global quota was reached. There is even wider agreement that the quota has outlived its usefulness and should be abolished if a genuine impetus is to be given to increasing cattle herds and improving their weight. Although experts unanimously agree that Paraguay's greatest potential lies in livestock development and meatpacking, a revision of government policies affecting this industry is required for investors to avail themselves of the country's natural advantages in these activities.

Estimated beef production in Paraguay in 1965 approximated 135,000 metric tons. Exports in that year amounted to about 18 per cent of production. Small quantities of horsemeat also are produced for export (since 1962). The horsemeat is exported to Japan in the form of frozen meat.

The International Products Corporation and Liebig's Extract of Meat Co., Ltd., operate the only canning operations in Paraguay, producing cans for their own meatpacking requirements.

LUMBER AND PRODUCTS

The 1963 industrial census reported 333 establishments in the lumber industry. These included sawmills, woodworking plants, container factories, and other woodworking activities (except the manufacture of furniture). These 333 establishments produced goods valued at ₲ 372.3 million (U.S. $3 million) and had a value added of ₲ 181.3 million, or nearly 50 per cent. There were 1,930 persons employed, of which 1,210 were workers. The industry utilized 7,864 horsepowers of energy.

There are estimated to be about ninety sawmills in Paraguay, but it is not known how many are in operation. Equipment varies widely. Only four or five sawmills may be characterized as modern, and not more than fifteen of the sawmills operate more or less efficiently. Many sawmills can work only one log during an eight-hour shift. There is substantial excess capacity in the sawmilling industry; the majority of sawmills work only one shift a day.

Outmoded machinery and increasing distances to supplies of timber have resulted in rising costs for this industry. Moreover, some 20 per cent of the sawmill output, in the form of splinter bars, rods, etc., is not exported because tariff concessions have not been obtained for these items in the LAFTA. In the domestic market, these small-dimension items are consumed as waste products. Many of the sawmills have attained such high costs of production that they have had to shut down.

Some 70 per cent to 80 per cent of Paraguay's lumber exports are in the form of logs, and virtually all of the remainder is sawed lumber. There is a very small exportation of finished products. A government policy that would favor exports of sawed lumber would do much to promote the sawmilling industry. In addition, financing is required to provide working capital to the industry as well as capital for the purchase of machinery and equipment.

With a view to controlling forestry operations, the Rural Welfare Institute, by Resolution No. 222 of March 23, 1966, established regulations governing the exploitation of forests. Lumber firms are required to maintain records of the movement of lumber from the cutting sites to ports or sawmills. Each log must be marked with tags provided by the Forestry Section of IBR and noted in the record book prior to movement. Moreover, no woodworking enterprise, sawmill, or related establishment may industrialize forest products without prior authorization of the IBR, to which application must be made for this purpose, indicating the origin of the lumber. Forest products, whether logs or sawed, that have not been registered as required above, are considered as contraband and are subject to the disposition of the IBR.

Plywood and Veneer

There were four laminating machines in the country in 1966, of which two were peelers and two were planers. Combined capacity was reported at 80 cubic meters a day, in three shifts of eight hours each. However, only two machines were in operation and these were working only single shifts. Nevertheless, even this level of output not only satisfied domestic demand for plywood but also left an exportable surplus. One obstacle to the development of the plywood industry has been the shortage of drying facilities for the wood prior to its processing into plywood. Another has been the undeveloped state of the internal market for laminated wood products.

Parquet

There is a growing market for parquet in Paraguay as well as a small export market for the product in Argentina. It is estimated that the production potential, with machinery presently installed, approximates 120,000 square meters a year. Agglomerated wood has not been produced in Paraguay thus far. However, a plant to manufacture some 20 cubic meters a day in three shifts was to be established in 1966.

TEXTILES

The production of cotton textiles and fiber is by far the largest component of the Paraguayan textile industry. In general the manufacture of cotton textiles is characterized by surplus capacity, duplication of production, and inefficient management. Moreover, the limited size of the local market, competition among domestic producers, and contraband or underpriced imports from neighboring countries suffering from sizable inflation have aggravated the precarious state of the Paraguayan industry.

The exception to the foregoing characterization is the Manufactura de Pilar S.A., in the city of Pilar. This company works three eight-hour shifts a day, using recently installed modern machinery. It is rated as one of the best textile plants in the LAFTA. Pilar's output has accounted for about 80 per cent of the country's yarn and piece goods production. The plant's manufacturing capacity was being expanded in 1966, as well as its electric power generating facilities. The company sells its surplus power to the city of Pilar. It also owns its own cotton gins and grows a part of its raw cotton supply. The factory, however, has had its special problem in that it is owned by an individual who, in 1966, was in his late seventies and there is no apparent means of assuring the continuity of the enterprise after his death. In July, 1966, the owner asked the American Embassy to seek the participation of an American textile firm in the Pilar plant, this participation to include both equity and management.

The 1963 industrial census reported forty-five establishments in the the textile industry, of which thirty-five manufactured thread and piece goods, eight produced knitted wear, one manufactured cordage, and one produced "unclassified" textile products. The forty-five establishments together employed about 1,800 persons and had a value of product amounting to ₲ 1.8 billion (U.S. $14.1 million). The value added in manufacture aggregated ₲ 597 million (U.S. $4.7 million) or 33.5 per cent. It is reported that the number of persons employed in the textile industry could be increased some 70 per cent if the industry were to operate at capacity.[4] Paraguay's output of cotton satisfies local needs, and its output of cotton fiber results in relatively sizable annual exports.

Of the forty-five textile enterprises reported in the 1963 industrial census, only four employed more than 100 persons each. These plants accounted for 43 per cent of the value of textile output and for about 65 per cent of the value added in the industry. Principal products are coarse cotton cloth, mixed woolen and cotton blankets, mattresses, canvas, and sacks for sugar and flour. Recently, the Pilar plant began to produce wash-and-wear fabrics. The size of Paraguay's textile plants and their relative efficiencies of scale, as shown in the 1963 industrial census, are given in Table 26.

Certain textile plants went into bankruptcy during the past few years (e.g., David y Bittar,[5] Fábrica de Tejidos Joaquín Grau S.A.). However, the Fábrica de Tejidos Joaquín Grau S.A., which went out of business in 1965, was bought by a new group and began operations in August, 1966. Output was to include bags for sugar and flour; knitted goods; linen, canvas, and duck; thread; and other cheap textiles. Its raw material input would be about 800 metric tons of cotton fiber a year. The company hoped to export 75 per cent of its output to member countries of the Latin American Free Trade Association. The plant's labor force, when full capacity was reached, would amount to about 400 persons.[6] Joaquín Grau, S.A., and Manufactura de Pilar, S.A., have been the largest producers of cotton textiles in Paraguay.

TABLE 26

Structure of the Textile Industry, 1963

Number of Establishments	Number of Persons Employed	Value of Product (₡ 1,000)	Value Added (₡ 1,000)	Per Cent Added
33	0 - 19	402,352	50,326	12.5
5	20 - 49	241,632	37,448	15.5
3	50 - 99	374,441	123,742	33.1
4	1000 - or more	761,019	385,171	50.6
45		1,779,444	596,687	33.5

Wool textiles are of minor importance in Paraguay; few sheep are raised in the country and climatic factors limit the market for such products. The manufacture of silk textiles, reported last in 1959, apparently has disappeared from the local scene since that time.[7] There is some production of burlap sacks made from imported jute.

Production of cotton textiles and fibers and of wool textiles, during the years 1955, 1960, and 1965, has been reported by the Central Bank as given in Table 27.

On the basis of the 1963 census data and reports from Manufactura de Pilar S.A., the figures of the Central Bank appear to be grossly understated. The Pilar factory alone has reported an output in excess of the total shown in the Central Bank's statistics.

While Paraguay produces cotton textiles with yarns ranging from eight through forty, it imports textiles of better quality from such countries as Italy, France, Japan, Switzerland, and the United States. These finer products may be purchased at prices not much higher than the rougher and heavier domestic textiles. Registered imports of cotton textiles, yarn, and other manufactures have remained more or less constant since 1957, running about $1.5 million a year, as shown in Table 28. Unregistered imports are believed to be sizable.

Registered imports of other textiles and manufactures during 1961 and 1966 are given in Table 29.

Imports by country of origin are available only as far as 1964. Of total imports of textiles and manufactures amounting to $2.658 million in that year, Japan accounted for approximately 50 per cent (cotton textiles, $795,000; silk and its manufactures, $446,000; other products, $19,000). The remainder came from the United States ($320,000), the United Kingdom ($223,000), various other European countries, and Argentina.

TABLE 27

Production of Cotton Textiles and Fiber
and Wool Textiles, 1955, 1960, and 1965

(Quantities in Millions of Meters; Values in Millions of *Guaranies*)

Year	Cotton Textiles		Cotton Fiber		Wool Textiles	
	Quantity	Value	Quantity	Value	Quantity	Value
1955	12.2	207.1	13.2	299.2	0.30	17.6
1960	13.6	434.8	4.3	225.0	0.06	10.3
1965	16.4	842.1	14.3	715.0	0.12	20.8

TABLE 28

Registered Imports of Cotton Manufactures,
Selected Years, 1957-65, and 1966

(Quantities in Metric Tons; Values in U.S. $1,000)

	Textiles		Yarn		Other Manufactures	
Year	Quantity	Value	Quantity	Value	Quantity	Value
1957	517	1,170	66	289	28	72
1961	851	1,118	54	102	203	83
1965	661	1,192	43	76	30	73
1966	561	973	43	84	41	103

Source: Central Bank of Paraguay.

TABLE 29

Registered Imports of Other Textiles and Manufactures, 1961 and 1966

(Quantities in Metric Tons; Values in U.S. $1,000)

Item	1961		1966	
	Quantity	Value	Quantity	Value
Wool fiber	170	100	109	40
Wool textiles and yarn	2	6	7	20
Wool manufactures	212	112	30	138
Silk and its manufactures	293	501	557	1,146
Burlap and its manufactures	1,003	389	1,067	471
Other items	354	284	231	200
TOTAL	2,034	1,392	2,001	2,015

VEGETABLE OILS

The production of edible and industrial vegetable oils is one of the leading processing industries in Paraguay. The principal source of both types of oil is the coconut, which grows naturally over most of the southern part of the country. Next in importance is cottonseed oil, extracted from seed that is acquired from cotton ginners. Production of tung oil has been increasing as new trees have reached bearing age. The production of peanut oil is relatively small. A newcomer in the vegetable oil industry in Paraguay is soybean oil, the beans being grown primarily by the Japanese settlers in the area of Encarnación. Other oilseeds (such as sunflower) are utilized for oil processing but their volume is quite small.

Paraguay has a wide variety of raw materials, as yet untapped, that could be utilized for the production of vegetable oils. For example, a systematic cultivation of avocados not only could provide a larger and cheaper supply of this item for human consumption, but an industrial oil may be extracted from this fruit that is used in the manufacture of cosmetics. Another palm tree, _yataí_, bears fruit from which may be obtained an oil similar to coconut oil. Although the areas where this tree grows are somewhat distant from existing oil processing plants, it may be worthwhile to investigate the feasibility of establishing a factory near the supply of raw material. The oil has duty-free entry privileges in Argentina, Brazil, Colombia, Ecuador, and Mexico. Castor beans also are available for processing within the country on a large scale.

There are about six oilseed processing plants of any significance in Paraguay. The largest of these, Compañía Algodonera Paraguaya, S.A. (CAPSA), is equipped with modern machinery and is considered to be the most efficient producer in the country. Concepción Industrial, S.R.L., also is a modern plant, having been inaugurated in August, 1964. The other processing plants have much older equipment, some of which requires replacement. The efficiency of extraction in these plants is relatively low, and a sizable amount of oil remains in the cake after the seeds are processed.

While virtually all of the edible vegetable oil produced in the country is consumed internally, practically all of the industrial oil is exported. The supply of raw materials needs to be increased to meet domestic and export requirements. Oil cake has a ready export market mainly in Europe. However, improved livestock production and feeding practices could easily expand the national market for oil cake. The exportation of vegetable oils is regulated by the Division of Vegetable Sanitation in the Ministry of Agriculture and Livestock.

As in the case of some other Paraguayan industries, there is an export tax burden on the vegetable oil industry. Considering the low unit value of these products, such export taxes represent a very substantial share of the selling price. Although the exporter pays these taxes, in the final analysis this outlay results in lower prices paid to producers of oilseeds and in greater difficulty in marketing the vegetable oils abroad. Because of increased competition from Brazilian _babassú_ oil in the Argentine market, the Paraguayan Vegetable Oil Producers Association petitioned the government for relief of export taxes on these oils and their by-products. In February, 1966, by Resolution No. 103, the Ministry of Finance reduced the pertinent export taxes.

Coconut Oil

The fruit of the coconut palm (_acronomía totai_) provides the raw material for both edible and industrial oils. The nut, when crushed and the oil refined, provides an edible coconut oil; from the pulp surrounding the nut, palm or pulp oil is extracted. The coconut oil is of higher quality and commands a much higher price than the pulp oil. The industrial uses of coconut oil are in the manufacture of fine soaps, special paints, and other products. Lower quality palm oil is used in the production of ordinary soap.

The major supply of raw material is collected in the central region of the country, where the majority of processing plants is located. A part of the crop is sold to middlemen who in turn sell the nuts to the factories. The remainder is sold directly by the farmers, after they remove the shell and the pulp to use as animal feed, to the processing establishments. The collection of coconuts has increased in recent years, as has the production of coconut oils. The latter has doubled between 1960 and 1965. The collection of whole nuts is estimated to have reached 120,000 metric tons in 1965.[8]

Currently, coconut oil is produced primarily for human consumption; some is utilized for the manufacture of soap, and the remainder is exported. Production and exports during 1961-65 are shown in Table 30.

TABLE 30

Production and Exports of Coconut Oil and Coconut Pulp Oil, 1961-65

(In Metric Tons)

	Coconut Oil		Coconut Pulp Oil	
Year	Production	Exports	Production	Exports
1961	3.0	1.5	2.5	0.2
1962	3.1	1.7	3.6	1.3
1963	4.2	3.9	5.4	3.9
1964	4.1	2.3	5.9	3.5
1965	5.1	3.2	5.0	2.5

The major markets for Paraguayan exports of coconut oils are the LAFTA countries, especially Argentina. Paraguay receives better prices in these markets than elsewhere because of the preference it enjoys within the LAFTA and because of the lower freight costs incurred in exporting to these countries.

If certain problems could be overcome, Paraguay could produce at least an additional 2,500 tons of coconut oils. The major problems affecting the industry are (a) lack of storage space for holding the coconuts; (b) in some cases, insufficient financing of the oil producers; (c) difficulties in transporting the raw material from more distant areas to the processing plants; and (d) deficient methods of collecting and gathering the nuts which affect their quality.[9] A major oil producing firm has had substantial success in the plantation cultivation of the coconut palm. Technical and financial aid to both growers and processors could do much to improve the efficiency of this industry.

Other Edible Oils

Cottonseed, peanut, and soybean oils are also produced in Paraguay. Output has been reported as shown in Table 31.

TABLE 31

Production of Cottonseed, Peanut, and Soybean Oils, 1961-65

(In Metric Tons)

Year	Cottonseed Oil	Peanut Oil	Soybean Oil[a]
1961	1,065	1,100	200
1962	1,560	1,370	275
1963	1,423	1,200	300
1964	n.a.	n.a.	n.a.
1965	2,400	1,200	2,000

[a]The first production of soybean oil was in 1960, when an estimated 100 tons were produced.

The balance sheet of Paraguayan requirements for edible oils shows that the country has been a net importer of these products to the extent of about 30 per cent to 40 per cent of its requirements. Although Paraguay has sufficient raw material to become a net exporter of edible vegetable oils, its production requires rationalized production of the raw materials and modernization of certain producing factories.

Other Industrial Oils

Tung and castor oils are growing in importance in the country's production and export trade. Output, virtually equivalent to exports of these products, has been reported as shown in Table 32.

TABLE 32

Exports of Tung and Castor Oils, 1961-66

(In Metric Tons)

Year	Tung Oil	Castor Oil
1961	4,583	--
1962	5,195	124
1963	4,456	62
1964	5,875	144
1965	4,552	30
1966	8,140	25

Exports of tung oil have gone chiefly to the United States, with small amounts to Europe and to the LAFTA countries. Argentina is the major producer of tung oil within the LAFTA and it exports to the same markets as Paraguay.

Although some 10,000 to 15,000 metric tons of castorseeds are produced annually, virtually all of these are exported to Europe. Because of the highly protected nature of the vegetable oil industries in the European countries and the relatively high price paid by Paraguayan producers for raw materials, local manufacturers have had little incentive to process the seeds domestically. However, duty-free entry of castor oil into certain LAFTA countries (Brazil, Colombia, Ecuador, Peru, and Uruguay) may provide such an incentive in the future.

Paraguay does not give advanced processing to its industrial oils and hence their use is limited. The initiation of more advanced processing methods will depend upon the country's ability to find new markets. Such advanced processing would include cooking, blowing, sulfurating, etc., and would add to the marketability of Paraguayan vegetable oils abroad.

SUGAR REFINING

The industrial census of 1963 reported the incredible number of 157 sugar refining establishments in Paraguay, with a value of product of ₲ 688.4 million (U.S. $5.5 million) and a value added of ₲ 315.3 million (U.S. $2.5 million). However, except for nine mills producing on a commercial basis, the others are small crude refineries using hand labor and animal power for grinding the cane. The nine important mills are located in an area that extends some 125 miles southeast of Asunción. About 30 per cent of the sugar cane harvested is ground by two of the nine mills which are relatively efficient. The three smallest of the nine mills apparently are very inefficient and reportedly obtain considerably below the average yield of sugar per ton of cane ground. The average yield for the commercial mills as a whole was approximately 85 kilograms (187 pounds) of sugar per metric ton of cane out of the 1963 harvest.

A substantial volume of the raw material is produced by the larger mills to assure part of their supply and thereby maintain a more stable rate of operation. These mills are well equipped to grow sugar cane and all of them use fertilizers to increase yields. Other growers use very little fertilizer because they are unable to finance its purchase. Most cane growers are small farmers who try to eke out a living from this one cash crop (see Chapter 2).

There is substantial excess capacity in the sugar industry. As shown in Table 33, refining capacity totals 62,000 metric tons a year for the nine mills; annual consumption is estimated at between 35,000 and 40,000 tons. Moreover, production exceeds national requirements, so that Paraguay has attempted (unsuccessfully) to obtain a quota of some 12,000 to 15,000 tons in the United States market.

The production of refined sugar has moved erratically from year to year. During the years 1954-65, output ranged from a low of 12,800 metric tons (1955) to a peak of 48,300 tons (1964). Output in 1965 amounted to 35,300 tons valued at ₲ 678.8 million (U.S. $5.4 million). Because of the various levels of technology found in this industry, the quality of the output is diverse and costs of production among mills differ markedly. All major mills use the lime-sulfur refining process, the lime for which is available locally; bleaching and other materials are imported. Paraguay is a marginal producer and exporter of sugar on a worldwide basis. Its high costs of production, because of the generally inefficient cane growing methods and high-cost milling operations, have made it unable to compete in world markets since the decline in sugar prices that began in 1963.* Consequently, Paraguay faces the prospect of piling up stocks of high-cost sugar unless domestic production is reduced or national consumption is increased. Intensive efforts are required to find new uses for sugar in the domestic economy.

There appears to be a large potential market for sugar in the local manufacture of soft drinks, preserves, bakery products, candy, other food products for human and animal consumption, and in the manufacture of alcohol. The development of sugar-consuming industries in the country would appear

---

*The World Sugar Council in London reportedly has established the minimum and maximum prices of refined sugar at the equivalent of ₲ 5.55 and ₲ 11.11 per kilo, respectively. Paraguay's average costs of producing sugar cane and refined sugar are ₲ 7.70 and ₲ 14.80, respectively.

TABLE 33

Capacity of Nine Major Sugar Refineries, as of July, 1966

Name of Refinery	Location	Annual Capacity in Metric Tons
Azucarera Paraguaya, S.A.	Tebicuary	18,000
Azucarera Friedmann, S.A.	Villarrica	14,000
Azucarera Iturbe, S.A.	Iturbe	10,000
Censi Y Pirotta, S.A.	Benjamin Aceval	5,000
Azucarera Guarambaré, S.A.	Guarambaré	5,000
La Felsina A.I.C.S.A.	Guarambaré	3,000
La Unión	Villarrica	2,500
María Auxiliadora, S.A.	Carapeguá	2,500
Azucarera Guairá, S.A.	Colonia Independencia	2,500
	TOTAL	62,000

Source: La Tribuna, July 15, 1966, p. 9.

to offer the most satisfactory solution to the situation of overproduction of sugar.

The price of sugar is controlled by the government, which receives the refined sugar from the mills and distributes it to retail outlets. A temporary scheme for subsidizing the exportation of sugar was introduced for the 1966 crop year, and refined sugar output was to be limited to some 38,500 metric tons. The fact that so many small farmers are engaged in sugar cane production makes the problems of the sugar industry politically sensitive. Substitute sources of income will have to be found for these cultivators if they are to stop growing high-cost cane.

ALCOHOL AND ALCOHOLIC BEVERAGES

Alcohol and Rum (Caña)

Sugar refiners and a few other operators produce alcohol and alcoholic beverages. The principal alcoholic beverages produced are (a) a type of local rum known as caña, derived from the processing of molasses; (b) grape wine; and (c) beer. The major sugar mills operate distilleries in which they process their own output of molasses in addition to supplies allocated to them by a government alcohol monopoly. The molasses also serves as the base for producing rectified spirits, denatured alcohol, and absolute alcohol. Registered production of alcohol had risen from 780,000 liters in 1940 to a peak of 3.1 million liters in 1963. However, in 1964 and 1965, this output declined to 2.9 million and 2.7 million liters, respectively. In the latter year, production was valued at ₲ 55.9 million (U.S. $443,000).

According to the 1963 industrial census, there were forty-eight establishments manufacturing (distilling, rectifying, and mixing) spiritous beverages other than wine and beer. Their output was valued at ₲ 468.3 million (U.S. $3.7 million), of which

₲ 177.3 (37 per cent) was added by manufacturing. The industry employed 769 persons, of which 478 were workers, and utilized only 625 horsepower of energy.

In 1941, the government created a Paraguayan Alcohol Corporation to control the production and monopolize the commercial sale of alcohol and rum. By Law No. 113 of October 6, 1951, this agency became the autonomous Paraguayan Alcohol Administration (Administración Paraguaya de Alcoholes--APAL). In theory, the profits of APAL are to be divided among its capital and reserves (25 per cent) and transfers to the Central Government (75 per cent). However, there have been no transfers made in many years, in spite of the increases in production mentioned above.

In July, 1966, a reorganization of APAL was undertaken and a new president and board of directors were appointed. The new administration immediately undertook an inventory of the situation of APAL. It found that this agency had not paid alcohol producers for some time and owed them ₲ 36.7 million, as well as a debt of ₲ 17.5 million to the Central Bank. The delay in payments on the part of APAL, combined with its imposition of production quotas and controls over consumption and exports, have created an unfavorable situation for the development of this industry. There is considerable clandestine production in the country. The new board of directors of APAL has estimated that such production deprives the Treasury of some ₲ 60 to ₲ 70 million a year in taxes.[10]

Wine

Paraguay produces red, claret, and white table wines. Fine wines are imported from Argentina, Chile, Germany, and Spain. Registered imports are very small and are consumed by those who can afford to pay the price. Average consumption of wine has been estimated at a mere 3 liters per capita per year.[11] The production, importation, and consumption of wine are subject to taxes. The 1963 industrial census reported forty wineries, whose output in that year was values at ₡ 97.1 million (U.S. $0.8 million), of which ₡ 51.3 million (U.S. $0.4 million) was added in the processing. The industry employed only 165 horsepower. Annual output is estimated at 6 million liters[12] and imports at about 200,000 liters. The grapes, the basic raw material for the wine industry, are grown chiefly in Colonia Independencia, Department of Itapúa, and to a much lesser extent in adjacent colonies. The main varieties of grapes grown include Oberlin, Clarete, Hebermont, Marta, and Seibel. In 1963, there were 1,366 hectares of wine grapes under cultivation, of which 1,034 hectares were in Colonia Independencia (with 337 producers) and 30 hectares in Villarrica (with 18 producers).

Major wineries include Vinos "La Copa," Vinos "Iturbe" S.R.L., and Vinos "Suabia." On May 14, 1956, a Winegrowers' Association (Centro de Vinicultores del Paraguay) was founded in the main wine-producing area of the country. It is composed of three major wine-producing cooperatives: Cooperativa "Ideal" de Villarrica, with 70 producers; Cooperativa "Independencia" of Colonia Independencia, with 150 producers and 40 winecellars; and Cooperativa "La Colmena," with 78 producers.[13]

Beer

One brewery, the Cervecería Paraguay, S.A., located in Asunción, satisfies most of the national market for beer. It produces chiefly light beer, both bottled and draft. Imports of beer are relatively small and are confined to certain European brands for the luxury trade. Local output was increased nearly fivefold between 1942 and 1953, reaching 5.7 million liters in the latter year. Production has risen rather steadily since that time, reaching 7.8 million liters in 1965. Nearly all raw materials used by the brewery are imported; the bottles also are purchased abroad.

The beer is produced under sanitary conditions and is quality controlled. In 1965, the Cervecería Paraguaya began to bottle Coca Cola, the only plant in the country to do so. Both the beer and the Coca Cola are marketed on a national scale, being transported by truck or river boat to local grocery stores (despensas), restaurants, and hotels. The Cervecería Paraguaya also is the nation's largest producer of carbonated water and ice.

The 1963 industrial census reported the following data for the Cervecería Paraguaya: value of product, ₲ 203 million (U.S. $1.6 million); consumption costs, ₲ 82 million (U.S. $650,000), including raw materials, ₲ 70 million, fuels and lubricants, ₲ 5 million, and electric power, ₲ 7 million; and value added in manufacture, ₲ 121 million (U.S. $960,000). This was related to a production of 7 million liters of beer.

TOBACCO PRODUCTS

There are three firms producing cigarettes and four producing cigars. The major cigarette factory is that of La Vencedora, S.A.; the others are Fábrica de Cigarrillos Nobleza and Lambaré, S.A. Production of cigarettes, without modern techniques and machinery, has remained virtually stagnant since 1954. Average output for the period 1954-56 amounted to 32.1 million packs (of twenty cigarettes each) a year, and this average remained the same during the period 1963-65. This stagnation of production does not indicate that consumption has remained constant, but rather that the contraband trade in cigarettes has increased markedly over the years. Registered imports of tobacco manufactures amounted to only $34,900 in 1965 (compared with $9,000 in 1964 and $2,000 in 1963). U.S. trade statistics, however, reported exports of cigarettes alone to Paraguay in 1965 at $4.6 million. While the majority of such imports--perhaps 80 per cent to 90 per cent--are transshipped to neighboring countries, the amount of contraband consumption would still be very sizable.

American brands of cigarettes are very popular in Paraguay and are hawked by little boys at all movie theaters and bus stops. Virtually all of the cigarettes sold in this manner are contrabanded, but little official effort is made to curtail this trade. Consequently, American brands sell on the street in Asunción at prices comparable to those in the United States. This situation may be expected to continue because of the taste preference which these brands enjoy in Paraguay. The price of American cigarettes is about ₲ 35 (about $.28) per pack compared with ₲ 15 - ₲ 20 per pack for Paraguayan brands.

There are four major producers of cigars in Paraguay: La Caoba; Fábrica de Cigarros "La Indígena"; Fábrica de Cigarros de Libusa Viuda de Wagner; and Antonio Herman. The "La Indígena" factory is in San Lorenzo and the Libusa factory is in Areguá; the other two plants are in Asunción. The general quality of cigars produced is poor, being considerably below that of cigars produced in neighboring countries. No production figures are available.

Unless the quality of Paraguayan tobacco is improved substantially, there is little prospect of improving the local tobacco products industry. The best grades of tobacco are exported.

Quebracho EXTRACT

Paraguay and Argentina are the only commercial suppliers of *quebracho* extract (tannin). This product, derived from the *quebracho* tree (see Chapter 4), is used in the tanning of leather. A small proportion of the *quebracho* extract is used in the domestic leather industry, but the bulk of it is exported, as shown in Table 34.

There are two firms in Paraguay producing *quebracho* extract: Carlos Casado, Limitada, at Puerto Casado, and Enrique Welbers S.A., at Puerto Pinasco. The latter factory, formerly owned by the International Products Corporation (IPC), was sold to a Swiss-German owner, Enrique Welbers, who also owns a similar factory at La Verde, Formosa Province, Argentina. IPC will continue to market the product abroad under the sales arrangement, handling both the Puerto Pinasco and the La Verde output. The transfer of ownership became effective July 1, 1965.[14] Heavy rains at times interfere with the hauling of _quebracho_ logs to the factories and, unless sizable stocks are maintained, the factories must cease operations until the roads are open.

The rated capacity of the two operating plants is about 36,000 metric tons and 27,000 tons, respectively. Thus, total output consistently has remained substantially below rated capacity. Local production of the tannin, moreover, requires the importation of sizable quantities of heavy chemicals, particularly caustic soda, soda ash, aluminum sulfate, and sulfur. Rapid depletion of convenient sources of _quebracho_ stands is another factor tending to raise production costs. With the displacement of _quebracho_ extract in important markets by other vegetable tanning agents, both natural and artificial, and the growing use of substitutes for leather (particularly in the United States), the future of the Paraguayan _quebracho_ extract industry is not very promising.

TABLE 34

Production and Exports of _Quebracho_ Extract, Five-Year Intervals, 1950-65

(In Metric Tons)

Year	Production	Exports
1950	38,738	38,738
1955	39,300	29,953
1960	30,800	33,499
1965	29,800	29,349

CHEMICALS AND PHARMACEUTICALS

Domestic manufacture of chemicals and pharmaceuticals is probably among the fastest growing industrial activities in Paraguay. Not only the volume of output but the number of products produced in Paraguay is increasing because of the foresighted management in this industry. The major producers are of Italian extraction and maintain contacts with European and United States firms to find additional lines of production or representation. Both domestic and imported ingredients are employed in manufacture, and many items are produced under license from foreign companies. The major lines produced are medicinal and pharmaceutical preparations; toiletries and cosmetics; detergents; laundry and cleaning products; and veterinary preparations.

In 1963, the ten firms reported in the industrial census employed more than 600 persons and had an output valued at ₲ 134.3 million (U.S. $1.1 million), of which ₲ 64.1 million, or nearly 50 per cent, was added by manufacture. Production includes analgesics, gargles, cough medicines, antibiotics, veterinary products, talcum and face powders, skin creams, lotions, balms, rouges and lipsticks, hair preparations, perfumes, and dentifrices. Distribution is made throughout the country. Prices of drugs and medicines are regulated by law. Many items, including raw materials and intermediate products, must be imported. Imports of chemical and pharmaceutical products averaged 3,100 metric tons a year during 1958-64, but surged to 7,421 tons in 1965, when they were valued at $2.1 million. The principal sources of imports of these products are West Germany, the United Kingdom, Argentina, and the United States.

WHEAT MILLING

There are three wheat flour mills in Paraguay with an aggregate annual capacity of between 128,000 and 140,000 metric tons. Nevertheless their current production of wheat flour amounts to only some 68,000 tons, consuming 93,000 tons of wheat in the process. The mills also produce some 25,000 tons of wheat by-products. The pertinent data for each of the three mills are shown in Table 35.[15]

Molinos Harineros del Paraguay, S.A., which has over 85 per cent of the national capacity, represents a capital investment of ₲ 421.3 million (U.S. $3.3 million). Some Paraguayan but mainly Argentine capital (Bunge and Borne) are invested in this enterprise. The mill consumes about 80,000 metric tons of wheat a year and employs 221 persons. The Concepción mill represents an investment of about ₲ 50 million (U.S. $0.4 million), all of which is Paraguayan capital. It consumes only 8,000 tons of wheat a year and has 32 employees. The Encarnación mill has 45 employees but consumes only 5,000 tons of wheat a year and represents an investment of only ₲ 18.5 million (U.S. $0.14 million). All of its capital is Paraguayan.

Because domestic production of wheat is only about 6,000 metric tons (1966), the bulk of national requirements must be met by imports. Registered imports of "wheat and its derivatives" over the years 1958-66 have averaged 74,000 metric tons a year, with an average annual value of U.S. $4.6 million.

These imports have come almost entirely from Argentina and the United States, purchases from the U.S. having been made through Commodity Sales Agreements under Public Law 480. While Commodity Sales Agreements concluded with Paraguay prior to 1966 were under Title I of P.L. 480 (loans repayable in local currency), the agreement of April, 1966, involving the sale of 40,000 metric tons of wheat, was made under Title IV (dollar sales, with up to twenty years for repayment).

All registered imports of wheat are made by the Paraguayan Government's wheat-purchasing agency, the Wheat and Flour Commission in the Ministry of Industry and Commerce. The Commission apportions the wheat among the flour mills and also sets the

TABLE 35

Data on Wheat Flour Mills, 1966

Name of Enterprise	Location	Annual Milling Capacity	Current Production	
			Flour	By-Product
Molinos Harineros del Paraguay, S.A.	Asunción	110,000-120,000	58,400	21,600
Molino Harinero de Concepción	Concepción	10,000- 11,000	5,840	2,160
La Industrial San José, S.A.	Encarnación	8,000- 9,000	3,650	1,350
	TOTALS	128,000-140,000	67,890	25,110

price of flour sold to bakeries and other end users. As domestic consumption of wheat has been estimated at approximately 100,000 metric tons a year, production at 6,000 tons (of which 1,000 tons are used for seed), average annual imports at 74,000 tons (1958-66), and stocks at 3,000 to 5,000 tons, it may be estimated that unregistered wheat imports, i.e., contraband, amount to some 12,000 to 15,000 tons a year.

The prices of wheat and flour in Paraguay are high. Transportation and storage costs add substantially to the F.O.B. price of the imported wheat, especially that coming from the United States. The difference in laid-down costs between wheat imported from Argentina and from the United States is of the magnitude of $42 a ton ($68 per ton for Argentina wheat; $110 per ton for American wheat). Nevertheless, Argentina's inability to ship larger quantities, combined with the delayed payment terms of acquisition for American wheat, have led the Paraguayan Government to request P.L. 480 wheat in almost every year since 1961.[16] Paraguayan law requires that bakeries add 5 per cent _mandioca_ flour to the wheat flour in producing bakery products.

The national wheat growing program was discussed in Chapter 2. At best, however, Paraguay will need to depend upon imported wheat to meet its requirements for at least the next decade.

Notes to Chapter 6

1. Technical Planning Secretariat, _Plan Nacional de Desarrollo Económico y Social Para El Bienio 1965-1966_ (Asunción, 1965), Vol. II, pp. 75-76.

2. In 1966, the International Products Corporation was absorbed by the Ogden Corporation.

3. Central Bank of Paraguay, _Producto Geográfico Bruto del Paraguay_, 1966, pp. 37-38.

4. Atilio Salomón, "Industria Textil," in Crítica y Analisis (Asunción, June, 1964), Vol. II, No. 7, pp. 8-9.

5. David y Bittar operated a rayon textile mill and a cotton textile mill.

6. La Tribuna, May 25, 1966, p. 7.

7. Central Bank of Paraguay, Boletín Estadístico Mensual, No. 97, June, 1966, p. 72.

8. Latin American Free Trade Association, Informe del Grupe de Estudio Sobre Paises de Menor Desarrollo Económico Relativo: Paraguay, June, 1966, pp. 87-88.

9. Ibid., p. 89.

10. La Tribuna, August 2, 1966.

11. Francisco Orúe Diaz, "La Actividad Vitivinícula en el Paraguay," in Crítica y Analisis, Vol. I, No. 2 (July, 1963), p. 4.

12. Francisco Orúe Diaz, "Sector Vinícola," in Crítica y Análisis, Vol. II, No. 7 (June, 1964), p. 10.

13. Felix F. Trujillo M., "Datos sobre el Vino Nacional," in Paraguay Industrial y Comercial, Vol. XXII, No. 261-62 (Asunción, June-July, 1966), p. 27.

14. La Tribuna, May 25, 1965, p. 10.

15. The data were provided by Juan José Adamo, Manager of Molinos Harineros del Paraguay, S.A., on August 23, 1966.

16. The first such agreement was concluded in 1956.

CHAPTER 7 MINING AND MINERALS

EXISTING INDUSTRIES

Paraguay possesses large quantities of certain nonmetallic mineral resources, notably clays for bricks, tile, and pottery; limestone and other raw materials for portland cement and lime; common and ornamental building stones; glass sand; talc; and mineral pigments. Except for iron ore, of which there reportedly are many small but rich deposits, Paraguay appears to be poorly endowed in most other mineral resources. It has a little manganese, copper, mica, and beryl. The country's geology indicates that salt, gypsum, and bauxite may yet be discovered.[1]

Exploration for petroleum in the Chaco has been undertaken by U.S. firms from time to time (for example, by the Union Oil Company, 1944-49, and by the Placid Oil Company, 1966), but thus far no large commercial discoveries have been made. Aside from wood and water power, the only known source of fuel or energy lies in some peat deposits near Pilar. Edwin B. Eckel has concluded that "by all odds the most valuable and promising of Paraguay's mineral resources are the water resources, both surface and underground, and the soils."[2]

According to Eckel, there is an excellent possibility of establishing several small new industries, or of modernizing existing ones, using local mineral resources and producing goods for local consumption. The 1963 industrial census data on the mineral-based industries in Paraguay are given in Table 36.

TABLE 36

Statistics on Mineral-Based Industries, 1963 Industrial Census

Activity	Number of Establishments	Value of Product[a]	Value Added[a]
Construction clay and brick tile	902	141.8	103.7
Glass and products	9	24.4	12.6
Ceramics (clay, china, and porcelain)	16	2.0	1.2
Cement	1	83.9	25.5
Lime	14	58.9	31.7
Cement, gypsum, and asbestos products	65	92.6	49.3
Other	7	44.4	13.1
Iron and steel products	10	18.6	8.5
Nonferrous metal products	4	7.4	4.9
TOTAL	1,028	474.0	250.5

[a]In millions of _guaranies_.

As seen from the data in this table, the production of mineral products is still very small in Paraguay. The main mineral industries are the production of clay bricks and tiles, cement, and lime. These are discussed in detail below.

Clay Bricks and Tiles

Virtually all important cities and towns are self-sufficient in bricks and tiles for local needs. Small establishments may be observed along all major roads in the country. Almost the entire output of the industry is produced by hand. The 902 establishments reported in 1963 consumed only ₲ 920,000 (U.S. $7,540) of electric power in that year and accounted for 987 horsepower and an aggregate of 980 workers. A few mechanically equipped establishments account for a small portion of the output. Ordinary building bricks sell for about one _guaraní_ apiece.

The Azucarera Paraguaya, S.A., at Tebicuary, has a small plant that produces refractory brick from nearby deposits of kaolin. These firebricks are made by hand, in wooden molds, in various sizes and shapes as desired by the customer.

The manufacturer of paving tiles is found in several of the more important cities, including Asunción, Concepción, Encarnación, Villarrica, Coronel Bogado, San Juan Bautista, and Luque. Some of these plants also produce mosaic and granite tiles. The plants in general are poorly or inadequately equipped.

Cement

There is one cement plant in the country, located at Puerto Valle-mí, near Puerto Casado, on the Paraguay River. It started production in 1952. The Paraguayan Government is a partner in the enterprise. The plant is a conventional rotary-kiln type which uses the wet-grinding ball-mill process. The equipment is antiquated, having been purchased secondhand from Belgium in 1948. The cement factory operates three kilns, two of which have rated annual capacities of 30,000 metric tons of finished cement each, and the third kiln (completed in 1954) has a capacity of 60,000 tons a year. The basic ingredients for this industry, limestone and shale, are readily available in sizable quantities; gypsum is the only material that must be imported. Production of portland cement has grown rapidly over the past decade, rising from 6,800 metric tons in 1954 to 37,400 tons in 1965. In the census year 1963, the plant produced 17,600 metric tons of cement having a value of ₲ 83.9 million (U.S. $0.7 million), of which ₲ 25.5 million (U.S. $0.2 million) had been added in manufacturing. It had 273 employees, of which 244 were workers, and it used 2,562 horsepower.

By Decree No. 17,687 of August 17, 1961, imports of portland cement into Paraguay were prohibited because the supply produced by Valle-mí, S.A., was adequate for domestic needs. However, demand has risen rapidly and currently exceeds what this factory can produce with its existing equipment. Imports of cement averaged 4,235 metric tons a year during 1958-61, declined to an average of 718 tons a year during 1962-65, and surged to a level of 7,575 tons in 1966 to meet the requirements of Paraguay's public works (electric power and road) programs. Therefore, Ministry of Industry and Commerce Decree No. 12,081 of June 23, 1965, established a National Cement Commission, composed of representatives of the Ministry of Industry and Commerce, Ministry of Public Works and Communications, Ministry of Finance, and Valle-mí, S.A. The representative of the Ministry of Industry and Commerce is its chairman. The Commission was charged with determining the level of cement imports required and to do the actual importation (free of customs duties and sales taxes) for public works projects in the public sector. The functions of this Commission were to expire as soon as planned expanded facilities of the company were put into operation.

The production costs of the Fábrica de Cementos Valle-mí, S.A., are high and it cannot compete pricewise with imports from Argentina, Brazil, and Uruguay.

Nevertheless, strong possibility exists for reducing production costs. The deposit of limestone utilized by the Valle-mí cement plant is a mixture of limestone and dolomitic limestone. As only the former can be used in making cement, the two minerals have to be separated, adding considerably to the cost of cement production.[3] However, the rejected dolomitic limestone is ideal for agricultural use and need only be crushed sufficiently to pass a 10-mesh screen. For some special applications a finely ground limestone (50 to 200 mesh) might be preferable but not absolutely essential. Klare S. Markley reported that mineral fertilizers and agricultural limestone were among the basic needs of Paraguayan agriculture, and he felt that "the production and distribution of limestone in Paraguay could be one of the greatest contributions to agriculture that could be made short of the introduction of balanced chemical fertilizers."[4]

The cement plant's management has attempted (since 1964) to obtain a loan from the Inter-American Development Bank to modernize its operations, but there have been differences of opinion concerning the alternatives of remodeling the existing plant, which is close to some sources of raw materials, or constructing a new plant, close to the principal consuming center, Asunción. In late 1966, there were rumors that a loan project for building a new plant was under consideration by the Inter-American Development Bank and that the Valle-mí project had been dropped.

Lime

There reportedly were fourteen lime plants, having 267 employees, in 1963, and using only 24 horsepower of mechanical energy. The value of product was ₲ 58.9 million (U.S. $470,000), of which ₲ 31.7 million (U.S. $250,000) had been added in manufacturing. Output has risen steadily from 10,600 metric tons in 1954 to 17,400 tons in 1963 and 18,500 tons in 1965. Local production supplies the country's requirements.

The manufacture of lime is concentrated mainly in the Department of Concepción, near the limestone quarries. The limestone yields about 60 per cent lime. Other output is found in or near Asunción, the raw material being brought to the plants by boat down the Paraguay River. The costs of production of these plants reportedly are higher than those farther north, in Concepción. Recently, the production of hydrated lime was begun at a plant in the Sajonia area of the capital.

In general, production is effected by traditional systems, in continuous ovens, using firewood as fuel. Another difficulty of this industry is a shortage of containers (asphalt barrels). Also, the frequent drops in the level of the Paraguay River delay shipments of the lime to consuming areas. Thus, to the extent that producers in the Asunción area can hold adequate stocks of raw material they may, in spite of higher production costs, have seasonal advantages in the downriver markets.

INDUSTRIAL POSSIBILITIES

Among the mineral-based industrial possibilities identified by Eckel are the following:

Iron

There reportedly is an excellent chance of developing a small local industry to produce several hundred tons per year of wrought and related forms of iron and even of steel. Iron deposits at Colonia Obligado and Paso Pindó need to be investigated in detail to evaluate the quality and extent of the reserves. The iron could then be converted into such end products as plowshares, crowbars, chains, machetes, anchors, ornamental grillwork, and many other items that normally have been imported. Such an industry once existed in Paraguay, during the War of the Triple Alliance. Charcoal for fuel and limestone for flux are available in the country in ample quantities, so that no imported materials would be needed once the furnaces were in operation.

Building and Ornamental Stones

Paraguay possesses a great variety of rocks that could easily supply all local need for ornamental stone and might even be developed into an export trade if regular production of superior material could be assured. Basaltic stone is quarried in the amount of some 400,000 metric tons a year. The output has three major uses: The quarry at Tacumbú produces crude and triturated stone for street paving and building constructions; the quarries located along Routes II and III provide stone for paving these roads; and the output of the Ñemby quarry is exported to Argentina for use in paving its Route 11. Such exports came to 166,000 metric tons in 1963. With the exception of the Tacumbú quarry, these operations were of a temporary nature, linked to the construction of the roads mentioned.

Many types of sandstone are produced in Paraguay. These range from white to red in color and many of them are quite attractive for flagstone walks, walls, and exterior facing for buildings. Large quantities of broken stone, mostly basalt or other dark-colored igneous rocks, are used for street paving, rough wall construction, and foundations of all kinds. All these materials are quarried by very simple methods and little or no attempt has been made to improve their natural appearance by cutting, polishing, or other dressing.

In addition to the above-mentioned rough building stones, it should be possible to produce many kinds of marble from the large deposits that outcrop along the Paraguay River from the mouth of the Apa River southward to San Salvador. These rocks range from uniform white or gray through mottled and striped rocks of various shades to what, according to Eckel, should be an excellent verd antique serpentine marble. Crushed and powdered marble of a high degree of chemical purity could be produced easily by the Valle-mí cement plant, which already has the requisite crushing and grinding equipment. Such ground marble is used in the sugar industry in appreciable quantities.

Several types of light-colored granite with very attractive texture, all durable and suitable for ornamental stones, exist in the general vicinity of Caapucú and Quyquyó, and probably elsewhere. There is also some beautiful and extremely tough black "granite" (alkalic shonkinite) at Mbocayaty.

The establishment of an ornamental stone industry would require technical knowledge and a substantial investment in equipment for quarrying, cutting, and polishing the stone. Import requirements would consist of small amounts of explosives for quarrying, and abrasives and acids for cutting and polishing. Exports of ornamental stone should be possible.

Glassware

Except for the small output of nine plants producing glass and glassware reported in the 1963 census, virtually all of Paraguay's requirements for such products are met from imports. Local output consists of small amounts of 5½-liter to 10-liter demijohns, ½- to 1-liter bottles, and some glasses. Although there was a small number of jars produced during the period 1958-64, no production was reported for 1965.[5]

The production of heavy water glasses, bottles, jars, and other glass containers is feasible for Paraguay, as silica sand and sandstone, much of it of excellent quality and purity for glassmaking, reportedly is available in the country. Feldspar and soda ash, the other chief ingredients of glass, are also believed to be available locally or, if not, would be cheaper to import than finished glass and glassware. Glass factories require comparatively small capital investments for machinery, and local wood or charcoal are adequate as fuels. Technical skill, if not already available in the country, could be imported. A feasibility study of this industry should be given priority, in view of the market offered by the production of soft drinks, wine and beer, milk, processed fruit and vegetables, and liquors.

Mineral Paints

There are three paint factories in Paraguay. In 1963 their combined value of output was only ₲ 13.7 million (U.S. $109,000), of which ₲ 3.5 million was added by manufacture. The plants had a total of twenty-two workers and utilized 36 horsepower of mechanical energy.

Paraguay uses comparatively large quantities of paint for both exterior and interior decoration. However, virtually all the paint needed is imported, either as pigment or as prepared paints. Nevertheless, there is abundant material locally to supply all the requirements for yellow, orange, pink, red, and brown colors that are used. This material exists in the form of rich iron ores near Caapucú, in low-grade lateritic ores that cover the surface in much of central Paraguay, as concretions of iron carbonate in some of the clay deposits, and in various other forms. The only treatment needed to produce excellent mineral pigments from such materials consists of washing, roasting under carefully controlled conditions, grinding, and grading as to color. The resultant pigments, according to Eckel, should be equal in most respects to imported products. A small pigment industry would require only a few hundred dollars worth of washing, grinding, and roasting equipment. Except for the initial machinery, no imports of raw materials would be needed to produce pigments regularly.

Locally produced tung, linseed, and castor oil are available to produce excellent vehicles for paints. If these oils were used, a fair share of the country's paint requirements could be met with no imports other than turpentine, small amounts of dryer, and containers for the final product. If high-grade modern paints were to be produced, then white lead, lithopone, and other ingredients also would have to be imported.

Clay Products

Paraguay contains abundant deposits of clay suitable for most grades of pottery, earthenware, and many other products. Several establishments, located principally in Areguá, Itá, Tobatí, and Itauguá, manufacture articles of baked clay, including pitchers, jars, plates, jugs, pots, toys, and ornaments. Very decorative articles such as cups and saucers, ash trays, pitchers, and vases are made of clay with gaily colored mosaic inlays. The household utensils are crudely made but are priced to permit their widespread consumption by low-income families. Production of higher quality products for middle-income families could be achieved with adequate modern machinery and careful technical control in the manufacturing process. With such improvement in quality, an export market for these novelties also might be developed.

Talc and Pyrophyllite

Deposits of talc and pyrophyllite are found at San Miguel and Caapucú, respectively. These raw materials may be used as fillers in insecticides, soaps, paints, and many other products for which a relatively large potential local market could become available.

Notes to Chapter 7

1. Edwin B. Eckel, Geology and Mineral Resources of Paraguay--A Reconnaissance (Geological Survey Professional Paper 327) (Washington, D.C.: U.S. Government Printing Office, 1959), p. 1.

2. Ibid.

3. Memorandum report by Dr. Klare S. Markley, vegetable oil specialist, cited in ibid., p. 87.

4. Ibid.

5. Central Bank of Paraguay, Boletín Estadístico Mensual, No. 97, June, 1966, p. 73.

CHAPTER 8 ELECTRIC POWER

The shortage of electric power in Paraguay has constituted an important obstacle to economic development. Wood, charcoal, and plant wastes are the principal sources of light and energy in most parts of the country. Moreover, electricity is extremely high-priced: For residential use, the cost is ₲ 8.50 (U.S. $0.0672) per kilowatt-hour (K.W.H.), and for industrial use, the cost ranges from ₲ 8.07 (U.S. $0.0640) per K.W.H. for amounts of 1,000 K.W.H. or less down to ₲ 6.95 (U.S. $0.0472) per K.W.H. for amounts in excess of 200,000 K.W.H.[1] The predominant type of current distributed for public use is direct current at 220 volts; however, alternating current at 220 volts, three-phase, fifty cycles, also is distributed.*

Although electric power consumption doubled during the decade 1955-65, it still was estimated at at only 65 K.W.H. per capita in the latter year.[2] While most of the consumption occurs in the area of Asunción, a growing number of private generating plants are selling power to interior localities. During this decade, Paraguay's installed capacity rose from 30,000 kilowatts to 58,000 kilowatts, and production of electrical energy grew at a compound rate of 7 per cent a year, from 70 million K.W.H. in 1955 to 134.7 million K.W.H. in 1965.**

---

*Both types are sold in Asunción.

**In 1950, installed capacity was only 12,000 kilowatts.

In the latter year, the public sector supplied 67 per cent of the energy generated (89.7 million K.W.H.), and the private sector 33 per cent (45 million K.W.H.).[3] The estimated production and consumption of electrical energy during the years 1961-65 have been as stated in Table 37.

Virtually all of the power plants in operation prior to the start-up of the Acaray plant were thermal generators. (One very small, recently installed hydroelectric plant was constructed in Alto Paraná for industrial use.) Some 75 per cent of the generating capacity was steam-powered and virtually all the rest diesel-powered. The enumerated installed capacity in 1963, by department and type of generation, is shown in Table 38.

Some 53 per cent of the installed capacity in 1965 was concentrated in the capital and neighboring cities (Luque, San Lorenzo, Lambaré) and was supplied chiefly by the National Electricity Administration (ANDE). The Central Department (including the capital) accounted for only 62 per cent of the total installed capacity in that year, compared with 70 per cent in 1963. While the majority of industries and the bulk of the population are concentrated in this area, the major expansion in installed capacity nevertheless has occurred outside the Central Department. This has been due to the growth of private generating facilities at individual industrial plants in the interior and to the expansion of other private industrial generating capacity to supply power to surrounding communities. Private generating facilities have been installed in twelve principal cities during the past decade.

During 1961-65, private electric power generation rose at a compound annual rate of 8.2 per cent, from 32.5 million K.W.H. to 45.0 million K.W.H. Thus, while average private generating capacity per power plant is small, the rate of growth of this capacity has exceeded substantially that of the public sector. During the past seven years, while ANDE's installed capacity remained at 27,700 kilowatts, private installed capacity increased at such

TABLE 37

Production and Consumption of Electrical Energy, 1961-65
(In Millions of K.W.H.)

	1961	1962	1963	1964	1965
Production					
Public sector (ANDE)	72.5	77.7	81.8	83.8	89.7
Private sector	32.5	35.0	38.0	41.3	45.0
TOTAL	105.0	112.7	119.8	125.0	134.7
Consumption					
Industrial	45.0	49.7	51.1	53.4	58.4
Residential and commercial	31.0	34.0	35.0	38.0	42.0
Plant consumption and transmission loss	18.0	19.0	22.0	23.0	23.5
Governmental	6.4	6.4	6.7	5.9	6.3
Public lighting	2.9	3.1	3.5	3.6	3.6
Streetcar	1.4	1.5	1.5	1.2	0.9
TOTAL	105.0	112.7	119.8	125.0	134.7

Source: Technical Planning Secretariat, Segundo Plan Nacional de Desarrollo Económico y Social, Bienio 1967/68, Annexo II, "Sector Industria y Energía" (Asunción, August, 1966), p. 68.

TABLE 38

Installed Capacity, 1963 Census
(In Kilowatts)

Department	Steam	Diesel	Hydro	Total	Per Cent of Total
Central	32,600	3,500	- -	36,100	69.9
Itapúa	800	2,900	- -	3,700	7.2
Guairá	2,900	600	- -	3,500	6.8
Ñeembucú	1,650	1,200	- -	2,850	5.5
Concepción	100	2,000	- -	2,100	4.1
Boquerón	950	350	- -	1,300	2.5
La Cordillera	100	500	- -	600	1.2
Presidente Hayes	180	200	- -	380	0.7
San Pedro	150	200	- -	350	0.7
Alto Paraná	- -	130	100	230	0.4
Paraguarí	- -	220	- -	220	0.4
Caaguazú	- -	200	- -	200	0.4
Misiones	- -	60	- -	60	0.1
Amambay	- -	30	- -	30	0.1
TOTAL	39,430	12,090	100	51,620	100.0

Source: Technical Planning Secretariat, Plan Nacional de Desarrollo Económico y Social Para el Bienio 1965-1966, Vol. II (Asuncion, 1965), p. 135.

a rate as to raise the country's total generating capacity to 58,000 kilowatts by 1965.

As indicated by Table 39, industry utilized some 43 per cent of the total electric power generated in 1965. Its demand has grown at a compound rate of 5.4 per cent a year during the years 1961-65. As previously mentioned, the major industrial consumption of electric power occurs outside of Asunción. Thus, ANDE's sales to industry have remained rather constant during the years, growing from 16.0 million kilowatts in 1961 to 15.7 million in 1965, as shown in Table 39.

The National Electricity Administration is the only generator and distributor of electric power in the public sector. It has a mandate under its organic law to coordinate the production and distribution of electric power for public use throughout the country. Currently, ANDE supplies Asunción and nearby cities with electricity. ANDE's production, as shown in the foregoing tables, has grown at a cumulative rate of 5.4 per cent a year during 1961-65. An additional 6,000 kilowatts of generating capacity was to be installed at its Puerto Sajonia plant in 1967.[4] ANDE is the only State enterprise that has shown an operating profit in recent years (₲ 133.5 million [U.S. $1.1 million] in 1965).

In view of the national power bottleneck, the government has undertaken to carry out an ambitious plan for developing the country's hydroelectric resources to provide adequate and cheap power for national needs. Ample resources of hydroelectric potential are found in Paraguay, mainly along its eastern border, making transmission over long distances necessary. The major resources are as follows:

(a) The Acaray-Monday Hydroelectric System

A project to build a two-stage hydroelectric project at Acaray was begun in September, 1965, and the first stage--to provide 45,000 kilowatts of power--is planned to go into operation

TABLE 39

Pattern of Consumption by ANDE's Customers, 1961-65
(In 1,000 K.W.H.)

Use	1961	1962	1963	1964	1965
ANDE's consumption	6,582	9,679	9,350	9,249	9,127
Distribution loss	11,354	9,227	12,894	13,769	14,210
Residential and commercial	27,830	30,108	32,077	36,177	39,805
Governmental	6,415	6,403	6,710	5,898	6,319
Industrial	15,997	17,646	15,833	13,893	15,706
Public lighting	2,874	3,147	3,413	3,602	3,604
Streetcars	1,448	1,490	1,517	1,212	929
TOTAL	72,500	77,700	81,800	83,800	89,700

around January, 1969. The second stage of construction, to double this capacity, was expected to be undertaken in 1969 and completed around 1972. The Acaray-Monday Hydroelectric System, when fully developed, was expected to have the following capacity: Acaray River, 240,000 kilowatts, generating 1,060 million K.W.H.; and the Monday River, 160,000 kilowatts of generating capacity, producing 690 million K.W.H. of power.[5]

The first stage of the project would serve some forty-two localities in the Departments of Central, La Cordillera, Paraguarí, Guairá, Itapúa, Alto Paraná, and Caaguazú, including the cities of Asunción, Hernandarias, Puerto Presidente Stroessner, Puerto Presidente Franco, Coronel Oviedo, Villarrica, Caaguazú, San José, Capiatá, and Paraguarí. In its second stage, the project also would serve the Departments of Ñeembucú and Misiones.

Once the Acaray hydroelectric project was in operation, ANDE's thermal capacity was to be shut down. This hydroelectric power was expected to reduce the cost of electricity some 30 per cent during the operation of the first phase of the project, and when both phases had been completed, the present cost per K.W.H. was expected to be halved (by 1980).

The Acaray project was estimated to cost the equivalent of $29.920 million. The financing is coming from an Inter-American Development Bank loan (47 per cent), suppliers' credits (43 per cent), and from ANDE's resources (10 per cent). The IDB's loan of $14.150 million, granted August 17, 1964, was for twenty-five years, including a five-year grace period. Interest was at 4 per cent a year. The suppliers' credits were for fifteen years, including a five-year grace period, with interest at 6.5 per cent a year. About 80 per cent of the inputs for the project were to be imported and the rest would be of national origin. An additional IDB loan of about $3 million was being considered during 1966/67 to finance rising costs of the project and interest payments.

(b) The Guairá Falls Reserve

The Guairá Falls, on the Paraná River, lie between Paraguay and Brazil. The boundary between the two countries has been much in dispute. However, it appears likely that joint development of this hydroelectric resource will be undertaken in the future. The potential at this site has been estimated preliminarily at 10 million kilowatts. A system of twenty-one groups of generators is visualized, of which two will have capacities of 250,000 kilowatts each, and nineteen will have capacities of 500,000 kilowatts each.[6] Calculated on the basis of a 6,000-hour utilization period (250 days) per year, output would come to 60 billion K.W.H.--the energy equivalent of 15 million metric tons of petroleum annually.

(c) Apipé Rapids (Yacyretá-Apipé)

These rapids provide an opportunity for a joint power project with Argentina. Average annual generation could be as much as 13.5 billion K.W.H., from an installed capacity of 2.1 million kilowatts, operating 6,420 hours a year. It is estimated that the project, when developed, would consist of thirty groups of generators having a capacity of 70,000 kilowatts per group.[7]

(d) Aquidaban River Project

A project to establish a 2,100 kilowatt hydroelectric generating facility at Pedro Juan Caballero, Department of Amambay, was being studied by the National Rural Electric Cooperatives Association (NRECA), under a contract with the U.S. AID Mission to Paraguay. This project may cost about $1.5 million of which 20 per cent to 25 per cent would come from local resources in the community served. A local cooperative (Cooperativa de Electricidad Amambay Limitada) has been formed on the Aquidaban River. The Agency for International Development (AID) would limit its financial contribution (about $1.2 million) to the first four years of the project.

According to the National Development Plan for 1967/68, projected electric power output during 1966-68 was to be as shown in Table 40.

TABLE 40

Projected Output of Electric Power, 1966-68

Sector	1966	1967	1968
	(In Millions of K.W.H.)		
Public sector (ANDE)	95.8	102.4	109.7
Private sector	48.0	51.0	55.0
TOTAL	143.8	153.4	164.7

It was estimated further that generation would reach 187.3 million K.W.H. by 1970 and 460.0 million K.W.H. by 1980. These projections included the implementation of ANDE's Electrification Plan for the interior of Paraguay, estimated to cost $5.5 million (₲ 436.5 million). The major portion of this investment was programmed for the period 1967-71.

Notes to Chapter 8

1. National Electricity Administration (ANDE), Resolution No. 49/65, Act No. 38, June 14, 1965.

2. Technical Planning Secretariat, _Segundo Plan Nacional de Desarrollo Económico y Social, Bienio 1967/68_, Annexo II, "Sector Industria y Energía" (Asunción, August, 1966), p. 65.

3. _Ibid._, p. 66.

4. _La Tribuna_, September 12, 1966, p. 4.

5. Comision Mixta Técnica Paraguaya--Argentina del Apipé, _Aprovechamiento del Rio Paraná en la Zona de las Islas Yacyretá y Apipé_ (August, 1964), Volume I, pp. 140-41.

6. _Ibid._, p. 143.

7. _Ibid._, pp. 119 and 174.

CHAPTER 9 TRANSPORTATION AND TELECOMMUNICATIONS

The establishment of an adequate transportation network is basic to all underdeveloped countries. For Paraguay, the problem has special significance in view of the country's "landlocked" location at the heart of the South American continent. Not only must Paraguay develop transportation arteries to integrate its national territory, but it must develop faster and cheaper means of reaching distant world markets. At the same time, Paraguay must attempt to become a crossroads or entrepôt of South America through improved land and air transportation facilities.

The national transportation system comprises chiefly the Paraguay-Paraná-Plate river system; highways, secondary roads, and feeder roads; domestic and international airlines; and a dilapidated State railway. Traditionally, the commercial and economic activities of the country have depended on its rivers, both for internal and external commodity movements and for communications. The population first tended to settle along the river banks, chiefly in the areas of Asunción and Encarnación. With the coming of the railway in 1861, and with the improvement of some roads, certain shifts took place in the location and economic activities of the population. This trend was accentuated with the growth of automotive transportation. A major share of present-day internal freight and passenger movement is by road, and productive areas are being extended increasingly throughout eastern Paraguay and in certain parts of the Chaco.

TABLE 41

Planned Investments in Transportation, 1966-68

Field of Investment	1966	1967	1968
	(In Millions of Guaranies at 1962 Prices)		
Highway network	602.3	1,177.7	988.5
River system	87.9	688.3	416.1
Railway	-----	-----	-----
Airlines and airports	45.3	241.5	367.0
Telecommunications	256.8	306.3	315.3
TOTAL	992.3	2,413.8	2,086.9

TABLE 42

Financing of the Planned Investment Program, 1966-68

Field of Investment	1966 Internal	1966 External	1967 Internal	1967 External	1968 Internal	1968 External
Highway network	299.7	302.6	402.0	775.7	338.2	650.3
River system	2.9	85.0	98.8	589.5	116.6	299.5
Railway	---	---	---	---	---	---
Airlines and airports	45.3	---	77.1	154.4	74.0	293.0
Telecommunications	147.8	109.0	73.7	232.6	65.4	249.9
TOTAL	495.7	496.6	651.6	1,762.2	594.2	1,492.7
	50%	50%	27%	73%	28%	72%

The Second National Development Plan calls for an investment program in transportation and communications during 1966-68 as shown in Table 41. External financing was to amount to between 50 per cent and 73 per cent of total investment in these fields, as shown in Table 42.

Thus far, transportation studies in Paraguay have been limited in scope. They have dealt with the Paraguay River, particular roads, the Asunción Airport, and the Port of Asunción. However, now that the more obvious transportation needs of the nation have been met, a global transportation study of the country is urgently needed to establish the relationships among the various forms of transportation and to determine the priority projects for each medium. In short, a transportation network needs to be developed for Paraguay to maximize the returns from the national investment in this type of infrastructure.

RAILWAYS

Paraguay has one of the oldest and one of the most outmoded railways in South America. This railway, formerly known as the Paraguay Central Railway, was started in 1856 and inaugurated in 1861, to run between Asunción and Paraguarí. After its sale to British interests in 1887, the line finally was completed to Encarnación (in 1913). A nearby ferry terminal, at Pacu-cuá, carries the railway across the Paraná River to the city of Posadas, Argentina, where it links with the standard-gauge General Urquiza Railway going to Buenos Aires. The distance from Asunción to Encarnación is 230 miles. At Borja, 105 miles from Asunción, a branch line was extended 40 miles to the town of Abaí in 1919. By Law No. 714 of August 21, 1961, the railway again was nationalized. A sum of £200,000 was agreed to be paid to the British company. The name of the railway was changed to President Carlos Antonio López Railway (Ferrocarril Presidente Carlos Antonio López--FPCAL) by Decree-Law No. 364 of February, 1964.

Although the line originally was wide-gauge, the size of track was changed to standard-gauge (4 feet, 8½ inches) by 1912 to permit through service to Buenos Aires. The line currently has 265 freight cars, 54 passenger cars, and 19 wood-burning locomotives and 2 oil-burning steam locomotives. Both the rolling stock and the right of way are in very bad repair and would require considerable investment to rehabilitate. Maximum speed under existing conditions is 6 miles an hour for freight trains and 12 miles an hour for passenger trains. Along most of the route, cheaper and more efficient highway transportation is now available. Buses and trucks run from Asunción to Encarnación in about eight hours, and when the highway is paved completely and a bridge replaces the ferry across the Tebicuary River, the time should be reduced to four or five hours.

In spite of efforts to improve the efficiency of its operations since 1961, the increasing competition from highway transportation makes the long-range financial situation of this railway untenable. The decline in economic activity of the railway over the past fifteen years is shown in Table 43.

The sharp downward trend in the number of passengers carried is directly related to the increasing availability of faster and cheaper road transportation (see Table 44). Those passengers still utilizing the FPCAL are traveling longer distances--from areas where highway transportation has not yet become available. A similar trend is noticeable in the movement of freight. There would appear to be no reason to expect significant increases in railway traffic unless freight and passenger rates were reduced to ridiculously low levels. Even so, costs would continue to rise so that the financial situation of the railroad would become even more impossible. The FPCAL has been losing money every year since 1958, as shown in Table 45.

TABLE 43

Operating Statistics of the State Railway, 1949-65

Year[a]	Number of Passengers	Passenger-Kilometers	Average Distance	Revenue Tons	Ton-Kilometers	Average Length of Haul
	(1,000)	(1,000)	(Kms.)	(1,000)	(1,000)	(Kms.)
1949/50	2,129	61,871	29.0	186.4	35,047	185
1954/55	1,696	47,480	28.2	125.5	26,694	207
1959/60	953	30,563	32.0	90.8	16,253	179
1964	551	39,377	71.4	112.8	20,389	181
1965	415	34,801	83.9	94.0	18,908	201

[a]In 1962, the operating year of the railroad was changed from July 1-June 30 to January 1-December 31.

Source: Presidente Carlos Antonio López Railway.

TABLE 44

Comparative Speeds and Costs of the Transportation Media in Paraguay

Type of Transport	Average Speed	Cost Per Passenger-Kilometer	Cost Per Ton-Kilometer
	(Kms. Per Hour)	(In *Guaranies*)	
Water	15.7[a]	2.60	1.78 (internal)[b] 0.60 (external)[b]
Highway:			
Microbus	60	1.40	----
Autobus	50	0.78	----
Truck	40	----	3.00
Railway:			
Passenger train	30	1.80	----
Freight train	13	----	3.01
Air[c]	285	3.61	18.30

[a]Average for both directions.

[b]Prices established by Decree No. 19,061 of November 13, 1961. Prices between Asunción and Buenos Aires of the State Merchant Fleet fluctuate between ₲ 0.80 and ₲ 0.40 per ton-kilometer.

[c]Data pertain to the military airline, T.A.M.

Source: Technical Planning Secretariat, *Plan Nacional de Desarrollo Económico y Social Para el Bienio 1965-1966* (Asunción, 1965), Vol. II, p. 160.

TABLE 45

Operating Results of the FPCAL, 1958-65

Year	Revenue	Expenditures	Loss
	(In Millions of Guaranies)		
1958	97.2	109.4	-12.2
1959	95.0	145.7	-50.7
1960	86.8	153.1	-66.3
1961	104.7	131.5	-26.8
1962	109.3	136.5	-27.2
1963	105.9	114.1	- 8.2
1964	125.7	138.4	-12.7
1965	121.6	152.5	-30.9

Source: Balance sheets of the Presidente Carlos Antonio López Railway.

The FPCAL no longer represents the vital link to the outside world that it signified in the past. River, highway, and air transportation have become more significant international transportation arteries for Paraguay since mid-century. Also, goods presently shipped by rail could be transported by truck to Encarnación, ferried across the Paraná River to Posadas, and railed or trucked to Buenos Aires.

In view of all the foregoing reasons, it has been recommended by transportation experts that the FPCAL be abandoned as soon as the highway from Paraguarí to Encarnación has been paved and physical access has been provided to the highway from points presently dependent solely on railroad transport. The present railroad way then could be utilized for access roads.

Industrial Railways

Ten short, narrow-gauge railways are found in the interior of the country, generally connecting logging and cattle-raising areas with the Presidente

TABLE 46

Data on Short-Line Railways in Paraguay

Line	Gauge		Length in	Main
	Feet	Inches	Miles	Commodity
Puerto Mihanovich	2	6	7	Logs
Puerto Guaraní	2	6	51	Logs
Puerto Sastre-Carrería	2	5½	47	Quebracho
Puerto Casado-Mile 100	2	6	125	Quebracho and cattle
Puerto Pinasco-Mile 59	3	3 3/8	67	Quebracho
National Northern Railway (Concepción-Horqueta)	3	3 3/8	35	Logs
Tebicuary-Azucarera Paraguaya-Mile 25	2	6	25	Sugar
Puerto Stopolio-San Antonio	2	6	20	Cattle
Abaí-José Fassardi	2	6	21	Logs
Yvapobó-San Antonio	2	6	20	Cattle

Carlos Antonio López Railway or the country's principal rivers. Nine of these industrial railways are privately owned; the National Northern Railway running between Concepción and Horqueta is owned and operated by the State. The pertinent data on these ten railroads are given in Table 46.

Two of these lines--the Abaí-José Fassardi and the Tebicuary-Azucarera Paraguaya--connect with the Presidente Carlos Antonio López Railway. The Puerto Casado and National Northern Railways provide public service for both passengers and freight. The former also provides a means for moving merchandise to and from the Mennonite colonies in the Chaco.

The National Northern Railway is in very poor physical condition. Its maintenance is in the care of an engineering section of the Paraguayan Army. The high cost and low yield of this line, which operates only one train a week, make it advisable to abandon this service. The bed of the railway could be filled and covered, and opened to automotive traffic.[1]

RIVER TRANSPORTATION

Although Paraguay is often considered a landlocked country, eastern Paraguay is actually a peninsula. The Apa and Paraná rivers form the boundary between Paraguay and Brazil in the north and east, and between Paraguay and Argentina in the south and southeast. The Paraguay River separates the Chaco area of Paraguay from Brazil and, flowing southward, crosses the country to form the boundary between southwestern Paraguay and Argentina. At the southwestern tip of Paraguay, the two rivers converge (at Confluencia) and flow into the River Plate, which empties into the Atlantic Ocean.

Both the Paraguay and the Paraná rivers have their headwaters in Brazil. Together with the River Plate, these rivers provide some 2,500 miles of navigable waterways connecting Paraguay with the Atlantic Ocean and the interior of Brazil. From

Buenos Aires to Confluencia the distance is about 770 miles, and from Confluencia to Corumbá, Brazil, the distance is 950 miles. The distance from Confluencia to Encarnación is 214 miles, and from Confluencia to Asunción, 242 miles.

For the most part, Paraguay has been dependent upon Dutch and Argentine vessels and Argentine ports for moving merchandise into or out of the country. The limited navigability of the Paraná River, because of various falls, and of the Paraguay River, because of sharp seasonal and cyclical drops in the water level, has made water transportation more costly than what it might be under more favorable navigation conditions. Between Confluencia and Asunción alone there are sixteen passes that reduce the water level and impede international river traffic.

The river level in the Asunción area often falls to such levels that vessels with a draft of more than 6 feet are unable to enter. Cargo movement into the country's major port comes to a standstill at such times. The economic loss to the country is considerable. It includes not only losses to the State Merchant Fleet and private shipping enterprises, but also losses to Paraguayan producers unable to export their products, and losses from the suspension of production because of inability to export. For example, the Ministry of Public Works and Communications has estimated that the loss to the State Merchant Fleet alone, because of the prevailing low-water conditions in 1962, approximated ₲ 50 million (U.S. $400,000).

The periodic, and sometimes prolonged, low-water stage of the Paraguay River often limits the draft and consequently the use of hold space of vessels using the river to about 70 per cent of their capacity. For this reason, auxiliary vessels are often employed to transport cargo to locations where prevailing depths of the river permit full loading of the principal vessel, which then proceeds to ports of the La Plata River. When cargo is handled in this manner, a surcharge is added to the normal shipping charges to cover the added cost and inconvenience of multiple handling.* It has been estimated that the combined costs involved during low-water and normal periods have resulted in average freight rates equivalent to about one half the delivered value of exported goods.

In addition to these national obstacles to river transportation, the actions of the Argentine Government concerning the navigation of the lower Paraguay River often have obstructed the movement of Paraguayan trade. Freedom of navigation of the Paraguay River is a cardinal point of Paraguay's foreign policy. After a protracted period of negotiations between the governments of Paraguay and Argentina, an Argentine-Paraguay Treaty of Navigation was signed, and ratified by Paraguay on March 14, 1967. This treaty hopefully will serve to eliminate the friction between the two countries concerning the navigation of their mutual river systems. Nevertheless, the costs of removing the physical obstacles to navigation are very high and political difficulties could recur to harass Paraguayan river commerce. Hence other routes and other forms of transportation might well be developed to relieve Paraguay from this difficult situation, and a change in the composition of exports should be sought, suitable to the alternative means of transportation developed.

For traditional exports--low-unit value, large bulk--river transportation still remains the cheapest form (see Table 44). Therefore, the Paraguayan Government as well as private interests have been interested in finding permanent solutions to the technical and political difficulties affecting river transportation. Several studies of the physical problems have been made,[2] but the recommendations have not yet been implemented.

---

*When foreign-owned ships are forced to navigate with less than a 9-foot draft, they add a 20 per cent surcharge to the freight rates. At times this surcharge has remained in effect for nearly six months of the year.

In 1941 a convention was signed which obligated the Argentine Government to maintain a channel in the Paraná-Paraguay River with a minimum depth of 21 feet between Buenos Aires and Rosario, 19 feet between Rosario and the city of Paraná, and 10 feet between Paraná and Corrientes, near Confluencia. Above Corrientes, the minimum depth of the Paraguay River was to be 6 feet. However, as this depth is inadequate for efficient transportation to Asunción, the principle of maintaining a minimum depth of 10 feet was established at a meeting of Paraguayan and Argentine experts in February, 1964.

If the Paraguay River is to be put in condition to support efficient vessel movement between Asunción and Buenos Aires, very substantial investments will have to be made in closing certain passes south of Asunción and in dredging certain parts of the river. Prior to undertaking such investments, the Paraguayan Government negotiated an agreement with the United Nations Special Fund on November 15, 1965, for a four-year study of the Paraguay River between Asunción and Confluencia and how to improve it. The study was to cost $1.680 million, of which Paraguay was to contribute $904,200 and the Special Fund $776,100. As of the end of 1966, the work still had not been started.

Ports

In addition to improvement of the river system, Paraguay needs to better its port facilities at Asunción and other principal embarkation centers. The main port, Asunción, has insufficient capacity to handle peak traffic loads that pass through it when the river is open to the international traffic. The resulting demurrage adds substantially to the transportation costs of Paraguay's exports and imports. At times, vessels have had to spend up to ten days in port.

To improve and expand the facilities at the Port of Asunción, the International Bank for Reconstruction and Development (World Bank) approved a loan equivalent to $2.750 million on December 15, 1965. Works to be undertaken at Asunción, by far the largest port in the country, would almost double its capacity, achieve substantial savings through speeding up the turn-around time of vessels and improving the efficiency of cargo handling, and materially contribute to Paraguay's development by providing a more efficient outlet for foreign trade.

The project being assisted by the World Bank loan included the extension of the main quay by 1,050 feet in order to provide more berth space alongside and more cargo-working space ashore. This extension would nearly double the length of the existing quay. A pontoon wharf was to be built to accommodate barges and other small craft. Two transit sheds with a total floor area of 75,000 square feet were to be built on the extended quay. New port operating equipment such as fork lifts, tractors, and other mechanized equipment were to be procured, as well as machine tools for the workshops and fire fighting equipment for the safety services. Auxiliary work to be undertaken included the relocation of a drainage creek which now obstructs operations, improvement of the port access road and paving part of the port area, construction of water mains, sewers, and a power transformer station.

The loan was to be made to the National Navigation and Ports Administration (Administración Nacional de Navegación y Puertos--ANNP), established by Law No. 1,066 of August 23, 1965, as an autonomous port authority responsible for the construction and operation of ports and the maintenance and improvement of navigation channels throughout the country. (The ANNP replaced the former Customs and Ports Administration.) The ANNP was to carry out the project with the assistance of engineering and port operations consultants. The project was expected to take four years to complete, at a total cost of $3,950 million. The World Bank loan would cover nearly 70 per cent of the cost, and the remainder was to be met from earnings of the port authority and a Central Government contribution.[3] This project is closely related to the penetration roads, access roads, and main highways which the AID, World Bank, and International Development Association (IDA) have been helping to finance. Primary functions of all these routes are to carry agricultural products, forest products, and livestock from the interior to Asunción, and to bring back imported commodities and local manufactures.

Other Paraguayan ports are expected to diminish in importance as expanded roat networks make faster transportation possible for internal freight movements. Nevertheless, with a view to facilitating lumber shipments on Paraguayan vessels, a new port is being contemplated at Confluencia, where the Paraguay and Paraná rivers join. This facility, with a depth of 13 to 14 feet, would also serve the southern part of Paraguay and would also be a transshipment point for cargo moving on these two rivers.*

With the completion of the new Route V between Concepción and Pedro Juan Caballero, the Port of Concepción may well become of greater importance in moving Brazilian products in transit to and from Argentina. The joint highway-river route is believed to be more economical than transport across Brazil to the Port of Santos and thence by ship to Buenos Aires.

Facilities at the Port of Villeta, near Asunción, also are to be improved. Law No. 781 of May 22, 1962, approved Decree-Law No. 218 of October 19, 1959, which ratified a treaty between Paraguay and Spain (signed in Madrid on June 25, 1959) providing for the establishment of a Free Zone for Spanish goods and for Paraguayan and/or Spanish raw materials. By Decree No. 13,877 of September 16, 1965, the Free Zone was located at Villeta. Inasmuch as the facilities at Villeta were inadequate to handle the anticipated volume of cargo, the Asunción branch of

---

*The Argentine Government prohibits the rafting of Paraguayan lumber south of Corrientes. Consequently, the logs are loaded on Argentine vessels at Corrientes for shipment to Buenos Aires.

the Banco Exterior de España offered a dollar credit to the National Navigation and Ports Administration to finance the construction of a reinforced concrete pier at this port.

Other ports mentioned in the 1967/68 National Plan for possible improvement were Humaitá, Pilar, Villa Oliva, Rosario, and Antequera on the Paraguay River, and Encarnación and Puerto Franco on the Paraná River. The privately owned ports presumably are cared for by the companies that build and operate them. Such ports are San Antonio; Ceballos-Cué; Ybapobó; Puerto Pinasco; Puerto Casado; Itapucu-mí; and Puerto Esperanza.

Merchant Marine

A Paraguayan Merchant Marine was first established by President Carlos Antonio López in 1854, and made substantial progress until disrupted by the Triple Alliance War. After the war, Paraguay's water transportation was dominated by Argentine, Brazilian, and British vessels. An attempt to reestablish a State merchant fleet in 1924 failed, and it wasn't until June 27, 1945, that the State Merchant Fleet (Flota Mercante del Estado--FLOMERE) was created as an autonomous government agency by Decree-Law No. 9,351. The principal reasons for establishing such a fleet were (a) to establish a stronger Paraguayan presence on the Paraguay-Paraná-Plate River system; (b) to compete with powerful Argentine and Dutch shipping companies that dominated Paraguay's foreign trade; and (c) to assuage national pride. As an autarchic entity, FLOMERE's financing comes from its own operations.

A Dravo Corporation study in 1950 concluded that flat-bottom barges of the type used in the push-towing system on the Mississippi and Ohio rivers would provide adequate navigation of Paraguayan waters, with an average of only 1.5 months a year of "time out of service." In spite of the recommendations of this well known firm, the Paraguayan State Merchant Fleet proceeded to acquire small ocean-going vessels. In 1962, five of its twenty-eight vessels had drafts of 11½ feet, eleven of its vessels drew 8½ feet, and the other twelve ships drew 6 feet. During the low-water year 1962, the first five vessels were completely inoperative, the next eleven vessels were out of operation 180 days, and only the last twelve vessels operated all year.[4] The combined loss amounted to 3.8 million usable ton-days, or 56 per cent of the State Merchant Fleet's usable-ton capacity in 1962.[5] In 1965 FLOMERE had thirty vessels with a usable cargo capacity of 18,839 metric tons and storage capacity of 36,539 cubic meters.

Paraguay's foreign trade is almost entirely (98 per cent) waterborne. The importance of FLOMERE in carrying this international cargo is shown in Table 47.

Internal and coastwise water transportation are performed chiefly by private vessels. There are 287 flat-bottomed vessels or barges engaged in this commerce, of which 50 per cent are of 70 tons, 30 per cent of 100 tons, and 20 per cent over 100 tons. In addition, there are 35 tugboats (50 per cent of 120 horsepower and 50 per cent of 50 horsepower) and 22 motor ships (80 per cent of about 60 tons and 20 per cent of over 100 tons). These vessels provide about 90 per cent of their service north of Asunción and about 10 per cent south of the capital and on the Paraná River. Two other motorboats provide regular service from Asunción to the north. The Argentine River Navigation Fleet (Flota Argentina de Navigación Fluvial) and Alfredo Mauro, S.R.L. are other companies operating on Paraguay's rivers.

The private companies engaging in internal and coastwise trade are encountering a series of difficulties, such as regulations requiring the employment of excessive personnel ("featherbedding"). To get around these regulations, the companies are using uneconomical small vessels of only 30 to 40 tons, to which the regulations do not apply. The larger-sized ships are tending to disappear. Also, a drop in the number of operating firms has

TABLE 47

Foreign Trade Tonnage and Proportion Carried by FLOMERE, in Selected Years, 1955-65 (In Metric Tons)

Year	Total	By FLOMERE	Per Cent of Total
	EXPORTS		
1955	256,189	11,791	4.6
1960	299,372	22,027	7.4
1965	465,760	81,974	17.6
	IMPORTS		
1955	174,032	41,967	24.1
1960	244,938	38,151	15.6
1965	331,420	192,223	58.0
	TOTAL		
1955	430,221	53,758	12.5
1960	544,310	60,198	11.1
1965	797,180	274,197	34.4

Sources: Central Bank of Paraguay, Boletin Estadistico Mensual, and State Merchant Fleet.

occasioned an underemployment in the shipping industry. The powerful Maritime Workers' Union (Centro de Obreros Marítimos) has insisted on maintaining the same number of workers in spite of the decline in the number of operating vessels. This labor force therefore works only part-time, by shifts, thereby creating considerable disguised unemployment.

International traffic is carried on ships of various nationalities, chiefly Dutch (the Holland-American Line) and Argentine. A decree-law of December 7, 1962, authorized special concessions to the Compañía Paraguaya de Navegación de Ultramar, S.A., which was created with a capital of ₲ 35 million (U.S. $280,000). Two small vessels of this company ply regularly between Paraguay and Europe. This operation is feasible economically only because of the high alternative transshipment costs and losses of cargo at Buenos Aires and Montevideo, occasioned by recurring periods of low water on the Paraguay River that make such transshipment necessary.

ROADS

The generally level to rolling terrain of the country makes road construction less of a problem in Paraguay than elsewhere in Latin America. Nevertheless, several important problems do exist. Much of the land is low-lying and poorly drained, necessitating the construction of extensive embankments and culverts. Moreover, road construction materials are scarce and poorly distributed, so that their transportation raises the costs of road building and maintenance. Asphalt and petroleum have to be imported. Also, the heavy rains that occur, particularly during Paraguay's summer months, delay construction and maintenance activities considerably and thereby add to their costs. In spite of the foregoing obstacles, Paraguay's road system has grown markedly since 1955, and particularly since 1960, as shown in Table 48.

TABLE 48

Paraguay's Road System, by Type of Construction, Selected Years, 1938-66
(In Miles)

Year	Asphalt	Gravel	Earth	Total
1938	---	99	37	136
1945	46	220	152	418
1950	48	294	172	514
1955	53	319	339	711
1960	115	405	810	1,330
1965	260	600	2,068	2,928
1966 (October)	436	594	1,968	2,998

The paving of the rest of Route I between Paraguarí and Encarnación would add about 186 miles to the country's paved roads. The sharp increase in road mileage since 1955 reflects the Stroessner Government's awareness of the importance of better roads to accelerate the political and economic development of the country. The accelerated road program has received substantial financial assistance from the U.S. Government and international lending agencies. The major national highways are listed in Table 49.

Penetration and Access Roads Proposed for Fiscal Years 1968 and 1969

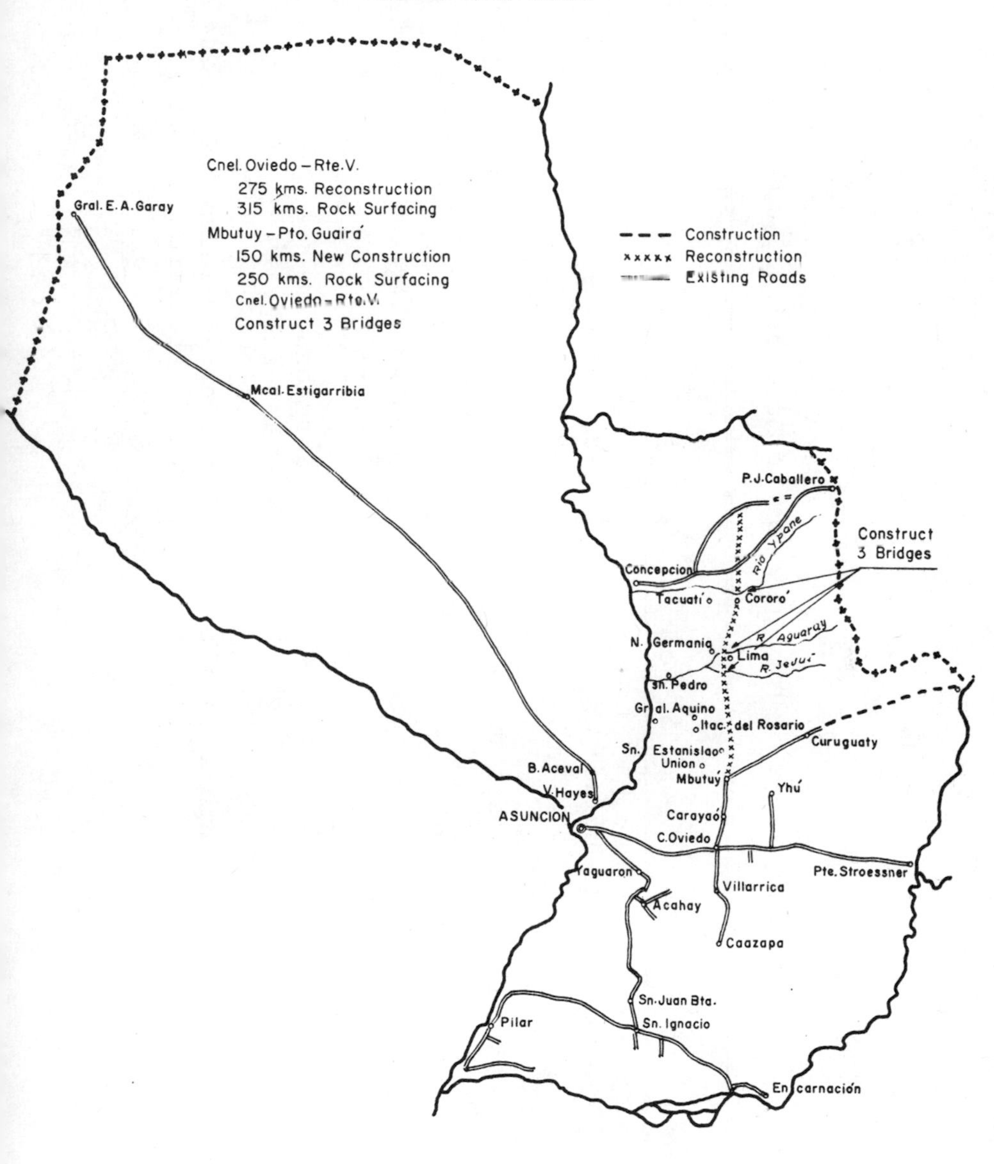

TABLE 49

Major Roads of Paraguay, as of December 31, 1966

Route	Name of Road	Terminals	Distance	
			Kilometers	Miles
I	Mariscal Francisco Solano López	San Lorenzo-Encarnación	358	222
II	Mariscal Estigarribia	San Lorenzo-Coronel Oviedo	122	76
III	General Elizardo Aquino	Asunción-Limpio-Emboscada	48	30
IV	General Diaz	San Ignacio-Pilar-Ita Pirú	210	130
V	General Bernardino Caballero	Concepción-Pedro Juan Caballero	244	151

VI	Dr. Juan Leon Mallorquin	Encarnación-Hohenau-Capitán Meza	86	53
VII	Dr. José Gaspar Rodriguez de Francia	Coronel Oviedo-Puerto Presidente Stroessner	197	122
VIII	Blas Garay	Coronel Oviedo-Villarrica-Caazapá	98	61
IX	Carlos Antonio López (Trans-Chaco)	Asunción-Fortin General E. A. Garay	773	479
X	Camino de las Residentas	Puerto Rosario-San Estanislao	95	59
XI	Juan de Lara	San Pedro-Nueva Germania	47	29
XII	Vice Presidente Sanchez	Chaco I-General Bruguez	167	104
Unnumbered	----	Coronel Oviedo-Route V	315	195

As a result of the determined increase in road facilities, automotive vehicles have increased at least threefold over the past decade. In 1965, there were 18,372 automotive vehicles in the country (not including 383 agricultural tractors), or one vehicle for every 110 inhabitants. A vehicle census made by the Transportation and Communications Section of the Technical Planning Secretariat showed the following vehicle registration in 1965:

Automobiles	5,442
Trucks	4,026
Pick-up trucks	1,834
Jeeps	885
Passenger buses	777
Microbuses	916
Rural pick-up trucks	654
Motorcycles	3,838
Agricultural tractors	383
	18,755

Some 57 per cent of the automotive vehicles in the country were privately owned. Private automobiles represented about 31 per cent of the total, and nine tenths of these were registered in Asunción. About 77 per cent of all automotive vehicles were registered in the Central Department, Asunción, and adjacent areas. An average of 1,325 automotive vehicles of all types are estimated to have been imported annually during the period 1962-66, for a total of 6,624. Of the total, 1,804 (29 per cent) entered free of duty.

Although trucks are the principal means of transporting cargo within Paraguay, they accounted for only 15 per cent of the total number of vehicles in 1965. Buses and microbuses accounted for 9 per cent. About 54 per cent of the cargo vehicles and 29 per cent of the commercial passenger vehicles (buses and microbuses) were over twelve years old. A large number of trucks and buses are imported as chassis and the superstructures are added locally, with little knowledge of weight limits, centers of gravity, or other engineering or safety features.

The average useful life of a truck or bus in Paraguay has been estimated at six years, logging about 35,000 miles on the average. At least 50 per cent of the commercial fleet therefore requires immediate replacement. Vehicle maintenance is little known in Paraguay and operating costs are high. An additional factor affecting the high cost of operation is that, for the most part, goods are carried in only one direction and the vehicles come back empty.

Now that the major highways have been built or are in process of construction, attention is being given to the development of feeder roads linking up with these major routes. The objective is to consolidate the advances that already have been made and assure the pay-off of the existing routes. The advancement of paved roads will depend on the volume of traffic generated over the respective highways. In spite of the fact that roads may be closed from 25 to 160 days per year because of rain, highway experts doubt that anything should be done about this situation until user pressure becomes sufficiently strong to bring about the necessary paving activities. They feel that principal attention at this stage of Paraguay's development should be given to completing the major routes, establishing the feeder road network, and developing an adequate maintenance program (including load limits on vehicles).

Local Road Boards (Juntas Viales) are responsible for the maintenance of strictly local roads in the country. There are fourteen regional boards, thirteen east of the Paraguay River and one in Olimpo in the Chaco. These regional boards have jurisdiction over a number of local boards. For example, the regional board that includes Asunción has some forty local boards under its jurisdiction. The regional boards are named by Executive Decree from lists of nominees submitted by the Government Delegates (Delegados del Gobierno) in the various departments of the country. The members of the local boards are named by the respective regional boards. The work of these Road Boards is coordinated by an Office of Road Boards (Dirección General de Juntas Viales) in the Ministry of Public Works and Communications. This office approves the Boards' annual investment plans and provides technical assistance in the laying out of local roads and in designing and constructing bridges and other structures. Greater mechanization and an improved system of financing is required to improve the efficiency of operations of the regional and local Road Boards.

AIRLINES

Air transportation is particularly suited to Paraguay's topography and geographic position. Not only does such transportation provide the readiest access to the outside world, but it also is serving to open Paraguay to outsiders. Dr. Natalicio González has written that the shortest route from South America to Europe is from Asunción northward along the 60° meridian until the parallel of New York City is reached. From that point, a plane can turn left to New York or right to Europe, according to its destination.

Paraguay is served by two national airlines within the country, and by Paraguayan and foreign airlines internationally. The Military Air Transport (Transporte Aereo Militar--TAM) serves the interior of the country, carrying passengers and cargo. Regular flights are maintained between Asunción and Villa del Rosario, Villa de San Pedro, Concepción, Horqueta, Pedro Juan Caballero, Bella Vista, Encarnación, Pilar, San Juan Nepomuceno, and Puerto Presidente Stroessner. Similar domestic passenger and cargo service is provided by Lineas Aereas de Transporte Nacional (LATN). This line was established as a private company in 1941, became a mixed corporation by Decree-Law No. 2,677 of January 27, 1951, but was nationalized by Decree-Law No. 37 of March 31, 1954. Its organic law was enacted on June 20, 1955 (Law No. 259). It is an autarchic entity dependent upon the Ministry of Defense. Charter planes also are available, either from the foregoing airlines or from private owners of small aircraft.

International air service is provided to and from Asunción by the airlines listed in Table 50.

The Paraguayan international air carrier (LAP) is an autarchic State-owned enterprise, dependent upon the Ministry of Defense. LAP was created by Decree-Law No. 337 of March 18, 1963. It is authorized to provide service both within the country and internationally, coordinating its activities with other national and/or international airlines, whether within or outside the country. The airline distances (in miles) to major Latin American cities from Asunción are as follows:

Caracas	2,400
Lima	1,600
Santiago, Chile	1,000
Rio de Janeiro	900
Sao Paulo	700
Buenos Aires	675

In recent years, both national and international air transportation services have increased substantially. Between 1961 and 1965, domestic air passenger traffic increased 56 per cent and air cargo traffic 130 per cent. During the same period, international air traffic rose 42 per cent for passengers carried and 408 per cent for freight. Virtually all international traffic, both freight and passenger, is carried on foreign airlines. The major international air carriers are Braniff International, which has two flights a week to and from Asunción, and Pan American Airways, which has one flight a week to and from the capital. A recent effort by Braniff to add a third flight was rejected by Paraguayan authorities for fear of increased competition with LAP on the Asunción-Buenos Aires run.

For economic and political reasons already mentioned, air transportation is expected to become a major element in Paraguay's transportation network, particularly in international passenger and cargo movements. The above-mentioned statistics on cargo movement, although significant, nevertheless represent rather small quantities of merchandise

TABLE 50

International Air Service, Paraguay

Company	Nationality	Equipment	Destinations
Lineas Aeras Paraguayas (LAP)	Paraguayan	Corvair	Buenos Aires Montevideo Curitiba Sao Paulo Rio de Janeiro
Lloyd Aereo Paraguayo S.A. (LAPSA)	Paraguayan	C 46-F	Montevideo Curitiba Sao Paulo Rio de Janeiro
Braniff International	United States	DC-7	Buenos Aires Lima Guayaquil Panama Miami Washington New York

Pan American Airways	United States	DC-3	Caracas New York Buenos Aires
Varig-Real S.A.	Brazilian	DC-3 Corvair Boeing 707	Iguazú Falls Curitiba Sao Paulo Lima Bogotá Caracas Mexico Miami Los Angeles
Primeras Lineas Uruguayas de Navegación Aera (PLUNA)	Uruguayan	Viscount	Montevideo Buenos Aires
Aerolineas Argentinas	Argentine	Avro 748	Formosa Corrientes Rosario Buenos Aires
Aerotransporte Litoral Argentino (ALA)	Argentine	DC-3	Resistencia Rosario Buenos Aires

trade. However, as the country industrializes and develops new and higher unit value export products, international air shipments should grow to substantial tonnages, aided by improved jet facilities in Paraguay and new international cargo planes and services.

The Agency for International Development, in August, 1966, authorized a loan of $4.7 million for the rehabilitation of Paraguay's only jet airport, near Asunción. The repayment period was to be forty years, including a ten-year grace period; interest was to be at the rate of 1½ per cent during the first ten years, and 2½ per cent thereafter. Specifically, the project involved the construction of a new runway 9,009 feet in length and 150 feet in width, with stopways, blast pads, and clear zones at each end. In the existing terminal area, a new connecting taxiway was to be provided at the north end of the present terminal apron. After this new taxiway had been built, the existing taxiway was to be removed and reconstructed as a parallel taxiway. A new drainage system was to be installed to serve the new runway area, and the existing drainage system was to be modified as required. High-intensity lighting was to be provided for the runway and approach systems, with sequenced flashing lights on the approach. In addition, a high-intensity Visual Approach Slope Indicator was to be provided on the north end of the runway.

TELECOMMUNICATIONS

The telephone system in Paraguay was established by the International Telephone Company (Compañía Internacional de Teléfono S.A.), which received a concession for this purpose by Law No. 850 of August 25, 1926. However, by Decree-Laws No. 20,725 and 20,727 of July 2, 1947, the company's properties were expropriated and a National Telephone Administration (Administración Nacional de Telefonos--ANT) was created as a dependency of the Ministry of Public Works and Communications. In the following year (Law No. 56 of October 24, 1948), the National Telecommunications Administration (Administración Nacional de Telecommunicaciones--ANTELCO) was established. Its present functions were defined in Decree-Law No. 2,340 of December 30, 1950. Thus, with limited exceptions, the operation of telecommunication services in Paraguay is a government monopoly exercised by ANTELCO. The Presidente Carlos Antonio López Railway also provides public service over its telephone and telegraph network. As of July 31, 1966, ANTELCO had 149 telephone and telegraph offices functioning throughout Paraguay, with a total of 9,896 subscribers. Of these, 8,456 were in the capital and 1,440 were in the interior.[6] The distribution of offices and subscribers, by districts, was as given in Table 51. In synthesis, Paraguay's

TABLE 51

Distribution of ANTELCO's Offices and Subscribers, by District, as of July 31, 1966

District	Number of Offices	Number of Subscribers
Asunción	23	8,456
Puerto Rosario	10	a
Concepción	9	94
Puerto Pinasco	4	a
Ypacaraí	11	92
Eusabio Ayala	12	25
Paraguarí	14	74
Villarrica	26	374
Encarnación	14	591
San Juan Bautista (Misiones)	12	101
Pilar	14	89
TOTAL	149	9,896

[a]No telephone service; telegraph only.

major telecommunications system as of July 31, 1966, was as shown in Table 52.

TABLE 52

Telecommunications System of Paraguay, as of July 31, 1966

	Asunción	Interior	Total
Number of districts	1	10	11
Number of employees	617	274	891
Number of lines	8,313	1,597	9,910
Number of instruments	12,441	1,748	14,189
Number of subscribers	8,456	1,440	9,896

On May 25, 1961, the United States Government loaned $1 million to Paraguay to modernize and expand its telecommunications facilities. This loan, which carried an interest rate of 3.5 per cent, was repayable 50 per cent in guaranies and 50 per cent in dollars over ten years, but with a maintenance of value provision governing that part of the repayment made in local currency. The loan financed about 50 per cent of the costs of new international radiotelephone, telegraph, and telex systems for Paraguay. On November 3, 1965, ANTELCO's new international telecommunication system was inaugurated. The new facilities represent an investment of some ₲ 250 million ($2 million), made over a two-year period. They reportedly are the most modern in Latin America. The project consisted of (a) the installation of a new receiving station at Isla Bogado (at Luque); (b) the renovation and expansion of the transmitting facility at Jardín Botánico; and (c) the construction of an international telegraph, telex, and telephone center at Ciudad Nueva. All of these locations are in the vicinity of Asunción. Paraguay now has radiotelephone and telegraph contact with Hamburg, New York City, Rio de Janeiro, Buenos Aires, and Montevideo. It also has telegraphic connections with Bolivia.

ANTELCO handles about 165,000 international telegrams a year which, at an average rate of ₲ 310 per telegram, provides a revenue from this activity alone of ₲ 51.6 million a year. International radio-telephone service handles about 26,400 communications a year which, at an average rate of ₲ 860 per message, provides an income of ₲ 22.7 million a year. Thus, ANTELCO's international operations provide no less than 38.5 per cent of its income; telephone service in the capital provides 39.7 per cent.[7]

A long-range National Telecommunications Plan is being developed, encompassing telephone, telegraph, and telex services. These services are intended to cover their costs, hence a schedule of priorities needs to be established. Also, the plan is to make provision for the country's long-term telecommunications needs. The basic study leading to the establishment of the national plan was carried out by a group of technicians sponsored by the International Telecommunications Union and was financed by the United Nations Special Fund. The study, which began in January, 1965, was to be completed in January, 1967. The ensuing plan was to cover a period of twenty years (1968-88).

During the period covered by the plan, it was estimated that some 37,000 new telephone lines would be added, of which 24,000 would be in Asunción. The telegram service was to be reorganized so that messages could be sent by telephone or teleprinter. The telex system also was to be based on the telephone network. Also, some 295 miles of bifilament line were to be installed between Asunción and Filadelfia in the Chaco, to provide a three-channel radio wave system. As demand increased, this system could be expanded to twelve channels and a low-frequency channel also could be added. A VHF system also could be installed to serve about 180 ranches as well as portable radios in transportation units in the Chaco. Better communications with the Army Engineer units charged with maintaining the Trans-Chaco Road also were to be provided. On July 1, 1966, a National Telecommunications by Satellites

Commission (Comisión Nacional de Telecommunicaciones por Satelitas) was established, headed by the General Administrator of ANTELCO. Its function is to study the feasibility of establishing a satellite communications program for Paraguay and having it join the COMSAT.

Aeronautic telecommunications in Paraguay are operated by Transporte Aereo Militar (TAM) for domestic flights. For international flights, the government has authorized (Law No. 247 of 1960) a private firm to provide these services. This firm is Radio Aerenautica Paraguay, S.A. (RAPSA); its activities are supervised by ANTELCO and the Civil Aeronautics Office. Its services include communications with aircraft, aids to air navigation, and fixed aeronautic services for both domestic and international flights. RAPSA, which functions from the International Airport in Asunción, operates connections with Argentina, Brazil, Bolivia, Peru, and Uruguay. A national air telecommunications plan exists that conforms with the recommendation of ICAO, the International Civil Aviation Organization of the United Nations. Meteorological services are operated by the Meteorological Office of the Ministry of National Defense. It does not have its own telecommunications system, but transmits its data through ANTELCO to TAM and to the Naval Transmission Service (Servicio de Transmiciones Navales). The Meteorological Office does have its own receiver to obtain information from other American countries. Weather messages are transmitted free of charge and have priority of dispatch. Mobile maritime communications are effected by the shipping companies operating in Paraguay. ANTELCO is studying the means of centralizing these services and linking them with the public communications services.

Radio and television activities are in the hands of private enterprise, except for Radio Nacional del Paraguay and a few small radio stations in the interior. A television station (Channel 9) began operation in September, 1965. Radio communications are had by means of medium, short, and very short waves. In addition to Radio Nacional del Paraguay, other stations in the country include Radio

Teleco; Radio Guaraní; Radio Guairá; Radio Concepción; Radio Comuneros; Radio Carlos Antonio López; Radio Ñandutí; Radio Presidente Stroessner; Radio La Voz del Amambay; and Radio Caritas. The United States Information Service publishes a monthly radio guide, "Guia," which it distributes free of charge to subscribers. Voice of America broadcasts are transmitted regularly to Paraguay during the hours of 7 A.M. to 10 A.M. and 7 P.M. to 12:30 P.M.

Notes to Chapter 9

1. Technical Planning Secretariat, Plan Nacional Económico y Social Para el Bienio 1965-1966, Vol. II (Asunción, 1965), p. 184.

2. The major studies are: (a) Preliminary Engineering Study of the River Transportation Between Asunción, Paraguay, and Buenos Aires, Argentina, as developed by Dravo Corporation for the Carlos Casado Interests of Asunción, Paraguay, January 19, 1950. (b) Bertram H. Lindman, The Transportation Problem of Paraguay (Asunción: Institute of Inter-American Affairs, Technical Cooperation Administration, Department of State, 1952). (Its Appendix A is the Dravo Corporation report.) And (c) Technical Planning Secretariat, Estudio sobre el Transporte Fluvial en el Paraguay (Asunción, June, 1964).

3. U.S. Department of Commerce, International Commerce, January 24, 1966, p. 41.

4. Estudio sobre el Transporte Fluvial en el Paraguay, op. cit., pp. 88 and 91.

5. Ibid., p. 92.

6. ANTELCO, "tele informativo," Vol. V, Nos. 53-54 (June-July, 1966), p. 21. Also several private firms operate telegraph or radio services in connection with their business operations.

7. ANTELCO, "Sistem Internacional de Radio" (a pamphlet distributed at the inauguration of the new facilities in November, 1965), p. 1.

CHAPTER 10 INSTITUTIONS, POLICIES, AND PROGRAMS

THE PRIVATE SECTOR AND PUBLIC POLICY

The private sector in Paraguay has been relatively weak. A tradition of strong, authoritarian government, combined with the country's turbulent history, has mitigated against the development of a well-founded free enterprise system. Therefore, the private sector has tended to be very conservative and timid in its outlook, content to carry on small-scale operations with varying degrees of efficiency, and with output limited almost entirely to a few basic needs of the country. However, since the signing of the Charter of Punta del Este in August, 1961, a "new look" has been developing in the Paraguayan business community. Since that time, a noticeable change in attitude has taken place, manifested in (a) the appearance of a young, well-educated, farsighted group of business leaders; (b) a realization on the part of these new business leaders of the need to cooperate with the government in promoting national as well as private interests, rather than remain in passive opposition; (c) the government's indicated willingness to accept private sector cooperation (The inception of the Technical Planning Secretariat in 1962 has led to closer consultation between the public sector and the private sector in matters relating to specific products and policies); and (d) government approval, forthcoming immediately, for the establishment of the private Development and Productivity Center and a private development financing corporation in Paraguay.

The official attitude has been favorable to private investment, both domestic and foreign. Fiscal incentives (tax exonerations of various kinds for stated periods) are offered on a nonexclusive basis to investors in new and existing plants and industries, and not only is there no discrimination against foreigners, but foreign investments have been favored under Paraguayan law. Government officials are particularly interested in attracting U.S. investment to Paraguay.

An Investment Guaranty Agreement was concluded in October, 1955, between the Governments of the United States and Paraguay, providing for specific-risk guarantees against inconvertibility and expropriation. An amendment to this Agreement, signed August 11, 1966, extended the specific-risk coverage to include risk of war and revolution, and added extended-risk coverage for housing and other investments. The extended-risk guarantees are used mainly to guarantee loans by U.S. investors to private foreign enterprises. Locally owned enterprises as well as U.S.-owned companies are eligible to borrow from U.S. lenders and have such loans guaranteed by AID against all risk. Extended-risk guarantees may also be used to guarantee U.S. equity investments in certain high priority local projects.

The foregoing developments have been aided substantially by the political and monetary stability that has characterized Paraguay during the past decade. A milestone marking the private sector's emergence into a new era was the Second Conference of Private Economic Entities held in Asunción during September 27-October 1, 1965.[1] This conference was sponsored by the Federation of Production, Industry and Commerce (FEPRINCO), an association of business associations in major economic fields (ranching, manufacturing, commerce). The President of the Republic attended the opening and closing sessions. Some seventy-five business organizations from all economic sectors and from all parts of the country were represented through more than 700 delegates. A keynote speaker was invited from Buffalo, New York, through the auspices of the U.S. AID Mission to

Paraguay (USAID). The views of the various Paraguayan groups were stated in a forthright manner, and the Conference undertook to cooperate with the government in the socio-economic development of the country.

The major business organizations in Paraguay, in addition to FEPRINCO, are vast and varied. Several business organizations that are also principal members of FEPRINCO are mentioned later in this chapter (see page 246). The private sector is represented on the Boards of Directors of the Central Bank and the National Development Bank. In addition, as problems arise affecting particular commodities, the government establishes national commissions composed of public and private sector representatives to formulate policy recommendations.

In general, the business associations suffer from inadequate financing and, in certain cases, from weak administrative organization. Moreover, as the custom in Paraguay in such organizations is for decisions to be reached by unanimous consent of the governing board, the time consumed in achieving such unanimity is considerable. Speedy action is rare. On the other hand, most of the businessmen with whom we have dealt in establishing the Development and Productivity Center and in promoting a private development financing corporation, have demonstrated full awareness of the country's needs and possibilities for private sector development and of how to go about this in Paraguay. These executives are quite knowledgeable and their willingness to participate, at much personal sacrifice, in continual meetings of their own associations as well as in creating the new institutional bases for the country's industrial development is worthy of sincere admiration.

Another encouraging factor at the present time is a growing awareness at certain interior points in the country--Encarnación, Villarrica, Coronel Oviedo, Concepción, Pedro Juan Caballero, etc.--of the need for local efforts to promote agro-industrial development in those areas. In some cases, local committees are being established, with local official and private representation, to formulate development programs and to find means of attracting enterprises to those areas. Unfortunately, municipalities in Paraguay have little autonomy. Nevertheless, they can make land available for industrial sites, stimulate the establishment of local utilities, streets, and roads, and help organize a labor force for new plants.

The National Development Plan for 1965/66, approved in July, 1965, called for diversification of Paraguayan production over the national territory, dispersion of industries to take advantage of local raw material and labor supplies, and the opening of new areas of the country to agricultural and manufacturing production. The government's colonization policies, if properly implemented, could assist materially in carrying out these objectives. The opening of new roads and the development of additional electric power resources at the Acaray River are expected to make major contributions to these ends. However, the Government of Paraguay has done very little by way of programming and promoting industrial development. The Ministry of Industry and Commerce, charged with these functions, has neither the trained staff nor the budget to implement them.

In the past several years, Paraguayan negotiations within the Latin American Free Trade Association have been left largely in the hands of private sector representatives. Government participation has been through second- or third-level officials. In part this phenomenon has resulted from the shortage of competent government personnel to deal with complex LAFTA matters. However, there undoubtedly has been official recognition of the primacy of private sector interests in these negotiations and, perhaps, a feeling that Paraguay's interests would be served best by its businessmen, who probably are more knowledgeable in the subject matter anyhow. It wasn't until early 1966 that the post of Subsecretary for Economic Affairs was created in the Ministry of Foreign Relations. The first occupant of this position took up his office in July, 1966.

Prior to 1940, access to markets and to a supply of electric power were the major location factors for industry in Paraguay. There were virtually no roads in the country, and electricity was found only in Asunción and in the neighborhood of tanning factories. Hence the few industries that existed were concentrated in or near the capital.[2]

Although Paraguay is still one of the least industrialized nations in Latin America in the manufacturing sense, approximately 50 per cent of its exports in 1965 consisted of processed products such as canned meat, tannin, vegetable oils, sawed lumber, yerba maté, essential oils, and cotton fiber. However, all of these involve a relatively simple transformation of raw materials.

The Paraguayan market is severely limited by its small size and the low average income of its population. Consequently, the scale of production is small, excess capacity, if found in most industries, and retail prices of local products are relatively high. Better quality and lower-priced items may be purchased in neighboring countries. Many Paraguayans visit such places as Clorinda, Corrientes, and Posadas, across the Paraguay River in Argentina, to do their shopping for food, shoes, and clothing. The stability of the Paraguayan currency has provided an added temporary advantage to these buyers, in the face of continual devaluations that have taken place in Argentina and Brazil.

A survey of six typical commodities imported into Paraguay from Argentina showed that, in relation to the U.S. dollar at the free market rate of exchange, prices had dropped between 20 per cent and 50 per cent between 1961 and 1965, with an average decline of 25 per cent. A similar comparison of six products normally imported from Brazil showed that their prices had fallen between 11 per cent and 75 per cent, with an average of 50 per cent during the same period. The effects of such monetary instability in these neighboring countries have been twofold: Paraguayan imports of these items (both registered and unregistered) have increased substantially and temporarily have adversely affected local production; and certain

Paraguayan exports to these countries have been reduced markedly because their relative cost has increased.[3] On the other hand, foreign merchandise tends to be much less expensive in Paraguay than in Argentina, Brazil, or Uruguay, where highly protectionist policies are in force to favor national manufactures.

The development of sound manufacturing industries in Paraguay constitutes a basic objective of its government. This will necessitate an evolution of the industrial pattern from the simple processing of raw materials to a more advanced stage of manufacturing involving higher levels of skills and technology. The goals of this industrialization are (a) to satisfy a larger proportion of national requirements from domestic production; (b) to increase exports of manufactured items; and (c) to provide more productive employment to the country's rapidly growing labor force.

The achievement of the foregoing goals requires the adoption of policies that will stimulate investment, permit cost reductions, and broaden the markets for local manufactures, especially export markets. Close cooperation between the public and private sectors is necessary for achieving efficient industrialization. In the next few years, it is anticipated that emphasis will be placed on improving output of traditional products, encouraging the establishment of economically sized plants (to replace the numerous small, poorly organized, low-technology enterprises), increasing the competitive position of Paraguayan products at home and abroad, and bringing local industry to a more advanced stage of production or processing.[4] Three major problems will have to be resolved in the process: (a) Market studies thus far have been almost entirely lacking, either as to internal or foreign markets. Virtually no attention has been paid to taste preferences in foreign markets, marketing and distribution methods, product promotion, or follow-up orders. (b) A shortage of medium- and long-term credit, especially for working capital needs, has inhibited national industrial development, both with respect to the creation of new enterprises and the improvement of productivity in existing ones. (c) Conflicting government policies with respect to taxes and incentive benefits made difficult the calculation of production costs by potential investors, and such investors heretofore could not be sure that advantages obtained at any given time would be better or worse than those available at some future date.

In part, the conflicts in policies arose because various State institutions have been involved in granting these benefits and each institution has acted independently of the others. Hence the conditions offered to investors have varied considerably and often have borne little relation to development needs. Such has been the case with respect to the aforo (valuation) system for imports, exchange surcharges, other taxes on imports and exports, consumption taxes, the discriminatory treatment of imported capital goods, tax exonerations, and similar policies. Accordingly, the 1967/68 National Plan recommended the establishment of an industrial development policy--coherent yet flexible and in accordance with defined objectives.[5] Such a policy is considered to be a precondition for increasing domestic and foreign investment in the industrial sector.

For the longer term, the 1967/68 National Development Plan recommended the creation of industries having greater dynamism and economic and social impact. These industries would be larger-scale activities, based on the exploitation of hitherto untapped resources, that would diversify the national output and facilitate inter-industry relationships both within the country and within the LAFTA complex.

Types of industries suggested by the Technical Planning Secretariat both for immediate and longer-term development are: (a) those that will give preference to utilizing raw materials of national origin; (b) those whose output will be destined for export; (c) those that will advance the degree of processing and the value of domestic raw materials; (d) those that will begin by using imported raw materials but will substitute these with national materials in the near future; (e) those that will fill unsatisfied domestic demand where no excess capacity exists, or if excess capacity exists, the productive unit is obsolete; (f) those that will locate in areas useful for the economic development of the country; and (g) those that will produce consumer goods of prime necessity or capital goods necessary to the productive sectors.[6]

INSTITUTIONS

The institutional structure for Paraguay's industrial development is still in the process of formation. The Ministry of Industry and Commerce and the National Development Bank are the major official entities in this economic sector. Closely related to these two institutions are the newly established private Development and Productivity Center, and the projected private development financing corporation (financiera). Together, these institutions will form the links of a development chain that should accelerate industrial growth in the country materially.

The Ministry of Industry and Commerce dates from August, 1950. It is responsible for promoting the nation's industrial development and trade expansion. Economic censuses (industry, commerce, electric power) also are effected by the Ministry. In addition, it maintains a small laboratory for testing locally processed commodities (e.g., vegetable oils, sugar) to assure that they meet at least minimum standards for export as well as for local consumption. The activities of this Ministry are inhibited by its very small budget and small staff. Nevertheless, in 1963, the Ministry was reorganized and expanded.[7] A Department of Export Promotion and Information was created, as well as a Department of Industrial Statistics and Censuses. In addition, an Industrial Planning Unit was authorized to plan and program public and private industrial investments in the country, coordinating this activity with the Technical Planning Secretariat.

This unit had yet to be established at the close of 1966. More recently the Ministry has attempted to improve its contacts with industry through weekly visits to manufacturing establishments throughout the country. In these visits, Ministry officials indicate their desire to cooperate with manufacturers in solving their problems. At the same time, Ministry staff and representatives of other development agencies (who go on these trips at the Ministry's invitation) obtain first-hand knowledge of industrial operations and problems in the country. This contact should help accelerate loan handling by the National Development Bank and the granting of industrial incentives by the Ministry of Industry and Commerce. As a rule, such visiting teams have representatives not only from the Ministry (including the Minister and/or Subminister), but from the National Development Bank, the Central Bank, the Technical Planning Secretariat, and, at times, foreign technicians as well.

Under the general jurisdiction of the Ministry of Industry and Commerce is the fairly recently created National Institute of Technology and Standards (Instituto Nacional de Tecnología y Normalización) This Institute, established by Law No. 862 of June 26, 1963, is responsible for developing and establishing standards for national manufactures and the industrialization of local raw materials. In sum, it was designed to be a research and development organization. The Institute was set up with the technical and financial assistance of the United Nations Special Fund. It is the second such institute in Latin America, after the Central American Institute for Industrial Research and Technology (Instituto Centro Americano de Investigación y Tecnología Industrial--ICAITI), established in Guatemala City in January, 1956.[8] However, financing and facilities have been inadequate thus far to permit the Paraguayan Institute to do much of a job. Should the situation change, the Institute may be in a position to work closely with the Development and Productivity Center in identifying new investment opportunities and in increasing the productivity of existing enterprises.[9]

A project for the creation of an Industrial Development Council under the aegis of the Ministry of Industry and Commerce was being developed in the fall of 1966. Its principal functions would be to coordinate the activities of all public and private institutions responsible for industrial development; orient the application and execution of economic policies with the industrialization goals of the country; and define the aims of industrial policy. Its decision would constitute recommendations to the respective institutions on the Council and to the National Economic Coordination Council. The Industrial Development Council was to be composed of representatives of the Ministry of Industry and Commerce, the Technical Planning Secretariat, the National Development Bank, and the Paraguayan Industrial Union, representing the manufacturing sector.

The National Development Bank thus far has been the only institution in Paraguay to offer medium-term credit for industrial development. It has obtained several foreign loans for industrial development purposes, as discussed in Chapter 5, and has contracted foreign consulting firms to provide technical assistance in specific industrial fields for the preparation of loan projects.

Credits granted for industrial purposes by the banking system, including the National Development Bank, during the period 1953-66, have been as shown in Table 53.

TABLE 53

Average Annual Banking System Loans for Industrial Purposes, 1953-57, 1958-62, and 1963-66 (In Millions of *Guaranies*)

Period	Total	NDB[a]	Per Cent of Total
1953-57	742.1	404.4	54
1958-62	980.9	150.9	15
1963-66	2,637.5	616.5	23

[a]Prior to December, 1961, Bank of Paraguay.

As seen from the foregoing tabulation, the ex-Bank of Paraguay once held a preponderant position in industrial lending. Since 1953, however, the Bank's role in this field declined sharply, partly as a result of the rise in commercial banks and partly because of the earlier dissipation of its resources. As previously mentioned, under new leadership, the National Development Bank is striving again to become an important force for industrial development in Paraguay. Its activities could be accelerated by the establishment of a private development financing corporation (as proposed by the USAID) that could join with the Bank in the financing of worthwhile projects that neither could handle alone. The Technical Planning Secretariat, in its National Plan for 1967/68, came out wholeheartedly in favor of this project.

In 1966, the NDB received a loan of $700,000 from the Inter-American Development Bank to round out a $1 million project for financing feasibility studies in the public and private sectors. The NDB was to give priority to studies of projects mentioned in the 1967/68 National Development Plan and to projects already being processed by the Bank. In its work to date, the NDB tentatively has identified thirty industrial investment opportunities in the country. Of these, twelve are in the export industries, others are import substitutive, and the rest remained to be analyzed. Manufacturing or processing activities under study by the NDB in late 1966 included: (a) lumber; (b) hides; (c) fruits and vegetables; (d) hard vegetable fibers; (e) hogs; (f) vegetable oils; (g) castor oil; (h) cattle feeds; (i) furniture; (j) mandioca; (k) essential oils; (l) iron; (m) construction materials, by modern methods; (n) fertilizers; (o) salt; (p) dairy products; (q) iron wire and bars for construction; (r) glass bottles and containers; (s) grilled chickens; (t) soaps and detergents; (u) modern slaughterhouses; (v) agricultural and industrial hand tools; (w) kitchen utensils; (x) manufacture of clothing on an industrial scale; (y) gelatins; (z) grain storage; (aa) packaging of peanuts and bananas; and (bb) beneficiation of rice, corn, and other agricultural products.[10]

The Institute of Sciences of the National University of Asunción is becoming increasingly important in such matters as analyzing national raw materials (e.g., citrus fruits, mandioca, fibers) suitable for industrialization and in making summary studies of particular industries. The Technological and Normalization Institute, intended to establish standards of quality for national manufactures and safety standards for industrial establishments, already has been mentioned. The financial and technical resources of both these institutes are quite small in spite of Paraguay's urgent need to develop unique and/or higher-unit-value commodities for export. A deliberate program of research and development in the industrial sector, although of vital importance, has not yet been undertaken. The Technical Planning Secretariat has been engaged in a program of commodity studies and also has attempted to evaluate the prospects for various industries in Paraguay. However, the studies had not been published by the end of 1966.

One of the most important obstacles to economic, political, and social progress in Paraguay has been the inadequacy of education of all types and at all levels.[11] There is only one Technical Vocational School in the country, established with the assistance of the Inter-American Educational Cooperative Service (SCIDE) in 1948. As of January 1, 1962, the school was absorbed by the Ministry of Education and Culture. However, although substantial progress has been made by the school since its founding, the quarters, curriculum, and facilities are far from adequate.[12] Also, because salaries are low, the school has had difficulties in retaining competent staff. The Technical Vocational School handles approximately 500 students a year and graduates about 150 annually. The courses run for three years and include bricklaying, cabinet making, precision machinery, welding, automotive mechanics, plumbing, basic electricity, radio and television, graphic arts, refrigeration, and drafting. The courses for the most part are given during the hours of 6:45 A.M. to 1:15 P.M.; a few are given at night. Students must have completed the six years of primary education to be enrolled in the school.[13]

The National Electricity Administration (ANDE) operates its own school for training its technicians. The school reportedly is well equipped and staffed. Certain religious orders provide rudimentary technical training at a few points in the interior of the country (e.g., Pilar, Encarnación, Coronel Oviedo, Villarrica). However, except in the case of ANDE's school for its own technicians, the lack of trained teachers limits the quality of vocational education being given in the country. The late Dr. Damon K. Kroh recommended that the Ministry of Education and the industrial sector cooperate in formulating a sound vocational educational program.[14]

In the private sector, Paraguay can count more business organizations than countries many times its size. The major organization is the Federation of Production, Industry and Commerce (Federación de la Producción, La Industria y el Comercio--FEPRINCO), organized in 1951 and established as a legal entity by Decree No. 15,332 of December 26, 1952. FEPRINCO basically is an association of business associations: its principal members are the Paraguayan Industrial Union (Union Industrial Paraguaya--UIP),[15] the Cattlemen's Association (Asociación Rural), the Importers' Association (Centro de Importadores), the Exporters' Association (Cámara de Exportadores), and the Chamber of Commerce and Stock Exchange (Cámara y Bolsa de Comercio).* Established initially to defend the interests of its various member associations as well as of individual members against State intervention and control of the economy, FEPRINCO in recent years has become a more forward-looking, dynamic force for industrial development in Paraguay. It speaks for the private sector in this country, and its voice is heeded by the government.

Under the sponsorship of FEPRINCO and the UIP, and with the encouragement and assistance of the U.S. AID Mission to Paraguay, the Development and Productivity Center was established in 1966 (Decree

---

*No stock exchange is yet in operation, in spite of the name of this organization.

No. 20,242 of July 27.* The Organization of American States and the United Nations, as well as other productivity centers in Latin America, have offered technical assistance to the new Center. Thus a problem of this institution will be the proper programming of the resources available to it. A consulting firm contracted by the USAID was to assist the Center and the private sector in general in, among other things, (a) identifying investment opportunities, (b) developing investment projects, (c) obtaining technical and financial assistance for these projects, and (d) promoting joint ventures. The consulting team also was to train Center personnel and assist the Center in programming and offering training courses.

POLICIES

Industrial policy in Paraguay consists of various fiscal, tax, monetary, credit, and regulatory laws that are executed by a host of State agencies, often without reference to each other and acting at cross purposes. These policies are discussed briefly below, according to the areas they affect. Tax policies are discussed in greater detail in Chapter 12.

Investment Incentives

In general, the Government of Paraguay favors the development of private enterprise and the entry of foreign private capital into the country. Paraguay has both an Industrial Development Law, affecting domestic investors, and a Regime for the Incorporation of Foreign Private Capital. Work has

---

*Prior to that time, Paraguay and Bolivia were the only countries in Latin America without a productivity center.

been going on for about two years to consolidate these laws, but a new bill had not yet been presented to the Congress by the end of 1966.

The Industrial Development Law (No. 202 of September 7, 1953, approving Decree-Law No. 30 of March 31, 1952) provided specified benefits to new and existing industries and firms. Benefits to new industries include exoneration from customs duties and other import taxes on machinery, parts, materials, and equipment required for the installation and operation of an industrial plant; exoneration from customs duties and other taxes on the exportation of the products or subproducts of a new industry; and technical and economic assistance that State entities could offer to increase and improve production in the plant or industry or to improve its economic development. These benefits may also be obtained by owners installing plants in industries which, although already in existence, have not been exploited during the three-year period prior to the request.

Benefits to existing industries may be granted to owners of industrial plants who enlarge and modernize their installations by at least 40 per cent of their value.* These applicants may receive benefits including exoneration from custom duties and other taxes in imports of machinery, parts, materials, and equipment required for the installation and operation of the plant; technical and financial assistance; and facilities and benefits of the State, at its convenience, for participation in fairs and expositions where national products will be shown abroad.

---

*This ratio is much too high to encourage improvements in existing industrial establishments. It again reflects the government's unwillingness to forego immediate income for longer-term economic benefits.

The Executive Power may authorize one, several, or all of the foregoing benefits according to the needs and convenience of the nation. The term of the benefits is determined on a case-by-case basis, and dates from their authorization. However, in no case may the duration of any of these benefits exceed ten years. When it is proposed to install new plants in already existing industries, to incorporate new facilities and modern production processes, the investor may obtain in advance one or all of the benefits enumerated above.

Benefits under this law are granted only if the applicant can prove that he has sufficient capital and resources for the installation and operation, or modernization and expansion, of the plant to be installed or already installed, as the case may be. Such benefits are not exclusive and may be granted to more than one enterprise in the same industry, so long as this expansion will be convenient to the national economy.

The beneficiaries under this law must make the investments, build their plants, and produce at the levels indicated in their proposals to the Ministry of Industry and Commerce, and must continue in operation during the period for which the benefits have been granted. They are required to permit Ministry inspection of their books and operations. The benefits obtained under this law may be transferred only by Executive decree, with the prior consent of a Council of Industry and Commerce. This Council of Industry and Commerce is an organ that reviews and grants benefits under this law and passes judgment on the technical and economic questions relating thereto.

A Regime for the Incorporation of Foreign Private Capital (Law No. 246, of February 25, 1955) established special benefits for foreign private capital invested in Paraguay, provided the capital is registered with the Central Bank. The investment may be made in cash or in investment goods, patents, trademarks, or gifts. Benefits may be conceded provided the investment accords with the economic and social development needs of the nation, as contained in the government's plans; that the capital goods brought into the country are new and are priced at the export prices prevailing when the goods are imported into Paraguay; and that the investment requires no other guarantees or benefits than those provided in this law. Registered foreign investments meeting the foregoing requirements may receive in whole or in part the following benefits: (a) exoneration from customs duties and additional taxes on imports of capital goods that will remain in the country; (b) exoneration from customs duties and additional taxes on exports of products and subproducts that did not appear in the regular list of exports as of the promulgation date of this law; (c) exemption from establishment taxes, and from taxes on contracts, inscription in the Commercial Register, and the issuance of shares and debentures; (d) a reduction of 25 per cent in the income tax; (e) availability of foreign exchange from the Central Bank for paying interest, profit, and dividends, and trademark, patent, and license fees, as well as for repatriation of registered capital at a rate no greater than 20 per cent a year; and (f) exemption for a five-year period from the obligation to employ a designated percentage of Paraguayan personnel in the enterprise. The time periods for benefits under (a), (b), and (d), above, are determined by resolutions of the National Economic Coordination Council, and may range from five to ten years, according to the economic importance and special conditions of each enterprise.

Should the Central Bank be unable to supply the foreign exchange required for the transfer of profits and dividends on registered capital, the Bank may authorize the investor to retain up to 25 per cent of the exchange earned on his exports for this purpose. When the investment is made for the purpose of utilizing raw materials of national origin, producing new products, or engaging in other activities of developing heretofore unexploited sources of national wealth, the National Economic Coordination Council may authorize the investor to retain between 25 per cent and 50 per cent of the exchange derived from the export of goods or services of his enterprise. The maximum period for this benefit is ten years from the date of the first exportation or first receipt of foreign exchange for services rendered. If, after the benefit period has expired, there remain amounts outstanding to be repatriated, the Central Bank will provide foreign exchange at a rate no higher than 15 per cent a year of that amount without affecting remittances for other services, which may not exceed 12 per cent a year of the capital originally registered with the Central Bank.

It is obvious from the foregoing that foreign investments receive much better treatment than domestic investments. Nevertheless, neither incentive law eliminates the requirement to pay the high exchange surcharges on imported capital goods. While the foregoing laws permit the granting of important benefits to private investors, they have not fulfilled their objective of stimulating industrial development. Of the total number of applications filed, only a small proportion had reached the execution stage by the end of 1966. This would indicate that (a) applicants have been irresponsible or incompetent; (b) the Ministry of Industry and Commerce had not performed an adequate screening of the applicants and projects; or (c) financing had not been forthcoming for the projects.

According to Paraguayan businessmen, a shortage of medium-term lending for working capital has been the reason why the benefits authorized under Law No. 202 have been utilized to the extent of only 35.5 per cent during the years 1959-65. Import duty exonerations under this law during the period amounted to ₲ 695.2 million, of which only ₲ 247.1 million was actually imported.[16] Moreover, these laws have provided little special incentives for the decentralization of industries, and none for encouraging the reinvestment of profits for plant improvement and/or expansion.

A Commission for the Revision of Laws 202 and 246 was established in early 1966, with representatives from the public and private sector entities involved in the country's industrial development. The representative of the Technical Planning Secretariat acted as coordinator. Major purposes of the proposed revision were to equalize the advantages for Paraguayan and foreign investors and to correct the abovementioned shortcomings in the laws. The Technical Planning Secretariat has recommended that a new Industrial Development Law contain the following basic provisions for granting benefits: (a) the beneficiaries are to be natural or juridical persons, nationals or foreigners, who make investments in national currency; (b) the investments are to be made in accordance with the government's development plans; and (c) investments in machinery and equipment preferably are to conform with the latest technological developments.

The benefits to be provided in the proposed new law would include (a) partial or total exoneration from import duties and charges, whether fiscal or exchange, for imports of machinery, accessories, and parts required for the installation and operation of an industrial plant, in accordance with each approved project; (b) similar exonerations for raw materials and other materials not produced in the country or produced in insufficient quantities; (c) partial exemption from payment of the income tax for a period of ten years from the start-up date of the enterprise; (d) partial or total exemption from the payment of income tax on profits reinvested in the enterprise; (e) a one-year exemption from taxes on legal papers and documents required to establish a new enterprise or modify the structure of existing ones, and on the issue or transfer of capital stock; (f) obligation on the part of Central Government and autonomous agencies to buy articles of national production, so long as these are of good quality and are priced competitively with imports; and (g) free technical advice from government agencies.

The structure of benefits was to be arranged according to the designation of enterprises as new industries or existing industries, and their relative priority within the proposed industrial development plan. Also, the administrative mechanism for reviewing applications and granting benefits under the proposed law was to be streamlined, and the applications would have to contain sufficient information to permit their proper evaluation. In addition, penalties were to be provided for investors receiving benefits but failing to implement their projects.

A new law for the Incorporation of Foreign Capital also was proposed, providing the same benefits to foreign investors as those indicated for local investors in the proposed Industrial Development Law. The only differences between the proposed law and the existing law affecting foreign investments would be in the manner of incorporating the capital, obtaining the foreign exchange for remittance of principal, interest, and dividends, and certain special benefits designed to foster the establishment of joint ventures.

While such revised incentive laws would serve to improve the investment climate in Paraguay, to make fuller use of their benefits it would be useful for the government and the private sector to undertake a joint study of the country's industrial potential, especially with reference to Paraguay's privileged position as a less-developed country in the Latin American Free Trade Association. Such a study is indispensable to achieving the "programmed development" desired by the Technical Planning Secretariat and accepted in principle by the government when it approved the 1965-66 development plan. In this connection, an input-output analysis of the LAFTA complex could provide much useful information on inter-country and inter-industry relationships.

The Paraguayan Government considers it desirable that export-oriented new industries be established, especially manufacturing activities. Certain export taxes have been reduced or abolished to further this policy. Moreover, determined efforts to install the public works--electric power, transportation facilities--and to provide sufficient credit for industrial development are being made. Also, persistent efforts are being made to expand the benefits that Paraguay might obtain as a member of the Latin American Free Trade Association. It is becoming more widely recognized that new forms of capital formation are required for the establishment of productive enterprises in this country. Thus, while no organized capital market yet exists in Paraguay, the Chamber of Commerce and Stock Exchange (Cámara y Bolsa de Comercio) was developing a project during 1966 to establish a securities and commodity exchange.

Import Policies

Imports are affected by various taxes and exchange surcharges, artificial valuations, prohibitions, quotas, and liberations. While these instruments could be utilized to promote industrialization without necessarily leading to strong protective policies, they often have worked as disincentives to investment.

Tariff Policy

The basic tariff law dates from September, 1924. It was amended in 1934, 1943, 1952, and 1957. The tariff is mainly for revenue, although its modifications added protective features for certain industries. Nevertheless, the tariff is not in tune with the country's industrial development requirements. For example, high tariff duties are levied on certain imported raw materials for industrial use, whereas the competitive finished products enter duty free. Also, excessive liberation of duties is granted to imports of competitive products. Undervaluation of imports and contraband imports cause additional problems for local manufacturers. It is imperative that the customs tariff be revised in a manner to make the duties more realistic and thereby reduce the incentives for contraband trade. Due attention will need to be given to the negotiations that Paraguay has undertaken within the LAFTA, as well as to its future path of industrial development under the conditions peculiar to Paraguay.

Exchange Surcharges (Recargos de Cambio)

Prior deposit of 100 per cent or more of the F.O.B. value of certain imports is required, and the deposit is retained for a period of 120 to 180 days. The government also levies surcharges on most imports, based on their C.I.F. value. While the surcharge on petroleum base fuels is 15 per cent and on wheat 19 per cent, most imports are subject to aggregate surcharges of 32 per cent. Imports of construction materials are subject to exchange surcharges of 31 per cent. During 1966, to amortize a government investment in a new radio station, the exchange surcharges on imported radios, radio equipment, parts, and accessories were raised to 35 per cent. In lieu of structural tax reform, the government continues to raise the so-called exchange surcharges when additional funds are required urgently. The "exchange surcharge" is actually a misnomer, as the taxes are levied on the value of imports.

The exchange surcharges do not apply to products which have been granted concessions by Paraguay when imported from LAFTA countries. Neither do they apply to imports of industrial and agricultural machinery from Spain entered through the Spanish Free Trade Zone at the port of Villeta.

These exchange surcharges adversely affect the industrial sector in two ways: The 32 per cent additional burden on imported machinery and equipment acts as a disincentive to investment by forcing the investor to have recourse to scarce, high-cost credit; and also, the tax is applied equally to imports of raw materials for the industrial process and to imports of finished products. Thus industries that could be developed locally but require certain basic imported materials are discouraged by the combination of high tariff duties and exchange surcharges.

Sales Tax

The sales tax is levied on the sales of goods intended for domestic consumption, the rate of tax ranging from 3 per cent to 10 per cent of the value of the product. In the case of imported commodities, the value is computed on a cost constructed by adding to the C.I.F. value any additional taxes, port charges, dispatch charges, etc., in the same manner as in computing a selling price, and then adding 30 per cent as imputed profit.* The sales tax is levied on all imports except those that the Ministry of Finance may specifically exonerate on a case-by-case basis.

Imports from the LAFTA

Under the Montevideo Treaty, Paraguayan imports from other countries in the LAFTA receive more favored treatment than those from other sources. However, the Paraguayan Government needs to be better informed concerning the country's industrial potential lest it prejudice the development of national industries through unwise negotiations.

Fiscal Policy

Direct taxes in Paraguay are low and provide a genuine incentive to prospective investors. The so-called income tax is really a business profits tax. The maximum income tax rate is 25 per cent, applicable to taxable income of ¢ 100,000 or more. Profits or earnings from various classes of activities are not subject to the income tax, e.g., farming; personal labor in a dependent relationship; practicing a liberal profession (doctors, lawyers, engineers, etc.); and government employment (including the military and police). Also, incomes from inheritances, legacies, or gifts, earnings from gambling, and profits from the sale of personal

---

*In the case of domestic products, the taxable amount is the gross value of all invoices representing the actual cost of operation.

property are not subject to this tax. Certain activities--ranching, meatpacking, foresting, and transportation--pay taxes on their respective exploitative operations "in lieu of income tax." This device of substitute taxes is employed when the government feels that it is not able to administer the income tax law in a particular economic activity, or where the returns under the income tax law appear to be less than warranted by the scale of the activity.

Other government policies tend to place Paraguayan exports at a disadvantage in foreign markets. For example, most export commodities are subject to duties ranging between 2½ per cent and 7½ per cent. While there has been some tendency toward reducing or eliminating these taxes,* their complete abolition would be desirable. The general problems affecting industry in an underdeveloped country, as well as the unusually high cost of transporting Paraguayan products to world markets, constitute important obstacles to the country's export trade without the additional burden of export taxes.

In addition to paying the foregoing taxes, exporters are required to sell their foreign exchange to the local commercial banks based on minimum export valuations established periodically by the Central Bank of Paraguay. As a rule, these valuations (*aforos*) purport to be equal to or less than the world market prices for such exports. However, the valuations differ from those established by the Ministry of Finance for purposes of levying the export taxes. There is a tendency for the *aforos* to lag behind changes in market prices, being either too high or too low. Hence the exporter cannot know his real costs until after he has sold his merchandise.

---

*The export tax has been eliminated on the following items: alcohol; kaolin; corn; fresh fruit; sawn lumber and wood products; carded cotton; palm hearts; *yerba maté*; *quebracho* extract; and *mandioca* starch.

Credit Policy

The problem of insufficient credit for industrialization was mentioned in the preceding chapter. The need for an industrial credit policy and the establishment of the necessary institutions for implementing the policy are basic to the country's industrialization requirements. The basic credit needs of the industrial sector are the financing of fixed capital investment, working capital, and exports. The Technical Planning Secretariat has recommended that a definite credit policy be established to channel credit into these activities. The policy would include the provision of exporter credits for periods up to 180 days, operating capital loans for at least 12 months, and fixed capital credits for at least 5 years. Interest rates would vary according to the type of credit, being lowest for the long-term loans.

Programs

Industrial programs in Paraguay should be directed to one or more of three basic objectives: (a) to provide remunerative employment to the growing labor force; (b) to establish broader bases for obtaining public and private savings; and (c) to increase national availabilities of foreign exchange. Existing incentive laws, as discussed above, could aid prospective investors toward these objectives. However, a "spirit of enterprise" must be developed widely, along with the identification of sound investment opportunities.

An editorial in the Colorado Party organ, Pátria, of September 1, 1966, reported that Paraguay, like other countries of the free world, was concerned with the problem of achieving full employment.[17] While the editorial mentioned various occurrences as indicative of government actions to implement this goal, the cases in point revealed that the editorial writer at least, did not distinguish between full employment and productive full employment. For example, attempts to continue the inefficient national railway in operation, the attempts made at arranging a temporary "solution" to the surplus production of sugar (see Chapter 2), and the maintenance of excessive personnel on the government payroll, scarcely qualify as sound full-employment measures. On the other hand, the Central Bank's assistance in reopening the Joaquín Grau textile factory, the proposed construction of a new cement plant, the initiation (at long last) of the government's workers' housing program, and the construction of the Acaray Hydroelectric Plant are definite steps in this direction.

A much greater realization of the aims of public policy was shown by Dr. Julio Sanabria, Subminister of Industry and Commerce, in a radio address on September 3, 1966, honoring the thirtieth anniversary of the Paraguayan Industrial Union.[18] After noting the important increase of 10 per cent a year (compounded) in the industrial sector product during 1955-65, Dr. Sanabria, an economist, cited the government's contributions to this development. These contributions, among other things, included the building of infrastructure; creation and modernization of institutions related to industrial development; negotiations of technical assistance and important foreign credits for financing investments; the opening of wider markets for manufactured and semi-manufactured products within the LAFTA; the establishment of the Institute of Technology and Standards; the reorganization of the Ministry of Industry and Commerce (1963); and the beginning of a project (in 1966) to create a National Industrial Development Council. The new industrial development policy, said Dr. Sanabria, is based on the idea of harmonious cooperation between private sector and public sector institutions, together seeking a type of development that will permit maximization of the physical and human resources available, provide stimuli to savings and investments, and serve to create new sources of employment and production. Thus new investments will be generated that, in turn, will make possible higher levels of living for important sectors of the population. Dr. Sanabria also emphasized the need for pre-investment surveys of industries on a regional scale to take advantage of the LAFTA market, and the need for financing such projects. In connection with the latter, he cited the studies being undertaken to establish a national securities market, for improving credit policy, and for providing maximum facilities for utilizing foreign credits.

The USAID was contemplating the continuation of a program begun in fiscal year 1966 (from July 1, 1965, through June 30, 1966) of sending ten-man teams (five from the public sector and five from the private sector) to the U.S. for short-term orientation programs offered by Conway Research Inc., of Atlanta, Georgia. The considerable success of the first effort in teaching the need for public-private cooperation at all levels of government for achieving national and area development[19] had led to requests by the Paraguayan Government and the private sector for continuation of this program. Representatives from interior points were to be included in the participant list each year, as was the case in fiscal years 1966 and 1967.

Notes to Chapter 10

1. The First Congress was held during April 18-21, 1951.

2. Juan Natalicio González, Geografía del Paraguay (Mexico City: Editorial Guarania, 1964), pp. 550-51.

3. Information from the Ministry of Industry and Commerce.

4. Technical Planning Secretariat, Segundo Plan Nacional de Desarrollo Económico y Social, Bienio 1967/68, Annexo II, "Sector Industria y Energía," (Asunción, August, 1966), pp. 4-7.

5. Ibid., p. 9.

6. Ibid., p. 12.

7. Law No. 904 of August 30, 1963.

8. "Un Millón de Dólares se Invertirá en el Instituto Nacional de Tecnología y Normalización," in Crítica y Analisis, Vol. I, No. 2, July, 1963, p. 47.

9. Only one standard--for mandioca to be used as an admixture with wheat flour in making bakery products--had been established by the end of 1966.

10. La Tribuna, September 3, 1966, p. 4.

11. Servicio Cooperativo Interamericano de Educación, Industrial Education and Paraguay's Future (Asunción, 1961), p. 117.

12. Dr. Damon K. Kroh, "Report on Visit to Escuela Técnica," November, 1963.

13. Haskell W. Sullivan, USAID Adviser in Vocational Industrial Education.

14. Kroh, op. cit.

15. The UIP celebrated its thirtieth anniversary on September 7, 1966.

16. CIAP, "El Esfuerzo Interno y Las Necesidades de Financiamiento Externo Para el Desarrollo del Paraguay," CIAP/39, OEA/Ser.H/XIV, September 7, 1966, p. 17.

17. Editorial entitled "Plena Ocupación."

18. "Hacia una Nueva Politica en el Orden Industrial," La Tribuna, September 4, 1966, p. 3.

19. Dr. Sanabria was the chairman of the first Paraguayan group to participate in this training.

PART III

FINANCIAL AND MONETARY TRANSACTIONS

CHAPTER 11 NATIONAL ACCOUNTS

There are no reliable data on the Gross National Product (GNP) of Paraguay. The Technical Planning Secretariat warns that: "The validity of such indicators as the per capita product and income for measuring the degree of the country's development must be taken with considerable reserve. Because of the lack of detailed studies of the income and its distribution, these indicators are used only for an approximation of the present economic and social structure."[1] Moreover, estimates of the GNP issued by the Technical Planning Secretariat and by the Central Bank of Paraguay have varied markedly from each other, even when issued almost simultaneously. And to confuse the situation further, the Second National Plan (for 1967/68) contains revised (higher) population statistics that reduce the per capita GNP figures substantially from earlier estimates. For example, the GNP per capita (in 1962 prices) for 1965, as a result of the various revisions, was reported in 1966 at $198 instead of the earlier figure of $207, a decline of 4.5 per cent. The revised population and GNP data are shown in Table 54.

The methodology employed in compiling the national accounts has been so poor, the number of persons working in the field so limited, and the budget for statistical investigation so insignificant, that the validity of the data is rather low. The Subcommittee of the Inter-American Committee on the Alliance for Progress (CIAP) that reviewed the Paraguayan economy in November, 1965, remarked upon the poor quality of the country's statistical information and urged an immediate improvement in Paraguay's statistical services, leading toward a total reform of the national statistics system.

TABLE 54

Population and Gross National Product in Current and Constant Market Prices, Actual 1961-65 and Projected 1966-68

		GROSS NATIONAL PRODUCT				GNP Per Capita	
Year	Mid-year Population	Current Prices	Constant Prices[a]	Current Prices	Constant Prices[a]	Current Prices	Constant Prices[a]
	(Thousands)	(In Millions of Guaranies)		(In Millions of U.S. Dollars)		(In U.S. Dollars)	
1961	1,801	39,419	42,733	313	339	173	188
1962	1,854	45,189	45,189	359	359	193	193
1963	1,910	48,251	46,207	383	367	200	192
1964	1,969	51,038	47,678	405	378	205	192
1965	2,030	55,803	50,739	443	402	217	198
1966	2,094	59,208	42,758	470	419	224	200
1967	2,161	63,683	55,722	505	442	234	205
1968	2,231	68,612	58,954	545	468	244	210

[a]Constant prices of 1962.

Source: Technical Planning Secretariat, II Plan Nacional de Desarrollo Económico y Social, Bienio 1967-1968 (Asunción, August, 1966), Table 27 and adjusted flow-of-funds table.

Comparative compound annual real growth rates of the national accounts components during the years 1961-66, according to the Technical Planning Secretariat, have been as follows:

	Rate Per Year (Per Cent)
Gross domestic product	4.1
Consumption	5.0
Gross real investment	3.1
Exports	9.2
Imports	4.0
Domestic savings	4.4
External savings	1.7
Disposable goods and services	4.7
Population growth rate	3.0
Persons employed	3.4
Installed capacity	4.7

A net import surplus has resulted in a faster growth rate for disposable goods and services than for the Gross Domestic Product (GDP).* According to these data, the per capita growth rate of the GDP averaged only 1.1 per cent a year during the period.

With respect to the sectoral distribution of income, "no detailed studies exist based upon scientific and technical criteria."[2] Nevertheless, the national plan shows an annual distribution of the Gross Domestic Product by economic activity for the years 1961-65.[3] These data indicate a virtual sectoral stagnation of the economy during these years; statistics for 1961 and 1965 are shown in Table 55. The alleged sectoral stagnation, however, does not accord with certain recorded facts. For example, in the important livestock sector, the value of registered animals slaughtered rose from ₡ 3,263 million to ₡ 5,443 million. Converted to constant values of 1962, the real increase approximated 41

---

*The Gross Domestic Product equals the Gross National Product plus net transfers to foreign factors of production.

TABLE 55

Estimates of the Gross Domestic Product,
by Economic Activity, 1961 and 1965
(In Millions of Guaranies at 1962 Market Prices)

Economic Sector	1961		1965		Change in Value, 1961-65
	Value	Per Cent	Value	Per Cent	Per Cent
Agriculture	9,204	21.4	10,900	21.3	+18.4
Livestock	5,015	11.7	5,838	11.4	+16.4
Forestry	1,611	3.8	1,931	3.8	+19.9
Hunting and fishing	43	0.1	49	0.1	+14.0
Mining	57	0.1	89	0.2	+56.1
Industry	7,112	16.5	8,016	15.7	+12.7
Construction	900	2.1	1,247	2.4	+38.6
Production of goods	23,942	55.7	28,070	54.9	+17.2
Electric power	223	0.5	278	0.6	+19.3
Water and sanitation	76	0.2	62	0.1	-18.4
Transportation and communication	1,638	3.8	1,925	3.8	+17.5
Basic services	1,947	4.5	2,265	4.4	+16.3

Commerce and finance	9,324	21.7	11,539	22.6	+23.8
Government	1,807	4.2	2,229	4.4	+23.4
Housing	1,545	3.6	1,738	3.4	+12.5
Other services	4,403	10.3	5,269	10.3	+19.7
Production of services	17,079	39.8	20,755	40.7	+21.5
Gross Domestic Product	42,969	100.0	51,110	100.0	+18.9
Net factor payments abroad	- 236		- 371		+57.2
Gross National Product	42,733		50,739		+18.7

per cent. Yet the value of product in the livestock sector is shown to have increased only 16.4 per cent between 1961 and 1965. Moreover, it has been estimated that at least an additional 10 per cent of animals is slaughtered annually without being registered and having the taxes paid. Construction and housing activities also are believed to be understated; the offical estimates of their product are based on permits granted, but a sizable proportion of such activities is carried out without permits, even in Asunción. Moreover, no value is imputed in the official statistics to the thousands of rural dwellings constructed each year by the growing farm population.

The industrial sector product also is believed to be underestimated in the official data. For example, the real increase in this sector between 1961 and 1965 allegedly was only 12.7 per cent. Yet the cotton textile industry alone, which accounts for about 10 per cent of the total industrial product, increased its output 21.7 per cent, in terms of 1962 prices.

A highly competent Belgian economist employed by the American Embassy in Paraguay has made an independent sectoral estimate of the Gross Domestic Product for 1962.[4] According to these figures, shown in Table 56, the GDP in 1962 would amount to $592 million, or $319 per capita, compared with roughly $193 per capita reported by the Technical Planning Secretariat. Dr. Ceuppens' estimates were derived through procedures utilized by the U.S. Department of Commerce; the Technical Planning Secretariat and the Central Bank have taken a much narrower view of what should be included in the GNP, as noted above.

Another criticism affects even the trend in the GNP. According to the official data shown in Table 56, the GNP per capita declined slightly from 1962 to 1963 and remained stable in 1965 (in terms of 1962 prices). However, Paraguay's exports increased $6.7 million in 1963 and $9.7 million in 1964; bank credits rose ₲ 1.6 billion in 1963 and

TABLE 56

Estimated Gross Domestic Product, by Economic Sector, 1962

Economic Sector	Millions of *Guaranies*
Agriculture	11,000
Livestock	7,000
Forestry	2,300
Hunting and fishing	450
Mining	100
Industry	15,000
Construction	2,200
Production of goods	58,800
Electric power	450
Water and sanitation	100
Transport and communications	2,200
Basic services	2,750
Commerce and finance	17,000
Government	2,000
Housing	6,500
Other services	8,500
Production of services	34,000
Gross Domestic Product	74,800
Net factor payments abroad	- 234
Gross National Product	74,566 (U.S. $592 Million)

Source: Dr. Henry D. Ceuppens, Economic Specialist, American Embassy, Asunción, Paraguay.

₡ 2.8 billion in 1964; and international reserves rose $1.8 million in 1963 and $5.0 million in 1964. The cost-of-living index (1962=100) rose only to 101.7 in 1963 and to 103.6 in 1964. The population increased at the rate of some 3 per cent a year.

Because of the poor quality and misleading impressions of economic activity in Paraguay presented in official national accounts statistics, as well as to give a more interpretative picture of Paraguay's development, certain other indicators of national growth are provided in Table 57.

TABLE 57

Socio-economic Indicators of Paraguay's Growth, 1955-65

a) Education

Education	1955	1965	Increase
Number of schools	1,910	2,632	38%
Number of teachers	9,111	12,761	40%
Students enrolled	267,643	364,640	36%

b) Agrarian Reform

In the forty years prior to 1954, land titles had been granted to only 11,268 new owners encompassing 549,225 acres. During the decade between 1954 and 1964, titles were given to 38,250 new proprietors encompassing 2.591 million acres.

c) Infrastructure

Prior to 1954, some 640 miles of road had been asphalted, filled with stone, or hard surfaced. In 1965, this figure reached 2,333 miles.

In addition to the foregoing indicators, Paraguay compares favorably, on an empirical basis, with other Latin American countries of similar population size and stage of development. The level of living of the mass of the Paraguayan population appears to be much better than in Honduras and Nicaragua, for example. While Paraguay does not have a wealthy class to bring up its average per capita GNP, as is the case in the Central American countries, the more evenly distributed income in Paraguay undoubtedly is at a higher level than the average per capita income of the masses in Central America. Hence, the additional wealth deriving from ranching operations in Paraguay, while not of the scale of coffee wealth in Central America, yet may well be sufficient to raise the average per capita product to the level at least of Honduras.

Without reliable data, it is difficult to determine total investment, consumption, and savings. Even the public sector statistics are unreliable because of the chaotic accounting methods practiced by the Central Government. Nevertheless, the latest available official information is shown in Table 58.

Thus, during the five-year period 1961-65, the investment rate averaged 17 per cent of the GNP; private investment represented 14 per cent and public investment only 3 per cent of the GNP. About one third of the gross investment is estimated to have gone for replacement of capital, thus leaving two thirds for net investment. Internal investment accounted for 76.5 per cent of total investment during the period, and external investment averaged 23.5 per cent of the total. An average output: capital ratio of .436 reportedly was attained in these years, a figure which appears rather high for Paraguay. The estimated sectoral distribution of gross investment in 1965 was reported as shown in Table 59.

In spite of the fact that private electric power facilities have been increasing rapidly (see Chapter 8), this activity is not identified in the private sector distribution of investment shown by the Technical Planning Secretariat.

Consumption during the period 1961-65, in real terms, rose at the rate of 5 per cent a year, according to the Technical Planning Secretariat.

TABLE 58

Gross Investment, 1961-65
(In Millions of 1962 Guaranies)

	1961	1962	1963	1964	1965	Average Annual Rate of Investment to GNP
Private investment	5,948	6,111	6,111	6,971	6,832	14%
Public investment	1,540	1,185	1,243	1,237	1,372	3%
TOTAL	7,488	7,296	7,354	8,208	8,204	17%
Net investment	5,062	4,744	4,682	5,420	5,281	11%
Capital replacement[a]	2,426	2,552	2,672	2,788	2,923	6%
Internal resources	5,567	5,870	6,070	6,298	6,661	13%
External resources	1,921	1,426	1,284	1,910	1,543	4%

[a]Calculated by the Technical Planning Secretariat as a flat 2.5 per cent of installed capacity.

TABLE 59

Sectoral Distribution of Investment, 1965

Economic Activity	Investment (₲ Million of 1962)			Per Cent of Total
	Private	Public	Total	
Agriculture, livestock, and forestry	1,085	27	1,112	14
Industry	1,170	44	1,214	15
Transportation	785	80[a]	865	11
Construction	1,642	493	2,135	26
Social	156	468	624	8
Electric power	---	260	260	2
Other	1,994	---	1,994	24
TOTAL	6,832	1,372	8,204	100

[a]Including communications.

Source: Technical Planning Secretariat, II Nacional de Desarrollo Económico y Social, Bienio 1967-1968 (Asunción, August, 1966), Table 33.

Public sector consumption (excluding the operating expenses of public enterprises) increased from 9 per cent of total consumption in 1961 to more than 12 per cent in 1965. The distribution of these consumption expenditures was reported as shown in Table 60.

TABLE 60

Consumption Expenditures, 1961-65

Year	Public[a]	Private[b]	Total
	(In Millions of 1962 *Guaranies*)		
1961	3,396	33,625	37,021
1962	3,760	35,514	39,274
1963	4,438	35,999	40,437
1964	4,646	37,901	42,547
1965	4,948	40,398	45,346

[a]Excludes operating expenses of public enterprises.

[b]Includes operating expenses of public enterprises.

As shown in Table 61, public sector investment declined from 8.6 per cent of the GDP in 1961 to 6.4 per cent in 1965. During the same period, its consumption rose from 7.1 per cent of the GDP to 8.5 per cent. These trends reflect the rise in Central Government current account outlays, especially for salaries, and the inadequate level of public sector savings to finance growing development needs.

The total amount of domestic savings in Paraguay is not known. For purposes of constructing the national accounts, the Technical Planning Secretariat has assumed a savings ratio of 13 per cent a year in relation to the real Gross National Product. On this basis, the Secretariat has estimated that the real growth in domestic savings has been 4.4 per cent a year between 1961 and 1965. The official estimates are as given in Table 62.

TABLE 61

Relationship of Public Sector Outlays to the Gross Domestic Product, 1961-65

(In Terms of 1962 Guaranies)

Year	Total Outlays	Consumption	Investment			
			Real	Transfers, etc.	Debt Amortization	Total
			(In Percentages)			
1961	15.7	7.1	3.6	2.1	2.9	8.6
1962	14.0	7.5	2.6	2.0	1.9	6.5
1963	14.3	8.4	2.5	2.0	1.4	5.9
1964	14.7	8.5	2.5	2.4	1.3	6.2
1965	14.9	8.5	2.7	2.3	1.4	6.4

Source: Technical Planning Secretariat, II Plan Nacional de Desarrollo Económico y Social, Bienio 1967-1968, Annex V, Public Sector, (Asunción, August, 1966), Table 2.

TABLE 62

Estimated Domestic Savings, 1961-65

(In Millions of Current *Guaranies*)

	1961	1962	1963	1964	1965
Central Government	854	995	301	186	1,185
Public enterprises	164	654	602	789	920
Private sector	4,127	4,221	5,421	6,142	5,202
TOTAL	5,145	5,870	6,324	7,117	7,307
(In Millions of 1962 *Guaranies*)					
Public sector	1,163	739	982	993	1,157
Private sector	4,404	5,131	5,088	5,305	5,504
TOTAL	5,567	5,870	6,070	6,298	6,661

TABLE 63

Public and Private Sector Savings, 1961-65
(In Millions of Current *Guaranies*)

	1961	1962	1963	1964	1965
Public sector savings[a]	1,018	1,646	903	975	2,105
Private savings and time deposits[b]	465	741	1,158	1,632	2,182
TOTAL	1,483	2,387	2,061	2,607	4,287
Annual increase	...	+61%	-14%	+26%	+64%

[a]Data from the Technical Planning Secretariat.

[b]Data from the Central Bank of Paraguay.

However, the rate of savings shown in Table 62 (13 per cent) does not appear to correspond with certain known facts: Public sector savings, in current prices, doubled between 1961 and 1965; private savings and time deposits in the banking system increased more than fivefold during these years; and the cost of living rose only 9.5 per cent during the period. Public sector savings, together with private savings and time deposits, during 1961-65, have been as shown in Table 63.

What is not known is the annual amount of domestic private sector savings held outside the banking system--hoardings, funds held abroad, undistributed corporate profits, and capital consumption allowances. Nor are figures readily available for private savings in the form of insurance premiums, social security funds, etc. The private sector savings level is a residual figure in Paraguay's national accounts and thus represents one of the major defects in their construction.

In sum, unless a sizable investment is made to improve the national accounts statistics, the available data will remain of little value, either for internal analysis or for international comparisons. The Technical Planning Secretariat is aware of the undervaluation of the national accounts data and hopes to undertake certain basic sectoral investigations if and when funds and trained manpower become available for this activity. It would be appropriate to make such studies in depth for a recent year, to be used as a base year, and to develop the appropriate sampling procedures by which to bring the base year statistics up to date.

Notes to Chapter 11

1. Technical Planning Secretariat, _II Plan Nacional de Desarrollo Económico y Social, Bienio 1967-1968_ (Asunción, August, 1966), pp. 31-32.

2. _Ibid._, p. 33.

3. _Ibid._, Table 4, facing page 38.

4. Dr. Henry D. Ceuppens, Economic Specialist, American Embassy, Asunción, Paraguay.

CHAPTER 12 PUBLIC FINANCE

A major change in government policy, introduced in the mid-1950's, has served to increase substantially the public sector's participation in the Paraguayan economy. This has taken the form of sizable public investments in infrastructure (roads, electric power, airports, ports, and telecommunications), including the creation of a number of autonomous State agencies and enterprises for implementing these investments. This policy contrasts markedly from the relatively passive role played by the government prior to that time.

In spite of the growing demands of the socio-economic development process for public funds, the financial condition of Paraguay's public sector has continued to be the weakest element in the country's economy. Savings have been too low to finance the development needs of the country; during 1961-65, public sector savings financed an average of only 48 per cent of public sector investments (in constant _guaranies_ of 1962), ranging from 33 per cent in 1961 to 71 per cent in 1965; the median rate was 39 per cent. Consequently, excessive reliance has been placed upon external borrowings. Relatively little effort has been made to raise the level of public revenues either through improved revenue administration or reform of the tax and rate structures.

The stability of the currency and the limited nature of the inflation in Paraguay since 1958 may be attributed to two factors: (a) a succession of Stand-by Arrangements with the International Monetary Fund (IMF), under which rather severe restrictions have been imposed by the IMF on Central Bank lending and (hence) on Central Government expenditures; and (b) a series of Surplus Commodity Sales Agreements between the United States Government and the Government of Paraguay under U.S. Public Law 480, by which local currency has been generated in a noninflationary manner for use in capital projects in the country. Because of, or in spite of, the existence of these financial "props" during the past decade, the Paraguayan Government has failed to avail itself of the opportunity to effect sound basic fiscal reforms.

Not only has the government failed to take comprehensive measures toward fiscal reform, but the national plans project substantially increased dependence upon external financing for the next several years. The actual operations of the public sector during 1961-65, the budget for 1966, and the Technical Planning Secretariat's Projections for 1967 and 1968, are shown in Table 64. It is seen from this table that, not only was the public sector depending increasingly on borrowed funds for its financing during the period 1961-68, but debt amortization resumed its upward trend in 1964, after sharp declines in 1962 and 1963. Moreover, operating expenses of the public sector were expected to increase substantially during 1967/68.

Paraguay's tax laws have been inadequate to the revenue needs of the country and, in many cases, actually have constituted bottlenecks to social and economic development. The existing tax structure is the result of an accumulation of numerous laws over time, such laws having been designed largely to meet immediate revenue needs of the government and having failed to take into account principles of equity and the possible economic consequences of their implementation. Moreover, continual changes in the revenue laws have created a vast body of uncodified laws that at times are contradictory, and an excess of liberations and exonerations therefrom.

Recommendations for tax reform made in 1964/65 by a joint mission from the Organization of American States and the Inter-American Development Bank

TABLE 64

Consolidated Statement of Public Sector Finances, Actual 1961-65, Budgeted 1966, and Projected 1967/68
(In Millions of Guaranies)

	1961	1962	1963	1964	1965	Budgeted 1966	Projected 1967	Projected 1968
Current revenues	4,501	5,405	5,302	5,557	6,867	7,045	7,759	8,602
Government revenues	4,597	5,128	5,027	5,230	6,499	6,508	7,131	7,916
Profits of state enterprises	96	277	275	327	368	537	628	686
Total expenditures	6,744	6,367	6,650	7,065	7,652	9,501	11,561	12,233
Operating expenses	3,061	3,380	3,904	4,118	4,362	4,491	4,904	5,177
Investments (gross)	1,540	1,185	1,182	1,178	1,372	2,931	4,535	4,833
Current account transfers	335	380	534	528	586	724	762	846
Capital transfers[a]	204	225	104	167	151	179	198	209
Loans and other financial transactions[b]	349	326	301	443	447	285	275	270
Debt amortization	1,255	871	625	631	734	891	887	898
a) Internal	(899)	(611)	(382)	(396)	(418)	(548)	(532)	(523)
b) External	(356)	(260)	(243)	(235)	(316)	(343)	(355)	(375)

Deficit	-2,243	-962	-1,348	-1,508	-785	-2,456	-3,802	-3,631
Financing the deficit	2,243	962	1,348	1,508	785	2,456	3,802	3,631
Capital receipts[c]	212	191	339	392	375	415	476	408
Borrowing:	2,003	693	1,006	1,092	559	2,185	3,538	3,601
a) Internal	(1,331)	(62)	(624)	(673)	(77)	(811)	(577)	(213)
b) External	(672)	(631)	(382)	(419)	(482)	(1,374)	(2,961)	(3,388)
Change in reserves[d]	+28	+78	+3	+24	-149	-144	-212	-378

[a]Capital transfers to the National Development Bank.

[b]Employee savings and loan associations.

[c]Sales of property, etc.

[d]Plus sign indicates drawdown of reserves; minus sign indicates increase in reserves.

Source: Technical Planning Secretariat, II Plan Nacional de Desarrollo Económico y Social, Bienio 1967-1968, Annex V, Public Sector (Asunción, August, 1966), Table 6.

TABLE 65

Ratio of Public Sector Investment to the Gross National Product
(In Constant Guaranies, 1961-68)

Year	GNP	Public Sector Investment			Per Cent of GNP
		Internal	External	Total	
		(In Millions of 1962 Guaranies)			
1961	42,754	1,163	377	1,540	3.6
1962	45,189	739	406	1,185	2.6
1963	46,217	921	261	1,182	2.6
1964	47,744	934	244	1,178	2.5
1965	50,869	1,157	215	1,372	2.7
Budgeted 1966	52,864	1,795	1,136	2,931	5.5
Projected 1967	55,862	1,740	2,795	4,535	8.1
1968	59,148	1,695	3,139	4,834	8.2

Source: Technical Planning Secretariat.

(OAS-IDB Mission) received minimum implementation. Basic reforms--such as a proposed new income-tax law and a simplified customs collection procedure--were emasculated or eschewed by the Executive Power. The income-tax bill, as revised by the Paraguayan Government, had to be withdrawn from the legislature because of popular pressure against the amendment to exonerate all government employees (including the military) from the income tax. These groups are exempt from the income tax under existing law. However, the proposal was to broaden the coverage of the income tax, so the government's amendments would have been especially discriminatory in favor of its civil and military employees.

The ratio of public sector investment to the GNP is very low in Paraguay, as shown in Table 65. The estimated doubling of the rate of investment in 1966 over that of 1965 and the projected continued rise in the investment ratio in 1967 and 1968 were to be financed primarily from increased public indebtedness, particularly to external lending agencies. According to the Technical Planning Secretariat, the financing of public sector expenditures during 1967 and 1968, expressed in constant values of 1962, was to be as shown in Table 66.

TABLE 66

Estimated Sources of Financing of Public Sector Investment, 1967 and 1968
(In Per Cent)

Sources of Financing	Government[a]		Public Enterprises	
	1967	1968	1967	1968
Internal	87	80	32	36
External	13	20	68	64
TOTAL	100	100	100	100

[a]Includes Central Government, decentralized agencies, and municipalities.

In its review of the Paraguayan economy in 1966, the Subcommittee of the Inter-American Committee on the Alliance for Progress (commonly known by its Spanish abbreviation, CIAP) reported that increasing public sector activity is required in the nation's development effort and that because of the need to raise the level of public investment, it is urgently required that current government revenues be raised accordingly, so that the programs contained in the national plan could be implemented and external funds be used more efficiently. These external funds have been used too slowly because matching local funds have been inadequate for stipulated uses. The Subcommittee unanimously was of the opinion that, if no rapid solution were found to Paraguay's fiscal problems, public sector investment and the use of foreign loans would be seriously affected. Moreover, without an immediate increase in its revenues, neither could Paraguay meet certain current high priority development expenditures, as in education and agriculture. The Subcommittee therefore recommended that the Government of Paraguay face up to a basic integral tax reform program, including reform of the income tax and sales and consumption taxes, and including an upward valuation of real estate for purposes of levying the property tax.[1]

Through an inter-agency agreement with the U.S. Internal Revenue Service, concluded in 1965, the USAID has been attempting to assist the Ministry of Finance in improving its income and property tax administration. A tightening-up of customs valuations was instituted in July, 1966, and a joint United Nations-USAID project enabled the Ministry to revise its fiscal accounting and control systems in 1967. An Inter-American Development Bank mission visited Paraguay in November, 1966, to consider the prospects for a basic tax reform program for the country in return for the IDB becoming the government's Financial Agent for negotiating external loans. The program was still under review in early 1967, including a loan package to be offered as an incentive for undertaking such reforms.

The elements of a comprehensive fiscal program will need to encompass (a) a widespread public relations effort to explain the tax system and revenue requirements of the government; (b) steps to control the contraband trade so that honest citizens are not placed at an economic disadvantage; (c) improved education at all levels to inculcate the ideas of civics and the obligations of a responsible citizenry; and (d) continued external technical assistance, combined with programmed external financing over a suitable but defined period in exchange for the preparation, enactment, and implementation of adequate fiscal reforms on the part of the Paraguayan Government. Such a period might cover ten or fifteen years and probably would require initially large external financing of local costs of capital projects, with the proportion tapering off as reforms were implemented.

CENTRAL GOVERNMENT FINANCES

The weakness of the Central Government's financial position derives from numerous factors. For one thing, the Executive Power, under the 1940 Constitution, has the exclusive right to initiate legislation concerning the general budget, estimates of revenues and expenditures, and monetary matters. Because of the failure to recognize the imperatives of socio-economic development and the concern with meeting the daily pressures of claimants for public funds, there has emerged a very distorted Central Government expenditure pattern, as will be seen below.

As a consequence of the foregoing situation, there has been little top-level communication between the Ministry of Finance and the Technical Planning Secretariat. The only points of coincidence between the budget and the plan have been with respect to those ongoing public works projects which the Technical Planning Secretariat automatically has incorporated into the national plans. Thus, the relationship between budgeting and planning has been the obverse of what it should have been: The plan has followed the budget rather than the budget having followed the plan.

Expenditures for the military establishment have been quite high in relation to the total Central Administration budget. Also, a well developed contraband trade has seriously reduced the government's revenues from customs collections and exchange surtaxes. Added to this situation has been the excessive liberation from customs duties resulting from political preferment, special concessions to the clergy and other institutions, and special privileges accorded to the military and various government officials.

On top of all the foregoing abuses must be added poor public administration, i.e., the failure to collect taxes due, inefficient tax collection and auditing procedures, and an inadequate tax structure for providing the government savings needed for accelerated economic development. The Technical Planning Secretariat has accused the government of "the absence of a global view of socio-economic development."[2] Thus, those autonomous agencies that have been created to carry out certain sectoral development functions, have operated without reference to the Central Government (except for certain transfer-payments) and have failed to provide a harmoniously functioning institutional basis for development.

A tendency in recent years toward strengthening the autonomy of the decentralized agencies has resulted in the adoption of diverse sectoral policies that, while providing satisfactory services in some instances, nevertheless have inhibited the satisfactory over-all coordination of public sector activities and the allocation of its resources. For example, while certain autonomous agencies have been operating profitably and have been increasing their investments, other such agencies have suffered chronic deficits and have had to be bailed out by Central Government subsidies.

The net effects of the virtual absence of a fiscal policy for development have been (a) a slowdown of ongoing projects; (b) chronic arrears in payments of debt service obligations to the United States, the Inter-American Development Bank, and other international lenders; and (c) the curtailment of credit to the private sector to offset the deficit financing of the public sector. If Paraguay is to reach the stage of self-sustained economic growth, it must begin at once the task of fiscal reform. It cannot and should not count indefinitely on the availability of surplus U.S. wheat to provide required local currency financing, nor on IMF Standby Arrangements to hold the floodgates of inflation in check in perpetuity.

The most serious threat to the Paraguayan economy is the fiscal irresponsibility of the Central Government. If this remains unchecked, the hard-won monetary and fiscal stability that has prevailed since 1960, and the increasing dynamism of the private sector in Paraguay, might be halted and then reversed because of runaway inflation, a shortage or investment funds, and growing government economic controls that inevitably would result from such conditions.

The Organic Budget Law

The Organic Budget Law (Law No. 845) of September 14, 1962, was prepared with the assistance of technicians of the United Nations Economic Commission for Latin America (ECLA). For the first time in Paraguayan history, provision was made for the presentation of a current account (operating) and a capital (investment) budget. Although the fiscal year is legally established as running from January 1 through December 31, in practice the budgets have been delayed in preparation so that, when passed, they have covered only ten-month periods (March-December). The first two months of the fiscal year have been covered by the "continuing resolution" method, so well known in the United States. A genuine effort was made to enact the 1967 budget on time; it covered the full year.

The General Budget of the Nation is presented to the unicameral legislature (House of Representatives) together with a budget message from the President. The General Budget is comprised of four parts: (a) the text of an annual budget law; (b) the government's budget, divided into that of the Central Administration and that of the "decentralized" or "autarchic" agencies;* (c) the budget of the public enterprises; and (d) an annex detailing the positions and salaries of personnel employed by the government. However, the legislature deals with and enacts only the budget of the Central Administration; the other budgets, also presented in current and capital form, are approved by Executive Decree through the Ministry of Finance. The Ministry may intervene in the functions of any of these agencies for the purpose of controlling its fiscal operations. Paraguay thus far has avoided the pitfall of requiring the presentation of a balanced budget each year, a practice which has proved so fruitless in other Latin American countries.

The importance of the decentralized agencies in the fiscal operations of the public sector is shown in Table 67 for the year 1965.

Thus the decentralized agencies, municipalities, and public enterprises together accounted for about 38 per cent of the public sector's aggregate revenues and expenditures in 1965. Also, on balance, the decentralized agencies and public enterprises produced an operating surplus of ₲ 1.4 billion, compared with a cash deficit of ₲ 319 million for the Central Government. The results of the operations of the decentralized agencies and public enterprises in 1965 are summarized in Table 68.

---

*The "autarchic" agencies are defined as (a) social security institutes, (b) economic development institutions, (c) autonomous educational institutions, and (d) public enterprises charged with the production and/or sale of goods and services in the market.

TABLE 67

Distribution of Public Sector Revenues and Expenditures, 1965

(In Millions of Guaranies)

	Revenues	Per Cent	Expenditures	Per Cent
Central Government	5,710	54	6,029	64
Decentralized agencies[a]	4,559	43	3,138	33
Municipalities	293	3	289	3
TOTAL	10,562	100	9,456	100

[a]Including public enterprises.

TABLE 68

Revenues[a] and Expenditures[b] of the Decentralized Agencies and Public Enterprises, by Economic Activity, 1965
(In Millions of Guaranies)

	Revenue	Expenditures
Social security agencies	1,270	831
Development:	1,473	379
National Development Bank	1,361	221
Rural Welfare Institute	97	117
Agricultural Credit Bank (CAH)	8	24
Capital Road Board	7	10
Office of Road Boards	---	4
Housing and Urbanization Institute	---	3
Public Enterprises:	1,816	1,779
Office of Transportation and Telecommunications	---	1
State Merchant Fleet	212	216
National Telecommunications Administration (ANTELCO)	254	200
Asunción Sanitary Works Corporation (CORPOSANA)	192	128
Paraguayan Alcohol Administration (APAL)	310	288
Office of the Port of the Capital	145	100
Lineas Aereas Paraguayas (LAP)	67	77
National Civil Airport Administration	20	14
Lineas Aereas de Transporte Nacional (LATN)	16	12
President Carlos Antonio López Railway	109	149
National Electricity Administration (ANDE)	491	594
Education (National University of Asunción)	---	149
TOTAL	4,559	3,138

[a]Excluding subsidies and borrowings.

[b]Net of debt amortization, interest payment, loans made, and increases in capital.

Source: Ministry of Finance

Fiscal Operations of the Central Administration

The Central Government's revenues are derived from two categories of income: (a) ordinary revenues, consisting principally of tax revenues, fines, and sales of public property; and (b) special-law revenues, derived chiefly from the exchange surcharges on imports (64.3 per cent in 1966) and from the proceeds of the National Lottery. Ordinary revenues are used to operate the administrative machinery of the government and to service the public debt. The special-law funds are allocated to various departments and autonomous agencies to be used mainly for financing capital development projects and other types of capital outlays (e.g., malaria control, health clinics, school construction). Such funds have been the main source of domestic financing for the capital budget. At times, however, these funds also have been used to liquidate portions of the floating debt. Revenues and expenditures under the special laws are supposed to balance (and often do) and therefore do not affect the size of the government deficit.

A program budget has been employed by the Ministry of Finance since 1963. This budget identifies the social and capital projects to be financed in the fiscal year and provides a brief description of their financing. Most of these projects are financed through the special laws, which serve to earmark certain revenues for specific purposes. For example, a decree-law issued in March, 1964, imposed a new tax on the exploitation of forests by private firms. The yield from this tax was to be transferred to the Rural Welfare Institute (IBR) to help finance the development of forestry and other IBR activities. While the earmarking of funds generally is considered to be unsound budget practice, nevertheless it has served to assure Paraguay's contribution to certain priority projects receiving external financial assistance.

Revenues

The bulk of Central Government revenues is derived from taxes, as shown in Table 69. During the years 1960-65, taxes accounted for between 90 per cent and 96 per cent of total Central Government revenues from both ordinary and special-law sources. The statistics shown in this discussion are to be taken as illustrative rather than definitive, as data published by the Central Bank, the Technical Planning Secretariat, the Ministry of Finance, the IMF, and the IBRD differ from each other. The Paraguayan Government's accounting system has been in a chaotic condition. The "official" figures have been changed periodically, without explanation, and reconciliation of data is extremely difficult because the collection of the information has been so poor.

As shown in Table 70, two thirds of the Central Government's tax revenues during 1960-65 have been derived from indirect taxes, and only one third from direct taxes. Moreover, when all import and export taxes and charges are taken into account, together they have provided over 60 per cent of government revenues during this period.[3] Such taxes have included customs duties on imports and exports, consular fees, exchange surcharges on imports and exports, and various internal taxes applied to imported commodities, especially fuels and alcohol. Thus the revenue of the Government of Paraguay, under the existing tax structure, has been highly vulnerable to economic, physical, and/or political impediments to the movement of Paraguay's foreign trade, the bulk of which passes on the Paraguay River.

Revenues obtained by virtue of special laws have constituted a substantial but diminishing share of total Central Government revenues. The shares of special-law revenues to total Central Government revenues during 1960-66, are shown in Table 71.

TABLE 69

Ratio of Taxes to Total Central Government Revenues, 1960-65

Year	Total Taxes	Total Revenues	Ratio of Taxes to Revenues
	(In Millions of Guaranies)		(In Per Cent)
1960	2,964	3,234	92
1961	3,347	3,480	96
1962	3,973	4,161	95
1963	3,784	4,220	90
1964	4,029	4,375	92
1965[a]	5,319	5,710	93

[a]During 1966, income and real property tax revenues rose substantially because of greater efforts on the part of the Ministry of Finance to collect delinquent taxes. Moreover, in the case of the real property tax, valuations of rural properties were increased during the year. During the first ten months of the year, the increases amounted to 17 per cent in income taxes and 13 per cent in real property taxes.

TABLE 70

Total Taxes Collected, 1960-65
(In Millions of Guaranies)

	1960	1961	1962	1963	1964	1965
Direct Taxes						
Foreign Trade:	380.7	344.0	373.6	331.6	272.9	325.2
Export duties	24.3	28.5	33.1	40.8	43.5	47.8
Foreign exchange charge on exports	356.4	315.5	340.5	290.8	229.4	277.4
Other Direct Taxes:	612.2	677.7	881.0	951.5	1,058.1	1,339.5
Inheritance, legacies, and donations	21.5	20.4	24.1	30.0	47.8	21.3
Contracts	6.6	10.3	11.4	11.4	12.8	29.3
Cattle and hides	32.2	26.5	104.7	103.1	98.5	268.5
Industrial production	0	41.9	25.5	21.9	51.7	24.8
Income	308.3	304.5	406.3	432.1	428.5	515.2
Real property	154.4	172.1	177.0	187.2	222.5	250.4
Social security	89.2	102.2	132.0	165.8	196.3	230.0
Total Direct Taxes[a]	992.8	1,021.7	1,254.6	1,283.2	1,331.0	1,664.8
Per Cent of Total Taxes	33.5	30.5	31.6	33.9	33.0	31.3

Indirect Taxes						
Foreign Trade:	1,053.1	1,263.3	1,599.0	1,391.2	1,574.1	2,164.7
Import duties	593.7	672.4	826.0	858.5	833.4	1,060.2
Exchange surcharge on imports	303.4	434.6	585.4	291.7	558.3	860.7
Consular fees	156.0	156.3	187.6	241.0	182.4	243.8
Other Indirect Taxes:	918.1	1,061.6	1,119.1	1,109.2	1,123.7	1,490.0
Commercial stamps	188.2	224.6	263.5	273.5	300.0	498.0
Admissions	5.7	6.2	6.7	6.9	7.6	7.5
Tobacco and matches	146.3	157.9	168.1	169.2	175.1	183.6
Alcohol	123.4	143.9	106.3	169.8	109.5	146.4
Gasoline and fuel oil	144.6	180.8	160.4	148.0	179.1	177.2
Sales	307.3	345.3	406.4	340.2	351.5	470.6
Various	2.6	2.9	7.7	1.6	0.9	6.7
Total Indirect Taxes[a]	1,971.2	2,325.0	2,718.2	2,500.6	2,697.7	3,654.6
Per Cent of Total Taxes	66.5	69.5	68.4	66.1	67.0	68.7
Total Taxes Collected[a]	2,964.0	3,346.8	3,972.7	3,783.7	4,028.7	5,319.4

[a]Totals may not add because of rounding.

Source: Ministry of Finance.

TABLE 71

Composition of Central Government Revenues, 1960-66
(In Millions of *Guaranies*)

Year	Ordinary Revenues	Special-Law Revenues	Total Revenues	Per Cent Special-Law Revenues of Total
1960	2,637	597	3,234	18.5
1961	2,843	637	3,480	18.3
1962	3,425	736	4,161	17.7
1963	3,497	723	4,220	17.1
1964	3,658	717	4,375	16.4
1965	4,786	924	5,710	16.2
1966	5,223	994	6,217	16.0

Source: Ministry of Finance.

The Tax System--Responsibility for tax collections in Paraguay is distributed mainly among four departments in the Ministry of Finance (Internal Taxes, Customs, Real Property Tax, and Income Tax); the Central Bank of Paraguay (exchange surcharges); the State alcohol monopoly (APAL); and the Rural Welfare Institute (IBR). The taxes collected by each collecting entity are as follows:

(1) Office of Internal Taxes

This office administers a wide variety of tax laws, including ordinary revenues and certain special-law funds. The major taxes coming under its jurisdiction are:

a) The Sales Tax, originating in 1952; the current law dates from 1957 (Decree-Law No. 130). The law applies to imported products and to national products leaving the factory; it also applies to every transfer of automotive vehicles. The rates range from 2 per cent to 10 per cent on national products, and from 5 per cent to 10 per cent on imported products. Exempted from this tax are imported equipment, machinery, parts, raw materials, and containers used in the manufacture of national products taxed by this law; the sale of national or imported items that are subject to the Consumption Tax; and also, live animals, wheat, wheat flour, serums and vaccines for veterinary use, agricultural instruments and tools, fertilizers, roadbuilding machinery, ships for the State Merchant Fleet, etc.

b) The Consumption Tax, originating in 1947; the present law dates from January 12, 1952 (Decree-Law No. 5). This tax applies to the manufacture, importation, exportation, circulation, or sale of merchandise, and is levied in addition to customs tariffs and other laws regulating the production and trade of these consumption items. The principal items taxed under this law are tobacco products, alcohols and beverages (alcoholic, carbonated, fruit juices, and raw materials), matches, and playing cards. Exports of national products are exempted from this tax.

c) The Stamp Tax, levied by Decree-Law No. 23 of 1952, applies to documents, contracts and obligations of a civil nature, papers submitted to government agencies, and other legal documents. Both fixed and proportional taxes are applied, depending on the nature of the document. The fixed tax ranges from ₲ 1 to ₲ 2,000 and the proportional tax from 3 per cent to 10 per cent.

d) Alcohol Taxes are subject to laws and decrees too numerous to enumerate. The basic law, however, is that of March 11, 1941 (Decree-Law No. 5,599), that established the system of producing, circulating, selling, and utilizing alcohols and alcoholic beverages, and fixed the taxes thereon. Alcoholic and carbonated beverages, beer, liqueurs, fruit wines, denatured and rectified alcohols, etc., are subject to this tax. On imported products, the tax is collected at the customs; on national products, the tax on Paraguayan rum and on rectified and denatured alcohol is collected by the state alcohol monopoly (APAL), while the tax on other items is collected directly by the Office of Internal Taxes. Theoretically, APAL is to turn its tax collections over to this Office every fortnight, but this has not happened since 1947.

The tax rates on imported products range between ₲ 6 and ₲ 100 per taxable unit, whereas the rates on national products are only ₲ 0.30 to ₲ 10 per unit for most items. However, the tax on Paraguayan rum (cana) is 35 per cent ad valorem, and on rectified alcohol, 75 per cent ad valorem. Such high taxes have led to substantial illicit production of these products.

Law No. 244 of October 26, 1954, which created the Asunción Sanitary Works Corporation (Corporacion de Obras Sanitarias de Asunción--CORPOSANA), established an additional 5 per cent tax (effective January 1, 1955) on the consumption of alcoholic and non-alcoholic beverages, the proceeds to be used for capitalizing CORPOSANA.

e) A Fiscal Patents (Patentes Fiscales) tax is paid annually by those juridical persons whose business activities are covered by Decree-Law No. 5,599 or are specifically mentioned as business or property owners in this law. The fiscal patents taxes are basic or fixed, depending upon whether levied on specific products or on types of businesses (manufacturing, importing, exporting, etc.).

f) Livestock Taxes, imposed initially by Decree-Law No. 11 of December 22, 1953, have been modified many times. Such taxes currently are levied on the transfer, slaughter, and exportation of livestock; on cattle hides; and on meatpacking establishments. Decree-Law No. 322 of March 31, 1962, established a tax,"in substitution for the income tax," of ₲ 200 per head of cattle slaughtered by the meatpackers. These taxes were discussed in Chapter 3.

g) Consular Fees are standard sources of income for most countries. They are fees collected by consuls stationed abroad for processing various documents and giving them legal status in the home country of the consul. Consular fees also are collected within the national territory for validating documents to be used abroad. The fees are uniform for all Paraguayan consulates, and are expressed in U.S. dollars.

h) Inheritance, Legacy, and Gift Taxes are governed by various laws passed between 1953 and 1963. The tax rates vary from 2 per cent to 50 per cent, according to the size of the inheritance, legacy, or gift, and the degree of relationship. Amounts less than ₲ 10,000 are exempt from these taxes.

i) The Tax on Gasoline and Other Fuels was levied initially by Decree-Law No. 59 of February 5, 1953. Since that time, additional taxes have been levied on these products. The proceeds of these taxes have been earmarked for various

TABLE 72

Retail Prices of Petroleum Products, as of June 30, 1966[a]

Product	Retail Price	Including Taxes		Ratio of Taxes to Retail Price
		Import Duty	Other Taxes	
	(In U.S. Cents Per Gallon)			(Per Cent)
Gasoline:				
Standard grade (80/90 octane)	45.0	4.4	16.1	45.5
Aviation grade (100/170 octane)	43.5	2.8	13.3	37.0
Kerosene:				
Standard grade	34.5	1.5	7.2	25.2
Motor lubricating oils:				
Grade 30	240.0	23.1	28.5	21.5

[a]These prices had been in effect since January 3, 1964.

purposes, such as school construction, public works, construction of the Military College and Ministry of Defense buildings, and construction of the Trans-Chaco Road. Retail prices and taxes on gasoline, kerosene, and motor lubricating oils, as of June 30, 1966, are given in Table 72.

j) A Military Service Tax (Decree-Law No. 68 of 1955) applies to all citizens legally exempted from military service.* The proceeds are earmarked to finance the needs of the Office of Recruitment and Mobilization. The tax is collected by the Office of Internal Taxes within the country, and by Paraguay's consuls from nationals living abroad. The tax is ₲ 200 a year for eight consecutive years for persons under twenty-six years of age; or if the person is older than twenty-six years and less than forty-five, he must pay ₲ 300 a year for eight consecutive years. The amounts due may be paid in lump sum if desired.

k) A Tax on Industrial Production, Decree-Law No. 322 of March 31, 1962, was levied on various industrial activities "in substitution for the income tax." As mentioned under f), above, the industrialization of cattle was made subject to a tax of ₲ 200 per head. In addition, taxes of ₲ 50 per log for internal consumption or export; ₲ 80 for each 200 kilos of cotton fiber for internal consumption or export; and ₲ 200 per metric ton of *quebracho* extract exported, were levied. These substitute taxes were imposed with a view to obtaining greater revenue yields from these economic activities in this direct manner; it had not proved possible to apply the income tax effectively in these fields.

(2) Office of Income Tax

This office is responsible for the administration of the income-tax law (Decree-Law No. 9,240 of December 29, 1949). This law applies to profits earned in Paraguay by physical or juridical

---

*In general, those who can afford to pay the tax are "legally exempted."

persons carrying out gainful economic activities in the country. In addition to the original law, there have been sixteen laws and decrees issued that are in effect. The present income-tax rate is quite low, ranging from 5 per cent to a maximum of 25 per cent on taxable income over ₲ 100,000. In practice, the tax is actually applied to business profits. Agricultural pursuits, government employees, professional persons (doctors, lawyers, etc.), retired and pensioned persons, and dependent workers are exempt from the income tax. By a law of 1959, certain economic activities in the interior of the country also are exonerated from payment of the income tax. Such activities are watchmaking and jewelry establishments; makers of men's and women's clothing; shoemaking; flower shops; barber shops; etc.

Law No. 1,171 of August 12, 1966, modified the income-tax law. It expanded the coverage of the law to foreign transportation companies (land, sea, and air) serving Paraguay. Such companies are now presumed to have a minimum taxable income of at least 10 per cent of the value of freight and passenger traffic booked in Paraguay. Insurance companies operating in this country also are brought under the income-tax law by Law No. 1,171. These companies are presumed to have a taxable income of no less than 6 per cent of the value of premiums collected net of cancellations. Besides the income-tax rates applicable under Law No. 9,240, Law No. 1,171 imposes 1.5 per cent additional tax on the value of premiums, net of cancellations, to be collected on the value of the policies at the time of their issuance. This additional tax is to be paid by the insured.

(3) <u>Office of Real Estate Tax</u>

The basic real property tax was instituted by Decree-Law No. 51 of December 24, 1952. The rate of tax is 0.10 per cent of the official valuation of the property (re-assessed every five years), or on the amount indicated by the Executive Power with the approval of the National Economic Coordination Council. The latter valuation may take into account such factors as the encouragement of agricultural, livestock, and forest development, the promotion of immigration and colonization, and other special factors. Additional taxes are supposed to be levied on unused or semi-idle lands in the capital area and around major cities.* However, the collecting office hasn't the means to implement the law.

Taxes also are imposed for street improvements. In suburban and rural areas the rates are between 0.10 per cent and 0.30 per cent, and for urban areas, from 0.20 per cent to 0.40 per cent.

Large rural landholdings are subject to an additional progressive tax, levied on each ₲ 1,000 of valuation (including improvements). For eastern Paraguay, the rates range from 0.03 per cent on tracts of 5,000 hectares or more, to 0.20 per cent on tracts over 200,000 hectares. For western Paraguay, the minimum rate applies to tracts of 18,750 hectares or more, and the maximum rate to tracts over 300,000 hectares.

(4) Office of the Customs

The basic customs tariff on imports and exports is Law No. 667 of September 27, 1924, as amended. Since 1957, the tariff duties have been computed in U.S. dollars as a means of eliminating the effects of any currency devaluation.

The import tariff consists of 1,239 taxable paragraphs, most of which carry specific duties. In addition to the duty-free list, the tariff law applies three groups of rates: (a) conditional duties, used chiefly for revenue purposes, which may be specific or ad valorem; (b) ad valorem duties only; and (c) mixed rates (specific and ad valorem). Decree No. 19,360 of 1943 established an

---

*On unused lands, 0.05 per cent to 0.30 per cent; on semi-idle lands, 0.05 per cent to 0.20 per cent.

additional duty of 15 per cent ad valorem on most imported merchandise; and those items exempted from the 1943 tax were made subject to an additional tax of 5 per cent by Article 2 of Decree-Law No. 151 of September 26, 1952. The incidence of the specific duties in terms of the per cent of the declared value of imports varies between 0.01 per cent and 19.0 per cent, and the additional duties between 5 per cent and 15 per cent. The average effective import tax rate (including both specific and ad valorem duties) approximates 40 per cent for the majority of imported items.[4]

Export duties in general are of the ad valorem type and are established on the basis of appraisals by the Central Bank and on sworn declarations. These specific duties on exports range between ₲ 1 and ₲ 200 per taxable unit, whereas the ad valorem duties amount to between 1 per cent and 2 per cent.

As a member of the Latin American Free Trade Association (LAFTA) since 1961, Paraguay has applied a policy of successive reductions in import duties on items coming from other LAFTA countries. The objective is to eliminate such taxes completely by the end of twelve years.

The magnitude of contraband activities in Paraguay and their long quasi-social and political acceptance in the country requires a special word on this subject. The contraband system appears to be well directed and controlled and relatively unmolested by the government.

Three broad categories of contraband may be distinguished:

(a) Contraband that is principally, although not exclusively, of the in-transit variety. This type covers whiskey, cigarettes, and other light consumer goods that are smuggled into the country from visiting vessels and small aircraft. Many local dealers, truckers, boatmen, and warehousemen derive their livelihood from this activity. While the quality of such imports undoubtedly is superior to products that might be produced locally, such tax-free imports probably tend to inhibit the growth and/or improvement of local manufactures and promote competitive tax evasion on the part of local producers. What is required is a shift in employment from contraband activities to legitimate productive enterprises that would satisfy local demands and also produce revenues for the government.

(b) Contraband in textiles from Brazil and Argentina. This contraband has flourished especially during the rising phases of periodic inflationary surges in Brazil and Argentina. Exporters in these countries during such periods unwittingly have sold their goods to Paraguayans below production costs. Such imports at times have benefited Paraguayan consumers and, in addition, have provided a competitive incentive to improve textile production in Paraguay. The growth of complementarity in this industry within the LAFTA should serve to eliminate this type of contraband.

Brazilian coffee at various times may have been smuggled into Paraguay for re-export to world markets. This happened when export taxes of coffee in Brazil became more onerous than those in Paraguay. At such times the Paraguayan Treasury collected the export taxes on such re-exports.* Conceivably the system could have been reversible, as in the case of live cattle movements across the frontier, depending upon relative prices in Brazil and Paraguay.

(c) The third type of contraband is the so-called ant trade, carried on at the retail level

---

*Paraguayan producers have instituted measures to eliminate this smuggling.

TABLE 73

Exchange Surcharges on Imports, in Effect as of December 31, 1966

Enactment	Date	Tax Rate	Purpose
Resolution 1, Act 25	February 16, 1959	5 per cent	2.5 per cent general revenues of the Treasury. 2.5 per cent for public works, especially feeds roads.
Resolution 3, Act 122	July 31, 1959	5 per cent	Originally for construction of the Trans-Chaco Road; in December, 1961, changed to financing asphalting of Paraguay's Encarnación Road and construction of a bridge across the Tebicuary River. Later, to finance the State railway.
Resolution 1, Act 54	April 8, 1960	5 per cent	Originally to pay the government's floating debt; later changed to capitalize the National Development Bank.

Resolution 2, Act 149	September 16, 1960	5 per cent	Finance the purchase of ships for the State Merchant Fleet.
Resolution 1, Act 88	June 28, 1961	4 per cent	General revenues of the Treasury.
Resolution 20, Act 154	November 9, 1964	4 per cent	General revenues of the Treasury.
Resolution 1, Act 20	February 2, 1965	2 per cent	1.5 per cent for financing the National Development Bank's contribution to the AID--financed ($3 million) agricultural credit project; and 0.5 per cent to finance Lineas Aereas Paraguayas S.A. (LAPSA)
Resolution 1, Act 153	September 22, 1966	2 per cent	Ø 800,000 per month to finance LAPSA and the remainder to go to general revenues of the Treasury.

Source: Central Bank of Paraguay.

by women and other small traders in border areas. Goods move overtly both ways in this trade. The "contraband" aspect, or failure to pay customs duties and charges, arises from the extremely difficult problem of administration involved in controlling so many individuals in their daily activities. Undoubtedly this trade is advantageous to the population on both sides of the border. As is often the case, such neighboring populations are in closer economic relationships than the respective areas with their own capital cities.

The control of the contraband trade would require a huge investment in policing facilities or a sensible restructuring of Paraguay's tax system (e.g., the elimination of exchange surcharges) that would eliminate the profitability of contraband. The former alternative is made difficult because of the government's poor fiscal condition and other considerations. The latter alternative must form part of an over-all tax reform program, which the Central Government thus far has not faced seriously.

(5) Central Bank of Paraguay

A series of Central Bank resolutions, beginning in 1957, have created numerous so-called exchange surcharges which really are additional taxes on the CIF value of imports. These exchange surcharges often have been the means of assuring urgently required government income and/or counterpart contributions to externally financed capital projects. The list of exchange surcharges on imports in effect as of December 31, 1966, was as given in Table 73. The total amounted to 32 per cent.

The surcharges in Table 73 generally have not applied to imports from bordering countries and from Uruguay. Usually, imports of petroleum fuels and wheat also have been exempted. A special exchange surcharge of 5 per cent (Resolution 2, Act 122, of September 14) was levied in 1961 on the importation (from any source) of radio receivers, record players, and parts and accessories therefor, the proceeds to be used for financing the enlargement of the government's radio station, Radio Nacional del Paraguay. A special set of exchange surcharges, shown in Table 74, applies to imports from neighboring countries and Uruguay.

Export taxes collected by the Office of the Customs are authorized by the Tariff Law of 1924, as modified by Decree No. 383 of March 15, 1940. The proceeds from the export tax on cattle hides are used for retiring the "Gold Bonds" issued to finance the Chaco War. In 1965, these proceeds amounted to ₲ 1.8 million. Other items subject to export tax are cotton, tobacco, _petitgrain_ oil, _quebracho_ extract, lumber, live cattle, and unspecified articles. Such taxes amounted to ₲ 46 million in 1965. The taxes are mixed, including both specific and ad valorem components, and they vary with each product. In general, the trend has been toward reducing these taxes, with a view to their eventual disappearance.

A second set of export taxes is levied by the Central Bank. A Resolution No. 6 of July 12, 1957, passed by the National Economic Coordination Council, authorized the Central Bank to make modifications in the exchange system according to the Economic and Financial Stabilization Program that was approved by that same resolution. Accordingly, by Central Bank Resolution 2, Act 142, of August 9, 1957, a "temporary" exchange surcharge of 15 per cent was imposed on an ascribed F.O.B. value of exports. By Article 14 of this resolution, the tax was to be reduced monthly, beginning January 1, 1959, until it was abolished completely by the end of that year. However, this provision still has not been complied with completely. Reductions in the rates have been made from time to time and the list of duty-free items has been expanded. Nevertheless, the rates currently in force on the remaining items range between 2.5 per cent and 7.5 per cent.

The third type of export taxes is that levied "in substitution for the income tax." Decree-Law No. 322 of March 31, 1962, applies such taxes to

TABLE 74

Exchange Surcharges Applicable to LAFTA Countries

Enactment	Date	Rate	Purpose
Resolution 2, Act 8	January 12, 1962	5 per cent	General revenues of the Treasury.
Resolution 1, Act 136	October 2, 1964	10 per cent[a]	General revenues of the Treasury.
Resolution 1, Act 136	October 2, 1964	24 per cent[b]	General revenues of the Treasury

[a]Applicable to imports of petroleum fuels.

[b]Applicable to all imports from these areas except petroleum fuels, wheat, and products included in the National Lists of the LAFTA.

established exporters of lumber, cotton fiber, and *quebracho* extract. The taxes are ₲ 50 per log or board, ₲ 80 per each 200 kilos of cotton fiber, and ₲ 200 per metric ton of *quebracho* extract exported.

Occasional exporters (i.e., those not having an established place of business) are subject to Law No. 879 of July 17, 1963. These taxes are applicable to exporters of raw materials, agricultural products, forestry products, and industrial commodities. The taxable profit of this type of exporter originally was presumed to be 8 per cent of the ascribed (*aforo*) value of exports. However, by Law No. 1,171 of August 12, 1966, the imputed profit rate was lowered to 4 per cent. For established exporters (except those covered by other laws),* the imputed profit rate under Law No. 1,171 is 10 per cent of the ascribed value of exports. The ascribed rates, set by the Central Bank for exchange purposes, are also to be used by the Ministry of Finance for tax purposes. Revenues from this third type of export taxes amounted to ₲ 9.9 million in 1965.

(6) Rural Welfare Institute

The Rural Welfare Institute (IBR) is authorized to collect the taxes levied on the exploitation of forests by virtue of Decree-Law No. 370 of 1964. The proceeds of this tax are earmarked for the forest products promotion activities of the IBR. This agency has about seventy persons on its payroll just to collect these taxes. The IBR derives about 30 per cent of its revenues from this tax, about 50 per cent from land sales, and the remainder from the Central Government.

---

*Exporters of processed meat, processed lumber, *quebracho* extract, cotton fiber, vegetable oils, sugar, and fresh and frozen meat are exempted from Law No. 1,171. Products of the meatpacking industry are covered mainly by Law No. 1,083 of 1965.

Expenditures

The following analysis of Central Government expenditures is divided into current account expenditures and capital account expenditures. Together these make up total Central Government outlays. This discussion is followed by the 1966 Capital Budget, and a summary of Central Government fiscal operations, 1960-66.

Current Account Expenditures--Current account expenditures include two groups of outlays. One group consists of administrative expenditures and the other group, of financial expenditures (servicing of the public debt, payment of pensions and retirement, transfers of funds to autonomous agencies, and payments for water, light, fuel, and telephone). Small amounts of special-law funds at times have been used for current outlays, although their primary use is for investment. At various times the Central Government also has borrowed from the Central Bank and even from abroad to finance its current financial requirements. As shown in Table 75, payments of current expenditures exceeded the amounts budgeted for these purposes in four of the six years (1960-65) under review, and were notably in excess of the budget during the past two years.

Whereas in previous years (1960-62) comfortable budget surpluses on current account were compatible with payments in excess of those budgeted, from 1963 on substantial current account deficits were incurred by such action, as shown in Table 76. In part, these deficits were produced by (a) larger payments on floating debt than had been contemplated in the budget; (b) increases in wholesale prices at faster rates than the growth of revenues in certain years;* (c) the establishment of new government offices and expansion of the activities of existing ones to meet the growing needs of the country; and

---

*According to the Central Bank, wholesale prices rose 12.8 per cent in 1961; 4.7 per cent in 1962; 2.5 per cent in 1963; 3.7 per cent in 1964; and 9.0 per cent in 1965.

TABLE 75

Budgeted and Paid Current Expenditures, 1960-65
(In Millions of *Guaranies*)

	1960	1961	1962	1963	1964	1965
Budgeted	2,730	2,933	3,339	4,240	4,090	4,493
Paid	2,760	2,997	3,266	4,074	4,344	5,131
Ratio of payments to budget	101	102	98	96	106	114

TABLE 76

Current Account Revenues and Expenditures of the Central Government, 1960-65
(In Millions of *Guaranies*)

	1960	1961	1962	1963	1964	1965
Revenues	2,883	3,012	3,641	3,794	3,893	5,005
Expenditures	2,760	2,997	3,266	4,074	4,344	5,131
Surplus (+) or deficit (-)	+ 123	+ 15	+ 375	- 280	- 451	- 126

(d) increases in salaries of government employees averaging 5 per cent a year during 1960-65.

To assist in financing its current account deficits and part of its capital investment requirements, the government issued bonds in the amount of ₲ 300 million in 1963, ₲ 402 million in 1964, and ₲ 344 million in 1965. These bonds were acquired by the Central Bank, which thus far has been the sole market for government securities in Paraguay.

Apart from the inadequacy of revenues already discussed above, major causes of the Central Government's deficits have been its heavy outlays for public debt servicing, national defense, and education (see Table 77). While outlays for education are substantially below national needs, it is questionable whether a country such as Paraguay needs to spend about one fifth of its budget for national defense (the percentage is greater if the police are included in defense outlays). Estimates of the civic action component of defense outlays range approximately between 15 per cent and 35 per cent. If the latter proportion were taken, defense outlays (exclusive of police) would still have amounted to about 12 per cent of the Central Administration's outlays in 1965.

The Central Government's expenditure budget alone, however, gives a very misleading picture of the sectoral activities of the Paraguayan Government. A truer picture is obtained when the operations of the decentralized agencies are added to those of the Central Government. Combined expenditures, by type of activity, for the year 1965, were approximately as shown in Table 78.

The 1966 budget showed that, excluding the Ministry of Defense, the Central Administration would employ 29,258 persons and the payroll would amount to ₲ 1.8 billion, or approximately 27 per cent of total budgeted outlays for the year. As at least 75 per cent of the military budget is believed to go for salaries, the total wage bill of the Central Government would appear to have approximated 40 per cent of its expenditures.

TABLE 77

Central Government Expenditures (Excluding Foreign Borrowings) by Selected Ministries, 1960-65

Ministry	1960	1961	1962	1963	1964	1965
	(In Per Cent of Total Outlays)					
National Defense	20	19	18	19	19	19
Interior[a]	9	8	9	9	10	9
Education and Culture	13	13	13	15	16	14
Public Works and Communications	11	9	9	7	7	6
Finance[b]	28	36	38	36	35	39
Public Health and Social Welfare	6	6	5	5	5	5
Agriculture and Livestock	3	2	2	2	2	2
Foreign Relations	4	3	3	3	2	2
All Others	6	4	3	4	4	4
TOTAL	100	100	100	100	100	100

[a]Includes the police.

[b]Includes service on the public debt, transfers of capital to domestic and foreign credit institutions, and payment of retirement and pension funds.

Source: Ministry of Finance.

TABLE 78

Public Sector Outlays, by Economic Activity, 1965
(In Millions of Guaranies)

Activity	Central Government[a]	Decentralized Agencies	Total	Per Cent of Total
Social security	---	831	831	9
Agriculture and industry	128	650[b]	778	8
Transportation	---	583[c]	952	10
Telecommunications	---	200	200	2
Health and sanitation	261	128	389	4
Electric power	---	594	594	6
Education	838	149	987	11
Housing	---	3	3	--
Defense and police	1,617	---	1,617	18
All other	2,816	---	2,816	32
TOTAL	6,029	3,138	9,167	100

[a]Ordinary and special-law funds.

[b]Includes the National Development Bank, Rural Welfare Institute, Agricultural Credit Bank, and the Paraguayan Alcohol Administration.

[c]Includes the Capital Road Board, Office of Road Boards, Office of Transportation and Telecommunications, State Merchant Fleet, Office of the Port of the Capital, Lineas Aereas Paraguayas, National Civil Airport Administration, Lineas Aereas de Transporte Nacional, and the Presidente Carlos Antonio López Railway.

Capital Account Expenditures--The Central Government's capital outlays during the years 1960-65 have been as shown in Table 79.

As Table 79 indicates, the Central Government's relative contribution to its investment program has varied markedly during the years studied, having ranged from 53 per cent in 1964 to 89 per cent in 1961. The ratio in 1965 approximated 73 per cent. The sources of foreign investment in the public sector have been as shown in Table 80.

The composition of domestic investments of the Central Government, 1960-65, is shown in Table 81. The preponderance of transportation (especially roads and ships) and the National Development Bank in these expenditures is noticed in all the years shown. In the more recent years, observable increases have been made in investments for school construction and seed improvement, and investments in a National Technological and Standards Institute (as an adjunct of the Ministry of Industry and Commerce) have been made in 1964 and 1965. An apparent sharp rise in Central Government outlays for public buildings took place in 1965, principally for the construction of a new building for the Ministry of Public Works and Communications (MOPC) and the amortization of debt for previous constructions. However, the steepness of this rise is misleading, as a detailed breakdown of the MOPC's investment became available only in 1965. In prior years, similar construction outlays often were included in "roads."

The investments shown for "mining" pertain to the MOPC's operations of stone quarries at Tacumbú and Ñemby. The former always have been owned by the government; however, the quarries at Ñemby formerly were in private hands but were expropriated by the government in August, 1961.[5] The stone from Tacumbú reportedly is used for road construction projects in the Asunción area, while that from Ñemby is exported to Argentina as triturated stone (187,032 metric tons valued at ₲ 23.1 million in 1965). Here, too, it is probable that investments for prior years were included in "roads."

TABLE 79

Central Government Capital Outlays, 1960-65
(In Millions of Guaranies)

Year	Total	Internally Financed	Per Cent	Externally Financed	Per Cent
1960	515.5	396.2	76.9	119.3	23.1
1961	622.8	551.9	88.6	70.9	11.4
1962	1,162.0	658.9	56.7	503.1	43.3
1963	738.1	426.5	57.8	311.6	42.2
1964	913.4	438.2	52.9	430.2	47.1
1965	898.5	658.8	73.3	239.7	26.7

TABLE 80

Sources of Foreign Investment in the Public Sector, 1960-65
(In Millions of *Guaranies*)

Year	DLF/AID	IDB	IDA	P.L. 480	Total
1960	119.3	---	---	---	119.3
1961	70.9	---	---	---	70.9
1962	248.3	27.2	6.2	221.4	503.1
1963	250.5	5.3	12.8	43.0	311.1
1964	301.7	---	4.6	123.9	430.2
1965	92.5	6.0	85.7	55.5	239.7

TABLE 81

Capital Investments of the Central Government, 1960-65
(In Millions of Guaranies)

Field of Investment	1960	1961	1962	1963	1964	1965
Administrative Functions	2.4	1.9	7.2	8.1	10.0	13.4
Banking:	76.8	196.6	325.3	152.0	186.5	191.0
Transfers to National Development Bank	--	121.5	184.4	148.7	177.8	161.2
Contributions to International Lending Agencies	76.8	75.1	140.9	3.3	8.7	29.8
Transportation:	421.1	400.4	780.5	559.0	658.3	621.8
Transfer to National Merchant Fleet	23.2	83.6	83.7	70.6	88.0	132.4
Roads	397.9	316.2	696.2	485.4	570.3	466.0
Ports (studies)	--	0.6	0.6	--	--	0.1
Asunción Airport (repairs)	--	--	--	3.0	--	10.4
Airstrip construction	--	--	--	--	--	1.0
Transfer to Lineas Aereas Paraguayas (LAP)	--	--	--	--	--	11.9

Agriculture:	--	--	28.2	6.4	1.7	3.0
Colonization (Puerto Pte. Stroessner)	--	--	27.2	5.3	--	--
Seed improvement	--	--	1.0	1.1	1.7	3.0
Education:	9.6	16.3	11.1	12.0	28.9	32.0
School construction	9.6	13.3	10.8	12.0	28.1	29.3
Other construction	--	3.0	0.3	--	0.8	2.7
Public Buildings (construction and maintenance)	5.6	7.5	9.7	0.6	0.7	11.7
Health (studies of sanitary facilities)	--	0.1	--	--	--	--
Industry:						
National Technological and Standards Institute	--	--	--	--	7.3	6.1
Mining	--	--	--	--	20.0	17.8
TOTAL	515.5	622.8	1,162.0	738.1	913.4	898.5
INDEX	100	121	225	143	177	174

Source: Ministry of Finance.

TABLE 82

Budgeted Capital Outlays of the Central Government, 1966
(In Thousands of Guaranies)

FINANCED WITH OWN FUNDS			
Transmitting equipment for Radio Nacional (partial cost)		87,234	
Capital transfers to autonomous agencies:			
To IPVU	24,331		
To CORPOSANA	12,220		
To LAP	13,560		
To State Merchant Fleet	126,000		
To National Development Bank	148,200		
To NDB, for AID agricultural credit program	39,600	363,911	
Road and bridge construction and maintenance:			
Asphalting road to Encarnación and construction of bridge			63,000
Maintenance of the highway network			88,000
Asphalting of Coronel Oviedo-Villarrica Road			29,000
Design road to Valle-mí			500
Construction of San Ignacio-Pilar Road			2,210
Construction of access road and bridge over the Acaray River			11,935
Construction of bridges over the Aquidaban, Ñeembucú, and Acaray-mí rivers			7,555
Asphalting of the Paraguarí-Piribebuy Road			5,000
Asphalting road to the Cavalary Division			2,000

Maintenance of dirt, stone, and asphalted roads		29,000
Maintenance of the airstrip (at Asunción Airport)		4,000
Advance payment of debts for road works		10,000[a]
Various projects		1,000
Amortization of Central Bank loan for asphalting road from Botanical Gardens to Benjamín Aceval		24,000[a]
Road construction by the Command of Engineers:		12,000
Villabín-Laureles	2,000	
Pozo Colorado-General Díaz	2,000	
Coronel Oviedo-Route V	4,000	
Mbutuy-Curuguaty	4,000	
Payment of debt to the Central Bank for road and bridge const.	6,800[a]	296,000
Purchases:		
Cessna plane	630[a]	
Quarry at Nemby	3,100	
Roadbuilding equipment	7,793	11,523
Construction projects:		
School buildings	21,766	
Building for MOPC	3,000	
Completion of health center in the interior	3,000	27,766
Conservation:		
Public buildings	6,800	
School buildings	14,234	21,034

TABLE 82 (Continued)

Contribution to operating funds of National Technological and Standards Institute		10,800
Ministry of Defense projects:		
Construction of Military School (bonds)	75,000	
Road maintenance	3,000	
Construction materials, machinery, vehicles, furniture, tools, office equipment, communications equipment, etc. Magnetrometric study	33,821	
Construction and repair of vessels; maintenance of vessels and other items	11,775	
Water supply systems	520	
Dredging and ballast	2,360	126,476
Subtotal		944,744
FINANCED WITH FUNDS FROM ABROAD		
From P.L. 480 funds		
Road construction:		
Itacurubí-Valenzuela and San Pedro-Nueva Germania	2,000	
Itacurubí-San Estanislao-Coronel Oviedo	2,000	
Coronel Oviedo-Route V-Curuguaty	13,000	
Coronel Oviedo-Cecilio Baez	350	
Coronel Oviedo-Route V	30,000	47,350

Conservation of equipment and training of personnel for road maintenance		4,000
Feasibility studies:		
Road from Coronel Oviedo-Route V; Mbutuy-Caraguatay-Salto Guairá	3,000	
New airstrip at Asunción Airport	1,512	4,512
Subtotal		55,862
From DLF/AID funds		
Road maintenance, Coronel Oviedo-Presidente Stroessner		12,350
From IDA funds		
Construction of road and bridges from Paraguarí to Encarnación:		
Asphalt paving	156,000	
Bridge over Tebicuary River	43,940	
Purchase of roadbuilding equipment	61,100	
Project supervision	11,544	272,584
GRAND TOTAL		1,285,540

[a]These payments are considered as legitimate capital outlays because the projects which created the debts had not been entered in the accounts at the time they were carried out.

The 1966 Capital Budget--The Central Government's capital budget for calendar year 1966 was shown as amounting to 1,572 million *guaranies*. However, if items erroneously included in the capital budget are excluded, budgeted capital outlays would be reduced to 1,285 million *guaranies* or 22.1 per cent of the total budget. Of this amount, 73.5 per cent was to come from internal sources and 26.5 per cent from abroad. The major projects, by source of financing, are shown in Table 82. Excluded are such noncapital outlays as the malaria eradication project; amortization of internal and external public debt; ferry service provided across the Tebicuary River; ferry services provided by the Ministry of Defense; and maintenance of certain transportation equipment.

Total Central Government Fiscal Operations, 1960-65--Expenditures of the Central Government during the years 1960-65 increased much more rapidly than its revenues, with the result that chronic substantial deficits have been produced each year. Between 1960 and 1965, current outlays increased 86 per cent as compared with 74 per cent for capital expenditures, as shown in Table 83. Capital outlays during this period, except in 1962, averaged only 16 per cent of total Central Government expenditures. In 1962, however, because of heavy foreign borrowings, the ratio exceeded 24 per cent. From 1962 on, drawings on external credits and on government reserves constituted important elements of public sector financing. The size of the annual deficit during 1960-65 and the sources of its financing are shown in Table 84.

During the years 1960-65, both revenues and expenditures of the Central Government appear to have risen faster than the Gross National Product, as shown in Table 85. While the GNP rose nearly 25 per cent, the revenue growth exceeded 37 per cent, all expressed in terms of constant values of 1962. Nevertheless, the proportions of revenues and expenditures to GNP have been lower in Paraguay than in virtually all other countries in Latin America. Moreover, inasmuch as the GNP statistics for Paraguay may be understated by some 10 per cent to 20 per cent, the ratios shown in Table 85 would be even lower than

TABLE 83

Central Government Expenditures, 1960-65
(In Millions of Guaranies)

	1960	1961	1962	1963	1964	1965
Current Expenditures	2,760.3	2,996.9	3,626.5	4,073.8	4,344.0	5,130.5
Ordinary funds	2,539.5	2,765.9	3,276.6	3,485.3	3,639.8	4,743.0
Special-law funds	220.8	191.6	198.8	231.7	203.8	187.6
Use of reserves or Central Bank borrowings	---	39.4	151.1	351.0	490.4	199.9
Foreign borrowings	---	---	---	5.8	10.0	---
Capital Expenditures	515.5	622.8	1,162.0	738.1	913.4	898.5
Ordinary funds	79.2	77.0	148.1	11.4	18.7	43.2
Special-law funds	317.0	474.9	510.8	415.1	464.5	615.6
Foreign borrowings	119.3	70.9	503.1	311.6	430.2	239.7
TOTAL	3,275.8	3,619.7	4,788.5	4,811.9	5,257.4	6,029.0
(In U.S. $1 million)	(26.0)	(28.7)	(38.0)	(38.2)	(41.7)	(47.8)
Ratio of capital expenditures to total outlays	15.7%	17.2%	24.3%	15.3%	17.4%	14.9%

TABLE 84

The Central Government Deficit and Its Financing, 1960-65
(In Millions of *Guaranies*)

Year	Fiscal Deficit	Sources of Deficit Financing	
		Internal	External
1960	42.1	+77.2[a]	119.3
1961	140.1	69.2	70.9
1962	628.2	125.1	503.1
1963	592.5	275.1	317.4
1964	881.5	441.3	440.2
1965	318.6	78.9	239.7

[a]Net repayment of internal debt.

TABLE 85

Relationship of Central Government Revenues and Expenditures to the Gross National Product, 1960-65 (In Millions of Constant Dollar Equivalents of 1962)

Year	GNP	Revenues	Expenditures	Per Cent of GNP	
				Revenues	Expenditures
1960	324	30.0	30.1	9.3	9.3
1961	339	27.5	31.2	8.1	9.2
1962	359	33.0	38.1	9.2	10.6
1963	367	32.5	37.1	8.9	10.1
1964	379	32.4	39.0	8.5	10.3
1965	404	39.1	41.2	9.7	10.2
Increase, 1960-65	24.7%	30.3%	36.9%	...	...

reported. It would appear that even at the present level of economic development Paraguay could support at least a 50 per cent increase in Central Government revenues over that of 1965.

In real terms, Central Government revenues during the years 1960-65 showed a slight upward trend. Annual fluctuations resulted chiefly from changes in economic activity in the country, from the introduction of a few additional taxes, from some tax rate increases, and from certain improvements in tax administration. The government has not attempted to evoke a rational budget policy, and revenue measures have consisted in the main of increasing traditional taxes (on imports and gasoline). Consequently, the tax structure has remained inadequate to provide for the mounting requirements of economic growth.

Notes to Chapter 12

1. Sub-Comite del CIAP Sobre Paraguay: Conclusiones y Recommendaciones, September 30, 1966 (six pages, hectographed). See also Organization of American States, Department of Economic Affairs, Reforma Tributaria en Paraguay (UP/G.15/4; June 21, 1966), a report of the joint OAS/IDB tax team that visited Paraguay during the period October, 1963, to June, 1965.

2. "...la ausencia de una visión de conjunto del desarrollo económico-social," II Plan Nacional de Desarrollo Económico y Social, Bienio 1967/68, Annexo V, Sector Publico (Asunción, August, 1966), p. 1.

3. Ibid., Table 11.

4. Organization of American States, Department of Economic Affairs, Reforma Tributaria en Paraguay (UP/G.15/4; June 21, 1966), p. 54.

5. Law No. 740 of August 31, 1961.

CHAPTER 13 PUBLIC DEBT

As in the case of the national accounts, data on the public debt also are incomplete. The principal element missing is the amount of public floating debt outstanding, known to be a sizable figure. Thus, this discussion of public debt necessarily is incomplete with respect to the internal public debt.

The outstanding known public sector debt of Paraguay at the end of 1965 amounted to ₲ 16,952 million (U.S. $134.5 million) and consisted of the following components, in millions of <u>guaranies</u>:

Internal:	
To Central Bank	5,519
Obligated but unpaid accounts, December 31, 1965	219[a]
External	11,214[b]
TOTAL	16,952

[a]The cumulative amount of this floating debt is unknown.

[b]Equivalent to U.S. $89.0 million.

This partial public sector debt represented some 125 per cent of current public sector revenues and about 102 per cent of total public sector expenditures in 1965. In the same year this debt amounted to as much as 30 per cent of the Gross Domestic Product. Because of a relatively favorable debt structure at this time, amortization payments accounted for only 11 per cent of public sector revenues and 9 per cent of its expenditures in 1965;

TABLE 86

Ratios of Public Debt Amortization Payments to Public Sector Revenues, Expenditures, and the Gross Domestic Product, 1961-65

Year	Ratio of Amortization Payments to:		
	Public Sector Revenues[a]	Public Sector Expenditures	Gross Domestic Product
	(In Per Cent, Based on Constant Values of 1962)		
1961	28	19	2.9
1962	16	14	1.9
1963	12	9	1.4
1964	11	9	1.3
1965	11	9	1.4

[a]The ratios of internal and external debt amortization to revenues were as follows, in percentages:

Year	Internal	External
1961	20	8
1962	11	5
1963	7	5
1964	7	4
1965	6	5

Source: Technical Planning Secretariat, II Plan Nacional de Desarrollo Economico y Social, Bienio 1967-1968, Annexo V, Sector Publico (Asunción, August, 1966), Tables 1, 2, and 3, following p.32.

these payments represented somewhat more than 1 per cent of the Gross Domestic Product, as shown in Table 86. Paraguay's immediate problem is not so much the servicing of the public debt--although payment on portions of its external debt are in arrears --but of providing the matching local currency funds to utilize the available external resources.

INTERNAL PUBLIC DEBT

Paraguay's total internal public debt is not known. However, data are available on the public sector's debt to the Central Bank of Paraguay. These data, for the years 1955-66, are shown in Table 87. Whereas the Central Government accounted for only about 15 per cent of the public debt owed to the Central Bank in 1955, the percentage had more than doubled a decade later. A similar rate of increase occurred in the indebtedness of the autonomous agencies to the Bank. Certain details of the outstanding public sector debt to the Central Bank are available for the years 1962 and 1963 and are shown in Table 88.

As shown in Table 89, the Central Government has relied very heavily on bond sales to the Central Bank for financing its internal indebtedness. From 1961 to date, these bonds have been utilized for converting and unifying internal debt, cancelling floating debt, financing construction of a military academy building, financing fiscal deficits. Prior to 1961, the bonded indebtedness represented almost entirely consolidated internal debt. (Information on the bonded debt no longer is published by the Central Bank.) In addition to bond issues, the Central Government also has received substantial amounts of short-term advances from the Central Bank. While such advances generally are made on a seasonal basis and are supposed to be cancelled within the fiscal year, sizable carry-overs have resulted in the period under review. Besides the Treasury's bonded indebtedness to the Central Bank and the arrears of the Ministry of Finance in repaying the short-term advances of the Central Bank,

TABLE 87

Outstanding Public Sector Debt to the Central Bank of Paraguay, 1955-66
(In Millions of *Guaranies*)

End of Year	Central Government[a]	Autonomous Agencies[b]	Ex-Bank of Paraguay[c]	National Development Bank	Total
1955	273.4	195.5	1,357.4	---	1,826.3
1956	425.1	257.5	1,593.8	---	2,276.4
1957	568.5	325.5	1,702.1	---	2,596.1
1958	631.2	310.5	1,719.5	---	2,661.2
1959	706.2	418.2	1,738.2	---	2,862.6
1960	767.7	620.7	1,787.9	---	3,176.3
1961	876.2	794.4	1,890.3	20.5	3,581.4
1962	1,055.5	906.6	1,885.4	39.2	3,886.7
1963	1,335.0	1,156.2	1,900.1	39.0	4,430.3
1964	3,776.2	1,257.8	1,950.7	118.8	5,103.5
1965	1,929.0	1,277.4	1,991.1	321.1	5,518.6
1966	2,052.6	1,363.9	2,027.0	556.6	6,000.1

[a]Includes bonded indebtedness.

[b]Including municipalities.

[c]Superseded by the National Development Bank in December, 1961.

Source: Central Bank of Paraguay.

TABLE 88

Public Sector Debt to the Central Bank of Paraguay, 1962 and 1963
(In Millions of Guaranies)

Creditor	1962	1963
Ministry of Finance	493.6	797.2
National Treasury (bonds)	561.9	537.8
Subtotal	1,055.5	1,335.0
Municipalities	4.6	4.8
Autonomous State Agencies	902.0	1,151.4
Agricultural Credit Bank	140.0	140.0
State Merchant Fleet	413.2	526.2
Sanitation Corporation	164.8	216.6
Others	184.0	268.6
Credit Institutions	1,924.6	1,939.1
TOTAL	3,886.7	4,430.3

Source: Central Bank of Paraguay, Memoria--1963, p. 45.

TABLE 89

Treasury Debt to the Central Bank on Behalf of the Central Government: Balances Outstanding at End of Year, 1962-65
(In Millions of *Guaranies*)

	1962	1963	1964	1965
Bonds	561.9	537.8	1,180.6	1,532.7
Short-term advances to the Ministry of Finance	351.3	794.8	526.5	295.3
Loans to other government agencies	--	--	62.4	26.3
Payment of diplomats' salaries	8.8	1.4	1.8	1.6
Payment of contribution to the IDB Special Fund	103.3	--	--	27.1[a]
NDB: Counterpart to IDA cattle loan	--	--	--	31.2
Interest due on loans, and miscellaneous	30.2	1.1	4.7	14.7
TOTAL	1,055.5	1,335.0	1,776.2	1,929.0

[a]Also, ₲ 54.5 million was contributed as letters of credit and is not shown in this amount.

there also have been large annual carry-overs of obligated but unpaid accounts which, during 1962-65, averaged ₲ 229.4 million a year.

The Treasury also has incurred substantial indebtedness to the Central Bank, on behalf of the municipalities and autonomous agencies, as shown in Table 90. The principal Treasury debts have been incurred on behalf of the State Merchant Fleet, the Asunción Sanitary Corporation (CORPOSANA), the Agricultural Credit Bank, and Paraguayan Airlines (LAP).

EXTERNAL PUBLIC DEBT

Paraguay's public external debt has been rising rapidly in recent years, as shown in Table 91. Between 1960 and June 30, 1966, this debt rose from $31.8 million to $120.2 million, an increase of 278 per cent. Fortunately, the country has had a favorable external debt structure: The average length of maturities on the outstanding debt is between fifteen and twenty years; grace periods average about five years; and the average interest rate on outstanding loans is about 4.5 per cent. Also, approximately one third of the outstanding foreign debt is repayable in local currency (and about two thirds in foreign exchange). Any significant departure from this pattern could generate an unmanageable debt service burden and adversely affect Paraguay's creditworthiness. The structure of the public external debt outstanding on June 30, 1966, was as shown in Table 92. Less than one half of the loans authorized had been disbursed as of that date.

The rise in external public debt since 1960 has corresponded with an increasing dependence upon external resources for financing investments by public enterprises in development projects (e.g., ANDE, ANTELCO, CORPOSANA, National Development Bank). Thus, as shown in Table 92, some 73 per cent of the total external debt outstanding on June 30, 1966, was accounted for by State enterprises and financial institutions; only 27 per cent

TABLE 90

Treasury Debt to the Central Bank on Behalf of the Autonomous Agencies:
Balances Outstanding at End of Year, 1962-65
(In Millions of *Guaranies*)

Agency	1962	1963	1964	1965
Municipalities	4.6	4.8	6.7	6.8
Agricultural Credit Bank (CAH)	140.0	140.0	140.0	140.0
Rural Welfare Institute (IBR)	0.9	0.9	0.8	0.8
National Electricity Institute (ANDE)	58.4	46.4	34.4	--
National Telecommunications Administration (ANTELCO)	17.1	10.7	4.0	--
Valle-Mí Cement Plant	6.7	6.7	6.7	6.7
National Airline (LATN)	5.6	3.9	2.6	18.8[a]

Alcohol Monopoly (APAL)	5.0	35.0	--	--
Paraguayan Meat Corporation (COPACAR)	38.5	17.8	40.0	32.9
Sanitation Corporation (CORPOSANA)	164.8	216.6	265.9	299.1
Carlos Antonio López Railway (FCAL)	--	4.6	4.6	4.6
Administrative Commission, Puerto Presidente Stroessner	4.0	4.0	4.0	4.0
Paraguayan Airlines (LAP)	--	89.8	108.2	125.8
State Merchant Fleet (FLOMERE)	413.2	475.0	533.4	542.0
Military Air Transport Service (TAM)	0.7	--	--	--
Trolley Line Administration (ATE)	--	--	--	1.1
Other Government Agencies	15.1	73.7	78.2	94.8
Interest on loans, etc.	32.0	26.3	28.3	--
TOTAL	906.6	1,156.2	1,257.8	1,277.4

[a]Includes ¢ 17.5 million for the purchase of airplanes.

Source: Central Bank of Paraguay.

TABLE 91

Public External Debt Outstanding, 1960-66[a]
(In Millions of U.S. Dollars)

Payable in Foreign Exchange	1960	1961	1962	1963	1964	1965	June 30, 1966
Central Government	7.2	15.7	14.7	13.6	12.8	16.3	18.9
Autonomous Institutions	15.5	14.9	13.4	21.3	28.1	30.7	49.6
Central Bank of Paraguay	4.9	3.3	1.5	3.3	5.3	4.1	11.8
Subtotal	27.6	33.9	29.6	38.2	46.2	51.1	80.3
Payable in Guaranies or Foreign Exchange							
Central Government	3.2	9.7	9.7	10.5	8.9	10.8	10.8
Autonomous Institutions	1.0	4.4	4.4	8.4	22.1	27.1	27.1
Subtotal	4.2	14.1	14.1	18.9	31.0	37.9	37.9
TOTAL	31.8	48.0	43.7	58.1	77.2	89.0	120.2[b]

[a]Including disbursed and undisbursed portions.

[b]Total includes a loan by the Crédit Lyonnais of Paris to the National Development Bank, in an amount equivalent to $2.0 million, for financing crude oil imports of the Refineria Paraguaya S.A. This loan is repayable in French francs.

TABLE 92

Structure of the Public External Debt Outstanding, as of June 30, 1966
(In Thousands of U.S. Dollars)

	Disbursed	Undisbursed	Total
Central Government	20,108	12,553	32,661
Autonomous Institutions	33,002	42,639	75,641
Central Bank of Paraguay	3,368	8,482	11,850
TOTAL	56,478	63,674	120,152

Source: Central Bank of Paraguay, "Deuda Externa, Ejecución de Préstamos Amortizaciones e Intereses Pagados y Saldos al 30 de Junio de 1966" (Single sheet; October, 1966).

of the external loans to the public sector had been made to the Central Government. The utilization of external loans to the public sector during 1961-65 has been shown in Table 93.

In spite of the sharp rise in external indebtedness on the part of Paraguay's public sector, the ratio of external financing to public sector outlays, in constant values of 1962, declines from 8 per cent in 1961 to 3 per cent in 1965; conversely, domestic resources (including internal borrowing) financed 92 per cent of public sector expenditures in 1961 and 97 per cent in 1965, as shown in Table 94.

The principal reason for this anomaly is that in spite of greatly increased contractual external indebtedness, the utilization of foreign credits has been declining because of the public sector's inability to provide the necessary local currency counterpart funds. Thus, for example, the public sector's investment program for 1965, as programmed in the first national plan (for 1965-66), was fulfilled to only 58.2 per cent of the projected amount. While bad weather, slow deliveries of equipment, and other causes affected the situation, an important consideration also was the lack of budgeted funds for executing the contemplated projects.

In addition, the Paraguayan Government's arrears on loans due the United States Government delayed the signature of already authorized loan agreements and could, if unresolved, result in a curtailment of disbursements on existing loans. The amount of payments arrears due to the United States Government on December 31, 1966, aggregated ₲ 98 million, equivalent to about U.S. $800,000. Of these arrears, ₲ 46 million represented interest due and ₲ 31 million represented past-due amortization of principal. On December 29, 1966, the Council of State authorized a special bond issue to pay these arrears.

Experience has shown that that portion of the public debt for which the Central Bank is responsible has been serviced promptly. However, the debt for

TABLE 93

Utilization of External Loans to the Public Sector, 1961-65
(In Thousands of U.S. Dollars)

	1961	1962	1963	1964	1965
Central Government	563	3,460	2,477	2,736	1,381
Decentralized Agencies	---	216	42	44	133
Public Enterprises	4,312	631	244	773	1,791
Financial Institutions	---	1,235	1,584	1,429	5,395
Municipalities	---	---	---	---	---
TOTAL	4,875	5,542	4,347	4,982	8,700

Source: Technical Planning Secretariat.

TABLE 94

Ratios of External and Internal Financing to Total Public Sector Outlays, 1961-65
(In Per Cent, Based on Constant Values of 1962)

Year	Total Outlays	Internally Financed	Externally[a] Financed
1961	100	92	8
1962	100	92	8
1963	100	95	5
1964	100	96	4
1965	100	97	3

[a]Including grants.

which the Ministry of Finance is responsible has been continually in arrears and, as in the case of debts due certain private companies, has required strong diplomatic representations for sporadic settlement to be achieved. The Minister of Finance at times has failed to include adequate provision for debt service in the national budget. For example, in the 1966 budget, provision for repayment of ₲ 666.5 million of external debt was made, compared with a requirement of ₲ 981.3 million.* Also, even when provision has been made in the budget for debt service payments, part of the funds at times has been diverted to other uses. Thus the creditworthiness of the Central Government appears to be inferior to that of the autonomous State institutions.

Payments of amortization and interest on the external debt during 1961-65 are shown in Table 95. Together they have averaged the equivalent of $3.7 million a year during this period, or about 8 per cent of the average value of exports as reported in the balance of payments statistics (see Chapter 15). The indicated service on the external public debt outstanding as of December 31, 1965 ($89.0 million), during the years 1966-70, has been calculated by the Central Bank as shown in Table 96. This table indicated a continued favorable debt position from the balance of payments viewpoint in that, within slightly declining over-all debt service payments, the proportion payable in local currency was calculated to increase from 32 per cent in 1966 to 63 per cent in 1970. Moreover, a larger share of the servicing would pertain to the autonomous State agencies rather than to the Central Government.

The composition of external loans to Paraguay from the Act of Bogotá (September, 1960) through

---

*Amount of debt servicing requirement estimated by the Central Bank of Paraguay. The Technical Planning Secretariat estimated ₲ 952.4 million.

June 30, 1966, is shown in Table 97. The Inter-American Development Bank (IDB) supplied some 40 per cent of these credits, the World Bank (IBRD and IDA) about 25 per cent, and AID 21 per cent. The remaining loans came from private foreign banks abroad and were for the purposes of industrial development and short-term export financing.

As previously mentioned, the Central Government's ability to provide internal financing to projects having external loan components has been far short of requirements. Moreover, the trend in debt service payments appears to call for rising local currency outlays, and the loans to the public sector projected for the next several years appear to be mainly to the Central Government which already is in arrears to the United States Government and smaller external creditors. Even if new external loans could be provided on the same favorable terms as in the past, it still would appear to be desirable to slow the rate of foreign lending until the Central Government has taken the self-help measures required to increase domestic savings materially, raise its foreign reserves to more comfortable levels, and bring its debt service payments to a current basis.

The Inter-American Development Bank has been negotiating with the Government of Paraguay to become its financial agent with respect to foreign borrowings. It is to be hoped that the IDB, together with the U.S. Government, will be sufficiently forceful in its views to bring about meaningful fiscal reforms (both administrative and structural) in Paraguay. As previously discussed, such reforms have been urged not only by the foregoing lenders, but by the CIAP, IA-ECOSOC, World Bank, and the United Nations. Presumably, positive steps toward such reforms could result in augmented external assistance programs. The Central Government, within that time, would have to create an Economic Development Fund of at least ₲ 800 million (U.S. $6.35 million), in addition to paying its past-due interest and

TABLE 95

Amortization and Interest Payments on the Public External Debt, 1961-65
(In Thousands of U.S. Dollars)

Amortization	1961	1962	1963	1964	1965
Central Government	942	1,081	1,042	1,112	496
Decentralized Agencies	---	---	28	14	28
Public Enterprises	1,664	988	941	866	1,035
Financial Institutions	---	---	60	366	489
TOTAL	2,606	2,069	2,071	2,358	2,048
Interest					
Central Government	210	210	382	514	477
Decentralized Agencies	---	2	7	4	7
Public Enterprises	879	963	987	834	1,060
Financial Institutions	87	23	88	175	215
TOTAL	1,176	1,198	1,464	1,527	1,759
Total Service Payments	3,782	3,267	3,535	3,885	3,807

Source: Technical Planning Secretariat, II Plan Nacional de Desarrollo Economico y Social, Bienio 1967/68 (Asunción, August, 1966), Appendix table, unnumbered.

TABLE 96

Calculated Debt Service, 1966-70, on Public External Debt Outstanding on December 31, 1965
(In Thousands of U.S. Dollars)

	1966	1967	1968	1969	1970
Payable in foreign exchange	3,875	3,472	3,329	3,110	1,886
Central Government	535	313	280	274	274
Central Bank	184	172	162	---	---
Autonomous State Agencies	3,156	2,987	2,887	2,836	1,612
Payable in *guaranies* or optionally in *guaranies* or foreign exchange	1,837	2,139	2,304	2,538	3,181
Central Government	813	783	803	822	840
Autonomous State Agencies	1,024	1,356	1,501	1,716	2,341
Total Service Payments	5,712	5,611	5,633	5,648	5,067

Source: Central Bank of Paraguay.

TABLE 97

Loans to Paraguay, by Sector, September, 1960 (Act of Bogotá), through June 30, 1966
(In Millions of U.S. Dollars)

Economic Sector	IDB	IBRD	IDA	AID[a]	OTHER	TOTAL
Agriculture and livestock	2.9	--	11.1	4.2	--	18.2
Industry	6.8	--	--	--	3.8	10.6
Transportation and communication	--	4.3	6.0	13.9	6.1	30.3
Electric power	14.2	--	--	--	--	14.2
Education	1.5	--	--	--	--	1.5
Housing	3.4	--	--	--	--	3.4
Colonization	1.7	--	--	--	--	1.7
Other	3.5[b]	--	--	--	2.0[c]	5.5
TOTAL	34.0	4.3	17.1	18.1	11.9	85.4

[a]Includes P.L. 480.

[b]To National Development Bank for "general development" and for feasibility studies.

[c]Export financing by private foreign banks abroad.

principal on existing loans and providing local-cost financing for ongoing projects. Unless the President of Paraguay authorized sweeping fiscal reforms, it is improbable that such a sum could be accumulated by the government within the specified period.

CHAPTER 14 MONEY AND BANKING

THE BANKING SYSTEM

The Paraguayan banking system comprises two government-owned banks, the Central Bank and the National Development Bank, and eight commercial banks. In general, the banking system is oriented toward the financing of foreign trade transactions. Only the National Development Bank and its predecessor, the Bank of Paraguay, have taken a relatively active role in development financing.

The Central Bank of Paraguay was established in 1952 when it was separated from the State-owned Bank of Paraguay, which combined both commercial and central banking functions. It has a five-man Board of Directors, one of whom is its President; all are appointed by the government. A Superintendency of Banks is part of the Central Bank, responsible directly to the Board of Directors.

The National Development Bank (NDB) also emerged from and succeeded the Bank of Paraguay, which was placed in liquidation in 1961. The NDB has a President and an Administrative Board of seven directors, all appointed by the government. However, three of these board members are representatives of the private sector. The NDB is organized into independent Development, Commercial, and Agricultural Departments, and operates both as a development and a commercial bank. The Bank, with head offices in Asunción, operates about forty branches and agencies throughout the country. These provide most of the banking services available in the interior.

Of the eight private commercial banks (i.e., not owned by the Paraguayan Government), three are branches of foreign private banks;* three are branches of foreign state banks;** and two are local private banks.*** Four of these banks, including the two Paraguayan institutions, opened during the period 1961-65. The capital and reserves of the commercial banks, shown in Table 98, increased nearly fivefold between 1960 and 1966. The rise was due mainly to the increase in capitalization of the National Development Bank. By 1963, the NDB accounted for 55 per cent of the capital and reserves of the commercial banks. Since then, the private commercial banks' resources have increased at a more rapid rate than the NDB's, so that by the end of 1966, the NDB's share of total commercial bank capital and reserves had declined to 48 per cent.

THE COMMERCIAL BANKS

The Banking Law (Decree-Law No. 20 of March 24, 1952) grants to foreign banks established in Paraguay the same rights and privileges as those enjoyed by any Paraguayan bank. All deposit banks operating in the country are subject to Central Bank regulation and are required to maintain, in addition to a minimum capitalization, reserves equivalent to at least 20 per cent of their assets;**** the Governing Board of the Central Bank

---

*The First National City Bank of New York; Bank of London and South America, Ltd; and Banco Holandes Unido.

**Banco Exterior de España; Banco de la Nación Argentina; and Banco de Brasil.

***Banco Paraguayo de Comercio and Banco de Asunción. The latter reportedly has private U.S. and Spanish capital participation as well.

****In addition to the required legal reserves against deposits (Resolution No. 5, Act No. 204 of the Central Bank, dated December 28, 1959).

TABLE 98

Capital and Reserves of the Commercial Banks, 1960-66

(In Millions of Guaranies)

Year	Private Banks	National Development Bank (NDB)	Total	Per Cent NDB
1960	352.6	151.2[a]	503.8	30
1961	480.3	420.3[a]	900.6	47
1962	589.9	611.3	1,201.2	51
1963	708.2	722.0	1,430.2	55
1964	897.6	839.8	1,647.4	51
1965	939.3	999.4	1,938.7	52
1966	1,258.4	1,147.3	2,405.7	48

[a]Bank of Paraguay, prior to December, 1961.

Source: Central Bank of Paraguay

TABLE 99

Interest Rates Established by the Central Bank

Interest Rates Charged[a]	Rate Per Year
Purpose	
Agricultural credits	9 %
Livestock, industrial, and anticipations of export letters of credit	10 %
Commercial credits	12 %
Any credits up to 180 days[b]	12 %
Interest Rates Paid[c]	
Type of Deposit	
Savings	6 %[d]
Fixed time:	
3 months	6½%
6 months	7 %
12 months	8 %

[a]Central Bank Resolution No. 563-Act No. 53 of April 20, 1954.
[b]Central Bank Resolution No. 1-Act No. 84 of May 26, 1960.
[c]Central Bank Resolution No. 2-Act No. 8 of January 14, 1959.
[d]An interest rate of 8 per cent is paid on contractual savings deposits.

may alter this reserve level to a minimum of 15 per cent or to a maximum of 30 per cent.

The Board of Directors of the Central Bank has established the interest rates, shown in Table 99, which the commercial banks may charge for loans and pay on deposits.

Except for the development loans of the National Development Bank, which carry the 9 per cent or 10 per cent interest rate, virtually all credits to the private sector are made at the rate of 12 per cent a year. However, to this rate must be added bank commissions of 3 per cent. Thus the effective interest rate charged comes to some 15 per cent a year. The curb rate of interest is at least 2 per cent a month. The interest rates charged on Central Bank loans to the government or to State agencies vary according to the circumstances but usually range between 4 per cent and 6 per cent per annum.

The three largest private commercial banks in Paraguay are branches of the First National City Bank of New York; the Bank of London and South America, Ltd.; and the Banco Exterior de España. The balance sheets of these institutions for the years 1964 and 1965 are shown in Table 100. These three banks accounted for 45 per cent of the total capital and reserves of the private banks in Paraguay at the end of 1965. While the First National City Bank of New York continued in 1965 to lead in total deposits, its percentage of increase (8 per cent) over the preceding year was smaller than that of its two principal competitors, the Banco Exterior de España (12 per cent) and the Bank of London and South America, Ltd. (15 per cent). The upward trend in savings deposits continued in 1965. Only in the Banco Exterior de España did demand deposits increase more than savings deposits, but even in this bank savings accounts continued to exceed demand deposits. The capital of all three major private banks increased in 1965 over 1964, although the Bank of London's decline in reserves offset the increase in its capital. The First National City Bank continued to be the principal

TABLE 100

Balance Sheets of Principal Commercial Banks, 1964 and 1965
(In Millions of *Guaranies*)

	First National City Bank		Bank of London and South America, Ltd.		Banco Exterior de España	
	1964	1965	1964	1965	1964	1965
DEPOSITS	1,026	1,112	615	706	633	711
of which:						
Demand	507	434	309	315	278	332
Saving	489	644	257	342	343	353
Other	30	34	49	49	12	26
CAPITAL AND RESERVES	104	117	205	205	78	103
of which:						
Capital	75	90	75	100	72	92
EARNING ASSETS	865	849	561	745	511	430
GROSS INCOME	142	144	92	123	84	110
of which:						
Commission	44	50	44	53	41	58
Interest	91	88	39	61	40	48
NET PROFIT	41	39	3	23	20	25
DELINQUENT LOANS	50	41	121	119	4	2
PAYROLL	27	29	41	43	15	17

profit earner in 1965, although the Bank of London showed a marked recovery from its poor showing in 1964.*

The major activity of the Paraguayan banking system has been the financing of commercial transactions for periods of 30, 60, 90, or 180 days. Such financing may include credits to agriculturists and industrialists as well as to merchants but, because of the short-term character of these loans, they all are classified as commercial credits. Credit activities of the banking system, in selected three-year intervals from 1953 through 1965, and in 1966, are shown in Table 101. The difference between the value of credit agreements negotiated and the credit balance outstanding in any particular year depends upon the utilization of these credits and the repayment rate. A sharp rise in loans to the commercial sector in recent years and increasing attention to the industrial and livestock sectors have characterized the period under review. On the other hand, credits for social development and for private construction have been very small throughout the period 1953-66.

The growth of medium-term loans to productive sectors became particularly important after the National Development Bank, which was created in March, 1961, commenced operations in December, 1961. Its main objective is to foster economic development through the promotion and financing of projects and programs considered basic to the national economy. By the end of 1966, the NDB accounted for 48 per cent of the commercial banks' capital and reserves and for 55 per cent of their loans outstanding. However, between 1962 and June 30, 1966, about 20 per cent of the NDB's credit activities were reported to have been of the short-term type, performed by its Commercial Department.

---

*The fourth largest private commercial bank, the Banco de la Nación Argentina, lost ₲ 6 million in 1965, after earning ₲ 2 million in 1964.

TABLE 101

Credit Activities of the Commercial Banks, by Economic Sector, at Three-Year Intervals, 1953-65, and 1966 (In Millions of *Guaranies*)

Economic Sector	1953	1956	1959	1962	1965	1966
	Loans Authorized					
Agriculture	213.3	238.0	205.1	158.0	543.4	421.1
Livestock	127.4	228.4	215.1	488.2	1,268.9	1,439.5
Industry	350.5	869.1	885.6	1,288.7	2,925.6	2,917.3
Commerce	117.6	979.3	807.3	3,276.0	6,882.0	9,001.8
Construction	2.7	13.1	7.1	1.6	147.6	66.1
Social Development[a]	0.6	8.8	4.7	--	--	--
Other	64.1	78.7	129.0	71.0	102.6	134.8
TOTAL	876.2	2,415.4	2,253.9	5,294.6	11,870.1	13,980.6

			Credits Outstanding[b]			
Agriculture	220.6	404.5	602.8	646.9	1,003.9	1,134.0
Livestock	97.7	318.0	271.8	400.4	972.0	1,327.1
Industry	230.4	991.5	1,041.2	1,239.4	2,076.2	2,384.9
Commerce	57.8	198.5	386.6	1,309.2	1,854.4	2,649.9
Construction	28.7	33.9	55.9	64.9	64.1	58.6
Social Development	2.9	12.3	14.4	12.7	10.0	9.6
Other	51.2	259.0	129.7	276.5	266.2	274.9
TOTAL	689.2	2,217.7	2,502.4	3,950.0	6,246.8	7,839.0

[a]No loan agreements signed since 1961.

[b]End-of-year balances.

Source: Central Bank of Paraguay, Boletín Estadístico Mensual, No. 103 (December, 1966), p. 10.

TABLE 102

Annual Change in Commercial Bank Operations, 1960-66[a]
(In Millions of Guaranies)

	1960	1961	1962	1963	1964	1965	1966
Domestic Credit	172	686	213	333	584	490	718
To private sector	103	605	168	188	495	355	465
Other assets and liabilities (net)	69	81	45	145	89	135	253
Financed by:							
Net Central Bank Credit	28	-222	-21	-239	-109	-495	-93
Loans and rediscounts	13	66	13	-22	7	-1	29
Currency and reserves[b]	15	-288	-34	-217	-116	-494	-122
Increase in Deposits	60	605	221	537	590	560	440
Demand deposits	54	382	-58	182	213	71	126
Time and savings deposits	63	211	245	377	369	476	321
Other deposits[c]	-57	12	34	-22	8	13	-7
Increase in Capital	95	128	110	118	99	131	319
Increase in foreign liabilities[d]	-11	175	-97	-83	4	294	52

[a]Excluding the National Development Bank.
[b]Excluding the 100 per cent reserve requirement against payments arrears.
[c]Including prepayment for imports.
[d]Increase (-).

Source: Based on data from the Central Bank of Paraguay.

TABLE 103

Annual Changes in National Development Bank Operations, 1962-66
(In Millions of Guaranies)

	1962	1963	1964	1965	1966
Domestic Credit	398	419	446	1,025	1,233
To private sector	381	408	391	818	1,070
Other assets (net)	17	11	55	207	163
Financed by:					
Net Central Bank Credit	24	54	60	276	281
Loans and rediscounts	17	109	37	223	205
Currency and reserves	7	-55	23	53	76
Increase in Deposits	56	121	131	141	184
Demand deposits	25	80	26	67	19
Time and savings deposits	31	41	105	74	165
Increase in Capital[a]	191	111	118	159	148
Long-Term Foreign Borrowing	116	130	121	455	655
Net Change in Foreign Assets[b]	11	3	16	-6	-35

[a]Includes unrecovered loans from the portfolio of the former Bank of Paraguay transferred to the NDB as part of its initial capital.

[b]Increase (-).

Private commercial bank operations (i.e., excluding those of the National Development Bank) during the period 1960-66 varied erratically from year to year. The principal determinants of their volume of credit activities have been the level of deposits, the reserve requirements against these deposits, and the banks' utilization of short-term foreign credits. The importance of these factors on commercial bank liquidity in the years 1960-66 is shown in Table 102. For example, nearly all of the increase in deposits in 1965 was used to meet a higher level of reserve requirements and to build liquid assets. Hence, the banks as a group supplemented their local resources by utilizing some ₲ 294 million of short-term external credits. Most of these funds were used to finance the meatpacking industry and for the pre-financing of agricultural exports.

The domestic credit activities of the National Development Bank have been determined in the main by its capital position and the availability of long-term external credits, including P.L. 480 funds, for development purposes. The annual changes in NDB operations during 1962-66 are shown in Table 103.

Sizable increases in credits to the industry, livestock, and agriculture sectors reflect the utilization of various external loans to the National Development Bank for these purposes (see Chapter 5). Within the combined agriculture and livestock sectors, the NDB has reported the distribution of credits by purpose, as shown in Table 104.

While the loans of the NDB for all agricultural purposes at least doubled between 1963 and 1965, the major increases in fixed capital loans went for enlarging cattle herds and for the acquisition of machinery and implements. Working capital loans rose more than fourfold during these three years. The NDB also expanded materially its loans to the industrial sector in these years, as shown in Table 105.

TABLE 104

National Development Bank Credits to the Combined Agricultural and Livestock Sectors, 1963-65
(In Millions of Guaranies)

	1963	1964	1965
Fixed Capital:	255.0	472.5	792.6
Cattle herds	126.0	220.5	465.3
Permanent crops	1.1	2.7	2.8
Land improvement	42.0	51.7	81.4
Machinery and implements	85.9	197.6	243.1
Working Capital	60.9	53.5	257.4
TOTAL	315.9	526.0	1,050.0

TABLE 105

National Development Bank Loans to the Industrial Sector, 1963-65
(In Millions of Guaranies)

	1963	1964	1965
Fixed Capital:	105.0	149.0	430.7
Machinery	72.9	100.3	316.1
Plant construction	16.6	28.9	47.7
Spare parts and tools	1.7	1.8	6.6
Installations	13.8	18.0	60.3
Working Capital:	212.4	218.8	292.5
TOTAL	317.4	367.8	723.2

It appears that in the industrial sector capital has been available most readily for fixed investment purposes, and loans for working capital have remained relatively static. Yet investigations regarding the feasibility of establishing a private development financing corporation in Paraguay in 1966 showed that the major financial gap in the industrial sector is working capital. Apparently, sufficient external loans are available to the NDB to meet fixed capital requirements. The notable increases in loans to the agriculture-livestock and industrial sectors suggest that with additional availabilities of working capital, substantial additional growth in these sectors could be attained easily.

While the commercial banks lend mainly against commercial paper (notes, warehouse receipts, shipping documents, etc.), the National Development Bank lends principally against mortgages and chattels. With the change in management at the NDB in 1965, a more conservative lending policy was instituted, as reflected in the far more tangible security required against loans in that year than in preceding years. In large part this change also reflected the pressures exerted upon the NDB by international lending agencies.

THE CENTRAL BANK AND MONETARY POLICY

The Central Bank of Paraguay has all the usual attributes of a central bank. It is the financial agent of the government and its institutions, it controls commercial bank activities, and it has the sole right to issue currency. In Paraguay, where as yet there is virtually no securities market, and where the Central Bank deals almost entirely with the government and state entities, monetary policy is oriented toward controlling seasonal pressures on the banking system. The only effective monetary control utilized thus far has been an adjustment of commercial bank reserve requirements against deposits.

Prior to October, 1965, the Central Bank attempted to maintain differential reserve requirements according to the type of deposit. However, deposits began to shift noticeably from sight deposits to savings and time deposits (probably with the encouragement of the commercial banks) so that lending operations to the private sector continued to increase. With a view to stabilizing this situation, the Central Bank, in October, 1965, established a uniform reserve requirement for all types of deposits. While the level of this requirement was changed twice during 1966 (in April and July), the principle of a uniform rate was maintained. The changes in reserve requirements from February, 1956, through July 31, 1966, are shown in Table 106. The 42 per cent reserve remained in effect at the close of 1966.

As shown in Table 107, the private commercial banks have kept fairly closely to the legal reserve requirements. There has been some tendency to maintain a slight excess of reserves against sudden upward changes in these requirements.

While the high reserve requirements coupled with sizable inflows of foreign exchange and P.L. 480 funds have kept the Paraguayan currency stable, there has been a definite limitation on funds available to the private sector for commercial and development purposes. The chronic fiscal deficits of the Central Government have been financed by the Central Bank largely at the expense of the private sector. The high reserve ratios have effected the transfer of funds from the private to the public sector, which the existing tax structure has been unable to accomplish adequately. The absence of a sound fiscal policy, therefore, would deter the commercial banks from getting into the longer-term lending field even if they were so inclined, and these government officials who complain about the passive role of the private commercial banks in fostering Paraguayan development fail to take account of the limited capabilities of these banks under existing fiscal and monetary policies.

TABLE 106

Central Bank Minimum Legal Reserve Requirements, 1956-66
(In Per Cent)

Type of Deposit	Feb. 1956	Mar. 1958	Dec. 1959	Nov. 1964	Oct. 1965	Apr. 1966	July 1966
Sight	30	34	40	40	40	39	42
Additions to sight deposits[a]	50	54	54	45	40	39	42
Savings	20	20	20	30	40	39	42
Time	25	29	29	30	40	39	42
Unutilized current account	20	24	24	--	--	--	--

[a]Applicable to sight deposits above the levels existing at the dates the laws were enacted.

Source: Central Bank of Paraguay.

TABLE 107

Legal Reserves of the Commercial Bank, 1961-66[a]

(Monthly Averages, in Millions of Guaranies)

Year	Total Deposits	Required Reserves	Actual Reserves	Surplus of Deficit of Reserves	Reserves as Per Cent of Deposits	
					Required	Actual
1961	1,769	667	674	+ 7	38	38
1962	2,079	781	783	+ 2	38	38
1963	2,508	838	900	+ 62	33	36
1964	3,029	1,082	1,074	- 8	36	35
1965:						
March	3,124	1,115	1,082	- 33	36	35
June	3,313	1,189	1,214	+ 25	36	37
Sept.	3,632	1,271	1,344	+ 73	35	37
Dec.	3,583	1,416	1,467	+ 51	40	41
1966:						
June	3,525	1,375	1,445	+ 70	39	41

[a]Excluding the 100 per cent requirements against payments arrears.

Source: Data from the Central Bank of Paraguay.

The rates at which the Central Bank discounts for the commercial banks are 6 per cent on commercial paper and 3.5 per cent on agricultural paper. A discount rate of 4 per cent for cattle ranch and industrial papers was established in December, 1956.* Commercial banks may seek accommodation at the Central Bank up to a limit of 50 per cent of the capital and reserve they held at the end of 1956. Discount operations exceeding 25 per cent of this limit are subject to a surtax of 50 per cent over the rates quoted above. Inasmuch as discount operations are performed mainly to meet seasonal credit shortages in the agricultural sector, these operations are rather limited and do not constitute a continuous source of credit to the economy.[1]

Since 1956, the International Monetary Fund has maintained a resident representative in Paraguay to advise the Central Bank on monetary policy and to supervise the various Stand-by Arrangements between the Fund and the Paraguayan Government. The Fund's intervention in this country has been a major factor in keeping the currency and prices stable and in generating the financing necessary for constructing basic public works projects in Paraguay. Given the virtual absence of fiscal policy in this country, the credit limitations imposed upon the Central Bank and the Ministry of Finance under the Stand-by Arrangements undoubtedly have been effective buffers against the persistent claims of government agencies, especially the military, for more and more public funds. Because of this situation, monetary policy has had to effect important shifts of savings from the private to the public sector during the past decade.

It is generally recognized by Paraguayan and foreign economists that private sector development cannot be sacrificed excessively to irresponsible fiscal practices. In its national plans, the

---

*Before May 1, 1954, the rate charged was 3.5 per cent, regardless of the purpose of the operation.

TABLE 108

Money Supply and Cost of Living, 1960-65

	1961	1962	1963	1964	1965
Rate of growth of Gross Domestic Product (%)	2.7	5.6	2.4	3.3	6.5
Circulating media (₲ millions)	3,548	3,883	4,216	5,187	6,151
Annual increase (%)	21.3	6.5	8.5	23.0	18.6
Variation in notes and coins (₲ millions)	396	-47	111	550	302
Variation in sight deposits (₲ millions)	247	283	221	421	662
Cost-of-living index	98.2	100.0	101.7	103.6	107.5

Source: Technical Planning Secretariat, II Plan Nacional de Desarrollo Económico y Social, Bienio 1967-1968 (Asunción, August, 1966), p. 11.

Technical Planning Secretariat has stressed the need to increase private savings and to change banking policy to achieve a better utilization of loanable funds, including a greater availability of credit to the business community.

As shown in Table 108, the money supply increased at a much faster rate than the Gross Domestic Product during 1961-65, while prices (the cost-of-living index for workers in Asunción) increased mildly. This pattern is consistent with substantial government investments in infrastructure, with sizable amounts of public funds going for imported capital goods, and raw materials not entering into the cost-of-living index.

With the imminent completion of much of the basic infrastructure requirements of the country, increasing attention will have to be given to stimulating private sector development. To accelerate the growth of this sector, adequate credit facilities will have to be made available through the banking system and other means. Obviously this will require a radical change in monetary policy. If this is to be accomplished within the framework of continued monetary stability, fiscal policy will have to be improved measurably. There is no substitute, in the long run, for basic fiscal reform; monetary policy cannot continue to substitute in this regard and yet provide for adequate private sector growth.

Notes to Chapter 14

1. International Monetary Fund, International Financial Statistics, Vol. XIX, No. 6 (June, 1966), p. 236.

CHAPTER 15 INTERNATIONAL TRANSACTIONS

FOREIGN TRADE

In the past two decades, Paraguay has ranked at or near the bottom of the list of Latin American countries with respect to the dollar value of its international commerce. In recent years it has exceeded only Haiti in this respect. Nevertheless, Paraguayan exports (F.O.B.) increased from $34 million in 1958 to a peak of $57 million in 1965, a rise of 68 per cent, and imports (C.I.F.) rose from $38 million to $51 million, or 34 per cent, during the same period.* As a result of factors discussed below, exports declined to $49 million in 1966. Imports, on the other hand, continued to rise, reaching some $58 million in that year.

Because of the sizable contraband trade into and out of Paraguay, both export and import statistics are understated. Moreover, the imposition of export and import taxes, including foreign exchange surcharges, encourages undervaluations, especially in connection with the valuation of imports. The magnitude of these understatements undoubtedly runs to tens of millions of dollars a year. However, a considerable amount of illegal imports into Paraguay are transshipped to neighboring countries, especially Argentina.

---

*These data are based on customs valuations and differ from those reported in the balance of payments statements.

Exports[1]

Paraguayan exports increased at a compound annual rate of 4.5 per cent in volume and 7.7 per cent in value during the years 1958-65. During 1958-60, exports declined because of a sharp drop in the demand for Paraguayan lumber and logs in the Argentine market. In 1961 and 1962 exports recovered their previous level, and in 1963-65 a strong sustained growth was noted. This growth was interrupted in 1966 because of (a) adverse weather conditions in the early months of the year that caused damage to certain export crops and to cattle herds; (b) Paraguayan Government policies regarding the slaughter of cattle for export that served to reduce the slaughter materially from authorized levels; and (c) declines in world prices of meat and meat products.

Paraguay's exports are unusually well diversified for a less-developed country, as shown in Tables 109 and 110. During the period 1958-65, exports of agricultural, meat, and industrial products increased in relative importance, while exports of essential oils and of forestry products declined in their relative share of the total value. In 1965, meat products and by-products accounted for 35.9 per cent of the value of exports; agricultural products for 28.6 per cent; logs and lumber for 23.1 per cent; vegetable oils for 5.6 per cent; industrial products* for 4.8 per cent; and essential oils for 2.0 per cent. The advantage of export diversification is shown in Table 111, which reflects the offsetting tendencies among the various export categories with respect to both quantity and value fluctuations. Those advantages could be enhanced by increasing the exportation of industrial products and vegetable oils in relation to other export categories.

---

*In certain presentations, meat products, vegetable oils, quebracho extract, and essential oils are included in industrial products.

TABLE 109

Paraguayan Exports by Commodity Group, 1958-65

	1958	1959	1960	1961	1962	1963	1964	1965
					Metric Tons			
Agricultural commodities	48,873	56,424	58,581	54,314	66,476	67,379	70,202	75,821
Meat products & by-products	31,302	34,785	28,949	31,303	26,163	33,095	36,373	40,632
Vegetable oils	5,354	6,695	5,410	6,206	8,257	12,276	11,812	10,304
Essential oils	208	265	288	304	311	379	434	366
Industrial commodities	10,999	10,532	8,518	14,335	20,331	15,277	29,076	27,745
Subtotal	96,736	108,701	101,746	106,462	121,538	128,406	147,897	154,868
Index	100.0	112.4	105.2	110.1	125.6	132.7	152.9	160.1
Forest products	244,894	127,489	197,627	234,886	232,838	178,714	249,867	309,953
Total	341,630	236,190	299,373	341,348	354,376	307,120	397,764	464,821
Index (1958=100)	100.0	69.1	87.6	99.9	103.7	89.9	116.4	136.1

Value in $000's, F.O.B.

Agricultural commodities	7,492.2	7,152.2	6,538.8	7.215.3	10,998.7	13,352.3	14,588.0	16,349.3
Meat products & by-products	10,295.2	13,359.9	9,527.8	10,760.4	9,370.5	12,209.5	16,739.3	20,540.2
Vegetable oils	1,509.8	1,675.5	1,541.6	1,882.8	2,333.4	4,424.2	3,983.1	3,195.6
Essential oils	795.4	956.3	1,008.5	1,054.8	1,079.1	1,273.2	1,456.0	1,123.8
Industrial commodities	791.7	431.7	379.2	650.9	772.9	959.6	1,879.6	2,756.1
Subtotal	20,886.3	23,575.6	18,995.9	21,564.2	24,554.6	32,218.8	38,646.0	43,965.0
Index (1958=100)	100.0	112.9	90.9	103.2	117.6	154.3	185.0	210.5
Forest products	13,216.1	7,619.1	7,982.1	9,111.5	9,190.1	7,536.9	11,124.6	13,230.8
Total	34,102.4	31,194.7	26,978.0	30,675.7	33,755.7	39,755.7	49,770.6	57,195.8
Index (1958=100)	100.0	91.5	79.1	90.0	99.0	116.6	145.9	167.7
Average value per ton ($U.S.)	99.8	132.1	90.1	89.9	95.2	129.4	125.1	123.0

TABLE 110

Percentage Share of Exports by Commodity Group, 1958-65

	1958	1959	1960	1961	1962	1963	1964	1965
				Volume				
Agricultural commodities	14.3	23.9	19.6	15.9	18.7	21.9	17.7	16.3
Meat products & by-products	9.2	14.7	9.6	9.1	7.4	10.8	9.1	8.7
Vegetable oils	1.6	2.8	1.8	1.8	2.3	4.0	3.0	2.2
Essential oils	0.1	0.1	0.1	0.1	0.1	0.1	0.1	0.1
Industrial commodities	3.2	4.5	2.8	4.2	5.7	5.0	7.3	6.0
Forest products	71.6	54.0	66.1	68.9	65.8	58.2	62.8	66.7
TOTAL	100.0	100.0	100.0	100.0	100.0	100.0	100.0	100.0
				Value				
Agricultural commodities	22.0	22.9	24.2	23.6	32.6	33.6	29.3	28.6
Meat products & by-products	30.2	42.8	35.3	35.1	27.8	30.7	33.6	35.9
Vegetable oils	4.4	5.4	5.7	6.1	6.9	11.1	8.0	5.6
Essential oils	2.3	3.1	3.8	3.4	3.2	3.2	2.9	2.0
Industrial commodities	2.3	1.4	1.4	2.1	2.3	2.4	3.8	4.8
Forest products	38.8	24.4	29.6	29.7	27.2	19.0	22.4	23.1
TOTAL	100.0	100.0	100.0	100.0	100.0	100.0	100.0	100.0

TABLE 111

Percentage Variation of Exports by Commodity Group, 1958-65
(1958=100)

	1958	1959	1960	1961	1962	1963	1964	1965
				Volume				
Agricultural commodities	100.0	115.5	119.9	111.1	136.0	137.9	143.6	155.1
Meat products & by-products	100.0	111.1	92.5	100.0	83.6	105.7	116.2	129.8
Vegetable oils	100.0	125.0	101.0	115.9	154.2	229.3	220.6	192.5
Essential oils	100.0	127.0	138.1	145.8	149.1	182.1	208.7	176.0
Industrial commodities	100.0	95.8	77.4	130.3	184.8	138.9	264.4	252.3
Forest products	100.0	52.1	80.7	95.9	95.1	73.0	102.0	126.6
TOTAL	100.0	69.1	87.6	99.9	103.7	89.9	116.4	136.1
				Value				
Agricultural commodities	100.0	95.4	87.3	96.3	146.8	178.2	194.7	218.2
Meat products & by-products	100.0	129.8	92.5	104.5	91.0	118.6	162.6	199.5
Vegetable oils	100.0	111.0	102.1	124.7	154.6	293.0	263.8	211.7
Essential oils	100.0	120.2	126.8	132.6	135.7	160.1	183.1	141.3
Industrial commodities	100.0	54.5	47.9	82.2	97.6	121.2	237.4	348.1
Forest products	100.0	57.7	60.4	68.9	69.5	57.0	84.2	100.1
TOTAL	100.0	91.5	79.1	90.0	99.0	116.6	145.9	167.7

TABLE 112

Exports by Purchasing Area and Economic Sector, 1963
(In Thousands of U.S. Dollars)

Destination Sector	LAFTA	EEC	EFTA	U.S.	All Other	Total	Per Cent
Industrial	1,572	2,976	3,760	7,853	4,322	20,483	51
Agricultural	4,272	2,990	854	984	4,184	13,284	33
Livestock	69	1,012	108	218	272	1,679	4
Forestry	4,744	---	---	---	---	4,744	12
Mining	---	---	---	---	---	---	--
TOTAL	10,657 (26%)	6,978 (17%)	4,722 (12%)	9,055 (23%)	8,778 (22%)	40,190 (100%)	100

Source: Central Bank of Paraguay, Memoria--1963, p. 77.

If the broader classification of "industrial products" is used, as was done by the Central Bank of Paraguay in its annual report for 1963,[2] then more than one half of the country's exports consisted of industrial products in that year. The main reason for this was the sharp rise in exports of meat products, particularly canned corned beef, which increased 25 per cent in volume and 42 per cent in value over the previous year. The composition of exports by sector and their regional destination in 1963 were as given in Table 112.

Meat Products and By-Products

The exportation of meat products and by-products since 1959 has constituted the leading category of Paraguayan exports. As shown in Table 113, the volume of these exports increased 29.8 per cent during 1958-65, whereas the value rose 99.5 per cent. During the period, slaughtering of cattle for export rose from 179,000 head to 233,000. Exports of frozen meat, which had been suspended during 1960-63, were reinstated in 1964. Markets for Paraguayan frozen meat appear to be available (e.g., Mexico, Peru, Spain), and this trade is expected to grow substantially. Also, since 1962, horse meat and hides have been exported, probably for the first time in Paraguayan history. During the period from 1958 through 1965, a strong world demand and favorable prices spurred the growth in value of meat exports. While Paraguay has extensive areas of land suitable for the expansion of cattle raising, government restrictions in the form of export slaughter quotas and uncertain tax policies burdening the industry restrain the growth rate of ranching operations in this country.

Agricultural Commodities

The value of exports of agricultural commodities more than doubled between 1958 and 1965, while their volume increased 55.1 per cent (see Table 114). These increases resulted from the emerging importance of certain new crops--coffee, soybeans, and castor beans--during the period, combined with

TABLE 113

Exports of Meat and Related Products, 1958-65

	1958	1959	1960	1961	1962	1963	1964	1965
				Metric Tons				
Canned meat	9,202	12,067	11,260	16,017	13,372	16,701	15,431	18,643
Frozen meat	950	263	-	-	-	-	1,902	4,789
Cured meat	3,152	2,809	-	-	-	-	-	-
Meat products	5,284	4,187	6,612	4,011	3,616	6,803	5,713	5,526
Meat by-products	2,573	2,627	1,143	2,645	1,278	1,752	3,190	2,469
Horse meat	-	-	-	-	304	50	1,982	795
Cured cow hides	9,179	11,352	8,453	7,954	6,818	7,304	7,051	7,893
Dried cow hides	750	1,232	504	516	454	268	304	270
Cured horse hides	-	-	-	-	58	-	206	-
Cattle on the hoof	-	3	743	-	26	-	181	-
Bristles	212	245	234	160	237	217	413	247
Total	31,302	34,784	28,949	31,303	26,163	33,095	36,373	40,632
Index (1958=100)	100.0	111.1	92.5	100.0	83.6	105.7	116.2	129.8

Value in $000's, F.O.B.

Canned meat	5,277.1	7,053.1	5,524.9	7,236.3	6,042.6	8,562.4	9,632.7	11,424.7
Frozen meat	244.6	89.2	-	-	-	-	838.2	3,017.3
Cured meat	806.0	1,144.0	-	-	-	-	-	-
Meat products	1,839.4	1,332.1	1,611.1	1,388.6	1,432.4	1,961.3	4,278.1	4,302.7
Meat by-products	38.5	41.9	23.3	33.4	28.6	34.1	66.3	62.7
Horse meat	-	-	-	-	45.0	6.0	352.8	156.8
Cured cow hides	1,811.6	3,229.0	2,069.0	1,898.8	1,587.5	1,462.5	1,244.4	1,312.5
Dried cow hides	172.2	329.0	135.5	111.7	98.1	57.7	52.2	49.1
Cured horse hides	-	-	-	-	3.5	-	11.0	-
Cattle on the hoof	-	0.7	38.0	-	2.0	-	13.8	-
Bristles	105.8	140.9	126.0	91.6	130.8	125.5	249.8	214.4
Total	10,295.2	13,359.9	9,527.8	10,760.4	9,370.5	12,209.5	16,739.3	20,540.2
Index (1958=100)	100.0	129.8	92.5	104.5	91.0	118.6	162.6	199.5

TABLE 114

Exports of Agricultural Commodities, 1958-65

	1958	1959	1960	1961
		METRIC		
Cotton	8,154	6,409	1,190	4,980
Rice	-	968	-	20
Sugar	5,221	15,420	1,380	3,300
Coffee	36	1,286	1,396	1,810
Fruits	5,213	4,410	6,253	5,651
Maize	19,282	11,988	20,772	10,398
Soybeans	-	-	360	265
Tobacco	2,476	2,355	6,119	5,898
Castor beans	2,621	5,197	5,423	11,359
Yerba maté	5,603	8,341	15,583	9,823
Miscellaneous	267	50	105	810
Total	48,873	56,424	58,581	54,314
Index (1958=100)	100.0	115.5	119.9	111.1
		VALUE IN		
Cotton	3,730.5	2,084.5	297.1	1,598.0
Rice	-	115.2	-	2.6
Sugar	586.6	1,066.5	97.2	335.3
Coffee	24.1	692.8	765.5	992.9
Fruits	315.8	192.7	220.9	223.8
Maize	688.5	421.9	733.5	321.3
Soybeans	-	-	21.8	21.1
Tobacco	694.2	640.6	1,587.4	1,528.2
Castor beans	160.1	311.1	325.1	680.5
Yerba maté	1,234.8	1,622.9	2,485.7	1,486.9
Miscellaneous	59.6	4.0	4.6	24.7
Total	7,494.2	7,152.2	6,538.8	7,215.3
Index (1958=100)	100.0	95.4	87.3	96.3

1962	1963	1964	1965
	TONS		
6,962	8,865	11,362	10,809
-	-	-	-
4,008	7,308	2,400	479
5,269	6,229	4,953	5,416
9,246	7,854	6,927	8,480
8,234	4,836	9,144	7,726
-	3,497	306	1,306
11,902	10,037	12,658	14,750
13,706	10,815	11,775	13,987
6,495	7,708	10,275	12,585
654	230	402	283
66,476	67,379	70,202	75,821
136.0	137.9	143.6	155.1
	$000's, F.O.B.		
2,469.2	3,198.5	4,197.1	4,688.0
-	-	-	-
281.0	1,476.0	376.8	61.8
2,835.4	3,226.0	3,181.6	3,627.5
307.2	338.7	404.5	558.0
249.9	145.1	288.2	245.2
-	194.5	13.3	85.2
3,092.5	3,105.9	3,741.3	4,284.5
821.5	775.3	982.1	1,132.0
920.8	878.5	1,348.7	1,603.7
21.2	13.8	54.4	63.4
10,998.7	13,352.3	14,588.0	16,349.3
146.8	178.2	194.7	218.2

TABLE 115

Exports of Forest Products, 1958-65

	1958	1959	1960	1961
		METRIC		
Quebracho extract	27,554	29,427	33,499	31,904
Sawn lumber	15,391	11,159	12,660	29,873
Broomsticks	-	40	-	-
Parquet	-	-	-	-
Logs	196,289	82,330	140,605	164,699
Poles	4,604	3,700	4,640	4,219
Posts	1,056	833	6,223	4,191
Total	244,894	127,489	197,627	234,886
Index (1958=100)	100.0	52.1	80.7	95.9
		VALUE IN		
Quebracho extract	3,473.6	3,556.1	2,949.8	2,648.3
Sawn lumber	1,432.4	956.6	750.0	1,762.0
Broomsticks	-	2.1	-	-
Parquet	-	-	-	-
Logs	8,075.1	2,920.9	3,840.7	4,400.1
Poles	189.8	148.3	190.0	157.8
Posts	45.2	35.1	251.6	143.3
Total	13,216.1	7,619.1	7,982.1	9,111.5
Index (1958=100)	100.0	57.7	60.4	68.9

1962	1963	1964	1965
	T O N S		
30,643	24,482	33,796	29,348
27,796	15,085	25,092	31,671
-	5	36	323
-	1	60	211
167,267	129,514	185,011	239,132
5,222	4,994	4,099	8,068
1,910	4,633	1,773	1,200
232,838	178,714	249,867	309,953
95.1	73.0	102.0	126.6
	$000's, F.O.B.		
2,531.0	2,806.4	3,977.4	3,465.5
1,744.0	856.2	1,644.3	2,238.4
-	0.2	4.0	38.1
-	0.3	6.0	76.1
4,650.2	3,532.4	5,264.9	7,109.0
190.6	182.7	158.0	251.4
74.3	158.7	70.0	52.3
9,190.1	7,536.9	11,124.6	13,230.8
69.5	57.0	84.2	100.1

a sustained growth in exports of fruits and vegetables and a surge in tobacco exports. Exports of agricultural commodities accounted for 28.6 per cent of the total in 1965 and represented the second largest group of products shipped abroad. Cotton, tobacco, coffee, yerba maté, and castor beans were the major agricultural products exported in 1965.

Forest Products

This category of exports ranked first in 1958, second during 1959-61, and third in subsequent years (see Table 110). The major item in this category is logs, which accounted for about two thirds of the volume and 55 per cent of the value in 1965. Quebracho extract (tannin) and sawn lumber are the other important commodities in this category. As shown in Table 115, the volume of forest products exports rose 26.6 per cent between 1958 and 1965, whereas the value of these shipments remained virtually unchanged. As discussed earlier in this study, a rationalization of forest products output and the domestic fabrication of lumber products for export are required to increase Paraguay's earnings from this resource category. The substantial differences in prices obtainable from the conversion of logs even to beams and sawn lumber are shown in the Central Bank's table of valuations for such exports, shown in Table 116.

The demand for plywood and veneer in the United States and European markets should provide incentive to producers in Paraguay. Evidence to date indicates that outside capital and technical assistance are required to bring local production operations to suitable quantity and standardized quality levels. The development of these new products and markets is indispensable to Paraguay. The tannin industry is declining sharply because of growing competition from synthetic products and it may be expected to disappear entirely within a decade. Logs and lumber go almost entirely to Argentina (90 per cent) and Uruguay (10 per cent). These markets are very unstable; and the successive monetary devaluations that have characterized the two countries have made it increasingly difficult for exporters in Paraguay to sell to these markets. At the same time, high transportation costs have made it uneconomic for Paraguay to export logs or lumber to more distant markets, such as Europe.

TABLE 116

Valuation of Lumber for Export, 1966

Species	Minimum Price in U.S. Dollars Per Cubic Meter, F.O.B. Paraguayan Port		
	Logs	Beams	Sawn Lumber
Cedar (Cedrela spp)	40	52	65
Trebol (Torresea cearensis)	60	74	95
Petereby (Cordia trichotoma)	48	78	81
Lapacho (Tabebuia ipe)	30	43	56
Guatambú (Balfourondendron riedelianum)	25	35	52
Ybyraró (Pterogyne nitens)	48	66	74
Incienso (Myrocarpus frondosus)	43	54	60
Curupay (Piptadenia mecrocarpe)	25	38	40
Ybyrapytá (Peltophorum dubium)	25	34	38
Others	25	34	38

Source: Data from the Central Bank of Paraguay.

TABLE 117

Exports of Vegetable Oils, 1958-65

	1958	1959	1960	1961	1962	1963	1964	1965
				Metric Tons				
Palm kernel oil	1,225	1,843	828	1,451	1,674	3,869	2,332	3,199
Palm oil	292	1,400	1,045	172	1,254	3,890	3,461	2,523
Tung oil	3,794	3,447	3,519	4,583	5,195	4,455	5,875	4,552
Castor oil	43	3	18	-	124	62	144	30
Crude fusel oil	-	2	-	-	10	-	-	-
Total	5,354	6,695	5,410	6,206	8,257	12,276	11,812	10,304
Index (1958=100)	100.0	125.0	101.0	115.9	154.2	229.3	220.6	192.5
				Value in $000's, F.O.B.				
Palm kernel oil	558.7	600.9	277.4	463.1	513.3	1,190.4	758.5	1,056.5
Palm oil	81.4	268.5	191.7	31.9	227.3	469.5	431.7	302.7
Tung oil	855.6	804.8	1,064.3	1,387.8	1,568.3	2,746.6	2,729.2	1,823.3
Castor oil	14.1	1.1	8.2	-	21.0	17.7	63.7	13.1
Crude fusel oil	-	0.2	-	-	3.5	-	-	-
Total	1,509.8	1,675.5	1,541.6	1,882.8	2,334.4	4,424.2	3,983.1	3,195.6
Index (1958=100)	100.0	111.0	102.1	124.7	154.6	293.0	263.8	211.7

Vegetable Oils

The entry of new investment into the vegetable oil industry and the increase in acreages of tung plantations have permitted Paraguay to double the value of its vegetable oil exports during the period 1958-65 (see Table 117). While growing and marketing conditions obviously affect the level of vegetable oil exports, Paraguay is in a strong competitive position in this field. Qualitative improvements and advanced processing of these oils could serve to increase the country's earnings from these exports.

Industrial Commodities

The list of industrial exports has been small. Until recently it consisted of three major items: unshaped straw hats, expellers and cakes (by-products of the vegetable oil processing plants), and wild animal hides and skins. Since 1962, however, a valuable new export item has entered this category--the heart of palm (palmito). By 1965, the value of exports of this item alone exceeded that of total industrial exports in any preceding year, as shown in Table 118.

Further expansion of this export is expected, but the rate of growth will depend upon the efforts taken by local producers and the government in promoting the product abroad. The markets for the traditional Paraguayan industrial exports appear to be growing; and with the development of safaris on a commercial basis and expansion of vegetable oil output, the production of wild animal hides and skins and of expellers and cakes, respectively, should expand steadily.

In spite of the foregoing, Paraguay needs to develop new manufacturing exports. Exports of cement disappeared in 1965 as Paraguayan requirements greatly exceeded national output. The National Development Bank (with the aid of Arthur D. Little, Inc.) is attempting to identify new industrial opportunities. The Agency for International Development (in cooperation with the Ministry of Industry

TABLE 118

Exports of Industrial Commodities, 1958-65

	1958	1959	1960
		M E T R I C	
Bran	-	250	802
Spirits & caña (rum)	10	52	7
Unshaped straw hats	151	41	46
Wild animal hides & skins	64	166	182
Expellers & cakes	10,274	9,983	6,368
Palm hearts	-	-	-
Cement	-	-	1,100
Miscellaneous	500	40	13
Total	10,999	10,532	8,518
Index (1958=100)	100.0	95.8	77.4
		V A L U E I N	
Bran	-	3.8	12.0
Spirits & caña (rum)	6.0	15.5	1.8
Unshaped straw hats	422.8	80.9	94.0
Wild animal hides & skins	58.0	96.3	115.1
Expellers & cakes	284.9	226.9	127.8
Palm hearts	-	-	-
Cement	-	-	26.4
Miscellaneous	20.0	8.3	2.1
Total	791.7	431.7	379.2
Index (1958=100)	100.0	54.5	47.9

1961	1962	1963	1964	1965
	T O N S			
3,850	5,470	850	1,194	400
-	329	84	173	62
105	309	96	104	73
295	191	201	247	297
8,307	12,944	13,298	21,293	22,944
-	85	501	1,388	2,499
1,675	540	100	165	-
103	463	147	4,512	1,470
14,335	20,331	15,277	29,076	27,745
130.3	184.8	138.9	264.4	252.3
	$000's, F.O.B.			
53.9	63.4	10.2	21.6	7.2
-	46.4	15.7	41.8	23.1
149.5	152.7	127.8	150.2	125.9
158.9	163.1	134.3	248.9	444.1
221.6	287.5	441.2	575.4	847.4
-	30.6	202.2	669.2	1,225.0
48.2	19.5	1.7	5.3	-
18.8	9.7	26.5	167.2	83.4
650.9	772.9	959.6	1,879.6	2,756.1
82.2	97.6	121.2	237.4	348.1

TABLE 119

Exports of Essential Oils, 1958-65

	1958	1959	1960	1961	1962	1963	1964	1965
					Metric Tons			
Petitgrain oil	171.7	224.7	236.3	250.7	250.6	299.2	343	251
Guaiac oil	34.8	37.3	45.0	48.0	49.1	71.1	82	77
Cedron oil	1.8	2.5	6.2	4.6	7.7	4.0	7	12
Lemon grass oil	-	-	0.2	-	-	-	-	25
Peppermint oil	-	-	-	0.3	3.2	5.0	1	-
Total	208.3	264.5	287.7	303.6	310.6	379.3	433	365
Index (1958=100)	100.0	127.0	138.1	145.8	149.1	182.1	208.7	176.0
					Value in $000's, F.O.B.			
Petitgrain oil	761.3	923.5	966.1	1,009.1	1,014.7	1,194.6	1,357.5	1,010.6
Guaiac oil	32.3	31.0	37.6	40.2	44.9	60.2	86.3	92.7
Cedron oil	1.8	1.8	4.7	4.1	6.2	4.5	9.0	15.0
Lemon grass oil	-	-	0.1	-	-	-	-	5.5
Peppermint oil	-	-	-	1.4	13.3	13.9	3.2	-
Total	795.4	956.3	1,008.5	1,054.8	1,079.1	1,273.2	1,456.0	1,123.8
Index (1958=100)	100.0	120.2	126.8	132.6	135.7	160.1	183.1	141.3

and Commerce and the private Development and Productivity Center) also is assisting in this search. However, the Government of Paraguay will need to invest much more in research and development activities to assist the private sector in identifying potential export-oriented industrial opportunities.

Essential Oils

Paraguay is the major world producer and exporter of *petitgrain* oil. Nevertheless, the quality of its product is below that of other supplying countries because of inferior technology employed. Other essential oils are produced in minor quantities; while it would be possible to improve the quality and quantity of domestic output of essential oils, the encroachment of synthetic products in this field suggests that careful study be made of the feasibility of further investment in the natural products. Exports of essential oils during 1958-65 are shown in Table 119.

Paraguay's traditional exports are sold principally to the United States and Argentina, each of which received about 25 per cent of the total value during 1963-65. As shown in Table 120, Paraguay's exports to the Latin American Free Trade Area (LAFTA) nearly doubled between 1960 and 1965, as did its exports to the European Economic Community (EEC). Its exports to the European Free Trade Association (EFTA) more than doubled during these years. During the same period, new markets appear to have been developed or expanded in Spain, Japan, and "other" areas. Significantly, the major markets for Paraguayan products (eight out of the ten leading markets) are highly industrialized countries where substantial investments in the development of synthetic or substitute products take place.

Imports*

Paraguayan imports follow a fairly typical pattern for a less-developed country. They consist

*Values are F.O.B. Paraguayan port.

TABLE 120

Direction of Foreign Trade, 1960-65[a]
(In Millions of U.S. Dollars)

	EXPORTS						IMPORTS					
	1960	1961	1962	1963	1964	1965	1960	1961	1962	1963	1964	1965
LAFTA	9.0	9.9	10.8	10.7	14.7	17.4	7.9	8.8	5.5	8.4	10.1	9.9
Argentina	7.7	8.7	9.6	8.6	11.6	14.7	7.4	8.3	5.0	7.6	9.4	8.9
Uruguay	1.2	1.1	1.1	1.5	2.9	2.2	0.1	0.3	0.3	0.3	0.3	0.2
Brazil	0.1	0.1	0.1	0.4	0.1	0.1	0.3	0.2	0.2	0.5	0.3	0.6
Other	- -	- -	- -	0.2	0.4	0.4	0.1	- -	- -	- -	0.1	0.2
EEC	4.3	3.7	5.8	6.3	6.0	7.8	5.2	5.6	6.5	5.0	6.7	11.5
Federal Republic of Germany	1.2	0.5	0.8	1.5	0.8	1.4	3.7	4.2	4.7	3.4	4.4	9.0
France	0.2	0.5	1.0	1.2	0.7	1.5	0.3	0.3	0.5	0.5	0.6	0.8
Belgium	0.4	0.3	0.4	0.5	0.7	0.9	0.5	0.4	0.5	0.5	0.6	0.5
Netherlands	2.2	2.4	2.7	2.6	2.6	2.7	0.5	0.5	0.5	0.3	0.7	0.5
Italy	0.3	0.1	0.9	0.5	1.2	1.3	0.2	0.2	0.3	0.3	0.4	0.7
EFTA	3.0	4.0	4.1	5.5	7.7	6.7	3.4	4.3	4.3	3.9	3.9	5.4
United Kingdom	2.8	3.6	3.5	4.5	6.7	5.7	2.3	2.7	2.6	2.5	2.3	3.1
Sweden	0.1	- -	- -	0.1	0.1	0.2	0.6	0.8	1.0	0.7	0.9	1.5
Switzerland	0.1	0.3	0.6	0.8	0.7	0.7	0.2	0.5	0.3	0.3	0.2	0.2
Austria	- -	- -	- -	- -	- -	- -	0.1	0.2	0.2	0.2	0.2	0.3
Other	- -	0.1	- -	0.1	0.2	0.1	0.2	0.1	0.2	0.2	0.3	0.3
OTHERS												
Canada	0.4	0.3	0.1	0.3	0.3	0.3	- -	- -	- -	0.2	0.2	0.1
United States	7.2	7.4	7.0	9.0	11.8	14.5	7.6	5.3	10.8	9.6	7.2	9.5
Netherlands Antilles	- -	- -	- -	- -	- -	- -	2.4	2.2	2.3	2.3	2.1	2.6
Spain	0.4	1.0	1.0	1.5	1.9	3.4	2.5	1.7	0.7	0.4	0.4	0.6
Japan	- -	- -	- -	- -	0.3	0.2	2.1	4.8	2.1	1.6	2.1	3.1
Other[b]	2.7	4.4	4.9	6.4	7.0	6.9	1.4	2.0	2.1	1.2	1.1	1.3
TOTAL	27.9	30.7	33.7	39.7	49.7	57.2	32.5	34.7	34.3	32.6	33.8	44.0

[a]Based on customs statistics.

[b]More than 80 per cent of the exports in this item are shipments through River Plate ports to unspecified destinations.

Source: Central Bank of Paraguay.

TABLE 121

Value of Imports, by Commodity Group, 1960-65[a]
(In Millions of U.S. Dollars)

	1960	1961	1962	1963	1964	1965
Consumption Goods	10.8	12.5	13.1	12.7	12.5	13.1
Wheat	4.3	4.7	5.3	4.9	4.8	4.5
Other foods, beverages, and tobacco	2.0	2.7	2.2	2.8	2.0	1.8
Textiles and manufactures	2.5	2.7	3.1	2.3	2.7	3.3
Chemicals and drugs	1.3	1.5	1.6	1.7	1.9	2.1
Paper and cardboard	0.8	0.9	0.8	1.0	1.1	1.4
Fuel and Lubricants	3.4	3.5	3.5	4.0	4.1	4.9
Vehicles and Accessories	3.7	3.9	5.0	3.7	4.1	6.4
Investment Goods	11.5	11.2	8.4	7.7	9.5	15.3
Agricultural implements	0.5	0.4	0.3	0.3	0.5	0.9
Iron, steel, and manufactures	1.9	1.6	1.6	1.5	2.0	3.1
Other metals	1.3	1.1	1.0	1.7	1.6	1.7
Machinery and motors	5.5	3.9	5.5	4.1	4.9	9.6
Ships	2.4	4.2	- -	- -	0.5	- -
Miscellaneous	3.0	3.6	4.2	4.4	3.6	4.3
TOTAL	32.5	34.7	34.3	32.6	33.8	44.0

[a]Values F.O.B. Paraguayan port.

Source: Central Bank of Paraguay, Boletín Estadístico Mensual, December, 1966.

of investment goods (machinery and motors; iron and steel and their manufactures; and other metals); consumption goods (mainly wheat and textiles); vehicles and accessories; and fuels and lubricants. The composition of imports during the years 1960-65 is shown in Table 121.

New investments in all subgroups of the consumption goods category may be expected to result in sizable import substitutions during the next decade. With the opening of a petroleum refinery near Asunción in 1966, imports of fuels (except aviation gasoline) are expected to disappear, but imports of crude oil should increase to feed into the refinery unless Paraguay succeeds in locating its own commercial oil deposits. Attempts thus far have not been successful. Lubricants will continue to be imported in the foreseeable future.

Imports of vehicles and accessories are expected to increase markedly as the Paraguayan road network is expanded, new areas come into production, and incipient efforts at regional development in various parts of the country begin to bear fruit. While the Italian automotive firm of Alfa Romeo received a concession in 1966 to assemble its lines in Paraguay, the size of the local market and the fact that Alfa Romeo is virtually unknown in the country would appear to cast considerable doubt on the success of this venture. For a profitable operation, Alfa Romeo would have to market its vehicles in neighboring countries and have the Paraguayan Government prohibit the importation of competing lines. However, Argentina and Brazil have excess capacity in their own automotive vehicle manufacturing enterprises; actually, Brazil exports vehicles to Paraguay. Moreover, the loss of customs revenues to the Government of Paraguay from any measures taken to protect Alfa Romeo would appear to be an excessive price to pay for the very doubtful benefits to be derived from this particular assembling operation.

During the years 1960-65, private imports accounted for between 50 per cent and 80 per cent of the total value of registered imports into Paraguay,

CHART 1

Indexes of Unit Values of Exports and Imports
(1958=100)

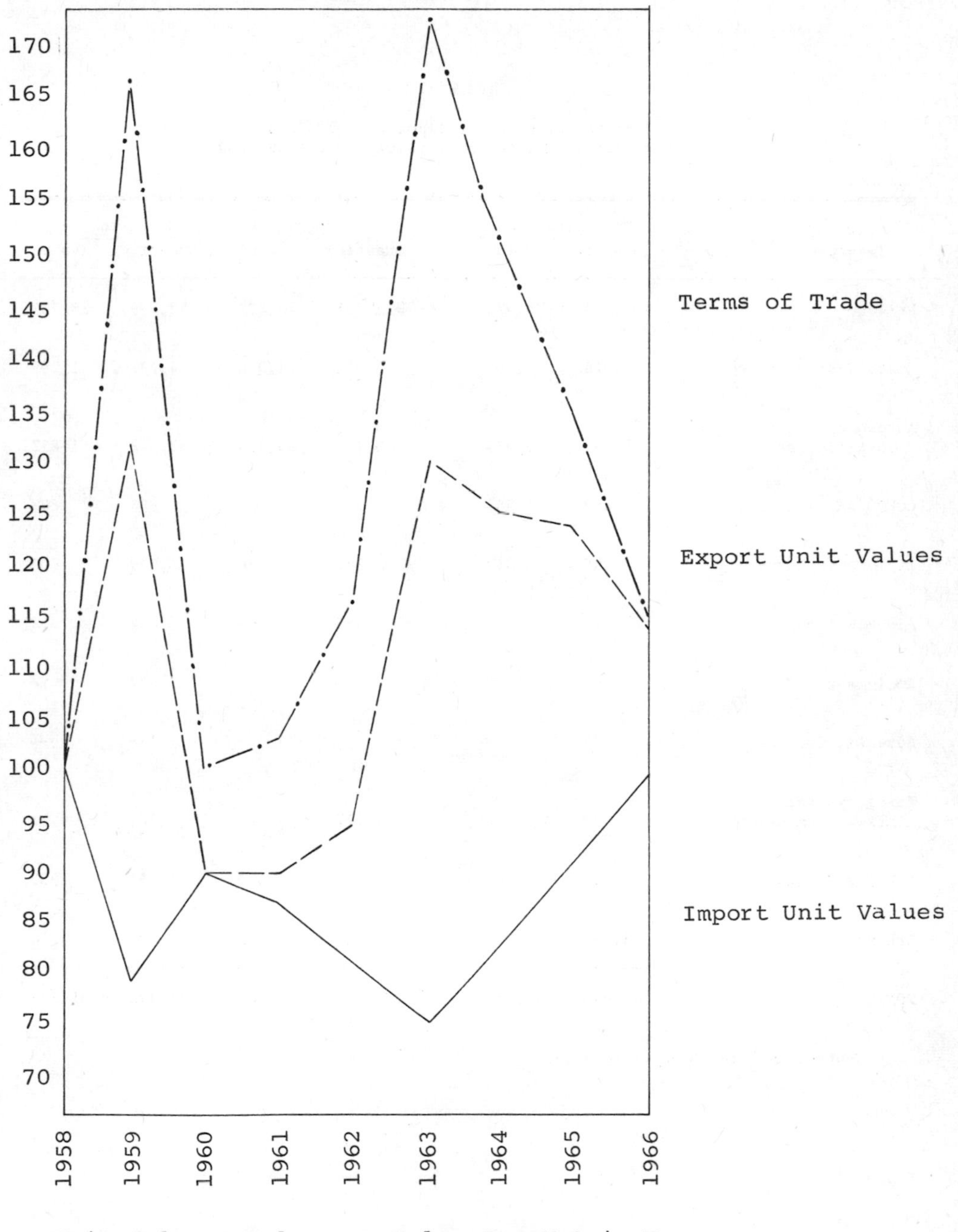

Unit Value = $\frac{\text{Value}}{\text{Tonnage}}$ = Value Per Metric Ton

TABLE 122

Imports, by Class of Importers, 1960-65
(Quantities in Metric Tons; Values in U.S. $1,000)

Class of Importers	1960		1961		1962	
	Quantity	Value	Quantity	Value	Quantity	Value
Private	195,363	23,976	211,065	24,202	243,339	28,729
State Institutions	7,018	1,354	5,341	1,015	6,732	1,299
Autonomous State Institutions	34,498	3,979	48,113	6,255	33,542	1,832
CORPOSANA	1,159	362	701	935	805	888
Diplomatic Corps	995	882	772	88	1,039	203
Aid Missions	895	790	485	544	254	332
Immigrants	98	78	124	90	87	52
Pure Oil Company	75	9	4	--	--	--
Paraguay-Brazil Mixed Commission	270	17	277	23	261	31
CARITAS Paraguay	569	89	6,162	1,469	1,195	803
Others	3,998	927	857	113	92	94
TOTAL	244,938	32,463	273,901	34,734	287,346	34,263

Source: Central Bank of Paraguay

1963		1964		1965	
Quantity	Value	Quantity	Value	Quantity	Value
233,422	25,766	223,078	26,951	258,456	34,529
8,294	1,272	11,504	1,417	15,721	2,168
43,249	1,801	38,100	3,064	52,062	4,856
724	986	912	841	740	909
878	84	155	64	612	109
947	621	1,300	1,015	1,069	638
99	52	41	20	39	31
--	--	--	--	--	--
186	17	111	4	600	33
7,847	1,976	1,640	385	2,099	698
39	29	26	7	22	38
295,685	32,604	276,867	33,768	331,420	44,009

TABLE 123

Capacity to Import, 1958-65
(In Millions of U.S. Dollars)

	1958	1959	1960	1961	1962	1963	1964	1965
Merchandise exports	33.6	35.4	36.5	43.1	39.6	38.7	45.4	60.0
Capital flow (net)	11.7	-1.5	7.2	10.7	4.7	6.6	12.6	11.6
Services (net)	-4.5	-4.7	-5.3	-8.5	-8.5	-9.1	-12.8	-16.1
Transfers (net)	1.6	2.8	3.4	4.9	4.3	6.3	5.0	3.4
TOTAL capacity to import	42.4	32.0	41.8	50.2	40.1	42.5	50.2	58.9
Merchandise imports, F.O.B.	-42.3	-36.5	-43.9	-47.8	-40.5	-38.1	-45.5	-52.2
Changes in gold and foreign exchange holdings[a]	+0.4	+5.0	+2.8	+0.3	+0.9	-1.8	-2.8	-3.9
Errors and omission	-0.5	-0.5	-0.7	-2.7	-0.5	-2.6	-1.9	-2.8

[a]Increase (-); decrease (+).

Source: Based on balance of payments data from the Central Bank of Paraguay.

as shown in Table 122. The Government of Paraguay accounted for some 10 per cent to 15 per cent of total imports in the same period, and the Catholic Relief Service (CARITAS) and foreign aid missions accounted for nearly all of the remaining imports.

The United States, Argentina, and the Federal Republic of Germany are Paraguay's leading sources of imports. The position of Germany improved markedly between 1960 and 1965, as shown in Table 120; in terms of value, imports from Germany rose 170 per cent during this period.

Terms of Trade

As shown in Chart 1, Paraguay's terms of trade have fluctuated markedly during the years 1958-66. The decline between 1959 and 1960 appears to have been caused by a decline in the value of Paraguayan exports and a sizable increase in the unit value of its imports. From 1963 on, the export unit values declined steadily whereas the unit values of imports rose sharply. This latter trend, however, may be attributed largely to a shift in the composition of imports from consumption goods to capital goods, vehicles and accessories, and fuel and lubricants (see Table 121). The increase in imports at higher unit values was made possible in part by rising exports and in part by large net inflows of foreign capital in the form of loans and grants, as shown in Table 123. These capital inflows also have helped to maintain the stability of the *guaraní* and to permit a recovery in Paraguay's foreign exchange holdings during 1963-66.

Foreign Trade Policies and Institutions

Paraguay's foreign trade policy nominally is to maximize national exports, to reduce imports of foodstuffs by achieving self-sufficiency in wheat, and to obtain advantages for the country's products within the Latin American Free Trade Association. Nevertheless, the country continues to levy taxes on exports and to tax imports of capital goods.* The short-term revenue needs of the government obviously conflict with its long-term development requirements, and until such time as a revised tax structure is adopted, with less dependence on customs duties and exchange surcharges, the two will remain irreconcilable.

To carry out its export-oriented development design, Paraguay needs to (a) increase the efficiency of its production through specialization and economies of scale; (b) establish plants to produce new, higher unit value export items, and try to develop distinctive Paraguayan products for sale abroad; (c) obtain financing for capital needs, operating costs, product and market research, and promotional activities; and (d) train specialists in project preparation and effectively incorporate these technicians into the enterprises resulting from such projects.

The Tariff

The Paraguayan tariff is principally for revenue purposes and, with the exchange surcharges, is high enough to occasion a very sizable contraband trade, as previously discussed. Although the Paraguayan Government for a while had begun to follow a policy of reducing taxes on exports so that the competitive position of Paraguayan products in foreign markets would be improved, legislation was enacted in 1966 which, among other things, applied a 3 per cent tax on the F.O.B. value of all exports not already taxed by special laws. The same bill levied a 3 per cent tax on all freight and passenger accommodations sold, thereby putting an additional tax on exports and also raising the cost of imports (the costs in all likelihood would be transferred to the consumer). These levies are "substitutes for

*Capital goods imported by the National Development Bank and financed by foreign credits usually have received special exonerations from import duties and charges.

income taxes," but in fact constitute regressive imposts detrimental to the country's legitimate foreign trade.

Paraguay is a privileged member of the Latin American Free Trade Association (LAFTA), but it has had difficulty in negotiating tariff reductions on significant items in that Association. Recently, Paraguay formed a tripartite association with Uruguay and Bolivia in an attempt to improve its trade position and to obtain the use of an Uruguayan port for its State Merchant Fleet. While Paraguay's trade with these countries has been quite small in the past, certain possibilities exist for Paraguayan exports of lumber, yerba maté, and other items in these markets.

The Exchange System

The Central Bank administers any exchange controls and supervises the foreign exchange operations of the commercial banks. A uniform exchange rate has been applied to all transactions since August, 1957, except those in bilateral agreement currencies which have been traded at discounts.* All payments transactions are subject to nominal controls, and there are restrictions on the provisions of exchange for travel and for capital transfers. A tax of 1.5 per cent is applied on all purchases and sales of foreign exchange.

Most imports are subject to surcharges in addition to tariff duties, and in many cases to prior deposit requirements. There also are special taxes on most exports. Exporters have been required to sell their foreign exchange proceeds to the banking system;** however there have been no legal sanctions

---

*Settlements with Spain under a bilateral payments agreement are made through a clearing account maintained in terms of U.S. dollars.

**However, Central Bank Resolution No. 3 of August 18, 1965, permitted coffee growers to retain 50 per cent of the dollar exchange earned from exfor noncompliance with this requirement. The banks have been required to sell 25 per cent of their gross exchange receipts to the Central Bank, and prior to the opening of the petroleum refinery in 1966, a further 15 per cent of exchange had to be sold by the banks to the oil companies to finance the importation of petroleum products.

Although the exchange rate nominally is free to fluctuate in response to market forces, the Central Bank has intervened in the market to maintain its stability since October, 1960, at ₲ 126 to the U.S. dollar. To cooperate with the Central Bank in maintaining exchange stability, the commercial banks--when necessary--allocate exchange among their customers. Consquently, the provision of exchange for import and other payments often has been subject to considerable delay. During the years 1962-65, arrears against import payments accumulated during the period of seasonal weakness in the exchange market (from September through March), and while they were reduced during the export season, they rarely have been eliminated entirely. Arrears outstanding amounted to $2.5 million at the end of 1964, $0.9 million at the end of 1965, and $2.5 million on June 30, 1966.

Until April, 1965, the system of exchange allocation was informal and its administration was left largely to the commercial banks, with occasional reference to the Central Bank. However, since April, 1965, the commercial banks have been required to submit formal accounts of their exchange transactions to the Central Bank, describing the sources and uses of exchange received and the final destination of the exchange they sold. Under these regulations the banks may sell exchange freely against specified documentation for import payments, for a

---

ports of coffee of certified Paraguayan origin, provided later conversion of such exchange into _guaranies_ was done through the banks at the official rate of exchange.

specific list of other current transactions, and for contractual capital payments. All other applications for exchange require the approval of the Central Bank. In July, 1965, limits were placed on the sale of exchange for travel. Since June, 1966, the Central Bank has required daily statements from the commercial banks on their sales of exchange.

A parallel market for foreign exchange operates freely in Asunción and other port cities. Receipts from many types of invisible transactions (e.g., tourist expenditures and family remittances) are negotiated in this market, as well as the earnings from the substantial contraband trade and from export proceeds in excess of the minimum surrender prices (aforos). At the close of 1966, the parallel market rate was virtually the same as the effective commercial bank selling rate (including tax and commission) of about ₲ 130 per dollar, as compared with ₲ 160 per dollar in July, 1965.

Import Controls

Except for temporary prohibitions on a few commodities, principally agricultural products in seasonal supply, imports are free from licensing or quantitative restrictions.* While exchange supposedly is made available freely for imports, in practice there often have been delays in the provision of exchange for reasons mentioned above. Since April, 1965, documentary proof of the transaction has been required. Import payments have been subject to a tax of 0.5 per cent on exchange transactions. In addition, surcharges--calculated on the C.I.F. value--are payable on most imports even if no foreign exchange payment takes place. These exchange surcharges were discussed in Chapter 12.

---

*For example, in June, 1966, prohibitions on imports of potatoes and onions were in effect until further notice.

Many imported products are subject to an advance deposit of 100 per cent of the F.O.B. value. This deposit is retained for 120 days or, if the deposit is made after the date of shipment, for 180 days.* However, imports from neighboring countries, imports from LAFTA countries of items on Paraguay's concession list, and other imports that are exempt from exchange surcharges, also are exempt from advance deposit requirement.

The use of suppliers' credits has become frequent in Paraguay during the 1960's; however, imports on credit for periods of more than six months require approval from the Central Bank. Such approval normally is granted only for imports of machinery and vehicles (other than private automobiles).

Export Controls

Certain exports are subject to licensing in order to assure domestic supplies. The proceeds of all exports (except coffee) are required to be repatriated and the exchange sold to a commercial bank. This requirement is enforced through a system of minimum surrender prices (*aforos*) established by the Central Bank. Special legislation permits coffee producers to retain 50 per cent of their earnings. Most exports are subject to taxes of 7½ per cent, 5 per cent, or 2½ per cent of their F.O.B. value; these taxes are collected by the banks and are payable in *guaranies*. Export receipts are subject to a 0.5 per cent tax on exchange transactions. Exchange proceeds from invisible transactions are not subject to surrender requirements.

Capital Movements

Capital transfers have been subject to control since April, 1964. The commercial banks may sell

---

*For nonexempt items imported through the Spanish Free Zone at Villeta, the deposits are retained for only ninety days.

exchange for liquidating contractual obligations against approved documentary evidence of the nature of the transaction. Other capital transfers abroad require prior approval of the Central Bank. Capital transfers also are subject to the 0.5 per cent tax on exchange transactions. When exchange is in short supply, arrears in capital transfers may occur.

Bilateral Agreements

Paraguay is a signatory to the Agreement for the Multilateral Compensation of Balances Between the Member Countries of the Latin American Free Trade Association. Under this agreement, bilateral payments accords were signed in May, 1966, between the Central Bank of Paraguay and the central banks of Argentina, Mexico, Chile, and Peru. There is a reciprocal credit swing of $865,000 under the agreement with Argentina and of $200,000 under each of the agreements with the other countries. Balances under these agreements are to be settled every two months in convertible currency. The use of these agreements by Paraguayan banks and traders is not mandatory as it is in certain of the partner countries.

Currently, Paraguay has one other payments agreement in effect--that with Spain, signed August 25, 1950, and effective since October, 1952. From 1959 through 1962, Paraguay was in a debtor position under this agreement, largely reflecting payments made against Spanish loans for the purchase of vessels by the State Merchant Fleet. However, Paraguay's exports to Spain have risen substantially since 1961, and since 1963 the bilateral account has been in favor of Paraguay. The exchange rate for Spanish agreement dollars was raised, in stages, from ₲ 79 per agreement dollar in 1959 to ₲ 125 in July, 1962. Under this agreement, trade lists and quotas govern commodity movements between the two countries. The purchase of Spanish ships by FLOMERE is done by means of supplier credit agreements.

The following ministries and offices are involved in Paraguay's foreign trade activities: the Ministry of Finance, through its administration of the customs and of taxes and charges on exports and imports; the Central Bank, through its management of foreign exchange and the balance of payments; the Ministry of Foreign Relations, through its negotiations of international treaties and agreements affecting commercial policy; the Ministry of Industry and Commerce, in recommending the application or removal of duties and charges to protect or promote Paraguayan industry, and in supervising the marking of Paraguayan exports; COPACAR, which recommends meat slaughter quotas for export; the National Foreign Trade Council; and the National Economic Coordination Council which has over-all jurisdiction over the national economy.

The Ministry of Finance--The conflict between the immediate revenue needs of the Ministry and fiscal policies required for longer-term national development already has been discussed, as well as the failure to control contraband trade and to remove its causes. A Tariff Commission, which was to work on a revision of the customs tariff, has been moribund for some time. The Directorate General of Customs, while not a policy organization, has made clearance procedures so complicated that the costs of foreign trade have been increased measurably.

Ministry of Foreign Relations--Paraguay is a country that invites foreign investment. The government has signed an Investment Guaranty Agreement with the United States, in 1966, adding extended risk guarantees.

Ministry of Industry and Commerce--A revised industrial development law, providing liberal fiscal incentives to enterprises coming into the country or expanding their capacity, has been drafted and was presented to the legislature late in 1966. Particular benefits were expected to be awarded to joint venture enterprises in which foreign capital would participate with Paraguayan private investments in the industrialization of the country.

A private Development and Productivity Center was established in October, 1966, with USAID assistance. This Center, in time, should have a positive effect on stimulating the establishment of new production and export activities in Paraguay. It is expected that the proposed private development financing corporation (financiera) will assist in financing such projects. The Ministry of Industry and Commerce has given its support to both the Center and the financiera and is very interested in regional development projects.

The Ministry has issued a promotional pamphlet, entitled "Paraguay: Land of Opportunity," in several languages. This Ministry, although understaffed and underfinanced, has shown definite interest in increasing its role in the development effort. With the initiation of a formal Private Enterprise Development project in the USAID in July, 1966, substantial technical support is being given to this Ministry so that its role may be enhanced and its budget enlarged.

COPACAR--The Paraguayan Meat Corporation is a mixed enterprise in which the government holds only 2 per cent of the stock but controls the organization. Established years ago to assure adequate supplies of meat at reasonable prices to domestic consumers, this entity appears to have outlived its usefulness. Its present functions include (a) recommending to the National Economic Coordination Council the annual cattle slaughter quota for export; (b) operation of an antiquated and unsanitary slaughterhouse near Asunción; and (c) selling meat at retail to keep prices down. The slaughter quota for exports has been a stumbling block to progress in the cattle industry and has tended to favor, at various times, the ranchers or the meatpackers, depending upon whether global or individual plant quotas were established.

National Foreign Trade Council--The National Foreign Trade Council (Consejo Nacional de Comercio Exterior) was created in 1962 to replace the National Free Trade Zone Council of 1960. The Council is comprised of representatives of the Ministries of Foreign Relations, Finance, Agriculture and Livestock, and Industry and Commerce; the Central Bank and the National Development Bank; and private organizations, such as FEPRINCO and the Paraguayan Industrial Union. The representative of the Ministry of Foreign Relations serves as chairman. The Council advises the government on commercial policies and takes an active role in LAFTA matters.

Gold and Foreign Exchange Holdings

The Central Bank's net holdings of international reserves at the end of 1965, excluding Paraguay's gold tranche position in the International Monetary Fund (IMF), reached a peak of $8.38 million in 1965. By the end of 1966, the balance had declined to $7.64 million as commercial arrears were reduced substantially in line with the government's commitments to the IMF. The net international reserve position of the Central Bank for the period 1953-66 is shown in Table 124. The improvement of the Bank's reserve position since 1963 probably is attributable to (a) a tightening of exchange transaction reporting that has served to reduce exchange leakages from the commercial banks to the black market and thereby has tended to increase the Central Bank's holdings; (b) a catching-up on commercial arrears; and (c) substantial net inflows of foreign capital to finance portions of the local costs of capital projects. Prepayment of exports by meatpackers and vegetable oil exporters (mainly foreign companies), who need to convert dollars into _guaranies_ for local expenses (including payment of taxes), also tends to raise the level of year-end exchange reserves of the Central Bank.

With respect to the Central Bank's holdings of convertible currencies, dollars formed the minor share during the years 1952-56, 1958, and 1960. In 1959, and from 1961 on, U.S. dollars have been the major convertible currency held by the Bank. This trend toward dollar reserves probably resulted from several factors:

(a) The monetary stabilization program introduced in 1957 undoubtedly created an incentive on the part of the government to hold the bulk of its international reserves in the form of U.S. dollars;

TABLE 124

Net International Reserve Position of the Central Bank, 1953-66

End of Year	Gold and Convertible Exchange			New Bilateral Balances	Net Holdings	Net IMF Position	Net Reserve Position
	Assets	Liabilities	Net				
1953	3.94	--	3.94	-1.67	2.27	--	2.27
1954	3.51	0.05	3.46	-2.72	0.74	0.38	1.12
1955	1.19	0.35	0.84	2.66	3.50	0.38	3.88
1956	1.24	0.12	1.12	6.09	7.21	-1.13	6.08
1957	1.56	0.02	1.54	4.51	6.05	-3.63	2.42
1958	0.36	0.59	-0.23	6.98	6.75	-4.38	2.37
1959	2.86	0.01	2.85	0.14	2.99	-2.56	0.43
1960	0.47	--	0.47	-0.50	-0.03	-2.38	-2.41
1961	2.44	--	2.44	-1.35	1.08	-0.44	0.65
1962	0.78	0.76	0.02	-0.70	-0.69	1.31	0.63
1963	1.40	1.50	-0.10	0.29	0.19	1.81	2.01
1964	3.15	0.60	2.55	0.45	3.00	2.31	5.31
1965	7.21	--	7.21	1.17	8.38	3.06[a]	11.44[a]
1966	7.29	0.05	7.24	0.40	7.64	3.75[b]	11.39[b]

[a]Includes $0.25 of IBRD bonds purchased by the Central Bank in September, 1965.

[b]Includes $0.25 of IBRD bonds, and $0.25 of IDB bonds purchased in April, 1966.

Source: Central Bank of Paraguay.

(b) At the same time the U.S. emerged as a more important market for Paraguayan exports, so that more dollars became available to the Central Bank (see Table 120);

(c) The bilateral payments agreements concluded by Paraguay in the postwar period were allowed to expire as the world dollar shortage dwindled and more flexible commercial policies were adopted by the major trading nations; and

(d) Inasmuch as Paraguay's exports to other multilateral payment countries have increased in recent years, it is likely that payments, in many cases, have been effected in dollars or in currencies that Paraguay converted into dollars.

In the postwar years 1949-54, Paraguay concluded several bilateral trade and/or payments agreements, most of them with European countries.[3] Between 1955 and 1958, the bulk of Paraguay's exchange transactions under payments agreements were with Argentina. These transactions dropped to very low levels during 1959-61 and disappeared completely in subsequent years. The only payments agreement currently in force is that with Spain. The balance of payments under this agreement has been in favor of Paraguay.

To arrive at the government's net gold and foreign exchange holdings, the country's gold tranche position in the International Monetary Fund (i.e., Net IMF Position) must be taken into account. This was done in Table 124.

The gold tranche position, as defined by the IMF, is: "The member's quota minus the Fund's holdings of the member's currency..." This tranche measures the amount a member may draw essentially automatically under the Fund's gold tranche policy. Thus, as of December 31, 1966, Paraguay's gold tranche position was as shown in Table 125.

TABLE 125

Paraguay's Gold Tranche Position, as of December 31, 1966

	Millions of U.S. Dollars
Quota	15.0
Gold	(3.8)
Currency	(11.2)
Net drawings	0
Fund holdings of currency[a]	11.2
Reserve position in the IMF	3.8
Gross fund position[b]	18.8

[a]Represents 75 per cent of quota.

[b]Represents twice Paraguay's quota minus the IMF holdings of *guaranies*.

Source: International Monetary Fund.

Between 1947 and 1966, the Government of Paraguay entered into at least seven stand-by arrangements with the International Monetary Fund. The most recent such agreement was that of August, 1966, for an amount of $7.5 million. Since 1961, this type of arrangement has been utilized by the Central Bank to justify its restrictions on credits to the Central Government, and by the Minister of Finance to withstand pressures by the military and other pressure groups to obtain excessive increases in appropriations. Paraguay's use of the Fund's resources during 1952-66 are shown in Table 126.

When the gold tranche position of Paraguay is added to the Central Bank's holdings of international reserves, total official holdings at the end of 1965 become $11.4 million, the highest level recorded during the years 1952-65. This level was maintained in 1966, thanks to the role of external resources in financing the country's imports.

TABLE 126

Paraguay's Use of International Monetary Fund Resources, 1952-66
(In Millions of U.S. Dollars)

Year	Purchases	Repurchases	Total Outstanding[a]	Quota	Fund Holdings of Guaranies as Per Cent of Quota
1952	0.88	--	0.88	3.5[b]	100
1954	--	0.38	0.50	3.5	89
1956	1.50	--	2.00	3.5	132
1957	4.00	0.50	5.50	7.5	148
1958	0.75	--	6.25	7.5	158
1959	--	1.50	4.75	8.7	129
1960	1.00	0.88	4.87	10.0	124
1961	--	1.65	3.23	11.25	104
1962	--	1.75	1.48	11.25	88
1963	--	0.50	0.99	11.25	84
1964	--	0.50	0.49	11.25	79
1965	--	0.49	--	11.25	75
1966	--	--	--	15.00[c]	75

[a]End of period.
[b]Original quota of $2 million increased to $3.5 million in 1948.
[c]In February, 1966, Paraguay's quota in the IMF was raised to $15 million.

Commercial bank net reserves of foreign exchange averaged $3.8 million a year during 1952-57. However, from 1958 on, these reserves were negative, even reaching an adverse balance of some $2.5 million (in 1961). These net deficits of reserves represent the excess of the banks' sales or commitments to sell foreign exchange to importers, over the amount of exchange actually received from exporters. The amount of exchange that the banks commit themselves to sell reportedly is determined by their holdings of export letters of credit. The negative balances are financed by short-term advances of reserves from head offices abroad.

The local commercial banks buy letters of credit at a discount from exporters and charge fees or commissions for doing so. In turn, the commercial banks discount these letters of credit with their head offices to obtain the foreign exchange advances for meeting their commitments to importers in Paraguay. The fees and commissions charged in the first instance presumably more than offset the discount loss in the second transaction. Until these letters of credit are liquidated, they constitute an exchange liability of the Paraguayan branches of the foreign banks.

The effectiveness of this financing device in equilibrating exports and imports depends, of course, mainly on the extent to which Paraguay's trade is conducted under the letter-of-credit procedure. Its advantage to the import sector is that even if payments against these letters are delayed, some exchange still will be forthcoming immediately through the system of advances previously described. On the other hand, because importers and exporters often are the same persons or enterprises, established clients of the banks undoubtedly have an advantage over newcomers having to purchase foreign exchange, even for more essential imports (from the national development standpoint) than those of the established traders.

Notes to Chapter 15

1. This discussion includes material from a report prepared by Dr. Henry Ceuppens of the American Embassy in Paraguay, dated May 5, 1966, entitled "General Analysis of Paraguayan Exports for the Period 1958-65." The values of exports are F.O.B. Paraguayan port.

2. Memoria--1963, p. 77. This was the latest annual report of the Central Bank in existence at the end of 1966.

3. See U.S. Department of Commerce, Investment in Paraguay (Washington, D.C.: Government Printing Office, December, 1954), pp. 93-96.

PART IV

PROSPECTS FOR ECONOMIC DEVELOPMENT

CHAPTER 16 DEVELOPMENT PLANNING

A Technical Planning Secretariat for Economic and Social Development was created in the Office of the President of the Republic in 1962. Its purpose is to analyze the national economy and establish its development goals. From the outset, the Secretariat was advised by a Tripartite Advisory Group, consisting of nominees from the Organization of American States (OAS), the U.N. Economic Commission for Latin America (ECLA), and the Inter-American Development Bank (IDB). It received P.L. 480 Title I loan funds from the U.S. Government to pay a portion of its annual operating expenses.

Two national plans have been produced thus far, the first covering the years 1965-66 and the second covering 1967-68. While the Tripartite Advisory Group was largely responsible for the first two-year plan, the Paraguayan staff of the Secretariat had the major role in the preparation of the second plan. Both plans were statistically weak and failed to develop a sound project base for national development. Moreover, the plans have failed to provide an ordering of events, combined with reliable time and cost estimates. Although widespread consultation was held by Secretariat personnel with counterparts in other government agencies and with the private sector, there was considerable initial opposition to "planning" by certain Paraguayan Government agencies, especially the Ministry of Finance. Although in general the opposition to planning abated markedly during and after the preparation of the second plan, nevertheless the national plans have not yet been incorporated into the national budget except for certain ongoing capital projects. Nevertheless,

TABLE 127

Institutional Progress of the Paraguayan Public Sector, 1961-66

Date	Law or Decree	Institution	Objectives
March 14, 1961	Decree-Law No. 281	National Development Bank	Promote and finance programs and projects to promote agricultural, livestock, forestry, industrial, and commercial development.
June 8, 1962	Decree No. 22,699	National Foreign Trade Council (Ministry of Foreign Relations)	Promote and direct Paraguay's trade with the LAFTA, GATT, and other common markets.
June 14, 1962	Ministerial Resolution No. 60	Planning Unit, Ministry of Public Health and Social Welfare.	Formulate a national health plan and coordinate, supervise, and evaluate its execution.
September 14, 1962	Law No. 841	Technical Planning Secretariat for Economic and Social Development (Office of the Presidency)	Analyze the economic and social situation of the country and formulate general socio-economic development plans.
September 18, 1962	Law No. 845	General Budget Office (Ministry of Finance)	Establish program and activity budgets (economic budgets)

March 22, 1963	Law No. 852	Rural Welfare Institute (IBR)	Promote and implement national agrarian reform.
August 30, 1963	Law No. 904; Decree No. 996 of October 18, 1963	Organization of the Ministry of Industry and Commerce	Promote the production and commercialization of national products, and foster the growth of domestic and international trade.
August 12, 1964	Law No. 966	National Electricity Administration (ANDE)	Satisfy the country's electric power requirements.
August 14, 1964	Law No. 970	Paraguayan Housing and Urbanization Institute (IPVU)	Construct low-cost housing, and plan and promote the orderly growth of cities and urban centers.
August 23, 1965	Law No. 1,066	National Navigation and Port Administration (ANNP)	Administer and operate all ports in the country and maintain the navigability of its rivers.
February 15, 1966	Decree Law	State Merchant Fleet (FLOMERE)	Provide passenger and freight services within the country and abroad.
June 15, 1966	Decree No. 19,244	National Council on Educational Planning (Ministry of Education)	Examine and approve development plans for education and suggest criteria for the formulation of the educational policies of the nation.

Source: Administration Division, Technical Planning Secretariat.

apart from fiscal reform, the Paraguayan public sector has taken certain steps under the Alliance for Progress to improve its institutional capability for development. A listing of these accomplishments in chronological order during 1961-66 is given in Table 127.

With the exception of ANDE, the foregoing institutions are relatively weak and require substantial technical assistance. Inadequate financing also is a problem affecting their operations. For the most part, the newly created institutions are autonomous agencies that have taken over ongoing inefficient activities and are trying, with limited resources, to improve the situation. While results thus far have not been entirely satisfactory, nevertheless an improved administrative structure has been created and could be molded into a reasonably efficient development tool.

The Technical Planning Secretariat, in its policy recommendations in both the 1965-66 and 1967-68 plans, has taken a broad view of socio-economic development and has set forth its views quite clearly. Because the Secretariat has been gaining support from both the business community and the public sector, and hence may be expected to exert greater influence on national policy formulation in the future, it is well to describe briefly the main views of this executive staff agency. As will be seen, the Technical Planning Secretariat appears to be well aware of current development theory, and its recommendations in general are sound.

PROPOSALS FOR DEVELOPMENT

National development must include consideration not only of economic factors but also of social and psychological factors which orient and activate the behavior of persons, groups, organizations, and institutions in the development process. Paraguay seeks national integration and consolidation just as developed countries do. However, the rising expectations of the Paraguayan people are creating pressures for short-term solutions. Within two or three decades the problems of national development must be solved. Therefore, it is imperative that there be created as soon as possible a governmental capacity to ensure development by means of a dynamic, objective, and national process of political and administrative decisions. Solid public administrative institutions are essential prerequisites to economic and social development. Various measures have been proposed by the Secretariat to improve both the government's operations and its public relations:

1. Measures to improve operations:

   a) Continue planning (studies, investigations, and projects) in order to orient public policies;

   b) Adopt a national policy of development and subordinate everything else to it;

   c) Make correlative political and administrative decisions;

   d) Create new types of activity and create or revise orientating or regulatory mechanisms of nongovernmental activity;

   e) Coordinate centers for the dissemination and utilization of scientific and technological knowledge;

   f) Offer new services and introduce new patterns to those services which are already provided;

   g) Increase its capacity to efficiently operate promotional activities in all the economic and social sectors;

   h) Increase its capacity to formulate, implement, and execute programs and projects; and

   i) Familiarize every level of the government with the potentialities and advantages of development.

2. Measures to improve public relations:

   a) Provide rational justifications of public policies;

   b) Strive for objective discussion of the most important matters at an institutional level; and

   c) Establish permanent channels of communication which effectively and positively interrelate individuals, institutions, and the government.

The concern of development administration is to enable the objectives of economic growth and increases in social welfare (expressed in public policies) to be effected through acts leading to economic and socio-cultural change. The key objective for all public administrative efforts, therefore, should be to establish a high and sustainable rate of growth of the economy, together with comparable normative levels in health, education, social welfare, and social security. Another main objective of public policy should be to obtain optimum utilization of existing resources; this can be achieved through planning. Planning aids in defining and expressing the future dimension of the country in a quantitative and qualitative manner, permits every national society and every government to anticipate events, and serves as an essential instrument for attaining a strict discipline in public investment and an adequate orientation of private investment. For this reason, administration for development requires a considerable degree of centralization in the planning and formulating of policies and strategy, as well as a considerable degree of decentralization in decisions and authority for the management and executory organizations.

SPECIFIC POLICIES

General Economic Policy

Economic policy consists of measures taken by the government to influence economic activity. In the present stage of Paraguay's economic development, such measures should be oriented mainly to facilitating a marked increase in export production. The economic potential created by improved infrastructure and accompanying large capital investments should be put to optimum use; equipment of the commodity producing sectors, especially the agricultural sector, should be improved; human resources should be capacitated; and administrative and managerial capacity should be upgraded and expanded.

The activity of the private sector is also increasing and will require administrative, managerial, and technical skills which are changing rapidly. To permit the private sector to keep pace, professional training and technical assistance at every level of management must be improved considerably, thereby permitting not only the absorption of technology but of the magnitudes of investment required for it. Consequently, actions and policies that should acquire significance in the short run should be conducive to (a) changing the productive structure and technology, especially in the agrarian and industrial sectors and their organization for export; (b) optimizing the use of investment resources, including available credit; (c) improving the administrative and technical capacities of the labor force; (d) obtaining the greatest possible knowledge of the potential of available natural resources; and (e) increasing the operative capacity of the State.

Foreign Trade Policy

Exportation is as important as production. Given the limited scope of the domestic market, recourse to foreign markets as a means of expanding national production is inevitable. The establishment of an adequate policy of orienting imports to achieve the best utilization of the import capacity of the country should also be a basic consideration.

Export Policies

The means proposed by the Technical Planning Secretariat to implement the program of increasing exports include establishing central markets for grading and classifying agricultural products for export; exploring commercial opportunities with neighboring countries and reaching effective agreement on the basis of supplementation in accordance with the provisions of the LAFTA treaty; promoting commercial treaties with countries outside the LAFTA; establishing a financing mechanism adequate to stimulate productive export activities; conforming the tax structure to the competitive capacity of exportable products; reducing to a minimum the processing and port handling costs of exporting; gradually bringing current commercial policy into conformance with a total integration of the Latin American market; supporting the creation of a financial organization to be responsible exclusively for financing intrazonal trade within the integrated area; setting up a compensatory mechanism for offsetting the losses resulting from any worsening in the terms of trade, such mechanism to have at least the function of stabilizing prices of raw materials; and requesting technical and financial assistance from international organizations in order to aid in the fulfillment of the program outlined for the foreign trade sector.

Import Policies

Policies in importation should include, among other things, the elimination of contraband, undervaluation, and fiscal fraud; attainment of a flexible policy which would permit temporal corrections of domestic prices and which would promote domestic production to substitute for imports; and carrying out the process of import substitution on sound economic bases, assuring its congruency with the policies of the LAFTA. In considering import substitution possibilities special attention should be given to incorporating frontier areas of bordering countries into the Paraguayan market.

Financial Policies

Two fundamental aspects in the development process are the utilization of credit as a stimulus to production, and the attainment of monetary and price stability to stimulate productive activity. Taking these principal aspects into consideration, the fundamental national objectives should be to expand domestic savings, increase financial aid from abroad, and formulate a complementary monetary policy whose purpose would be to adapt the means of payment to the increase in the Gross Domestic Product. Therefore, it will be necessary to strengthen the mechanisms of savings and direct investment; give limited financial assistance to the rural areas and to the housing sector in order to execute programs that later can be continued with their own saving capacity; concentrate such assistance in areas or nuclei which are able to attain a satisfactory rate of growth in a relatively short time; amend the banking laws to permit the banking system to receive savings deposits under a revaluation clause (in case of currency depreciation), such deposits to carry a lower interest rate than those not carrying this clause; enhance credit facilities abroad for financing national exports; negotiate long-term credits for important activities presently undercapitalized; and study the possibility of creating a National Inter-Bank Committee to coordinate the financing of national projects receiving external aid.

Tax Policies

The deficient tax structure and its sequel of counterproductive effects require a new planning of tax policy, taking into account the development needs of the country. The general strategy should include:

(a) Consideration of a tax structure that contemplates a high proportion of direct taxation, in order to tax the taxpayer according to his ability to pay. For this purpose, and as an item of priority in the short run, a program which contemplates specifically the reorganization of the income and real estate tax structures should be undertaken.

(b) Preparation of land maps and soil studies for classification of soils in the rural areas, and a scientific cadastral survey accompanied by improvement in the efficiency of real estate tax administration and the abandonment of outdated practices.

(c) Inasmuch as almost 20 per cent of the periodic income of the Central Administration is obligated for predetermined purposes, elimination of earmarked taxes and their reincorporation into the general budget should be realized to obtain greater fiscal flexibility.

(d) Revision of policy on tax exemptions and franchises, to obtain greater revenues for the government.

(e) Simplification of tax legislation, eliminating the multiplicity of relatively insignificant taxes and clarifying the laws in such a way as to form a group of clear, precise, and coherent legislation enactments, thereby simplifying their application.

(f) Reorganization of the offices in charge of administering the tax laws, in a gradual manner.

(g) Attraction of as many private resources as possible, thereby permitting them to respond to the financial needs of the development program.

(h) Granting of preferential treatment to incomes in certain sectors of production that would serve to stimulate further investment. Such measures could include accelerated depreciation of fixed assets; partial or total exemption from taxation on reinvestment of profits; partial or total exemption from taxes on specific activities according to their location; exemption from export duties; and conformance of tariff policy to the need to stimulate or discourage specific imports.

Employment, Salary, and Income Distribution Policies

Those sectors having the lowest productivity have had the highest percentage of persons employed. Policy should establish the conditions by which underutilized labor could be transferred to sectors having greater productivity and by which jobs necessary to take care of the growing labor force could be created. In the case of rural employment, such policy would require acceleration of agrarian and colonial reform, establishment of a hierarchy of occupations, execution of programs of seasonal employment, and facilitation of selective medium- and long-term credits for work incentive programs. In the case of industrial employment, the program should include a gradual transfer of workers from artisan production to the manufacturing sector; an increase in the proportion of occupations that may be classified as highly productive; oriented programs of technical and financial assistance; and expansion of public works and services.

In the medium and long run, increasing participation of wage earners in the distribution of urban and rural income is required. Therefore, it is recommended that a general policy of dynamic salaries be created in accordance with the productivity of the system; that salary scales be established that would encourage professional training and the assumption of additional responsibilities; that salary scales be revised periodically in accordance with the rise in productivity of the economic system; and that social security coverage be expanded and its cost adapted to the various wage levels. Moreover, the educational system should provide the means for improving equality of opportunity, mobility, and the formation of human capital (manpower). Therefore, maximum attention should be given to developing educational projects geared to improving individual capacity and qualifying available manpower to participate in the economic development process.

Improved Domestic Marketing Policy

The promotion of exports should constitute the fundamental dynamic stimulating the agro-industrial production of the country. Expansion of the domestic market will be the multiplier effect of this strategy. Consequently, the Secretariat recommends that programs be adopted to improve internal as well as external marketing conditions and means of communication; that these programs be coordinated with technical and financial assistance to cooperatives and community development activities; that the most suitable production lines and zones be identified; that the demand levels and taste preferences of the internal market be studied; that small rural artisan industries be developed; and that industrial production be decentralized in order to expand effective demand in the regions benefited by these policies.

Investment and Resource Allocation Policies

Investment policy should attempt to achieve a more rapid maturity of the productive potential of Paraguay. Investments should encompass fixed capital requirements and should be complemented, where necessary, by State investments in directly productive activities. Investment policy should be directed at two basic programs which overlap: (a) a general investment program that permits the more dynamic economic sectors to develop within the areas and sectors identified as of priority importance; and (b) particular investment programs of accelerated modernization in areas and/or activities of a priority nature. Within this general framework, public investment policy and private investment orientation should contemplate that: (1) resources destined for public works be directed in greater proportion toward facilitating internal and external marketing of national products; (2) investment in infrastructure should keep pace with economic development needs; (3) investments in social infrastructure be directed toward a better use of existing facilities and the servicing of new areas of the country; (4) reinvestment of capital be stimulated; (5) investments conform with the size of projects, the technology employed, and the actual or potential availability of raw materials; (6) new production destined for the domestic market should be able to compete with the output of existing enterprises and with products from other LAFTA countries; (7) investments tending to improve the utilization of existing installed capacity be favored; and (8) interrelated investment and financial programs be established.

Agrarian Policies

There are relatively few Secretariat recommendations in this basic sector of the Paraguayan economy. This is not because of failure to recognize the importance of this sector, but that many of the policies previously mentioned pertain particularly to the production and marketing of agricultural products. Specific recommendations in the field of agrarian policy therefore were confined to the following: (a) consolidate new areas of production; (b) integrate properties in the Central Zone into more economic farm units; (c) establish improved programs of experimentation, demonstration, farm administration, and credit; (d) introduce tax reforms beneficial to agriculture; and (d) effect economic and physical cadastral surveys leading to improved land use.

In sum, the strategy of Paraguay's macro-socio-economic development plan is to increase the export orientation of the economy. This is to be accomplished through regionalization of production and its specialization. The future increases in income resulting from this process are to be spread among a larger number of the productive population. When this is accomplished, Paraguay can begin to produce for a growing local market, as well as for export. The concept of decentralization, or regional development, extends also to the provision of social services (schools, health facilities, and water supplies).

With respect to financing the development program, the Technical Planning Secretariat relies heavily on foreign capital. Nevertheless, it recommends the adoption of policies that will permit greater participation of local capital resources in the development effort. This might be accomplished through tax reform and other means of capturing private savings, such as an issue of development bonds for financing specific projects, and permitting commercial banks to accept savings deposits with a revaluation provision as a hedge against inflation.

In the past few years, the Technical Planning Secretariat has been thinking more and more in terms of regional development. It has come to feel that perhaps this approach would be more fruitful than a global approach to development. Certainly, local attempts at development planning in at least six major areas of the country have tended to reinforce this point of view.* For such planning purposes, the Secretariat has divided the country into seven zones, designated as shown in Table 128.

TABLE 128

Areas Proposed for Regional Development

Zone Number	Designation	Principal City or Cities
I	North Zone (Zona Norte)	Concepción; Pedro Juan Caballero
II	Central Zone (Zona Central)	Asunción; Villarrica
III	Eastern Zone (Zona Este)	Coronel Oviedo
IV	Southeast (Sur-Este)	Encarnación
V	Southwest (Sur-Oeste)	Pilar; Ita-pirú
VI	Southern Chaco (Chaco Sur)	Pozo Colorado
VII	Northern Chaco (Chaco Norte)	Mariscal Estigarribia

*The first regional office of the Technical Planning Secretariat was established at Encarnación, Department of Itapúa, in late 1966. It is staffed largely by personnel of that area.

In order of priority, the zones to be addressed are IV, III, I, V, VI, II, and VII. As previously mentioned, a regional planning organization already has been established for Zone IV and an inventory of its physical resources has been completed. Similar organizations are expected to be established in Zones III and I within the next two years. Much will depend, however, upon the success of the experiment in Zone IV, continued AID financing of regional planning efforts, and the availability of competent personnel to staff these planning organizations in the interior. An AID contribution to this effort, albeit modest in scale, could be the key to the success of the regional development effort; training of Paraguayans, technical assistance, and the financing of a few local technicians would be all that was required. The self-help component of such activities would represent a very high proportion (at least 75 per cent) of total inputs.

Not only is the private sector interested in regional development, but the Ministry of Industry and Commerce sees in this approach a vast opportunity to stimulate decentralized industrial development in the country. Exposure of Paraguayans to this type of activity in the United States in 1966 and 1967, under USAID sponsorship, has been an important element in promoting the regional approach in Paraguay.[1] Personal contacts between the author and members of the Technical Planning Secretariat and Ministry of Industry and Commerce also have helped to promote this concept. And the USAID's willingness to finance a local technician to work on the Zone IV plan (as part of a three-man team) has been of major importance in getting this experiment under way in 1967.* All parties expect that through the regional development approach,

---

*The other two members were to be financed by the Department of Itapúa and the Technical Planning Secretariat, respectively.

government ministries and autonomous agencies will be able to focus better on development problems and bring them into manageable proportions on a priority basis. It is anticipated also that the private sector will be guided by these priorities and, as infrastructure becomes less of a limitation, other location factors will come to bear on the distribution of manufacturing and processing facilities about the country.

Notes to Chapter 16

1. The author was responsible for organizing this training program while serving as Economic Adviser with USAID/Paraguay.

CHAPTER 17 PARAGUAY'S FUTURE

The long-term trend in the Paraguayan economy is upward, and Paraguay has the potential human and material resources to achieve modest self-sustained economic growth by the end of the century. Certain public sector agencies are becoming increasingly development-minded and are building infrastructure (electric power, roads, improved ports, and airports) and giving more attention to encouraging agriculture and manufacturing. An institutional framework for development has been created in both the public and private sectors and, with modest technical and financial assistance from external sources, these institutions could become efficiently operating implements of sectoral plans (e.g., housing, agrarian reform, shipping, credit). Paraguay currently is the only country in South America that can boast political and monetary stability sustained over a period of years. The re-election of President Stroessner in February, 1967, for another five-year term, would appear to indicate a continuation of these conditions.

While the government's financial resources have fallen far short of the nation's development requirements, public investments have been growing substantially in recent years in relation to the total national budget. Although no sweeping fiscal reforms have been made, improvements are taking place in fiscal administration. Improved collection of certain taxes, combined with favorable business conditions, have resulted in a rise in tax revenues even without major changes in the rate structures. Nevertheless, the major obstacle to Paraguay's economic growth continues to be the absence of a fiscal policy that could provide adequate public savings for socio-economic development. This has been reflected in the low level of implementation of national plans, in the onerous taxes levied on the livestock industry and on foreign trade, and in the chronic arrears in debt service payments by the Ministry of Finance to the United States Government and certain other creditors. It is doubtful that the President of the Republic is fully aware of this situation. He often has remarked upon Paraguay's creditworthiness and its promptness in paying external obligations. While this has been true of debts payable by the Central Bank, it certainly has not been the case with respect to the debts of the Ministry of Finance.

It would appear to be of crucial importance that the President have a Financial Adviser to keep him informed of the public sector's fiscal condition and to make recommendations for fiscal improvements on both the revenue and expenditure sides. Such an adviser should be able to recommend a fiscal reform program consonant with the development needs of the country. An AID program loan or similar device probably would help materially in having such a self-help program implemented. This proposal would be consistent with CIAP, AID, and IDB recommendations regarding self-help efforts on the part of Paraguay.

Improved fiscal policies also are indispensable for permitting the proper operation of monetary policy in Paraguay's development process. Heretofore, monetary policy has been utilized very largely to transfer savings of the private sector to the public sector through the Central Bank. At the close of 1966, the commercial banks had the use of no more than 58 per cent of their deposits. The inadequacy of monetary policy to provide adequate financing of the public sector has been reflected in the growing external debt of Paraguay and the need (since 1956) of continual IMF Stand-by Arrangements, primarily to enforce limitations on public sector borrowings from the Central Bank and very secondarily to protect the country's balance of payments.

Paraguay has relied excessively on external financing for its public sector projects. While the debt service burden has not been unduly oppressive because of the liberal terms offered by foreign lending institutions, changes in the credit policies of these lenders and the continuation of the Ministry of Finance's dilatory tactics in servicing its external obligations could effect significant changes in this situation. Moreover, there presumably are limits to the country's absorptive capacity for foreign borrowing, the principal limitation being that of providing matching local funds.

Inasmuch as adequate fiscal reforms would have to include the elimination of contraband activities and a stabilization or reduction of military outlays, it is obvious that the government must become less dependent upon the military for its existence. A broadly based representative government must be achieved to make this possible. It appears that Paraguay is moving slowly in this direction. All major political parties have been recognized. In addition, certain personnel changes were begun in 1966, and perhaps a more development-minded attitude will emerge in the near future. The emergence of deliberate self-help efforts at the regional and municipal levels is a recent development of considerable interest and potential value, both economically and politically.

The President has come to rely increasingly on the Technical Planning Secretariat for advice and information. If the Secretariat could be linked more closely to the top level National Economic Coordination Council, the importance of the Secretariat would be enhanced and it would be in a stronger position to influence the implementation of its plans. At such time, the Secretariat should become deeply concerned with the development of human resources, which thus far has received relatively little attention.

With regard to the private sector, prior to the signing of the Charter of Punta del Este in 1961, this sector might have been characterized as having been very conservative and on the defensive against government encroachments. Mistrust of the government was widespread, and the country's sad experiences with inflation prior to the monetary reforms of 1957 added substance to the private sector's attitude. The numerous business associations that were formed during the late 1940's and early 1950's originated in a need to protect particular private interests against government intervention (economic controls, regressive taxes, discriminations against nonparty members, State monopolies, etc.) that was accentuated by wartime requirements during World War II and the Korean War. Moreover, Paraguay's chaotic history also had inhibited private sector initiative and had served effectively to discourage foreign investment in the country. Until the Stroessner Administration had demonstrated its ability to maintain political stability and, with U.S. and IMF assistance, to maintain a semblance of monetary stability, the private sector kept to its traditional defensive position.

Since the signing of the Montevideo Treaty in 1960, opening new possibilities for Paraguay's output, and the signing of the Charter of Punta del Este in 1961, committing the Government of Paraguay (along with other signatory nations) to adopt a development posture, there has been a marked awakening in the country's business community. The main factors involved have been a more liberal attitude on the part of the government toward businessmen and its willingness to work with the major business associations in the country; the injection of young, technically qualified leaders into these associations and their willingness to collaborate with the government in formulating economic policies rather than obstructing them; the maintenance of political and monetary stability in Paraguay during most of the past decade; and improving exports and business conditions in general during the past several years, as reflected in the economic indicators (other than GNP statistics).

As a result, FEPRINCO held the Second Conference of Private Economic Entities September 27-October 1, 1965 (the first since 1951). Some seventy-five business organizations from all economic sectors and from all parts of the country were represented through more than 700 delegates. The President of the Republic attended the opening and closing sessions. The views of the various groups were stated in a forthright manner, and the Conference undertook to cooperate with the government in the social and economic development of the country.

With the help of the USAID, a private Development and Productivity Center was established in October, 1966. A second private sector project in which the USAID has been involved is that of creating a private development financing corporation. This corporation is expected to make loans for industrial and agro-industrial projects, including working capital loans, and to complement the activities of the National Development Bank in these fields. Official approval has been obtained for this project. AID and ADELA were expected to participate in this project along with Paraguayan investors and other participants. Recently, interest has been shown in establishing savings and loan associations.

A reform of the industrial incentives laws has been drafted and was expected to be enacted during 1967. This reform would equalize benefits to Paraguayan investors and, in addition, would provide special incentives for technological innovation and the decentralization of industry, as proposed in the national development plans. It is noteworthy that the National Development Bank has utilized its external credits for industrialization rather rapidly (once initial difficulties were overcome regarding conditions precedent to disbursement of the loans) and was negotiating new foreign credits in 1966-67. The NDB could expand its development loan portfolio as rapidly as its capital and reserves would permit. The demand for credit in the agricultural, livestock, forestry, and manufacturing sectors greatly exceeds the availability of loanable funds. And the monetary policy of the Central Bank has virtually eliminated the commercial banks from development activities. Private sector interest in the financiera, therefore, is substantial.

Continued attention is being given to the incorporation of Paraguay more firmly into the Latin American Free Trade Association. The government has succeeded in negotiating special Paraguayan concessions with other member countries. However, investors need to develop projects for taking advantage of these opportunities. The Development and Productivity Center and the proposed private development financing corporation should be able to assist materially with the identification of opportunities, formulation of projects, and their financing.

Paraguay has had to begin its development on four separate occasions: after independence from Spain, after the Triple Alliance War, after the Chaco War, and after the internal strife that prevailed during much of the period 1947-54. The current effort--abetted by relative internal tranquility, a stable currency, and sizable foreign technical and financial aid--shows definite promise of success. The institutional base for this development, although very imperfect, is stronger than ever before in the country's history. And its available resources--both of manpower and capital--although limited, are of magnitudes never before attained by Paraguay. Its people have become development conscious, and the private sector has begun to take a leading role in national development. Closer cooperation among businessmen, farmers, and government officials is taking place not only in the capital city but at key points in the interior of the country. The discernible trend toward local self-help should be encouraged fully by the Paraguayan Government and external aid donors. The development of stronger local administrative units would certainly assist in accomplishing the national objective of integrating the national territory into the political and economic life of the country. It also would tend to develop a more responsible citizenry, with a stronger voice in government policy formulation.

Geographic isolation historically has been a serious deterrent to Paraguayan development. Its actual resources are quite similar to those in the much larger and wealthier neighboring nations (Argentina and Brazil), and its costs of production and transportation have been substantially higher than in those countries. Consequently, Paraguayan products have had difficulty competing in the national market as well as in markets abroad. If this country is to achieve economic viability, it must find the means of (a) converting its raw materials into quality products of high unit value; (b) establishing itself as a service and/or assembly center for the South American continent; (c) maximizing its complementary relationships with other LAFTA countries and even with those of the Central American Common Market; and (d) improving its productive efficiency in traditional lines of production so that, through price reductions, its output may be consumed more widely within the country and in neighboring border areas.

To accomplish the foregoing, the nation will have to make a substantial investment in research and development activities, including the strengthening of such institutions as the Faculty of Agronomy and Veterinary Sciences, the Faculty of Engineering, and the Science Institute of the National University; the Institute of Technology and Standards; and the Agricultural Experiment Stations. An incentive program to generate research activities in the private sector is needed, as only one or two of the largest firms are engaged to a limited extent in any such work at this time. The attraction of foreign capital into such programs would be eminently worthwhile, especially in view of the fact that most of Paraguay's benefits to date under the Montevideo Treaty have been granted on items that it does not produce.

Since Paraguay is a potential crossroads of South America, the development of service industries to accompany the expanding infrastructure is becoming increasingly important. In this, too, emphasis on technological innovation is required. Paraguay's principal resource is its people, who must be brought to a high level of technical proficiency to establish the country's international reputation for quality and performance. The people are intelligent and they work hard. They are willing and anxious to learn how to build their country, in which they have tremendous pride.

In sum, Paraguay's long-term economic growth depends upon its ability to convert its geographic disadvantages into economic assets, e.g., by becoming a Switzerland in South America. The intelligence, diligence, pride, and integrity of the Paraguayan people; their past accomplishments in the face of tremendous natural and man-made adversities; and current trends toward regional development, improved agricultural production and marketing, decentralized industrialization, agrarian reform, and improved education and health lead us to conclude that moderate optimism in Paraguay's economic future would be well justified.

GEOGRAPHIC APPENDIXES

BY

TIMOTHY G. SMITH

APPENDIX A THE PHYSICAL GEOGRAPHY OF PARAGUAY

Paraguay is a country of low plains whose ecological and topographical development has been determined largely by four elements: The Andes, to the west, have contributed the alluvial material forming the sediments of the Gran Chaco (57 per cent of the total land area), and they block any east-west movement of air which might modify the climatic regimen; to the east are found basalt flows upon which the dense forests of the Alto Paraná have developed; the Paraguay and Paraná rivers have built up the low fields and swamps covering 15 per cent of the national territory; and the climatic elements control precipitation and provide some of the highest temperatures of the continent, affecting the development of soils and vegetation. The combined actions of these forces have produced three regions: the Gran Chaco, the highlands of the Alto Paraná, and a central basin formed by the major rivers and their tributaries, where they flow between the previous zones.

Paraguay is unfortunate in that it has no abundance of petroleum, coal, iron, or other minerals demanded by the world's markets. A country three times as large as New England, its resources include rich forests, extensive areas of fertile, agriculturally suited soils and grasslands, and powerful cascades of water that can provide for the development of this landlocked country and hold keys to unlock future benefits for its young population. This discussion of the physical geography of Paraguay will try to present the landscape, its climate, fauna and flora, and each of the three regions, to present the complex picture of the interactions of elements that make up the physical landscape.

THE CLIMATE

Paraguay is situated in a zone of convergence of northeastern winds, warmed during their journey across the Amazon Valley, and the cool polar maritime air of the Southern Atlantic. It was noted 200 years ago by the Jesuit historian Dobrizhoffer that

> The sirocco, a very hot wind coming down from Mato Grosso near the equator, makes the air stifling, even at night. The Southern wind sweeping north from the colder Magellanic region causes lung complaint, arrests the vegetation, and occasionally destroys the crops...[1]

During the warm season of the year, the predominant winds are northeasterly, importing humid air, warmed over central Brazil. With a change of season the southeasterly winds crossing southern Brazil, or winds moving north along the eastern slope of the Andes from Patagonia and the polar ice mass of Antarctica, are predominant. Where an intermixing of these two air masses occurs, temperatures can change rapidly, such as a change from 35.2° C. to 4.2° C., experienced one afternoon as a cold front moved from the southeast over Puerto Presidente Franco.[2] Although Paraguay lies in a tropical latitude, polar air of the Southern Atlantic brought snow flurries, in 1965, to the colonies east of Encarnación.

Breezes are always present in Asunción, but at times the winds reach hurricane proportions. On September 22, 1925, winds of more than 100 miles an hour destroyed the commercial center and the then new dock facilities of Encarnación.

Mean annual temperatures decrease from north to south, with the high recorded in January and the low in July. Data for selected stations are:

	January	July
Bahia Negra	29.1° C.	21.0° C.
Concepción	23.7° C.	19.7° C.
Asunción	22.7° C.	18.3° C.
Encarnación	21.6° C.	16.1° C.

Most precipitation in Paraguay is conveyed by the humid northeasterly winds. The rainy season tends to occur during the spring and summer. But the southeastern corner also receives precipitation from winter winds as they rise over its hills and those of neighboring Argentina and Brazil, recording rainfall averaging 1,800 millimeters annually, without notable seasonal differences. This is the highest frequency of precipitation, which progressively diminishes toward the northwestern border of the Chaco, where one third of that amount (600 millimeters) is noted. The Chaco, because of intense heat and frequent winds, has a higher rate of evaporation than the rest of the country, and statistics often fail to present a full picture of its tropical semi-arid condition. A further constraint on moisture in the Chaco is the Sierra de Chaquita along the northern border of the Chaco, in Bolivia, which blocks moisture-laden winds from reaching the area to its south.

The Chaco claims a hot-dry climate, and the eastern section of Paraguay has a moderate to warm climate, divided into the north, where the rainfall is concentrated in the summer, and the south, where it is recorded throughout the year. This classification is based on data recorded at nine meteorological stations that have been in continuous operation since 1941.

Due to the higher rainfall in the southeastern corner, a forest of tropical character has developed along the Río Paraná near latitude 27° S. Toward the north, closer to the equator, the plant cover becomes increasingly subtropical in appearance as the winds for the southeast lose their moisture content.

THE CHACO

The sediments of the Chaco are composed of debris transported from the Andes by the Pilcomayo and Bermejo rivers, as they flow toward the Río Paraguay which covers continental sediments from the Brazilian Shield, resting in turn on marine sediments of Devonian and Cambrian periods. These sediments have been warped into a structural trough, possibly resulting from the uplifting and folding of the Andes, aided by the increasing weight of the sediments themselves. The general slope of the Paraguayan Chaco is about 1 per cent, 450 meters elevation in the northwest corner to about 100 meters above sea level, at the confluence of the Pilcomayo and Paraguay rivers.

The Paraguayan Chaco may be subdivided into northern and southern regions on the basis of physical characteristics and associated land use. The northern Chaco, north of 23° 30'S., includes some 16.6 million hectares covered by a xerophytic deciduous forest which developed in the region's tropical, semi-arid climate. This forest land, of little current economic utility, represents about half of the total forest in the country. An exception is the diminishing stands of red quebracho (Schinopsis lornzzi, Engl.) supporting one of the principal industries of Paraguay: the extraction of tannic acid.[3]

These alluvial soils have a fairly heavy sandy-loam composition. The sandier soils, 15-30 centimeters in depth, are found in the stream channels, while shallower bushland soils, 12-15 centimeters in depth, are derived from silt deposited during flooding. Both soil types are affected by concentrations of salt which remain after floodwaters containing soluble material, washed down from the western slopes, have evaporated. Where water remains on the surface for a period of time, it leaches the finer material which forms a subsurface of hard clay and merges into a layer of lime, a feature which prevents the penetration of deep root systems.

The sandier soils support a grassy cover, whereas the heavier soils are characterized by a denser cover of scrub brush, similar to mesquite, with occasional large trees such as quebracho, acacia (Acacia farneciana, Will.), or palo santo (Bulnesia sarmienti, Lor.). Rainfall in the northern Chaco decreases from about 1,000 millimeters near the Paraguay River to 600 millimeters at the western extremity. The vegetation tends to correspond to this pattern as larger trees and denser growth are found closer to the Río Paraguay and less frequently as one moves toward the west.

The most extensive use of this area is for cattle grazing and lumbering. Along the Río Paraguay, often on plantations, are groves of palms raised for the oil of their nuts. The only extensive agricultural use of this region is in the Mennonite Colonies around Filadelphia and Mariscal Estigarribia and along the river near the towns. In the 1940's the Union Oil Company drilled several test wells in search of suspected oil deposits, only one of which turned up traces of oil and gas. However, the subsurface structure of the Chaco suggests that oil and other valuable minerals may be present, probably along the western edge.[4]

The southern section of the Paraguayan Chaco is covered by more recent alluvial deposits than the northern and has a somewhat higher frequency of rainfall. The soils of this zone are of a more uniform consistency, with a lighter structure and a deeper profile, than those previously described.

The vegetation cover, in this zone, is in a state of transition. It is being actively invaded by a low and spiny plant cover mixed with herbaceous scrub forest, similar to mesquite, that can be compared in origin and composition to the *caatinga* found in northeastern Brazil.[5] The local name of this plant cover is *algarrobo*, and its expansion is greatly reducing lands available for cattle grazing. In 1932-33, before the Chaco War, over 500,000 head of cattle grazed along the Pilcomayo River on some of the best grasses in the country. Most of these cattle were killed during the War. Today, this area has been invaded by *algarrobo* and contributes very little toward livestock production.

Intermittent streams flowing into the Río Paraguay are lined with trees forming strip forests of heavier vegetation extending back into the Chaco. Near the Río Paraguay, the creeks are lined with palm trees and an undergrowth of hard aquatic grasses. Further upstream, this cover gives way to *algarrobo*, interspersed by grass which is in turn replaced by hardwood forests in the higher elevations.

The Pilcomayo River, which flows into the Río Paraguay, forms part of the border between Paraguay and Argentina. This river transports much of the sediments which cover the Chaco. However, its load of silt has been deposited in such a way that it actually forms a barrier to the waters of the upper Pilcomayo, causing most of the waters to be diverted into the Río Negro and the Río Monte Lindo. Water entering the Río Paraguay via the Pilcomayo is drained from a smaller watershed within the Chaco. The upper channel of the Pilcomayo River, where it flows through the Cordillera Real, possesses an untapped potential for development of hydroelectric power which could greatly facilitate the Chaco's development process.

THE HIGHLANDS OF THE ALTO PARANA

This province covers about one third of eastern Paraguay. The average elevation is 200 to 600 meters above sea level. The appearance of this zone, rolling to gently hilly, is greatly influenced by the Serra Geral lavas: basaltic lavas, with interspersed thin beds of red sandstone and shale.[6]

These flows rest on a massive red sandstone exposed on the western extremity, which can be delimited by a line running almost directly north from just west of Encarnación. The flows are part of a larger formation of the same name, extending across Brazil almost to the Atlantic Coast and covering approximately 880,000 square kilometers. Outliers of these traps and related igneous activity occur throughout eastern Paraguay in the form of isolated mesas or hills such as those near Acaray, Yaguaron, and Lambare.

The flat upland surfaces are generally covered by a dark, chocolate-red soil, 1 to 3 meters in depth, which supports a luxuriant natural vegetation with more than 150 commercially valuable species of trees and a dense undergrowth. These soils have a high water-holding capacity and a nutrient content that ranges from medium to adequate, but they also have a fairly light structure that can be easily compressed if worked by heavy machinery, such as bulldozers. They respond rapidly to local agricultural practices and are considered among the best coffee-growing lands in both Paraguay and southwestern Brazil.

Flood plains in local stream channels are covered by a very fertile, almost black clay-loam. On these frequently inundated areas are found low forests, bamboo, and other herbaceous vegetation, as well as areas of open grass cover, locally known as playas.

Precipitation is more frequent in the southern end of this province and decreases northward. Encarnación, with a moderate temperate regimen and adequate rainfall in all seasons, is typical of the southern Alto Paraná, while Puerto Presidente Franco (between the Acaray and the Monday rivers) and Pedro Juan Caballero (further north) enjoy warmer temperatures but have a rain deficiency in the winter.

Few large deposits of economically valuable minerals have been found in this province. However, near Encarnación a small blast furnace to process native iron ore is being considered. Gem stones, such as agates, amethysts, or beril, may be found in cavities in the basalt. Reports of copper deposits are frequent.

The best examples of exposed Serra Geral lavas in Paraguay are along the banks of the Río Paraná, which for most of its course lies in a structural trough: the geosynclinal basin of the Paraná. Along with its headwater tributary, it flows more than 2,250 kilometers. From the falls of Guiará, the Paraná River flows through a steeply walled canyon, to just west of Encarnación, where it leaves the basalt and immediately widens from 1 kilometer to 8 to 10 kilometers and continues in a meandering path through braided channels to its confluence with the Río Paraguay some 350 kilometers to the west.

The basalt is both so thick and so resistant to erosion that while the river itself came into existence near the beginning of the Cretaceous era, the Paraná still presents a very youthful appearance with almost vertical walls and little, if any, flood plain, unless it happens to cut across a bed of sandstone--as it does near Hohenau, 50 kilometers east of Encarnación. Its tributaries follow faults in the basalt and lines of least resistance in often-incised sinuous patterns until they plunge over its flank, frequently in spectacular cascades such as those on the Ríos Acaray, Monday, and Iguazu, which offer many sites for the installation of local hydroelectric facilities. Because of the dense vegetation cover and a low gradient between cascades, the water of the tributaries is clear even after a prolonged rainfall, since vegetation prevents most erosive sheet wash and slack water allows the deposit of detritus to build the fertile soils of the flood plains.

The Paraná cuts into the basalt at Guiará Falls near the Paraguayan-Brazilian border, above which the river is about 4 kilometers wide, with an average depth at low water of about 1 meter. After a series of 18 cascades over 120 meters, in 60 kilometers, it is only 75 meters wide, with over a 30-meter difference between high and low water.[7] These falls have the largest volume and are also geologically one of the oldest in the world.

Perhaps better known than the Guiará Falls are the Iguazu Falls 12 kilometers east of the Río Paraná, across from Puerto Presidente Stroessner, with a mean fall of about 80 meters and a volume said to be greater than that of Niagara's. These falls are a mecca for European and American tourists, and each of the neighboring countries has opened good hotels. The Paraguayan Hotel and Casino are located above the Río Paraná, at Puerto Presidente Stroessner, commanding a sweeping view of the river from a pleasant tropical setting.

THE CENTRAL BASIN

The Paraguay River originates in the western Mato Grosso, separated from the Amazon River basin by a slight elevation. It meanders along the eastern edge of the Chaco more than 2,500 kilometers until it joins the Paraná River at the southern tip of Paraguay, 1,170 kilometers above Buenos Aires. Characterized by a low gradient, it descends only 90 meters from its source (at 150 meters) to 60 meters above sea level, where it meets the Alto Paraná.[8] This lack of gradient not only makes it difficult to utilize its force for the creation of hydroelectric power but even to impound its waters in a reservoir. Due to this feature, and to the low surrounding landscape, there develops an interior sea in the upper reaches of the watershed during periods of excessive rain, and in 1966 many Paraguayans were driven from their homes as the floodwaters washed over the banks of the river at Asunción and Pilar, causing damage to crops and property. Where the waters of the Paraguay and the Paraná overflow their channels, they replenish the soil's fertility with silt, but they also leach many minerals and leave concentrated salts on the surface if they remain undrained for long periods of time.

During drier periods, the volume of water is reduced greatly and the load is deposited, often prohibiting deep draft vessels from reaching Asunción. This problem is less critical below the confluence with the Río Paraná because differences in the climatic regimes along their respective courses brings them to flood stages during different seasons of the year. Except for periods of extremely low water, the Río Paraguay is navigable for 1,530 kilometers, as far north as Corumba, Brazil, by ships of 3 meters draft. It is navigable another 800 kilometers to San Luis Caceres by small craft, providing (except for air and radio) the only media of transportation and communication through the center of South America and the only connection between much of northern Paraguay and Asunción.

The area east of the Río Paraguay, to the base of the highlands, presents a series of vegetation belts. Along the river are found lower fields and swamps, often with palm trees. Further inland is a central basin, with islands of forest located on the higher ground and cover of prime quality pasture lands on the intermediate and low areas. Finally, foothills covered by forests have developed on exposed red sandstone and form a transition zone between the basin and the lavas further east.

Swamps and low fields, with scattered palm trees, occupy much of the area near the river. These lands usually have heavy soils and a plant cover adapted to frequent inundation. Included in this category are the low lands bordering the tributaries of the Río Paraguay. One large area which parallels the Río Paraguay extends south of Asunción to the Río Paraná and in places is over 100 kilometers wide. When these areas are covered by water, only isolated islands of higher land remain dry. On these places are found palm trees, scrub growth, hardwoods, and pasture grasses. Palm trees are more frequent in the warmer zones and decrease in frequency toward the south, as well as away from the Río Paraguay.

Areas of higher grasslands, between the uplands and the swamps, extend from Paraguarí, 60 kilometers southeast of Asunción, toward San Juan Bautista, Misiones. T. S. Darrow suggests that this gently rolling topography, which represents the original and the highest-quality cattle lands in Paraguay, was originally covered by forests that were transformed through time into grasslands.[9] Possibly this resulted from periodic burning or flooding, causing a change in the soil structure and composition.

East and south of Asunción are areas of mixed grasslands. These lands, once open pastureland, are being actively invaded by scrub forests, not unlike what is happening in the Chaco. The local soils are red sandy clays, which erode easily and lose their organic content with misuse. This results in frequent abandonment and consequent invasion by scrub forest. These soils, actually the poorest in the country, are used by the majority of the Paraguayan farmers.

These same soils, residual from the red sandstone, are found along the western extremity of the basalt flows where the parent material is exposed. The hills here form a transition zone between the Alto Paraná and the central basin and are covered by dense forests, providing the largest remaining timber reserves in Paraguay. It is locally considered to be part of the Alto Paraná.

One exception to the previously described pattern is an area, near the confluence of the Río Apa and the Río Paraguay, covered by a dense forest with some open lands used for cattle grazing. This is an area of rugged hills underlain by a formation of pre-Cambrian rocks covered by limestone deposits.

The mineral resources in this zone are limited to building materials, such as clays, and some small deposits of minerals found on scattered outcroppings. In the north, around the Río Apa, limestone provides material for production of cement. Traces of bauxite, lead, and some semiprecious stones have been noted.

FLORA AND FAUNA

Complementing the variety of Paraguayan landscapes, which range from semi-arid to grasslands and tropical forests, are as wide a variety of native fauna and flora. Animals, such as the jaguar, the ocelot and puma, wild boars and deer, abound in the Chaco and the Alto Paraná. The word "Chaco" itself derives from a Quecha word "chacu," referring to an abundance of animal life. In the Chaco are found a myriad of snakes, from the beautiful but deadly coral to the anaconda, in the north, which reaches over 40 feet in length and drops from trees on unwary victims. The rivers provide a home for crocodiles as well as for fish like the dorado, pacu, armado, corbina, and surubi (the more popular game species), while the piranha and its carnivorous habits remains the least popular. These rivers are also inhabitated by the lungfish which seals itself in mud during dry periods, a visitor from past epochs. Birds add their calls to the woods and are imitated by verse and song of the Guaraní folklore, a folklore built heavily on the features of the countryside.[10]

The vegetation is varied and in places has an archaic cast--with Arucarians, tree ferns, and primitive angiosperms being common to the Alto Paraná. Several studies have indicated that this region, as well as the Chaco, may have been a center of origin and dispersal for much of the present fauna and flora of South America.

One contribution, whose origin is still in dispute, is maize (Zea mays), which it is claimed came from the lowlands of either Paraguay or Bolivia rather than Mexico as so often cited. This evidence is based on the work in 1939 of Mangelsdorf and Reeves, who suggested that maize might have originated in Paraguay since the earliest traces of pod corn are found there. A species locally called avati quaircuru (Zea mays tunicata) still flourishes and was first classified by Saint-Hilaire, in 1829, as being an ancestor of the modern-day varieties.[11]

Moises S. Bertoni, in his laboratory on the bank of the Río Paraná, studied the Paraguayan environment for most of his life and provided basic work for most studies on Paraguay, including the classifying of over 160 indigenous varieties of manioc.[12] Manioc (Manihot utilisima), possibly originating in the Amazon Valley, has become the food for much of tropical Africa and Asia as well as America under the names of yuca, cassava, or tapioca. Another plant, the wild pineapple (ananas guaraniticus), reportedly was smuggled out of the country and developed to its present characteristics in the Caribbean and the Hawaiian Islands.

Among the trees native to Paraguay are the lapacho (Tabebuia Gomez), which produces flowers of white, blue, yellow, and red and is a hard straight-grained wood and the national tree. Yerba maté (Ilex paraguayas) produces a tea that is consumed at the rate of about 0.25 kilogram per day per person in Paraguay and is the object of an active industry. Red quebracho, native to the Chaco and the area just east of the Río Paraguay, has for years provided one of the largest volumes of exports from Paraguay; now, however, it is diminishing in importance. More than 279 trees and shrubs have been documented as being used for medicinal purposes by Paraguayans, treating everything from an upset stomach to arthritis and cancer.[13]

Orchids adorn trees and cliffs in shady, damp sites; banks of poinsettias are seen along the streets of Paraguayan villages, while the perfume of jasmine, the national flower, drifts across Asunción for almost half the year, giving strong credence to Paraguay's claim of being a paradise.

Notes to Appendix A

1. P. T. Sulsona, A Reconnaissance Soil and Land Classification of Paraguay (Asunción, 1954), p. 29.

2. R. F. Sanchez, *El Clima del Paraguay* (Asunción: Dirección de Meteorologia Asunción, 1963). (Typed copy.)

3. M. Michalowski, *Arboles y arbustos del Paraguay* (Asunción: Ministero de Agricultura y Ganaderia, STICA). All references to plant species will be taken from this source.

4. E. B. Eckel, *Geology and Mineral Resources of Paraguay: A Reconnaissance*, U.S.G.S., Professional Paper #327 (Washington, D.C.: 1959).

5. C. A. Rizzini, *Nota Previa sobre a divisão fitogeografica do Brazil* (Asunción: Instituto Brasileiro de Geografía e Estatistica, Ministerio de Agricultura y Ganaderia, STICA, 1956), p. 4.

6. C. L. Baker, "The Lava Field of the Paraná Basin, South America," *Journal of Geology*, Vol. 31 (1926), p. 67.

7. *Ibid*., p. 68.

8. J. L. B. Sanchez, *El Río Paraguay*, Monografía Hidrografíca (Asunción, 1962), p. 22.

9. T. S. Darrow, *Manual del Estanciero* (Asunción: Ministerio de Agricultura y Ganaderia, STICA, 1956), p. 5.

10. For an interesting discussion of the relation of Paraguayan fauna and flora with Guaraní folklore, see H. G. Warren, *Paraguay: An Informal History* (Norman, Okla.: University of Oklahoma, 1941), Chap. 1.

11. P. C. Mangelsdorf, "The Origin and Evolution of Maize," *Advances in Genetics*, Vol. 1 (1947).

12. N. González, *Geografía del Paraguay* (Mexico City: Editorial Guarania, 1964).

13. M. Michalowski, *Plantas Medicinales del Paraguay*, Manual #173 (Asunción: Ministerio de Agricultura y Ganaderia, n.d.).

APPENDIX B THE HISTORICAL DEVELOPMENT OF LAND USE PATTERNS IN PARAGUAY

The development of land use patterns in Paraguay has been profoundly influenced by the centralization of political and economic activity in Asunción. Presently, through the increased transportation facilities and communication with markets, the diversification and expansion of agricultural activities is being encouraged, with the support of both the Government of Paraguay and private groups. Until efforts to encourage development by the Government of Paraguay were begun during the 1950's, most economic activity outside of the capital was initiated by private groups. In the early 1950's, the Government of Paraguay started to construct a series of highways which have linked the population centers, provided farmers with a means of reaching new markets, and made the hinterland areas accessible for development.

The most important of these roads was built from Asunción east to Coronel Oviedo (1954) and later extended to the Brazilian border at Puerto Presidente Stroessner (1963). This road reduced a trip of several days to several hours, and its impact can be seen by the increasing agricultural activity along its length and the growth of several towns. The most notable town is probably Coronel Oviedo, which in 1950 had a population of 5,804 and grew to 9,431 in 1961.[1] As this path through the semitropical hardwoods of the Alto Paraná was opened, agricultural colonization on the rich basalt residual soils became feasible. These colonies have been used for the resettlement of farmers from crowded minifundia around the capital, to encourage the repatriation of Paraguayans in Argentina and Brazil, and as a site for settlement of foreign immigrant groups.

The highway south from Asunción to Encarnación, and beyond to the private colonies, has diverted to Asunción those products that formerly went to Argentine markets, much in the same way that the roads to the north will, and are, encouraging the shipment to Asunción of foods that once went to Brazil. More recently, a road through the Chaco to Bolivia, completed in 1965, has strengthened the ties between the Mennonite Colonies of that region and Asunción. These roads also can influence the distribution of crop types by offering to farmers an incentive for growing new crops and encouraging the expansion of areas under construction. The lack of transportation in the Chaco and in the forest zones has also placed a definite constraint on the expansion of arable lands to the north of Asunción, as compared to the open grasslands further south. The grasslands are also closer to the channels of the Paraná and Paraguay rivers, which serve as media of transportation and in some localities as sources of power.

Poor drainage is probably one of the prime factors in the lack of agricultural development of the grasslands and the Chaco. While the low grasslands of the southern part of the country and the central basin are used extensively for cattle grazing, only the intermittent islands of higher, better drained soils are arable. Much of this zone is frequently inundated, and it is not unusual to find cattle grazing in water reaching to their middle.

P. T. Sulsona suggests that "some Chaco areas could be developed into large scale farming with the introduction of drainage and irrigation systems, control of plant diseases and pests and soil fertility practices."[2] Proof of this is shown by the extensive development of an oasis-type environment in the Mennonite Colonies, currently flourishing in the center of the Chaco.

The skewed distribution of landownership prevalent in Paraguay evolved from the historical tendency of Paraguayans to locate around Asunción, leaving most of the country in unsettled or unfarmed land--which became the property of a very few persons. But, according to the Agricultural Census of 1956, only 20 per cent of the area occupied by the minifundia zone surrounding the capital is occupied by farms; more than half is used for cattle grazing. Within this 20 per cent (268,000 hectares) are some 77,000 plots, or approximately half of the total number in Paraguay, with a median size of 3.5 hectares. In this same zone are 1,100 cattle ranches which occupy more than 743,000 hectares. For the country as a whole, only 5.2 per cent of the farms occupy 92.2 per cent of the total area included within the agricultural census, whereas the remaining 94.8 per cent are on 7.8 per cent of the land area.[3]

When considering these figures, one must remember that approximately 64.4 per cent of the total population of Paraguay live in the rural areas and that some 985,000 of them derive their living from agricultural activities.[4] At the same time, 1956, it was found that the percentage of farmers with clear title to their land was 38.1 per cent, and they owned over 80 per cent of the land counted. Families who rented land represented 12.3 per cent and squatters 48.6 per cent, although 15 per cent of the latter do have provisional titles.[5]

There have been improvements in the tenure problem since the 1956 census, because the Institute of Rural Welfare has presented titles to some 30,000 farmers, with a total land area of 730,000 hectares.[6] But even so, the number of farmers without title and sufficient land remains high and provides one of the principal obstacles to the development of the agricultural potential.

One reason for this problem developed during the War of the Triple Alliance, when many landownership records were lost. Although there is a law that allows persons who have lived on land without title for ten years to have an option to buy that land, most farmers are hesitant to improve their plots during that ten-year period beyond a bare minimum for fear the legal owner will claim the improvements or crops. Compounding this problem, the registration of land titles is difficult for most farmers, because it is usually necessary to go to Asunción--a trip involving time and money. As a result, when farms are divided among a family, as is often the custom, the title may be kept by the father. The paucity of records makes interpretation of landownership and tenure patterns difficult. There is no cadastral survey of Paraguay.

The constraint of insecure tenure has limited the domestic supply of food by encouraging farmers to grow, on a small scale, a diversity of crops for self-consumption. Such diversification is encouraged by the uncertainty of market prices and buying power. In other words, a farmer who produces a variety of crops has a better chance of selling his products than one who produces just one crop. One result of this is that only one area of monoculture by small-scale farms is found. This is the sugar cane cultivation near Guarambare, outside of Asunción.

Areas of specialty crops are common, but these crops are usually intermixed with others. Examples are areas of pineapple cultivation on the hills above Paraguarí, the grape arbors of Colonia Independencia, the cotton and wheat around General Artigas or Coronel Bogado in Itapúa, or the corn and manioc around San Juan Nepomuceno. Those areas specializing in specific crops, such as grapes, cotton, tung nuts, <u>yerba maté</u>, soybeans, coffee, or rice, are often the sites of foreign colonies or exploitations whose owners are immigrants. For example, soybeans were introduced within the last five years by the Japanese.

The present pattern of land use in Paraguay did not develop within the last two or three decades but results from historical events extending over many centuries. Before settlement by Europeans, Paraguay was occupied by several tribes of Indians, most notably the Guaraní. Locally, these Indians have been cited for many achievements. However, their impact on present land use has been lost except where they consistently burned the vegetation to create open grassland. One such location is around Trinidad (in Itapúa), another around Pastoreo (west of Puerto Presidente Stroessner). The presence of a family-based tribal organization, rather than a strong social structure such as that developed by the Incas of Peru, encouraged the Guaranís' absorption into the Spanish-*mestizo* milieu.[7] This intermixing with the Spanish and the attacks made on these tribes by slave raiders from Brazil help explain their lack of permanence in the Paraguayan landscape. However, the isolation of the country from other centers of Spanish population did foster several outstanding characteristics of the Guaraní: the common use of the Guaraní language, *yerba maté* and medicinal herbs, and the patterns woven into textiles. Nevertheless, most traces of the Guaraní Indians have disappeared.

The City of Asunción was founded in 1537 by Gonzalo de Mendoza and Juan de Salazar, who, while "sailing downstream until the east bank of the Paraguay, where a small peninsula makes a bay, landed and built a stockade, a *casa fuerte*...and called it Nuestra Señora de la Asunción, in homage to the Virgin Mary."[8] Asunción remained a base of military operations and exploration for several years.

Beginning about 1590, missions were established by the Jesuit priests at eight sites in what is now southern Paraguay. This activity presented the first large-scale changes made in land use in Paraguay by Europeans. At their height, each mission contained about 3,500 Indians and two missionaries, serving--in addition to their work of religious mentors--as doctors, judges, overseers, school teachers, and agricultural advisers. One goal of these missions was material self-sufficiency. Meat came from their herds of cattle; *yerba maté*, sugar, tobacco, corn, small grains, fruits, vegetables, cotton, honey, and wax also were produced on the mission lands.[9]

But in 1767, "by the stroke of the pen, a Spanish king destroyed the heroic work of two hundred years."[10] And, in 1814, a traveler reported "where once flourishing orchards bore fruit for the entire community, nothing but stumps could be seen... fields lay untended, overgrown with brush and weeds."[11] Even the cultivation of yerba maté ceased until the 1930's, when it was again planted on a large scale in Misiones, Argentina, and later in Itapúa, near Hohenau.

With the closing of the Jesuit missions, activity centered about the capital city and its immediate hinterland. For the next several decades, the most common form of European settlement and land use outside of the cities was the encomienda, which represented the first large ranches on the Paraguayan grasslands. Indians were moved onto these tracts of land and required to work in forced labor. But the encomienda system was found impracticable and unprofitable, and by 1803 it was abolished. It was replaced by a system of communal labor (minga) on the part of the indigenous population, who were allowed to live in their own villages rather than on the ranch itself. The encomiendas were located around Asunción in the central basin and the area now in the Department of Misiones.

During this period, the centralization of activity in Asunción was still dominant. Under the rule of José Gaspar Rodriguez de Francia, president and dictator of Paraguay from 1814 to 1840, the frontier of Paraguay was effectively sealed to foreigners and foreign trade, isolating the population from outside influences. As a consequence, the population became almost completely dependent upon Asunción for any marketing, economic, civil, or social activity.

Carlos Antonio López, who replaced Francia in 1841, again opened the routes to the hinterland and encouraged movement into the countryside. This was promoted through the building of a railroad from Asunción 60 kilometers southeast to Paraguarí in 1858. Before its construction, the Central Zone was reportedly a deserted area without population. But in 1904, over 80 per cent of the population of the country (an estimated 495,000) lives within the railroad's sphere of influence.[12] This movement is witnessed by the string of towns that developed between Asunción and Encarnación along the present 358-kilometer right-of-way. But the War of the Triple Alliance in 1865-70 again forced centralization of activity and population. Most Paraguayans wanted to be near Asunción for its security and protection by the Army. This centralization under Francia, and later under Solano López during the War of the Triple Alliance, resulted in a densely populated zone of minifundia or small subsistence and mixed subsistence/commercial farms surroundint the capital. In this area is found a majority of the arable land in the country. Since the Chaco War, however, the population in this area has drastically increased; almost 80 per cent of the population live within 100 kilometers of the capital.

At the turn of the century, two more land use types were introduced. First was the exploitation of the natural yerba maté groves in the forests of the Alto Paraná, mainly in the southeastern corner of the country near Encarnación. Second was the growth of a tannin extract industry based on the extraction of this oil from quebracho trees, which grew in profusion around Concepción. These two activities encouraged land development and construction of local railroads to carry raw materials to the rivers, where they could be processed or shipped to Asunción or Buenos Aires. During this time, a boom town atmosphere prevailed and the local economies flourished to such an extent that the "ladies of Concepción bought their dresses in Paris."

Both of these land uses have almost ceased and have disappeared from the current picture of eastern Paraguay; they were replaced by the exploitation of timber. But the land opened by the construction of the roads and railroads was often settled by agricultural colonists who immigrated from neighboring countries and Europe. This movement of immigrants began in the late 1800's and included persons from Brazil, Germany, Argentina, Poland, Russia, France, England, Canada, Australia, and, more recently, Japan and Korea. The earlier settlements were located around the capital; later colonies spread to lands near Encarnación, into the Chaco, and in the northeastern forestlands, near Concepción. Their activities are reflected on the present landscape by the introduction of crops, techniques, and cultural traits of their homelands and by the development of small- and large-scale industries to process their products.

Future possibilities for changes in land use patterns in Paraguay are greater than at any time in the past. Three general trends probably will be followed in the foreseeable future.

First is the increased colonization of forest areas, especially those along the Paraná River--an area with rich soils; high rainfall; accessibility to the markets of Paraguay, Brazil, and Argentina; and local sources of hydroelectric power in the tributaries of the Río Paraguay.

Second is the expansion of areas of _minifundia_ in the central basin, which will place additional pressures on the limited amount of farm land available and also on the government services needed to relieve this problem. One solution to this is the growth of mixed agricultural-industrial complexes in such a manner that people will be attracted to them instead of to the capital, which is approaching its capacity to absorb unskilled labor. These growth centers might also discourage Paraguayans from leaving the country and attract others from Brazil and Argentina, where it is reported that as many as 800,000 persons of Paraguayan birth may now reside. Currently, interest in regional development is increasing in cities in the countryside (especially in Concepción, Pilar, Encarnación, and Coronel Oviedo), and industrial activities are developing around the site of the Acaray Dam near Puerto Presidente Stroessner.

The third trend may be in the creation of arable land from frequently inundated grasslands of southern Paraguay or from the forest scrub lands of the Chaco. Both regions have soils that are better suited, with less initial cost for development and with proper irrigation, to agricultural activity than are the structurally lighter forest soils.

THE PRESENT LAND USE OF PARAGUAY

A summary investigation of information on land use in Paraguay reveals little more than generalized statistical data, such as that in the Agricultural Census of 1956 and 1961. The only detailed land use maps available were done in 1965 during the colonization feasibility study of the Plan Triangulo, at a scale of 1:100,000. The reconnaissance included an area formed by a triangle, with Asunción, Puerto Presidente Stroessner, and Encarnación as its apexes.

While it is possible to gather a picture from statistical surveys of the economy, further information in a form useful for economic analysis can be drawn from land use data. Land use data serves first as a quantitative and qualitative agent in inventorying the actual conditions of the economy. Secondly, it shows the spatial relationships among various elements of the economy, presenting complex statistical information in a manner useful for comparison and including information on soils, geological structure, landownership, or transportation studies.

Land use data, when compared with information on forestry activities, can indicate locations for possible future development based upon the analysis of market and supply zones. Compared with soils, the influence of the physical characteristics of the land can be seen and areas of high adaptability to conditions can be marked for future investment zones. The increased effectiveness of investments in roads, schools, power lines, or other rural services can be facilitated through an observation of the levels of the agricultural economy drawn from a comparison between land use and demographic data.

These examples show a static picture of the current situation. However, a series of land use studies can effectively point out the strength and weakness of any development activity. The expansion of crop land or individual crop types, the movements of populations, and the changes in the level of rural life can be identified more rapidly and with less expense than through traditional methods of statistical gathering.

About 2.6 per cent of the land in Paraguay is classed as arable; most of this is located around the capital and in the central basin. Outlying arable areas are near Concepción, Pedro Juan Caballero, in the Chaco, and along the bank of the Río Paraná in Itapúa. The majority of the land (59.4 per cent) is in forest, including forest lands that are penetrated by agricultural activities, classed as domestic woodlots, and virgin forest land that is used for commercial exploitation and inhabitated only by occasional slash and burn farmers and an estimated 30,000 Indians, most of whom live in the Chaco. Pastureland occupies 35.1 per cent of the total area. Urban settlements occupy 0.6 per cent and the rest is classed as swamps and rock or sand outcroppings (Appendix Table 1).

Land use in Paraguay can be grouped into eight types, based on the predominant land cover and on land tenure patterns, available technology, and infrastructure within the types. These classifications were reached after extensive field work, including mapping with aerial photographs at a scale of 1:50,000. It is hoped that these eight types of "land use" will be indicative of the Paraguayan landscape in such a way as to isolate and spacially delimit the various levels of rural development, locate the intensity of utilization, and note any trends of changing land use. These types are grouped according to the physical regions wherein they are predominantly found, as shown on page 474.

APPENDIX TABLE I

Land Use in Paraguay, 1966

		Area Hectares	Per Cent
Urban Areas[a]		25,000	0.6
Arable Lands[b]	(847,000-100%)	847,000	2.8
Horticulture	(3,650-0.4%)		
Tree crops	(107,172-12.7%)		
Annual field crops	(534,560-63.1%)		
Artificial pasture	(17,490-2.1%)		
Fallow	(184,140-21.7%)		
Natural Pasture Lands[c]		14,323,000	35.1
Forest Lands[c]	(24,223,000-100%)	24,223,000	59.4
Domestic woodlots[b]	(5,549,999-24.6%)		
Commercial forest	(18,764,000-75.4%)		
Other Use Types[c]		1,257,000	2.9
Total Land Area		40,675,000	100.0%

[a]Secretària de Planificación, Interim Report, Plan Triangulo, Appendix "A": "Land Use" (Asunción, 1966), p. A-20.

[b]Ministerio de Agricultura y Ganaderìa, Resultados Preliminaries del Censo Agropecuario 1961 (3a. publicación) (Asunción, 1965), p. 3.

[c]Secretaria de Planificación, Sintesis del Diagnostico Sector Agropecuario y Forestal del Paraguay (Asunción, 1964), p. 32.

In the central basin is found the greatest diversity of land uses, including most of the urban areas, the zone of minifundia which surrounds Asunción, and an extensive area of mixed small-scale and intermediate-scale farming that is found throughout the grasslands of eastern Paraguay. Predominantly within the zone of the Alto Paraná are found the colonies of Itapúa, where emphasis is placed on tung nuts, yerba maté, and soybeans; the areas of pioneer agriculture in the colonies east of Caaguazú; and the coffee plantations around Pedro Juan Caballero. All of these land uses are decreasing the area of commercial forest in eastern Paraguay, also considered a land use type. Finally, the Chaco is presented as a single unit due to its lack of development, except for several outstanding examples of pioneer agriculture and extensive cattle ranches.

Urban Areas

The only urban area of major importance in Paraguay is Asunción, the capital city. It occupies about 6,500 hectares near the junction of the Pilcomayo and the Paraguay rivers. It is situated on a series of ridges that rise 10 to 30 meters above the river and the surrounding lowlands. Most industrial, wholesaling, export, import, educational, and governmental activities are located in Asunción, which grew almost 47.7 per cent from a population of 206,634 in 1950 to 305,160 in 1962. This growth compares with an over-all growth rate of 36.1 per cent for the entire country during the same period.[13]

Five other urban areas should be noted, including Encarnación, Coronel Oviedo, Villarrica, Concepción, and Pilar.

Encarnación, a town of 17,888 persons, is located at the southern tip of Paraguay, on the Río Paraná. The city and its environs traditionally have been isolated from the capital by wide grasslands and dense forests, and, as a result, they have developed somewhat apart from Asunción. Encarnación has served as an entrance for immigrant groups from Brazil and Argentina, and the Department of Itapúa contains almost one fourth of the immigrants in Paraguay. Its present influence as a commercial center, however, is overshadowed by the presence of Posadas, Argentina, across the river, and by Asunción, which--because of the connecting highway that was recently improved and paved in 1966--is now within eight hours travel by truck.

Coronel Oviedo, with a population of 9,485, is located near the International Highway that connects Asunción and Brazil. Its more than 90 per cent growth in the last decade has been strongly affected by the improvements and extension of this road, as well as by the opening of a road to the northern part of the country, which starts at Coronel Oviedo. The town is mainly a retail trading center, with some tertiary industries. It claims a fairly young population since many Paraguayans who live in the countryside send their children to Coronel Oviedo to attend school.

Villarrica, with a population of 14,393, is located in the central basin, south of Coronel Oviedo, next to the railroad between Asunción and Encarnación. During the first half of the century, Villarrica was considered the center of Paraguayan culture and was the birthplace of many Paraguayan poets and musicians. It is now a trading center, serving much of the Central Zone and those living in the German colonies to the east; it is also a processing center for the sugar cane produced nearby. Villarrica is experiencing a period of economic decline, reinforced by the movement of many people from its environs to the more active zone of Coronel Oviedo.

Concepción, with an 18,200 population, is located on the Río Paraguay, 310 kilometers north of Asunción. In the first half of this century, it was the center of an active lumber and tannin extract industry, but for several years it has been in a generally stagnant position. New life is being injected through an increase of trade, resulting from the construction of a new road between Concepción and the Brazilian border at Pedro Juan Caballero, and the opening of several plants for processing of agricultural products. North, at Valle-mí, on the eastern bank of the river is a cement plant, which has been in operation since 1952.

Pilar, with a population of 5,230, is south of Asunción, on the Río Paraguay, and is the site of Manufactura de Pilar, S.A., a Paraguayan firm that produces the majority of the textiles used in the country. It is a retail and educational center for the southwestern corner of the country.

Zone of Minifundia

Surrounding Asunción is a zone of small farms, which occupy about 268,000 hectares. About half of these, within the immediate environs of the capital, supply the majority of the truck crops and more perishable fruits for market. Farms further from the capital tend to produce commercial crops of a less perishable nature, i.e., bananas, tobacco, pineapples, manioc, and corn. All of these producers work on a very small scale; the median area of the some 77,000 plots in this zone is 3.5 hectares. Other crops common to this area include beans, sweet potatoes, sugar cane, mangoes, papayas, oranges, lemons, and grapefruits. Most farms also have a small vegetable garden, beside the house, and keep several pigs and chickens.

Mixed Small and Intermediate Farms of the Central Basin

East and north of the previously described areas is a zone of small- and intermediate-sized family farms, which extends the entire length of the central basin, south to Coronel Bogado, west of Encarnación. These farms are located on an island of better-drained soils, supporting a natural forest cover, and rise several meters above the surrounding grasslands.

Many of these farms are _minifundia_; their average size is less than 7 hectares. Emphasis is placed on cultivation of subsistence crops for self-consumption. The other farms are generally larger, ranging from 15 to 25 hectares, and often produce commercial crops as well as subsistence crops. The _minifundia_ of the central basin, in contrast to those surrounding the capital, may have developed from a combination of dividing farms among the sons of a family, restriction of tenure on the expansion of the area under present cultivation, and the poor drainage of the surrounding lowlands, which prohibits the expansion of arable land under the current level of technology. While the area occupied by _minifundia_ is increasing, the intermediate-sized farms appear to be decreasing in number. The consequence of this change in land use is the intensification of pressure on the land's capacity for agricultural activity. The same crops found around the capital are present here, but there is some local specialization. In the south is found more rice and cotton, while nearer Villarrica is more manioc, corn, and sugar cane.

Grasslands of the Central Basin

The grasslands of eastern Paraguay occupy 49 per cent of the total province. However, their use is limited largely to cattle grazing, averaging in density about 0.52 head per hectare. Rice is cultivated in some areas, but it has been successful only in Misiones and Itapúa, where the development of a calcium hard pan, below the surface, has not been as extensive as further north. Only a very small percentage of these grasslands have ever been plowed or planted with non-native grasses.

The grasslands in Misiones and Itapúa should be seriously investigated as to the benefits of a large-scale drainage of the wet areas for the future expansion of arable land. During the study of the _Plan Triangulo_, it was suggested that the cost of draining these lands for development as arable land was less than that of clearing forest areas for the same purpose. The soils of this area, when drained, are richer in nutrients and minerals than the forest soils. Only one farmer in Itapúa has employed extensive irrigation and the use of pumps to control the amount of water on his fields.

The Colonies of Itapúa

In the southeastern corner of Paraguay is an area of tung nut and yerba maté cultivation, stretching over a landscape farmed by Paraguayans and immigrants from more than thirty-five countries. The more extensive areas of these plantations are in the Japanese colony of Alto Paraná and the German colonies of Hohenau, Obligado, and Bella Vista. Two tung nut presses in the region process about half of the harvest, the surplus being sent to Asunción.

Tung nuts produce an oil used in linoleum and oil paints. An estimated 21,990 hectares of tung is grown in Paraguay, 98 per cent of which is found in Itapúa.[14] The plant takes about four years until it can be harvested, and until then it is often interspersed with annual field crops, especially soybeans, which provide a source of income. Yerba maté, or "Paraguayan tea," is the most popular beverage consumed by Paraguayans, who daily drink almost a quarter kilogram per person. In a natural state, the trees grow 20 to 40 meters, but they are cultivated only to about 2 meters high and harvested every other year. In 1964, an estimated 5.718 million kilograms (55 per cent of the total Paraguayan production) were exported from Itapúa.[15] Other products exported from this region include cotton, wheat, citrus fruits, and swine.

Itapúa may be considered one of the better-developed agricultural zones of Paraguay, benefiting from a favorable climate, good soils, and a mixture of Latin, Asian, and European population groups that possess a variety of skills and cultural traditions.

Colonies of the Alto Paraná

In the forests east of Caaguazú, several agricultural colonies are being developed. Their land use patterns are typical of similar colonization activity in Itapúa, the Chaco, or around Pedro Juan Caballero. Quite often this activity is classed as "pioneer settlement" or "pioneer agriculture," since it represents the first permanent agricultural use of an area. In the areas around Caaguazú, the development is characterized by strips of cleared land in virgin forests. After an area is declared open for settlement, the first settlers locate a water source for personal and crop use, construct rough lean-tos, and begin clearing ground to plant food crops. In many of these areas, heavy machinery has been found to be impracticable to clear the forest because it tends to pack the soil, making it difficult to grow common field crops without first reworking the land. After subsistence crops are planted, the farmer usually plants a commercial crop. He then can turn to domestic activities, often improving his house. Next, some of the land is cleared for a pasture, and, finally, a more secure house is built, usually out of brick.

This last stage takes from three to six years in the Alto Paraná. At this point, an equilibrium between the inputs and outputs of production has been reached, and the marginal return is not high enough for the farmer to put more work or improvement into his farm.

The National Development Plan has estimated that between 7 and 8 hectares is the maximum that an average family, with occasional seasonal help, can efficiently cultivate. In many government colonies of 20-hectare farms, only a small proportion of the acreage has been cleared and converted into arable land when this final stage of equilibrium is reached. In many of the private colonies--where a higher level of technical skill, available capital and equipment, and a more refined marketing structure are present--almost 75-80 per cent of the land (on plots averaging 25 hectares or more) is generally under cultivation.[16]

Pedro Juan Caballero

The Paraguayan coffee industry has been developed around the border town of Pedro Juan Caballero, due mainly to the efforts of Clarence Johnson, a planter from Texas, who has been promoting its cultivation since 1953. His corporation has experienced several setbacks, including a bankruptcy, which left several hundred Japanese stranded. Currently, however, an active coffee industry is in operation; in 1963 an estimated 6,000 bags of coffee were exported to the United States. In this area there are 329 farms, cultivating more than 5 million plants--68 per cent of the total grown in Paraguay.[17]

Most of the population live near the Brazilian frontier, across which is carried on an active interchange of trade. One planter in Pedro Juan commented to this writer that most of the economic growth in the region and the major source of income resulted from the coffee plantations on the Paraguayan side of the border, whereas most of the services and retail trade derived from Ponta Porá, Brazil, separated from Pedro Juan by 100 meters of grass. There are differences between the two not only in their economic bases but also in language, food, house types, and popular music. With the improvement of the road from Concepción to Pedro Juan, reducing a trip of two days to four hours, there has been an increased flow of products between these towns and a corresponding increase of trade between Concepción and the Brazilian towns.

Forestlands of Eastern Paraguay

Although forest covers almost 60 per cent of eastern Paraguay, only about half of it is of commercial value. The high forests (30-50 meters) of prime quality timber are found on the better-drained ridges, in the southern Alto Paraná and in the wide shallow valleys of the northern Alto Paraná. The less-valuable forests consist of lower-height varieties and second growths recovering from previous cutting, wind damage, and agricultural use. The lower, noncommercial forests are usually in the valleys and on poorly drained sites and are often intermixed with bamboo and other herbaceous vegetation.

To harvest the commercial forest, it is necessary to build a road to each tree so that, after cutting, the tree can be hauled out by oxen. The construction of an extensive network of logging roads has resulted. Once the trees have been cut, the land is declared by national law as open for agricultural settlement. This use is destroying the prime forestlands in lieu of the poorer forestlands that have no commercial value. Ironically, the noncommercial forests are usually located in the river valleys on soils better suited for agriculture.

Two further uses are made of these forestlands. Scattered areas of pioneer settlement penetrate and consequently reduce the area of prime commercial growth. This activity is mainly on the fringes of the forestlands, where the dominant vegetation changes to grasses. A second use is industrial, employing a combination of the hydroelectric potential of the tributaries of the Río Paraná, the forest reserves, and the river itself for transportation. The most active area is around the Acaray Dam Project. Near Caaguazú, and in Itapúa, there are more than sixty saw mills and other processing facilities, including a plywood mill. However, their development is very limited; almost 80 per cent of the forest products exported from Paraguay are uncut logs.

The Chaco

The Chaco, with less than one person for every 3.3 square kilometers, is probably one of the least-inhabited areas in South America. Only 0.3 per cent of its land (29,714 hectares) is arable or in tree crops. Most of this acreage is in the Mennonite Colonies, scattered along the western bank of the Río Paraguay, or the immediate environs of Villa Hayes.

Forests cover 36.5 per cent of the agricultural lands, and pasture land occupies 55.2 per cent, or 3.4 and 5.2 millions of hectares, respectively. Agricultural lands represent only 38 per cent of the total area of the Chaco. The most extensive use of these lands is cattle grazing; 2.7 million cattle were noted in the 1961 Agricultural Census.[18] This represents a density of 0.24 head per hectare, about half that found in eastern Paraguay.

Commercial crops grown in the Chaco include cotton, kaffir, peanuts, oranges, tangerines, and bananas. Food crops are the same as found in eastern Paraguay. Most families have several fruit trees and also plant trees for construction materials, which may have prompted the recent introduction of eucalyptus into the zone.

With the opening of the road from Asunción to the Bolivian border (built by the joint efforts of the Mennonite Colonists, the Paraguayan Army, and the United States Agency for International Development), the colonists in this area have transportation for sending their crops to market--other than overland by airplane, a trip of several days. Bulky items that once were prohibitive because of the cost of transport can now be imported for use in the colonies.

Other Land Use Types

Other agricultural land uses (not included in the previous descriptions) are prevalent throughout the countryside, usually on river banks or in places where settlers have access to the capital or other markets--be they in Paraguay, Brazil, or Argentina. Most of these farms are of a subsistence nature and are small family-sized operations.

Recreation and tourism are being introduced into some sections of the Chaco, Alto Paraná, and southern Paraguay. The country has many good fishing and hunting facilities, but these facilities are only beginning to be developed.

Notes to Appendix B

1. Dirección General de Estadistica y Censos, _Datos Censo de Población y Vivienda de 1962_ (preliminary data)(Asunción, 1965).

2. P. T. Sulsona, et al., A Reconnaissance Soil and Land Classification of Paraguay (Asunción, 1954), p. 60.

3. Ministerio de Agricultura y Ganaderia, Censa Agropecuario 1956 (Asunción, 1961).

4. Secretaria Technica de Planificación, Sintesis del Diagnastico del Sector Agropecuario y Forestal del Paraguay (Asunción, 1964), p. 8.

5. Ibid.

6. Ibid.

7. J. H. Steward and L. C. Foram, Native Peoples of South America (New York: McGraw Hill, 1959), p. 332.

8. H. G. Warren, Paraguay: An Informal History (Norman, Okla.: University of Oklahoma Press, 1949), p. 45.

9. Ibid., p. 92.

10. Ibid., p. 98.

11. Ibid., p. 100.

12. R. C. Berjarano, Vias y Medios de Communicaciones del Paraguay (1811-1961) (Asunción, 1963), p. 147.

13. Dirección General de Estadistico, op. cit. The population of the urban areas is taken from the 1962 census. The actual urban areas are usually of a fairly small size, but the populations surrounding these locations are usually larger than indicated by the census.

14. Overseas Technical Cooperation Agency, Report on the Survey for the Development Plan of the Forest Resources in Paraguay (Tokyo, Japan; April, 1965), p. 12.

15. Aurelio Belda, _Consideraciones Sobre la Yerba Maté_ (Encarnación, 1965).

16. Data from a survey of 132 farms in Itapúa, 1965.

17. Ministerio de Agricultura y Ganaderia, _op. cit_.

18. _Ibid_.

APPENDIX C CHARACTERISTICS OF IMMIGRANT GROUPS IN RURAL PARAGUAY

Twice within the last century, Paraguay had to rebuild its population: first, after the War of the Triple Alliance--when only 28,000 men remained in a population of less than 300,000; again, after the Chaco War of the 1930's. Much of this rebuilding and repopulating of the countryside was done by immigrants.

The demographic impact of immigrants in Paraguay was minor, when compared with their economic and cultural impact. Between 1880 and 1958 about 66,900 immigrants entered the country, a little more than 800 a year.[1] Much of the industrial and commercial development in Asunción and other towns was financed and managed by these persons or their descendants. Outside of the urban areas, they have been prominent in the development of agricultural processing industries and in introducing new skills, crops, and customs.

Information on the approximately 12,000 urban immigrants is scarce. This appendix will attempt to present the impacts, problems, and tendencies of immigrant groups on the agricultural development of rural Paraguay, with particular emphasis on the Germans and the Japanese.

In 1961, there were 44,535 immigrants living in Paraguay. The largest contingent came from other Latin American countries, especially Argentina and Brazil. However, many of these were either second-generation European immigrants or foreign born of

Paraguayan parents. It is not uncommon for peasants to travel to Argentina for the birth of their children, so that the children will be eligible for Argentine social benefits. It is also very difficult to control the flow across borders, especially along the Río Paraná where many persons cross annually to Argentina or Brazil to work in the harvests. Consequently, among those classed as Argentine and Brazilian are many sons of European and Paraguayan parents.

Although Europeans are the second largest group, their influence on Paraguay's development has probably been the most significant. Yet, between 1950 and 1962 there was a decrease in their number due to deaths and emigration (especially from the Mennonite Colonies). The most notable declines in the number of Europeans were among the Germans, Russians, Polish, Spanish, and Italians (Appendix Table 2).

The largest increase in the past decade was by the Japanese, who began large-scale colonization in the Alto Paraná in the early 1960's. Immigrants from the United States also increased during this same period due to the development of the coffee industry. The number of Canadian Mennonites decreased almost 20 per cent.

Most of the immigrant population live in Asunción and the Department of Itapúa. Others settled in the Chaco, Pedro Juan Caballero, the central basin near Villarrica, Caaguazú, San Pedro, and north of Asunción. During the last decade, there was an increase in the proportion of immigrants in the capital, Pedro Juan Caballero, and the forestlands east of Caaguazú, while corresponding decreases occurred in the Chaco, Itapúa, and San Pedro.

In a seminar on population in Río de Janeiro in 1957, it was suggested that immigrants who are professionally trained and those with skills are necessary for an underdeveloped economy, and that the benefits to a host country are dependent on this level of training of the immigrants. In a report by the Economic Commission for Latin America (ECLA) it is stated that although many countries have a high population density and an unemployment problem, trained immigrants actually improve the possibilities of employment through the creation of new jobs and an inflow of capital goods.[2]

This inflow of capital goods and cash is exemplified by the nearly $2 million given by the Mennonite Central Committee in the United States over the last thirty years to their colonies of the Chaco, the pensions of postwar German settlers, or the tools and supplies furnished by the Japanese migration companies to the colonies in the Alto Paraná.

In the agricultural sector, immigrants have influenced the national capital stock by transforming formerly unproductive lands and raw materials into agricultural and industrial goods. The Mennonites provide much of the poultry and eggs for Asunción. The coffee industry was started by a group of Americans in the zone of Pedro Juan Caballero. And in Itapúa, under the encouragement of German colonists, and now the Japanese, the forestlands were transformed into the third largest center of tung oil production in the world.

Whether skilled or unskilled, most of the immigrants to Paraguay are from countries that have a higher level of living. They have developed habits of consumption of economic goods and, consequently, a higher level of hopes than have the local residents. They are also accustomed to a monetary environment and usually are not hindered by local social and group pressures, allowing them more freedom in decision-making.

Immigrant groups acted as a direct stimulus to agricultural development by the introduction of crops and farming techniques and the construction of roads. For example, the intensive method of farming, which the Japanese employ when growing truck crops, was adopted by neighboring Paraguayans. The Polish wagon, brought from Eastern Europe, is replacing the oxcart in the southern regions, as it

APPENDIX TABLE 2

Foreign Nationals in Paraguay, 1950 and 1962

Country	1962	1950	Per Cent Change (1950-62)
Latin America			
Argentina	16,454	20,889	-22.07
Brazil	8,608	6,243	37.9
Uruguay	487	866	-43.8
Bolivia	234	292	-19.9
Chile	167	150	11.3
Others (14 countries)	134	138	- 2.9
Europe			
Russia	2,713	3,204	-15.3
Poland	2,111	1,999	5.6
Germany	1,759	2,977	-40.9
Spain	1,169	1,742	-32.9
Italy	944	1,889	-50.0
Australia	289	447	-35.3
Czechoslovakia	228	613	-62.8
France	223	345	-35.4
Switzerland	143	333	-57.1
England	97	319	-99.7
Hungary	94	165	-43.0
Yugoslavia	87	166	-41.6
Others	338	403	-16.1

North America			
Canada	1,770	2,215	-20.1
United States	635	511	24.3
Asia			
Japan	5,372	412	1,203.89
Others	74	56	32.14
Middle East			
Lebanon	109	141	-22.67
Syria	221	514	-57.00
Others	66	72	- 8.33
Africa			
South Africa	9	2	---
Summary			
Latin America	26,084	28,688	- 9.75
Europe	10,195	14,602	-30.18
North America	2,405	2,726	-11.77
Asia	5,446	468	1,060.00
Middle East	396	727	-45.52
Africa	9	2	---
TOTAL	44,535	47,113	- 5.42

Source: Dirección de Estadistica y Censos, Asunción, 1966.

is more mobile and lighter--although an oxcart still gets through mud faster than any other vehicle in common use.

The colonists of eastern Itapúa built a road network within their colonies that is as good in quality as any in the country. They also opened penetration roads into once-isolated forests and stimulated the construction of roads by the Paraguayan Government.

New tastes, such as cheeses, wines, and processed meats, were introduced by immigrant groups and were readily accepted into the indigenous culture, adding to the diversity of rural activities.

The influence of the Mennonites as a stimulus to development of the Chaco as an agricultural rather than purely ranching zone was also important; these colonists demonstrated to the native Paraguayans the advantages of a strong cooperative organization and its leverage in dealing with the predominantly feudalistic marketing structure of Paraguay. Furthermore, they demonstrated that traditional domestic crops, when managed and cultivated in the right manner, can be produced on a scale efficient enough for profitable commercialization.

In sum, there appears to be a growing assimilation and mutual adoption of many rural practices. Many colonists have adopted Paraguayan styles of houses and use adobe or bricks, rather than wood, for the greater insulation it provides from the sun. Food (including manioc, yerba maté, and corn) and Guaraní expressions are common throughout the colonies. The Japanese often learn Guaraní before Spanish. In exchange, the Paraguayans have adopted the tools, wagons, and wheat of the Polish; the dairy products of the Ukrainians; Japanese soybeans and truck crops. The Germans have developed the tung nut industry, among other contributions. These examples suggest that immigrant groups may be of value to the economic development of Paraguay if afforded an opportunity to involve themselves with the native population.

Until recently, most immigrant groups settled in isolated areas of the countryside away from the influence of the national culture. Consequently, the amount of social and economic interaction between an immigrant and the native Paraguayans depended on the former's purpose for migrating to Paraguay. Some groups were looking for the isolation and religious autonomy that is readily found in the Paraguayan forests. One such group in Itapúa desires isolation so it can practice its rituals of periodic fasting. Another, the Hutterites, founded their colony, Primavera, in the northeastern forest in an attempt to provide their followers with a location to practice their unique form of communal religious life. But other groups (such as the Japanese) were looking for a source of income or wanted to own land or have settled in Paraguay for political refuge.

These differences in attitudes among colonists lead to "open" and "closed" settlements. Most of the private European colonies are examples of closed colonies, where both settlement of nongroup members as independent farmers and contact with the Paraguayan environment are limited. Contrasted to this attitude are the Italian settlements around Villeta, or the Polish and Japanese settlements in Itapúa, where immigrants of any one nationality are scattered among the indigenous population.

Isolation of colonists from native populations limits their perspective. As colonists lose contact with their home country, they infrequently develop a proportionally active interest in Paraguayan affairs. Rather, the colony becomes their only real object of interest and discussion. When a committee from Itapúa traveled to Asunción for a conference on national economic problems in 1965, several leaders of the German colonies, twenty-five to thirty years old, mentioned that this was the first time they had ever left their colony for more than a few days, and it was also the only time they had ever been to Asunción. When construction of a road between Capitán Meza and the populated centers of Itapúa was proposed, the local population was apathetic toward its completion, preferring to carry on general trade with the Argentine towns across the river.

Many colonies in Paraguay have developed to a substantial degree due to the strength and organization offered by a closed social order or, as Fretz states, "a freedom to develop their own subculture."[3] Their contact with the national economy is usually limited to that with businessmen in Asunción. In these situations, the social, cultural, and even economic benefits to the national economy have been impeded, leaving colonies such as Capitán Meza and towns such as Pedro Juan Caballero literally "islands of prosperity" until integration with other areas was forced upon them.

Integration appears to be occurring more rapidly with the Japanese than it did with the Europeans. The newer Japanese colonies include almost 20 per cent Paraguayans in their number, in contrast to their near-total exclusion among early European settlements. The settlement pattern of the Japanese colonies, with a central administrative core and several subnuclei, provides for frequent meetings of colonists and a common ground for discussion of mutual problems of adjustment to new farming methods, soils, tools, and crop types. It also affords an opportunity to exchange ideas on a daily basis: for Paraguayans to experiment with methods of intensive cultivation and for newcomers to learn the idiosyncrasies of Paraguayan life.

A major problem of acculturation is the conflict between the cultural traits of ethnic groups. In theory, the involvement of foreigners with Paraguayan culture is a good idea. It "adds new blood to the country" as is often suggested by Paraguayans in Asunción. But, in practice, many comments are heard about the "ugly Orientals" and reference to blond foreigners is often made as "gringo" plus an uncomplimentary adjective. When immigration laws were first proposed in 1903, Orientals were prohibited entrance to Paraguay. This prohibition was abolished in 1924,[4] but integration is still discouraged by locating most Orientals away from the populated Central Zone; those arriving under contracts are not allowed to live in Asunción. In 1965, a group of 250 Korean refugees, immigrating on their own funds, arrived in Asunción and bought land near Aregua, 20 kilometers east of Asunción, where they now manufacture craft items and grow vegetables. Although it is too soon to assess this situation, it will be interesting to observe the development of this colony, which is not now accepted by many Paraguayans, during the next few years.

H. Hack offers the following criteria as important in the acculturation process: the degree of differences between cultural patterns of the immigrants and the native population, measures taken by the government, the location of the settlement, and the form of the settlement--whether open or closed.[5]

An increase in the total population, or an addition to the total agricultural production by immigrants, does not in itself promote economic development. Rather, to be considered an effective force in economic change, an immigrant should participate in an interchange of products, ideas, and customs with the native population.

> Only when the Dutch method of farming becomes an example to the whole economy is it possible to speak of a successful economic integration....These colonies are a lasting success only when they become radiating points for the development of their environments, so that the native population becomes integrated with their economic activities.[6]

German-Speaking Immigrants in Paraguay

Since the first German colony was founded in 1881, an estimated 12,000 German-speaking persons have settled in Paraguay, assuming a vital role in its economic and cultural development.[7] Among their descendants are counted the current president of

Paraguay, General of the Army, Don Alfredo Stroessner; and numerous military, professional, commercial, and cultural leaders.

A lack of census data on migration makes it difficult to locate their distribution. But a study of place names suggests a predominance in Asunción. In the rural areas, they are found in the central basin and in the Department of Itapúa, east of Encarnación, where approximately half of the German citizens in Paraguay reside and where a consulate of the German Federal Republic is located. Those in the Mennonite Colonies number about 6,500, a majority of the total number of German-speaking immigrants.[8]

Most of the German colonies are of a closed social structure; little intermixing occurs among the individuals of these colonies and other national groups. It was noted by Fretz that a socio-economic barrier often exists between the native groups and the European settlers as exemplified by the Germans, who tend to isolate themselves from the national culture.[9]

Until recently, the Paraguayan Government has given little attention to the affairs of these colonies, and many of the colonists have had little reason for contact with Asunción, aside from legal affairs. In the southern part of the country, even today, trade relations may often be easier with Argentina than Asunción. These areas, until recently, were often economically part of Misiones, Argentina, rather than Paraguay. Within the colonies, there generally exists a lack of cultural and recreational diversions, except for an occasional dance or football game. The colonists mix little among themselves and have even less opportunity for contact with the national culture.[10] Quite often the colonists have considered themselves to be socially superior to the national population or to other immigrant groups.

At present, there are increasing opportunities for contact between the German colonies and the native populations. First, there are increasing constraints on the expansion of the colonial areas into forestlands. This results from the local tenure patterns and the proximity of many of these colonies to national colonization projects. The colonists are left with a choice of intermixing their farms with those of other groups, moving into other areas of Paraguay, or resettling. Second, improved communication facilities make contact with Asunción easier than in previous times. Third, and most important, the present Paraguayan Government has shown active interest in the colonists and their needs.

The earliest German settlers arrived in 1881 and 1887, locating, respectively, in Colonies San Bernardino and Nueva Germania, east of Asunción. These immigrants largely were persons searching for a "socialist utopia" and a new way of life, such as that proposed by Friedrich Nietzsche, whose sister was the wife of the latter colony's leader. They settled in the forests of Paraguay, because they regarded the presence of a forest to be an absolute requirement for pioneer settlement.[11] Partly because of their location away from main highways and partly due to internal problems of organization, these colonies suffered many hardships. They are currently considered municipalities, rather than colonies, and are well integrated by native Paraguayans. Actually, few of the original families now live in either town; their descendants often founded their own colonies, such as Altos--10 kilometers northeast of San Bernardino. San Bernardino is currently a major resort area with many fine homes fronting on Lake Ypacaraí, a pleasant forty-five minute drive from Asunción.

In 1900, German settlers established the colony of Hohenau, east of Encarnación. This colony and its daughter colonies of Obligado, Bella Vista, and Fordii were founded by colonists migrating from Germany and by others coming from previous colonization experiences in the state of Paraná, Brazil. These pioneers transformed a once-virgin forest into one of the more highly developed agricultural landscapes in Paraguay.

The original emphasis in these colonies was on the production of subsistence crops and on yerba maté as a commercial crop. With the introduction of tung after World War I, most farmers concentrated on its cultivation--to the extent that 98 per cent of the tung grown in Paraguay is found here, including some 12,000 hectares in Obligado. These farmers formed cooperatives and invested in facilities in Obligado, which, along with another press in Encarnación, processes approximately 50 per cent of the total production exported to the United States, Europe, and Japan.[12]

Capitán Meza, founded in 1907, is an example of a colony that remained detached from the Paraguayan economy until the early 1960's, when a road joined it with the larger population centers of Itapúa. Until then, communication between the colony and Encarnación had been by river boat, and general trade had been more convenient with the Argentine towns across the river--at this point, only about 0.5 kilometers wide. Crop types farmed in Capitán Meza, taken from an average of the twenty-one members of one of the two cooperatives, are as shown in Appendix Table 3.

The prevalent settlement pattern in these colonies is the classic strassendorf, or street village, developed in Germany between 1050 and 1350.[13] Hohenau, 25 kilometers long and 3 kilometers wide, has one road that extends the length of the town. The farmsteads are along this road, their fields spreading directly back from the houses. As a consequence, most of the houses and population are scattered throughout the colony. At the intersection of the colony's highway and the main route to Encarnación are the town's few amenities: a bank, doctors' offices, a pharmacy, general stores, and hotels. In Bella Vista, a newer colony, most service establishments are along its main road. Obligado has a larger center, where are found the cooperative's warehouses, tung nut oil presses, and a high school.

Between Obligado and Hohenau is a newly constructed hospital with modern facilities. Several

APPENDIX TABLE 3

Crop Types and Land Use of an Average Farm, Capitán Meza, Itapúa, Paraguay, 1965

Land Use	Area	
	Hectares	Per Cent
Horticulture	10.00	10.9
Annual Field Crops		
Manioc	1.40	1.5
Corn	2.83	3.1
Soybeans	0.10	0.1
Tree Crops		
Tung	7.61	8.3
Yerba maté	5.40	5.9
Oranges	7.14	1.2
Pasture Lands	6.98	7.6
Forestlands	56.02	61.2
TOTAL	91.52	100.0

good secondary schools are found in this region, and the construction of a hydroelectric power station is planned. Through cooperative effort, some of the best roads outside of the capital have been constructed in these colonies. All of these elements provide the colonists and nearby farmers with some of the basic infrastructure necessary for sustained economic growth.

In 1920, 1931, and 1934, several groups of German-speaking immigrants were given plots of land east of Villarrica in the area of Colonies Independencia, Carlos Pfannl, and Sudetia, respectively, the latter being occupied by German-speaking immigrants from Czechoslovakia. These colonies are representative of situations in which a strong social structure promoted the stability and unity necessary to survive obstacles and promote internal growth. Crop types grown here were influenced by a combination of local physical elements and cultural traditions; this is the center of viniculture in Paraguay, including over 50 per cent of the total acreage. Other crops in this region are cotton, corn, manioc, vegetables and fruits.

After World War II, an influx of German settlers entered Paraguay, many of them settling east of Encarnación at Cambyretá (which, literally translated, means "the place of milk"), and began producing milk and dairy products. Only a small proportion of their production is sold, the rest being used for self consumption; in 1965, these farmers formed a dairy products cooperative to process and market their products.

The Japanese in Paraguay

Since 1936, when Japanese settlers first arrived in Paraguay, colonies have been established in the central basin, around Encarnación, Pedro Juan Caballero, and more recently near Puerto Presidente Stroessner.

These settlement attempts by the Japanese have been more organized than any other colonization project in Paraguay--except possibly the Mennonites in the Chaco--and their success must be considered relevant to the problem of immigrant group assimilation. The relations between the Japanese and others in Paraguay may indicate several reasons for this development.

First, the Japanese hire more local help than other migrant groups, giving a basis to local claims that they are more closely integrated with the economy than are other groups.

Second, although comments of "ugly Orientals" are common, the Japanese are respected by the Paraguayans because they work hard, all of them work, and they work alongside of the Paraguayans.

Third, the Japanese consider themselves more culturally advanced than the natives or the Europeans. One Japanese store owner commented that the Paraguayans and Europeans "will do things that we would never think of; they shout across the room, put their arms around you and are rough in their language." But they place a high value on maintaining good interpersonal relations.

Finally, the Japanese colony in Alto Paraná does not extend credit on the basis of future harvests. To join the cooperative, one must buy shares in advance. This necessitates a capital investment, but it also eliminates the feudalistic system of obligations prevalent in most districts of Paraguay--where usurious rates of interest are commonly charged, preventing the farmer's accumulation of capital stock.

The colony of La Colmena was founded by 540 persons, 120 families, in 1936. World War II, which isolated the colony from any contact with Japan and also from the Paraguayan population, influenced the predominance of subsistence crop cultivation, which is the major difference between this and the other Japanese colonies. Currently, the area of vineyards and tree crops is expanding, but traditional methods of farming persist, as indicated by the presence of rice paddies still scattered over the landscape. Produce currently is marketed through a cooperative. In 1963, a road connecting La Colmena to the main route to Asunción, 90 kilometers to the northwest, was opened.

The Japanese Colony at Pedro Juan Caballero, on the Paraguayan-Brazilian border, was formed in 1953 by a Texas coffee planter, Clarence Johnson, who first imported Japanese as workers on the coffee plantations in return for their passage and a parcel of land. However, his corporation went bankrupt, stranding many of the Japanese, some of whom moved to colonies in Brazil. The less than 100 Japanese remaining now supply truck crops for the two towns, Ponta Pora and Pedro Juan Caballero, and have become a well-organized and economically stable settlement.

These early efforts at colonization were not as well organized as are the present schemes. In 1959, a Joint Paraguayan-Japanese Commission was given the responsibility to plan basic immigration and colonization programs and to investigate areas of Paraguay where Japanese colonies might be established. This group advises the two governments on measures facilitating the flow of Japanese and on their settlement into colonies, as well as on the general development of these colonies.

Actual colonization is carried out by two organizations. The Compania Pro-Fomento de Migracion Japonesa, S.A., was established in Japan in 1955 to promote, facilitate, and finance emigration projects. A quasi-governmental corporation operating with Japanese and United States loans, it selects and purchases lands in foreign countries (principally Latin America) and then resells them to colonists on a continued payment plan. In Paraguay, the amortization period extends up to eight years, and the loan carries an interest rate of 6.4 per cent. The company often finances construction of roads and houses, as well as the purchase of agricultural implements and machinery from Japan. The Federación de las Asociaciones Emigratorias, which is wholly supported by the Japanese Government, advertises immigration programs in Japan and provides assistance to the colonies in construction of medical clinics and schools and in general agricultural development.

In 1955, the Japanese Corporation for the Promotion of Migration bought and surveyed land for settlement in Colony Federico Chavez near the city of Encarnación. These colonies were largely on land that had been cleared by earlier Polish settlers. Today, these farms, averaging 26.5 hectares each, are divided into the land uses shown in Appendix Tables 4 and 5.

Subsistence crops (including corn, manioc, wheat, rice, beans, and vegetables) occupy approximately 21.13 per cent of the area under cultivation. Paraguayan farms of comparable size, in the area surrounding this sample, plant almost 32 per cent of their lands in the same crops. The Paraguayans place more emphasis on yerba mate and less on tung, soybeans, or cotton.

Soybeans were introduced into Paraguay by the Japanese less than ten years ago. The crop was quickly adopted by the farmers, but the native farmers did not know how to grow soybeans or how to use the bean for domestic consumption. They planted them as they would have planted potatoes, because of their similarity. This lack of knowledge caused a large part of the Paraguayan soybean crop to spoil while in the ground. The price for Japanese soybeans in 1965 was approximately twice that for Paraguayan soybeans. The Japanese had introduced a profitable crop--until the world market became swamped--which was adopted by local farmers, European and Paraguayan alike. But the transfer, due to a lack of extension services and communication, was not completed, creating a source of antagonism between the Japanese and other groups.

In 1961, the Colony of Alto Paraná was formed. It was to occupy 85,000 hectares; 30,000 hectares of forest were cleared and then divided into 500

APPENDIX TABLE 4

Land Use on Japanese Farms,
Colony Federico Chavez, Itapúa

Type Use	Area	
	Hectares	Per Cent
Annual Field Crops	11.9	45.0
Tree Crops	8.0	30.0
Forestlands	5.7	21.5
Pasture Lands	0.9	3.5
Total	26.5	100.0

APPENDIX TABLE 5

Average Crop Types on 15 Japanese Farms,
Federico Chavez, Itapúa

Crop Types	Area	
	Hectares	Per Cent
Annual Crops		
Corn	3.17	11.92
Manioc	0.28	1.05
Cotton	2.28	8.60
Soybeans	4.95	18.67
Wheat	0.19	0.71
Rice	0.13	0.49
Beans	0.44	1.66
Vegetables	0.45	1.69
Total	11.89	44.79
Tree and Permanent Crops		
Tung	6.66	25.13
Yerba maté	0.37	1.39
Fruits	0.98	3.69
Total	8.01	30.21

lots, which were occupied by 400 Japanese and 100 Paraguayan families in 1965. The original agreement called for a total migration of 85,000 Japanese families to Paraguay. However, the Japanese administrators pointed out to the Paraguayan officials that 85,000 families was an unrealistic number to expect, because Paraguay had to compete with countries offering an easier life, as well as with increasing employment opportunities in Japan.

A typical family, which has lived in the colony for four years, cleared 30 hectares of forest, 7 of which were later cleared of logs and used for the pasturing of twenty-four animals. Almost all of the land was planted in tung nuts, interspersed with soybeans during the four years before tung trees produce a crop. All available land was planted in crops as soon as the fires to clear the brush cooled. The gardens are planted right up to the roads, in perfectly straight rows, ignoring the contours of the hills and general conservation practices. A good storage barn, dry and above the ground, and a pleasant two-story house with a landscaped garden were built. Near the house were a vegetable garden and plots of subsistence crops. Many of the wooden houses and administrative buildings in the colony are slowly being replaced by brick buildings, more suitable to the environment.

Colony Alto Paraná influences the region of Itapúa in at least two aspects of its activities. First is its extensive cultivation of tung nuts, which occupies almost 36 per cent of the total area of 21,990 hectares under cultivation.[14] Obligado, a nearby German colony, has 12,000 hectares of tung nuts. As a result, there are plans to install a new tung oil press. In addition, the construction of the only port facilities on the Paraguayan side of the Río Paraná capable of handling the potential freight of the zone is being considered.

Another aspect is its settlement pattern. The colony is organized around an administrative core platted for urban amenities, with six outlying centers to serve the rural neighborhood. These subnuclei include a cooperative store, a school, a warehouse, and general repair shops. A modern hospital, with an air-conditioned operating room, and an agricultural experiment station (which works with the University of California at Davis) also have been established. The colonial administration plans to attract an urban population and to develop a trading center with related external economies to serve the colonists.

Colony Yguazu, straddling the International Highway 270 miles east of Asunción, has 87,763 hectares, divided into lots of 30 hectares each. Like Colony Alto Paraná, it is divided into a series of blocks, each centering around local administrative centers. Opened in 1960 with room for 2,000 families, only 90 families (including 14 Paraguayans) occupied the area in 1965.

The colonists are all members of a cooperative and grow commercial crops (selected by a central committee), including soybeans, wheat, cotton, rice, corn, and tomatoes. The average family farm has cleared 10 hectares: 5 are in wheat, 2 in soybeans, and 3 in pasture (or 2 in pasture and 1 in rice). Tomatoes are sold in Asunción or shipped unripened to markets in Argentina.

One constraint to its rapid development is that the forestlands cannot be cleared by bulldozers without collapsing the soil structure and blocking root penetration. Consequently, the land must be repeatedly tilled by tractor, and it generally yields only one half that of land cleared by hand for the first five years.

Notes to Appendix C

1. J. W. Fretz, Immigrant Group Settlement in Paraguay (North Newton, Kansas: Bethel College, 1962), p. 17.

2. UNESCO, Immigration and Economic Development in Latin America, E/CN.12/250, 1959. (Mimeographed.)

3. Fretz, op. cit., Preface.

4. See Ley de Octubre 6, 1903, and Ley Nº 691 de Octubre 31, 1924.

5. H. Hack, Dutch Group Settlements in Brazil (Amsterdam: Royal Tropical Institute, 1959), p. 59.

6. Ibid., p. 60.

7. Fretz, op. cit., p. 51.

8. As few records are available on descendants of immigrants these figures can only be estimated. See Fretz, op. cit., p. 51. See also, US/AID, Las Colonias Mennonitas del Chaco Paraguay (Asunción, 1966). (Typed.) Since this was written the 1961 Census of the Population has become available in Asunción.

9. Ibid., p. 128.

10. Ibid., p. 73.

11. Ibid., p. 57; and N. González, Geografía del Paraguay (Mexico City: Editorial Guarania, 1964), p. 423.

12. Overseas Technical Cooperation Agency, Report on the Survey for the Development Plan of the Forest Resources in Paraguay (Tokyo, Japan; April, 1965), p. 11.

13. J. M. Houston, A Social Geography of Europe (London: Duckworth, 1963), p. 86.

14. Overseas Technical Cooperation Agency, op. cit., p. 12.

STATISTICAL APPENDIX

U.S. ASSISTANCE TO PARAGUAY

APPENDIX TABLE 6

AID Assistance to Paraguay During Five Years of Alliance for Progress Grant Funds, 1962-66
(In $000)

Activity	Fiscal Year--Gross Obligations						Fiscal Year 1967 Tentative
	1962	1963	1964	1965	1966	Total thru: 1966	
Agricultural Productivity and Institutional Development	391	506	441	523	747	2,608	876
Road Construction & Maintenance Training	212	708	220	291	218	1,649	202
Rural Health Development	99	145	50	16	-	310	-
Potable Water (SANOS)	-	17	67	74	28	186	-
NATIONAL UNIVERSITY							
Admin. & Organization of Higher Education	-	-	15	12	111	138	18
Faculty of Agronomy & Veterinary Medical & NMSU Contract	39	219	30	58	264	610	51
Medical and Nursing Education	109	299	156	369	173	1,106	50
School of Public Administration	22	97	18	4	-	141	-
Supervision & Administration	-	-	-	-	29	29	47
Total University	170	615	219	443	577	2,024	166
Rural Education Development	622	696	1,099	530	136	2,993	196
Fiscal Reform & Economic Planning	46	89	77	108	83	403	-
Private Enterprise Development	-	-	-	-	-	-	250
Government Management & Organization	88	94	86	99	170	537	186
Technical Support	281	253	249	256	332	1,371	404
Airport Improvement	-	-	-	79	3	82	-
Special Development Activities	-	-	32	25	-	57	25
TOTAL:	$1,909	$3,123	$2,450	$2,444	$2,294	$12,220	$2,305
American School	-	-	12	29	26	67	-
GRAND TOTAL:	$1,909	$3,123	$2,642	$2,473	$2,320	$12,287	$2,305

APPENDIX TABLE 7

Summary of U.S. Assistance to Paraguay During Five Years of Alliance for Progress, 1962-66
(In $000)

Source	Amount					
	Fiscal Year 1962	Fiscal Year 1963	Fiscal Year 1964	Fiscal Year 1965	Fiscal Year 1966	TOTAL
AID						
Development Grant Funds	1,909	3,123	2,450	2,444	2,294	12,220
DLF Loan (Brazil Road)	7,100	-	-	-	-	7,100
AID Loan (Agric. Credit - BNF)	-	-	-	3,000	-	3,000
Total	9,009	3,123	2,450	5,444	2,294	22,320
FOOD FOR PEACE						
PL 480--Title I--Total Sales Agreements	5,975	3,300	1,700	3,000	-	13,975
PL 480--Title III--Voluntary Relief Agencies	988	916	1,655	271	1,160	4,990
PL 480--Title IV--Dollar Credit Sales	-	-	152	-	2,545	2,697
	6,963	4,216	3,507	3,271	3,705	21,662
Less: Planned U.S. Uses (Title I)	896	759	557	732	-	2,944
	6,067	3,457	2,950	2,539	3,705	18,718
Total	15,076	6,580	5,400	7,983	5,999	41,038
(See Appendix Table 10 for details of utilization of P.L. 480 funds during this period.)						
OTHER U.S. ASSISTANCE						
Social Progress Trust Fund	-	2,900[a]	-	4,900[a]	-	7,800[a]
Export-Import Bank Long-Term Loans	-	-	-	-	-	-
Military	200	1,300	1,200	1,500	1,300[b]	5,500
Total	200	1,300	1,200	1,500	1,300	5,500
GRAND TOTAL	15,276	7,880	6,600	9,483	7,299	46,538

[a]Not included under U.S. Assistance. Included under IDB contribution. See Appendix Table 9.

[b]Estimated.

APPENDIX TABLE 8

Total U.S. Assistance to Paraguay
Fiscal Years 1946-61
(Millions of Dollars)

	Amount		
	Grant	Loan	Total
ECONOMIC			
AID	16.1	15.9	32.0
Export-Import	-	10.4	10.4
PL 480 - Title I	-	2.1	2.1
PL 480 - Title III	2.6	-	2.6
	21.5	28.4	49.9
MILITARY	0.2	0.4	0.6
Total	21.7	28.8	50.5

APPENDIX TABLE 9

Summary of Major Other Donors' Loans and Grants
During Five Years of Alliance for Progress, 1962-66
(In $000)

Source	Amount
LOAN	
IDB	34,000.4
IDA	11,800.0
The Paraguay Central R.R. Co. Ltd. (England)	560.0
First Nat'l. Boston Bank of New York	375.0
Chase Manhattan Bank	1,000.0
Bankers Trust Co. (New York)	1,000.0
Government of Spain	5,500.0
Manuf. Hanover Trust & Co.	375.0
Kreditanstalt für Wiederaufbau (German Bank)	3,000.0
	57,610.4
GRANT	
UNTA	5,200.0
UNSF	2,500.0
	7,700.0

APPENDIX TABLE 10

Utilization of PL 480-Title I Funds, 1962-65
(In $000)

	Sales Agreements				
	Fiscal Year 1962	Fiscal Year 1963	Fiscal Year 1964	Fiscal Year 1965	Total
LOANS TO GOVERNMENT FOR:					
Agriculture	635	497	477	149	1,758
Roads	1,465	415	-	36	1,916
Airport	143	-	-	12	155
Planning Secretariat	77	-	-	55	132
Industrial Census	69	-	-	14	83
	2,389	912	477	266	4,044
LOANS TO PRIVATE INDUSTRIES (COOLEY) TO:					
Pan Western Enterprises, Inc.	296	530	-	-	826
International Products Corp.	3	213	220	-	436
	299	743	220	-	1,262
GRANTS FOR ECONOMIC DEVELOPMENT TO:					
Nat'l. Develop. Bank	-	-	-	280	280
Ministry of Finance	-	-	-	2	2
	-	-	-	282	282

SELECTED BIBLIOGRAPHY

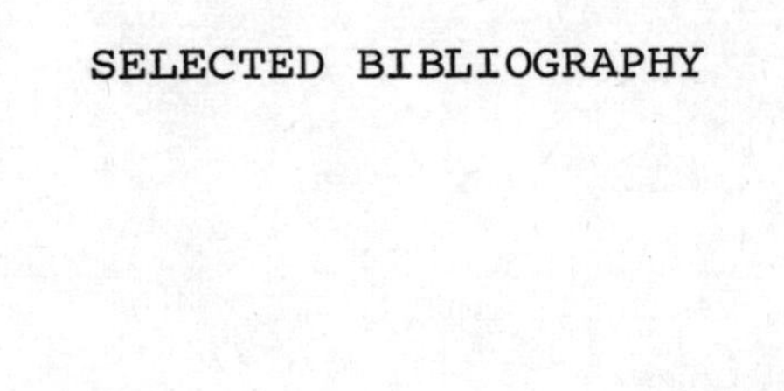

SELECTED BIBLIOGRAPHY

Books

Fretz, Joseph Winfield. Immigrant Group Settlements In Paraguay. North Newton, Kansas: Bethel College, 1962.

________. Pilgrims In Paraguay. Scottsdale, Pennsylvania: Herald Press, 1953.

González, Juan Natalicio. Geografía del Paraguay. Mexico City: Editorial Guarania, 1964.

Raine, Philip. Paraguay. New Brunswick, New Jersey: Scarecrow Press, 1956.

Sapena Pastor, Raúl, and Sapena Brugada, Raúl. A Statement of the Laws of Paraguay in Matters Affecting Business. Washington, D.C.: Pan American Union, 1962.

Warren, Harris Gaylord. Paraguay: An Informal History. Norman: University of Oklahoma Press, 1949.

Official Publications

Banco Nacional de Fomento. Memoria.

Ministerio de Hacienda. Presupuesto Anual.

________. Monthly statement of accounts. (Unpublished.)

Ministerio de Industria y Comercio. Paraguay Industrial y Comercial. (Published irregularly.)

Secretaría Técnica de Planificación del Desarrollo Económico y Social. "Paraguay: Informe Sobre la Evolución Económica y Social en el Quinquenio 1961-1965." Asunción, March, 1966.

________. Plan Nacional de Desarrollo Económico y Social Para el Bienio 1965-1966. Asunción, July, 1965.

________. II Plan Nacional de Desarrollo Económico y Social, Bienio 1967-1968. Asunción, August, 1966.

U.S. Government Publications

Ceuppens, Henry C. "General Analysis of Paraguayan Exports for the Period 1958-1965." Asunción, American Embassy, May 5, 1966. (Unclassified.)

Eckel, Edward B. Geology and Mineral Resources of Paraguay--A Reconnaissance. Geological Survey Professional Paper 327. Washington, D.C.: U.S. Government Printing Office, 1959.

Report of U.S. Department of Agriculture, Land Grant College, and International Development Survey Team. Agricultural Development in Paraguay. Asunción, February 17, 1965.

U.S. Department of Health, Education, and Welfare, Public Health Service. Encuesta de Salud, Nutrición y Alimentación, República del Paraguay, Mayo-Agosto 1965. (Preliminary Report.)

International Organization Publications

International Monetary Fund. International Financial Statistics. (Monthly.)

________. Balance of Payments Yearbook.

Kalnins, Arvids. "Tentativa de Estimación de la Existencia de Ganado Vacuno del Paraguay, Años 1956-1964." Asunción: Central Bank of Paraguay, September, 1964. Dr. Kalnins is a United Nations Adviser to the Central Bank.

Organization of American States, Department of Economic Affairs. Reforma Tributaria en Paraguay (UP/G.15/4). June 21, 1966.

Articles

Smith, Tim G. Itapúa: Notes On the Economic Environment. Unpublished paper submitted to the University of Oregon as a Master's thesis, October 17, 1965.

The First National City Bank of New York, Foreign Information Service. "Paraguay: Building Foundations for Growth." Asunción, December, 1964.

Newspapers

La Tribuna. Independent morning daily, with some Colorado Party bias.

Pátria. Organ of the Colorado Party; morning daily.

ABOUT THE AUTHOR

Joseph Pincus is presently a Private Enterprise Development Officer to the United States AID Mission to El Salvador and was, until recently, an Economic Adviser to the U.S. AID Mission to Paraguay. He has had extensive experience in Latin American economic affairs and served previously as an economist with the U.S. Tariff Commission, Latin American Studies Project; the U.S. Department of State, Division of Research for American Republics; and as Tariff Adviser for the International Cooperation Administration to the United States Operations Mission in Honduras.

Dr. Pincus is the author of *The Central American Common Market*, *El Sistema Tributario en Honduras*, *Breve Historia del Arancel de Aduanas de Honduras*, and several other publications. He received his doctorate in 1953 from The American University, Washington, D.C.